ARMOURED THUNDER

ARMOURED THUNDER

THE CANADIAN SHERBROOKE FUSILIER REGIMENT IN THE NORMANDY CAMPAIGN

DANIEL M BRAÜN

Pen & Sword
MILITARY

AN IMPRINT OF PEN & SWORD BOOKS LTD.
YORKSHIRE · PHILADELPHIA

First published in Great Britain in 2024 by
PEN AND SWORD MILITARY
An imprint of
Pen & Sword Books Limited
Yorkshire – Philadelphia

Copyright © Daniel M. Braün, 2024

ISBN 978 1 39905 142 2

The right of Daniel M. Braün to be identified as Author of this work has been asserted by him in accordance with the Copyright, Designs and Patents Act 1988. Sherbrooke Fusilier Regiment Cap Badge reproduced with the permission of DND/CAF (2020).

A CIP catalogue record for this book is available from the British Library.

All rights reserved. No part of this book may be reproduced or transmitted in any form or by any means, electronic or mechanical including photocopying, recording or by any information storage and retrieval system, without permission from the Publisher in writing.

Typeset in Times New Roman 11/13.5 by
SJmagic DESIGN SERVICES, India.
Printed and bound in the UK by CPI Group (UK) Ltd.

Pen & Sword Books Limited incorporates the imprints of
Archaeology, Atlas, Aviation, Battleground, Digital, Discovery, Family History, Fiction, History, Local, Local History, Maritime, Military, Military Classics, Politics, Select, Transport, True Crime, After the Battle, Air World, Claymore Press, Frontline Publishing, Leo Cooper, Remember When, Seaforth Publishing, The Praetorian Press, Wharncliffe Books, Wharncliffe Local History, Wharncliffe Transport, Wharncliffe True Crime and White Owl.

For a complete list of Pen & Sword titles please contact:

PEN & SWORD BOOKS LIMITED
George House, Units 12 & 13, Beevor Street, Off Pontefract Road,
Barnsley, South Yorkshire, S71 1HN, England
E-mail: enquiries@pen-and-sword.co.uk
Website: www.pen-and-sword.co.uk

or
PEN AND SWORD BOOKS
1950 Lawrence Rd, Havertown, PA 19083, USA
E-mail: uspen-and-sword@casematepublishers.com
Website: www.penandswordbooks.com

Contents

Preface vi

Chapter 1	Preparations for D-Day	1
Chapter 2	6 June: The D-Day Landings	25
Chapter 3	7 June: The Battle for Carpiquet	40
Chapter 4	Operation CHARNWOOD: The Battle for Caen	70
Chapter 5	Operation ATLANTIC: The Battle for Verrières Ridge	103
Chapter 6	Operation TOTALIZE: The Drive towards Falaise	121
Chapter 7	Operation TRACTABLE: Closing the Falaise Gap	154
Chapter 8	The Pursuit to the Seine	178
The Aftermath		212
Conclusion		217
Annex A	Honour Roll	219
Annex B	Decorations and Awards	221
Annex C	Command Appointments	223
Annex D	Order of Battle	225
Annex E	German Forces opposing the Canadians in Normandy	229
Annex F	Abbreviations	231
Bibliography		234
Endnotes		241
Index		249

Preface

I joined the Sherbrooke Hussars, a Canadian Army Reserve armoured regiment in the city of Sherbrooke, Quebec, in July 1971. I enrolled as a trooper and quickly rose to the rank of master warrant officer before taking my commission to the rank of captain. In 1996, I was promoted to the rank of lieutenant-colonel and I took command of the regiment. The regiment perpetuates the Sherbrooke Fusilier Regiment, an armoured regiment raised in Sherbrooke in 1940 which landed on the beaches of Normandy on D-Day, fought in all the major battles involving First Canadian Army and was fighting in Emden, Germany, on the last day of the war.

I am a history buff, and the history of the regiment has always appealed to me. I graduated from Bishop's University with a BA and an MA in history, before undertaking a PhD in history at Cambridge University in England. Although I never completed my PhD for economic reasons, I always maintained an intense interest in history, and particularly that of the Sherbrooke Fusilier Regiment. Therefore, over the years, I conducted research in my free time into the activities of the regiment. On several occasions, I attended the annual reunions of the Sherbrooke Fusilier Regiment Association and got the chance to talk to veterans of that regiment. The Sherbrooke Hussars holds a copy of the Sherbrooke Fusilier Regiment's War Diary, and I was able to gain access to it. I also travelled to Ottawa, Ontario, on several occasions to consult the Canadian military archives stored there.

The result of my endeavours is a two-volume set: *Armoured Thunder* describes the fighting history of the Sherbrooke Fusilier Regiment in Normandy during World War Two, and *Armoured Fist* describes the regiment's fighting through Belgium, Holland and Germany till VE-Day. In this first narrative, I describe the origins of the regiment and its preparations for D-Day. The regiment trained first in Canada and then in the United Kingdom before being selected to take part in the invasion of Europe. The tanks of the regiment landed on D-Day on Juno Beach in support

PREFACE

of 9th Canadian Infantry Brigade, the exploitation force of 3rd Canadian Infantry Division. They fought the first Allied tank battle the next day against the tanks and *Panzergrenadiers* of *12.SS-Panzerdivision (Hitlerjugend)*. The regiment then went on to fight in every major Canadian battle to the end of the conflict: the capture of and subsequent breakout from Caen, the night advance towards Falaise in Operation TOTALIZE, the closing of the Falaise Gap, and the pursuit of the Germans to the Seine River. In the second narrative, I describe the fighting to clear the right shoulder of the Scheldt Estuary, to clear the Rhineland, to liberate Holland, and the assault on Germany. When the war ended, the regiment returned to Canada in January 1946 and was disbanded on 15 February 1946.

Units and formations – both Allied and German – are identified once using their full name and then the abbreviated name in parentheses, all except those units or formations which are referred to only once in the book. For a detailed list of the Canadian Order of Battle, including the abbreviation used for each unit, see Annex D; see Annex E for a list of the German formations facing the Canadians in Normandy. For the Allied armies, formation designations are often the same for the Canadian, British, Polish or American formations. Therefore, a designator has been added to differentiate them (Cdn = Canadian; Brit = British; Pol = Polish and US = United States). Likewise, care has been taken to use abbreviations whenever possible. All the Allied ranks are given in an abbreviated form and these are given in Annex F at the back of this book, along with any other abbreviation used. The first time an individual is referred to in the book, their name is complete using both given names or initials if known. However, when the same individual is subsequently referred to, then the given names are dropped.

I must give thanks to the Sherbrooke Hussars, and its commanding officers, who over the years encouraged my research and gave me free access to the historical documents held by the regiment. I must also thank those veterans who were generous with their comments regarding this text or who were available to clarify their actions in events in which they participated. Unfortunately, most of the veterans of the Sherbrooke Fusilier Regiment have passed away and are no longer with us. Nonetheless, I hope that this book will serve to perpetuate their gallant contributions in the elimination of Nazi tyranny. I want to also thank the members of the Sherbrooke Hussars Senate, and any past members of the regiment, who have always encouraged me with the completion of this project.

Most of the photographs used come from the Library and Archives Canada in Ottawa, the Imperial War Museum in London or the Bundesarchiv in Germany. Since the fifty-year copyright period has expired, all are now in the public domain and, as such, are accessible to the general public to use in as much as the credits for the photographs, where known, are identified. I drew all the maps included to improve the comprehension of the events affecting the Sherbrooke Fusilier Regiment, using the original World War Two maps of the regiment which were salvaged and brought back to Sherbrooke by its members. The towns and villages are identified using their original names as they existed on those maps in 1944 and 1945 – for example: les Buissons and Villons-les-Buissons were two independent hamlets in Normandy but are now known as Villons-les-Buissons, and Vieux Cairon has become Cairon le Vieux.

Special thanks are given to my children William and Michelle, and to my spouse Manon, for their continued support during the research and the writing of this book.

Any errors or omissions are mine alone. Should anyone notice an error, I would be grateful if they informed me so that future copies of the book can be revised and maintained as accurately as possible.

Daniel M. Braün
January 2024

PREFACE

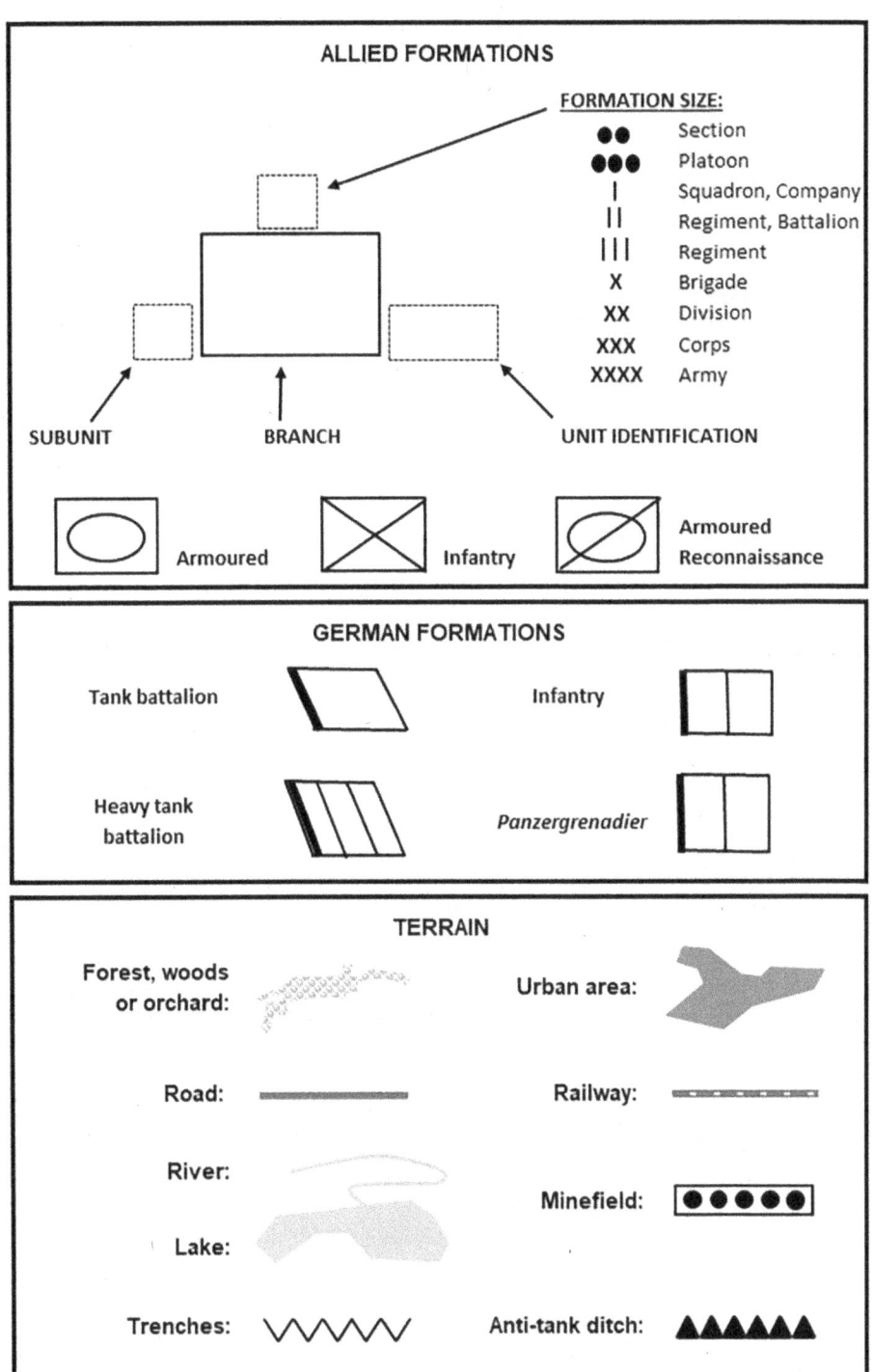

ARMOURED THUNDER

ALLIED FORMATIONS

When identifying formations or units, should the description of the map identify that the movements shown are for a single battalion or regiment, then the identification of the battalion or regiment is dropped. The same goes for identifying troops, squadrons or companies within those battalions or regiments.

EXAMPLES:

Symbol	Abbreviation	Full Name
XXXX ⊠	1 CDN	First Canadian Army
XXX ⊠	2 CDN	Second Canadian Corps
XXX ⊠	3 BRIT	Third British Corps
II ◯	SFR	Sherbrooke Fusilier Regiment
II ⊠	NNSH	North Nova Scotia Highlanders
II ⊠	SD&GH	The Stormont, Dundas and Glengarry Highlanders
I B◯	SFR	Baker Squadron, SFR
II A◯	FGH	Abel Squadron, Fort Garry Horse
••• 3◯	C	3 Troop, C Squadron, SFR
••• ⊘		Recce troop, SFR

Chapter 1

Preparations for D-Day

Canada Goes to War

In the early hours of 1 September 1939, Adolf Hitler sent the *Wehrmacht* across the Polish frontier at four points of entry, while the *Luftwaffe* bombarded several Polish cities. Immediately, the Polish government informed His Majesty's government in London that it considered that this constituted a case of aggression as defined in Article 1 of the Anglo-Polish Treaty of Mutual Assistance. In an emergency meeting of the British Cabinet later that morning, British Prime Minister Neville Chamberlain proclaimed that there was no possible question as to where Britain's duty lay. The Cabinet decided that a stiff warning should be given to Hitler that world war could only be averted if Germany ceased its hostilities and withdrew her troops from Poland. That same day, the French Council of Ministers decided to order the immediate mobilisation of its military and to summon the French Parliament – only the French Parliament could declare war. That evening, both governments jointly warned Germany to desist from further aggression and to remove her troops from Poland.

The next day, the British Cabinet met again and decided that if Germany requested more time to comply with the Allied demands, the time limit could be extended to noon, or even midnight, on 3 September. The same day, after some Cabinet members and members of the opposition opposed that stance, Chamberlain told the House of Commons at 23.30 that an ultimatum would be given to the German government at 09.00 on 3 September which would expire two hours later. The ultimatum would be presented jointly to Joachim von Ribbentrop, the German Foreign Minister, by the British and French ambassadors in Berlin, Neville Henderson and Robert Coulombe, and would state that:

> unless no later than eleven a.m. British Summer Time today, September 3, satisfactory assurances to the above effect have been given by the German Government ... a state of war would exist between the two countries as from that hour.[1]

When no answer was received by the appointed deadline, Chamberlain told the House of Commons at noon that a state of war existed between Great Britain and France against Germany.

Canada, as a member of the British Commonwealth of Nations, had already informed His Majesty's government that she would offer aid and assistance in the case of war. However, as of 1 September 1939, she was unprepared for war. Prior to 1914, no permanent military force existed in Canada. After the Great War, the Canadian Army was organised into the Permanent Active Militia (PAM), the Non-Permanent Active Militia (NPAM), the Royal Canadian Air Force (RCAF) and the Royal Canadian Navy (RCN). A peacetime establishment was created which allowed the PAM to include 6,925 officers and other ranks while the NPAM was set at 134,843 all ranks. However, due to the high cost in casualties sustained during the war, the public sentiment was averse to military matters and recruiting was therefore difficult. During the early 1930s, budgetary compressions had an impact on defence expenditures and the Canadian militia could not maintain its peacetime establishments. Unit strength returns for 30 June 1939, for example, indicated that the PAM numbered only 3,688 officers and other ranks while the NPAM counted only 51,287 all ranks. As the skies of peace began to darken over Europe and diplomats began to predict another global conflict, Canada's military forces could muster no more than 54,975 all ranks – less than half its peacetime establishment. During the period prior to the German invasion of Poland, the military did not have the equipment or the necessary funds to adequately train its personnel. NPAM units were authorised to draw pay for only ten days of training per year. As a result, units were only training essential personnel: officers, warrant officers and specialists. The units were drastically under strength.

As a result of the dwindling numbers, the newly elected Liberal government of Prime Minister William Lyon Mackenzie King put forth a five-year plan in September 1936 which called for an increase from the planned 1936–1937 military expenditures of $30 million, to an allocation of $199.4 million spread over a five-year period.[2] The first year's allotment was established at roughly $65 million. The House of Commons, however, did not believe that the European situation warranted as yet such excessive expenditures, nor did it believe that the Canadian population would accept the additional fiscal burden. As a result, the initial budget request was cut to $36 million for the first year. As a consequence, the military was reorganised and a new peacetime military establishment was put in place on 31 December 1938: the PAM was set at 4,268 officers and other ranks and the NPAM was set at 51,418 all ranks. Although the Canadian government increased its defence expenditures for the 1939–1940 fiscal year from $36.3 million to a still inadequate $64.7 million, the Cabinet adopted a list of priorities which gave first priority to resources to the neglected RCAF and the humiliated RCN. Now, for the first time in Canadian history, the Militia was relegated to the lowest priority in the military. This decision would ultimately mean that when war actually did erupt in September 1939, both the PAM and the NPAM would not have the adequate personnel, nor the equipment and materiel necessary to train units to their full establishments. In 1938–1939, only 46,251 men trained as compared to 55,000 in 1913.

In response to the German remilitarisation of the Rhineland in March 1936, the Chief of the General Staff, Lieutenant-General (Lt-Gen) Ernest Charles Ashton had presented Defence Scheme No. 3 to the Minister of National Defence, Ian Alistair Mackenzie, on 15 March 1937. The plan called for the Militia to only be used for local defence and internal security. On mobilisation, a 'Mobile Force' could also be created as an expeditionary force for employment with other British Empire forces overseas should this be the decision of the Canadian government. Provisions were also made for forces to man coastal defences and to guard 'vulnerable points' in Canada. When the Nazi-Soviet Non-Aggression Pact was announced on 21 August 1939, and the Canadian High Commissioner in London, Charles Vincent Massey, reported to Ottawa the next day that all the evidence available at the British Foreign Office pointed to a probable German attack on Poland between 25 and 29 August, the Cabinet approved a plan to introduce a precautionary stage of war preparation. General Order No. 124 called out the ninety-nine NPAM units identified in Defence Scheme No. 3 to guard vulnerable points: defence establishments, railways, canals, oil depots, dry docks, grain elevators, wireless stations, potential enemy landing points, bridges, aerodromes, and other potential targets of attack or sabotage. When German troops finally crossed the Polish frontier in the early hours of 1 September, the Canadian government ordered general mobilisation and organised the Canadian Active Service Force (CASF). However, Canada had no troops ready for immediate deployment, except for local coastal defence against very small raids. The NPAM was incapable of immediate effective action of any sort against a formidable enemy; this was due to its limited strength, obsolescent equipment and rudimentary training. Nonetheless, the Canadian House of Commons authorised a declaration of war on Germany on 9 September, and King George VI gave his Royal assent the next day.

An evaluation of the armed forces in Europe on 1 September 1939 showed a certain degree of parity between the Allied and Axis powers, with the level of the Soviet forces uncertain:

British-French Alliances		**Berlin-Rome Axis**	
France	1,000,000	Germany	1,750,000
Britain	600,000	Italy	950,000
Poland	500,000	Hungary	200,000
Turkey	300,000		2,900,000
Romania	275,000		
Greece	200,000	**Other**	
	2,875,000	Soviet Union	2,000,000[3]

Canada's military establishment, on the other hand, was almost non-existent:

Navy	2,000	PAM troops
	1,000	NPAM troops
	2	minesweepers
	6	destroyers (4 new, 2 old)
Air force	3,048	PAM troops
	1,000	NPAM troops
	8	squadrons
	37	combat worthy planes
	82	Vickers machine-guns
Army	4,261	PAM troops
	51,000	NPAM troops
	10	Bren guns
	5	mortars
	4	anti-aircraft guns
	2	light tanks[4]

On 15 September, the Chiefs of Staff presented a new plan to the cabinet for the next year of the war. The plan recommended that Canada raise three divisions: one would go overseas immediately while the other two would be recruited and trained in Canada. The plan would put 60,000 men under arms. The cost was set at $491 million. Cabinet, however, decided that it could not

PREPARATIONS FOR D-DAY

afford the expenditure. Instead, it decided that it would adopt a modest war effort and cut back the number of divisions from three to two, a saving of 20,000 men. The budget was set at $314 million. Canada therefore mobilised First Canadian Corps (First Cdn Corps) of the CASF, comprised of two infantry divisions, each composed of three infantry brigades. 1st Canadian Infantry Division (1st Cdn Inf Div) was to include 1st Canadian Infantry Brigade (1st Brigade)[5], composed of units from Ontario; 2nd Brigade, formed from Western units; and 3rd Brigade, composed of units from Quebec and the Maritimes. 2nd Canadian Infantry Division (2nd Cdn Inf Div) was to be composed of 4th Brigade, from Ontario units; 5th Brigade, formed from Quebec units; and 6th Brigade, composed of Western units. Each brigade would be made up of three infantry battalions and one machine-gun battalion. Other than the infantry, each division was given a tank regiment and a cavalry regiment. 1st Cdn Inf Div left for the United Kingdom in December, while 2nd Cdn Inf Div was kept under arms in Canada. However, on 25 January 1940, it was announced that 2nd Cdn Inf Div would be sent overseas as soon as possible.

The region of the Eastern Townships is located east of the city of Montreal in the province of Quebec. At its heart is the city of Sherbrooke which is situated at the confluence of the St Francis and Magog rivers. The region had a population of approximately 75,000, of which more than 45,000 resided in the city of Sherbrooke alone. The area had a strong military heritage and was well represented in the NPAM. Citizens from the region had served in the war of 1812, in defence against the Fenian Raids (1866 and 1870), in the Boer War (1900–1902) and in the Great War (1914–1918). Two infantry battalions – The Sherbrooke Regiment (MG) (Sher R) and Les Fusiliers de Sherbrooke (Fus de Sher) – along with 35th (Howitzer) Battery (35th (How) Bty) were part of Military District No. 4. The 7th/XIth Hussars (7/XI H) was part of Military District No. 5 and had independent squadrons in most of the small towns surrounding Sherbrooke. Its headquarters was in Richmond, about 30 miles from Sherbrooke.

With the outbreak of hostilities, the members of the Sherbrooke militia units anxiously awaited the creation of an active unit in Sherbrooke. On 3 September, No. 1 General Base Depot was created using volunteers from both local infantry units. Lieutenant-Colonel (Lt-Col) L.M. Watson, the commanding officer (CO) of the Sher R, was named as the commander of the new unit. The unit was used to guard vulnerable points in the region before it was shipped to the United Kingdom on 25 January 1940. There, it provided guards for vulnerable points until it was disbanded on 6 July 1940 and its members distributed among the units of 1st Cdn Inf Div. 35th (How) Bty was also mobilised on 5 September 1939 under the command of Major (Maj) C.G. Grier and was established on the exhibition grounds of the Eastern Townships Agricultural Association. Recruiting offices for both units were set up in Lennoxville and in the Belvedere Street Armoury in Sherbrooke.

The period from October 1939 to April 1940 has been called the 'Phoney War'. French and German troops stared at each other across the no-man's-land between the French Maginot Line and the German Siegfried Line. However, on 9 April, the Phoney War was shattered when German troops invaded Norway and Denmark. Then, on 10 May, German troops bypassed the Maginot Line and pushed through Belgium and Holland to attack France. That afternoon, the War Committee of the Canadian Cabinet held an emergency session to review the situation and to consider methods by which Canada might give further assistance to the British government. It was decided to send 2nd Cdn Inf Div to England in June and July – rather than in July and August as planned – and to send a battalion of infantry to Jamaica to relieve the British battalion garrisoned there for other duties. By 17 May, the German Army had taken Holland and had pierced the British-French line of defence. The Allies were therefore forced to fall back from Belgium or risk being encircled. In response, the Canadian Cabinet decided to form a Canadian corps in the field and raise 3rd Canadian Infantry Division (3rd Cdn Inf Div) for service in Canada. When the war situation deteriorated even more with the collapse of the Allied front and the encirclement of the British Expeditionary Force at Dunkirk, it was decided on 24 May to also create a fourth division through General Order No. 184. The creation of 4th Canadian Infantry Division (4th Cdn Inf Div) would be made up of nine infantry battalions organised in three brigades and mobilised in June and July.

With the departure of No. 1 General Base Depot from Sherbrooke, military circles in the city had continued to lobby for the creation of an Eastern Townships battalion for the CASF. It was feared by both the Sher R and the Fus de Sher that the best soldiers would leave to join other units being raised in Montreal and Toronto and, if formed too late, it would only get leftovers or soldiers of poor quality. On 4 June, an editorial entitled 'Give the Eastern Townships a Chance to Serve' appeared in the *Sherbrooke*

Daily Record, a local newspaper. It pointed out that although it had been announced that Canada would create a third and a fourth division, the Eastern Townships had been neglected. Although the area had two well-established militia units, an artillery battery and a Signals Corps unit in Sherbrooke, along with cavalry units or artillery batteries in nearly every town or large village, it had been overlooked when the first two divisions had been created. Instead, the area's commitment had been restricted to two artillery batteries, a base depot and a company of engineers. Another *Sherbrooke Daily Record* editorial on 10 June again criticised the government for its lack of action. It argued that there were thousands of young men who were eager to do their bit but were not being called upon because the government had preferred to follow a half-hearted course of action rather than face the true needs of the situation.[6]

Towards the end of June, both the Sher R and the Fus de Sher received orders to mobilise up to their full war strength as part of the NPAM. This meant that the battalions could enrol part-time soldiers to fill any empty position on their establishments. The 7/XI H, however, was incorporated into the Royal Rifles of Canada on 8 July to mobilise an Anglophone battalion in Quebec City for Military District No. 5. But in Sherbrooke, editorials continued to apply pressure on Ottawa for the creation of a Sherbrooke unit. Although the government had announced its desire to enrol another 40,000 men into the CASF, there were still no provisions made for an Eastern Townships regiment, even though there were enough men in Sherbrooke and its vicinity ready and able to serve their king and country. Finally, on 23 July, it was announced that a new bilingual CASF battalion would be formed as part of 4th Cdn Inf Div from the amalgamation of the Sher R and the Fus de Sher, to be known as 'The Sherbrooke Fusilier Regiment, C.A.S.F.'. On 28 July, under Authority Serial 1044 HQS 3498-10-D, FD 36, the new battalion was authorised to mobilise to full infantry (rifle) strength – 934 all ranks – and was allocated block numbers D-46000 to D-50999 inclusive.

The Creation of the Sherbrooke Fusilier Regiment

When the Sherbrooke Fusilier Regiment was created in July 1940, Colonel (Col) Mathias William McA'Nulty took a reduction in rank to become its first CO and Maj Aimé Biron was named as the deputy commanding officer (DCO). Over the course of the summer, the battalion was organised into four rifle companies and an administrative company. Able Company (A Coy) and Charlie Company (C Coy) were Anglophone companies under Maj Eugene William Langler Arnold and Maj William Lyman Tomkins respectively. Baker Company (B Coy) was a Francophone company under Maj Alphonse Jules Camirand and Dog Company (D Coy) was designated as a bilingual company under the command of Maj Déodatus William Beaudry. To fill the position of the officer commanding (OC) Headquarters Company (HQ Coy), Lt-Col McA'Nulty turned to Maj Bertram Dawson Lyon. Regimental Quartermaster Sergeant Gerald Cuthbert Henry Barlow was promoted to the rank of warrant officer, first class (WO1) and was named as the battalion's first regimental sergeant-major (RSM). Most of the officers and the non-commissioned officers (NCOs) came from either the Sher R or the Fus de Sher.

Immediately, the new battalion set up recruiting stations in both NPAM armouries. The ideal recruit was a man between 18 and 45 years of age with a chest measurement of at least 34in (32in for 18 and 19 year olds). The minimum height for the infantry was 5ft 4in tall. Privates would be paid $1.30 per day. A married man would earn the same daily pay as a single man, but his wife would receive $35.00 per month and $12.00 per month for each of his first two children. Tradesmen would get an extra supplement varying from 25¢ to 75¢ per day depending on the trade they held. Recruitment went well from the start. On 25 September, it was reported that the battalion had enrolled 33 officers and 676 other ranks, for a total of 709 men. Over the course of that autumn and winter, the battalion got down to the arduous task of converting civilians with little or no knowledge of military affairs into a cohesive fighting unit. Training was under the responsibility of the company commanders and, other than those lessons usually attributed to basic military training, included small arms training, the phases of mechanised warfare, signalling, bayonet drill, bush craft, and map using. The officers attended lessons in the evenings on tactics and field procedures using sand tables, map-using and navigation, leadership, and man management.

On 28 March 1941, the *Sherbrookes*, as the battalion came to be known, received word that the unit would leave Sherbrooke sometime in May, provided the weather and road conditions justified travelling and sleeping out at night. The battalion was to move to the Militia Training Centre (MTC) in Farnham. The move was to take place on foot, and along the way the battalion was to hold parades in support of the Victory Loan Campaign in the various towns and villages it crossed. The battalion was informed on 10 May that the march would begin on 29 May. At 12.10 on the given day, the first fighting company began its march to Little Lake Magog, the site of the first night's camp. Over the next eight days, the *Sherbrookes* marched forward towards its destination in Farnham. Once it arrived at the MTC, a ten-day training syllabus was put in place and the companies got the chance to use the rifle ranges. On 19 June, the battalion left Farnham and headed off in the direction of St Johns on the Richelieu River, arriving at St Johns Barracks the next day. A week later, the battalion was ordered to again move off, this time towards Mont St Bruno Camp. It arrived on 28 June, after having covered a total distance of 170 miles but two weeks later it was ordered to proceed on foot to the Connaught Ranges, a short distance outside the nation's capital of Ottawa. Unfortunately, the men had hoped that since they were so close to the Port of Montreal, their next stop would be a ship heading for overseas duties. Instead, the men faced an eleven day trek of another 156 miles. The battalion arrived in Ottawa on 25 July. Once again, a training syllabus was put in place.

The battalion's stay in Ottawa would prove to be a short one. On 5 August, word came in that the *Sherbrookes* were to travel to the British colony of Newfoundland[7] and participate in the coastal defence of the colony. The advance party left two days later, followed by the main body of the battalion on 10 August. The men travelled by train to Quebec City where they boarded the *Lady Drake* for passage to the colony. The rear party was the last to leave Ottawa on 20 August. On its arrival, the battalion relieved the Royal Rifles of Canada in the Lester's Field Barracks; the latter being shipped to Hong Kong with the Winnipeg Grenadiers to free up two British battalions stationed there for other assignments. The camp was a small town in itself with about eighty buildings all told. The mission given to the *Sherbrookes* was to guard the new airport at Torbay and to conduct coastal defence duties and surveillance. The battalion reported back to W Force, which in turn reported back to the St John's Defence Command. Six areas of concern had to be defended if the enemy attempted an invasion of the colony: Portugal Cave, St Philips, Topsail, Petty Harbour, Capes Spear and Torbay. A series of schemes were conducted over the ensuing months to practice the companies in their deployment in the case of an enemy attack. The nominal roll for the beginning of January 1942 showed that the battalion had an effective strength of 35 officers and 762 other ranks. RSM Barlow, who had been the first man enrolled when the *Sherbrookes* were mobilised, left the battalion on 8 January; he had been selected for an officers' preparatory course. He was replaced by Warrant Officer, Second Class (WO2) Edward J. Wolfe.

Conversion to the Canadian Armoured Corps

At the beginning of the war, Canada had very limited armoured resources. However, with the successes of the tank in leading the German *blitzkreig*, the Canadian Defence Committee authorised the creation of the Canadian Armoured Corps (CAC) in August 1940. Subsequently, 1st Canadian Armoured Division (1st Cdn Armd Div) was created.[8] In mid-November 1941, the British War Office informed the Canadian government that it would welcome the arrival of a second armoured division and another independent tank brigade to the United Kingdom. The Cabinet acquiesced but it judged that it did not have the financial resources to create another division from scratch. Instead, it decided to convert 4th Cdn Inf Div into an armoured formation. 4th Canadian Armoured Division (4th Cdn Armd Div) and 2nd Canadian Army Tank Brigade (2nd Cdn Army Tk Bde) were officially created on 26 January 1942. The decision was taken to assemble the new division in Debert, Nova Scotia, to conduct conversion training. On 8 February, the first draft of the *Sherbrookes* left St John's for Halifax Harbour. The second and final draft left Newfoundland on 16 February and the infantry battalion was established in Debert as the 27th Canadian Armoured Regiment (The Sherbrooke Fusilier Regiment), CAC. The battalion became a regiment, the four fighting companies were reduced to three and renamed as squadrons, and the platoons were now troops. The change would mean a reduction in strength by nearly 220 men. To make the final selection of who would stay with the new regiment, a board of review was set up to choose the men in the regiment most suited to the new establishment. Those men not classified as Category 'A' would be returned to a Base Depot for reassignment.

On 6 April, the regiment began in earnest its first courses in wireless, gunnery, driving and maintenance (D&M), and military training. Each course would last six weeks. That same day, the men were issued with black felt berets and tank badges to be worn on the right sleeve of their tunic. Each of the men took another course every seven weeks in rotation until he had taken all four courses. After a second re-board, the officers were divided among the squadrons. Over the next few months, the regiment lost several important members. Eighteen officers, including Lt-Col McA'Nulty, and forty-seven other ranks left for the United Kingdom to follow advanced armoured courses. On 8 April, Maj Camirand left and, on 30 April, Maj Biron, the DCO and acting CO in Lt-Col McA'Nulty's absence, was struck off strength. He had been promoted and was given the command of

PREPARATIONS FOR D-DAY

The United Kingdom.

2e Bataillon, Fus de Sher. On 4 May, Maj John Clifford Cave was taken on strength as the new acting CO.

The regiment spent the months of May through September conducting armoured conversion training. The number of available tanks was limited but the men got the chance to fire the Ram's 6-pdr main gun at Spencer's Point Ranges, to practice seaborne landings on McNab and Lawlor Islands in Halifax Harbour, and to conduct training in crew drills. In early September, the *Sherbrookes* were informed that 4th Cdn Armd Div would be shipped overseas over the course of the next few months. The regiment was supposed to leave Halifax on 23 September, but after several delays the move was finally called off. After a series of postponements, the advance party finally left for Halifax on 26 October. Two days later, the remainder of the regiment moved off from Debert. In Halifax, the men embarked on the *Queen Elizabeth*. The luxury liner, now converted into a troop transport ship, finally cast off on 30 October. During the night of 3–4 November, as the men slept, the ship pulled into the Firth of Clyde and dropped her anchors outside the harbour boom. The next day, the squadrons transferred to lighters for the trip to shore and then boarded trains for transport to Aldershot station. Warburg Barracks became the new home for the *Sherbrookes*.

With the arrival of the regiment, Lt-Col McA'Nulty resumed his command of the *Sherbrookes* and the squadrons got down to training the men. Unfortunately, there was little equipment available to the men: a few trucks, no universal carriers and the first Ram tank only arrived in camp on 13 November. Therefore, gunnery and D&M training was limited. Wireless training had to be conducted indoors as there were no vehicles in which to mount the radios. By the end of the month, the regiment had received four tanks and therefore only one troop could train on them at a time. To practice individual tank drills and troop tactics, the remainder of the troops resorted to using fence rails tied in an 'H' formation and assigning the men to crew positions. The officers supervised the training during the day, and two nights each week were set aside to give them any training they could not get during the day. Unfortunately, a few days after Christmas, Lt-Col McA'Nulty was stricken off strength for medical reasons and Maj Lyon was put in temporary command. Finally, on 8 February 1943, Lt-Col Melville Burgoyne Kennedy Gordon arrived in Warburg Barracks as the new commanding officer of the *Sherbrookes*. During the spring, the regiment experienced more changes in its senior leadership: Maj Lyon was stricken off strength on 4 March and returned to Canada; Maj Beaudry suffered the same fate on 1 June; and RSM Wolfe left the regiment on 9 July and Squadron Sergeant-Major (SSM) J.G.L.L. Dufault was named the new RSM on 3 September. By the end of the month of August, the reorganisation of the regiment was complete and only Maj Arnold remained from the original senior leadership of July 1940. He remained as the officer commanding A Sqn, while Maj George Stuart Mahon commanded B Sqn and Maj Vincent Owen Walsh commanded C Sqn. Maj Frederick Hosking Baldwin was in charge of HQ Sqn.

The conduct of the war in North Africa and the Soviet Union demonstrated that the proportion of armour to infantry in the armoured divisions was too high. It also showed that the effectiveness of an infantry division was multiplied if independent armoured brigades were available for close support in offensive operations. As a consequence, the British Army undertook a major reorganisation during the summer of 1942. Beginning in January 1943, the First Canadian Army (First Cdn Army) also underwent an extensive reorganisation of its armoured formations to bring them in line with the British organisation. Each Canadian armoured division consisted of two armoured brigades. They were now modified to consist of one armoured brigade and an infantry brigade. Therefore, six armoured regiments were displaced. As a consequence, the First Hussars (Hussars), the Fort Garry Horse (Garrys) and the *Sherbrookes* were converted to army tank regiments and joined the newly formed 3rd Canadian Army Tank Brigade (3rd Cdn Army Tk Bde). 2nd Cdn Army Tk Bde was still in Canada awaiting shipping space for transport to the United Kingdom. It was decided that once it arrived a competition between the six regiments of both tank brigades would take place and the best three regiments would be retained on the order of battle. The competition took place on 5 July and covered each regiment's operational capabilities. On 28 July, the *Sherbrookes* were informed that the three regiments of 3rd Cdn Army Tk Bde had scored higher than the regiments of 2nd Cdn Army Tk Bde and that the *Sherbrookes* would be retained on the Canadian order of battle. With effect from 22 July, 3rd Cdn Army Tk Bde was regrouped as 2nd Canadian Armoured Brigade (2nd Cdn Armd Bde). The change in terminology from a tank regiment to an armoured regiment was aimed at expressing the concept of strategy and tactics which had become necessary due to new developments in equipment by Germany. The German Army had increased its supply of heavy anti-tank weapons. It was therefore realised that the tanks would have to fight alongside the infantry because if they tried to dash ahead, they could find themselves boxed in and annihilated by a screen of anti-tank guns which the Germans were able to place with deadly swiftness. Rather, it was envisioned that the tanks and infantry would advance together. This reorganisation also marked the end to the regimental conversion training programme.

Training for Operation OVERLORD

On 3 July, Lt-Gen Henry Duncan Graham Crerar, the commander of First Cdn Army, was informed that 3rd Cdn Inf Div had been selected for assault training with the view to taking part in the assault in Operation OVERLORD. 2nd Cdn Armd Bde would come under the command of the division for the assault. On 8 July, First Cdn Army Headquarters (HQ) issued a memorandum to 3rd Cdn Inf Div which set forth the evolution of the training to be conducted in preparation for Operation OVERLORD. The training program was divided into four stages. The first stage was named 'preliminary training'. The months of August and September would be a period of intensive familiarisation with the mechanics of amphibious assault operations. The division was to learn the basic drills up to a full-scale brigade landing. The tank crews were to focus on loading and unloading with landing craft, tank (LCT) and landing ship, tank (LST). They would then make repeated landings on various beaches in both day and night. The second stage was 'basic training', and it would consist in a series of battalion-level and brigade-level amphibious exercises during the period from September to the end of October. The training was considered 'basic training' only in the sense that it was carried out without practice in the fire fight or reference to particular enemy defences. The third stage, from November to the end of January, was 'assault training' by brigade groups, characterised by increased realism. Later exercises would include live fire from artillery guns aboard LCT and smoke screens laid by aircraft. The final stage would culminate in collective assault training beginning in February. The exercises would be rehearsals for the landing in France in Operation OVERLORD.

The *Sherbrookes* immediately got into the training mode. Due to the lack of sufficient tanks to equip all three regiments of 2nd Cdn Armd Bde, a composite regiment was created with the *Sherbrookes* supplying C Sqn. For the remainder of the month of July, the squadrons practiced driving the tanks onto LCT, chaining them down and then sailing over water towards a beach. The tanks were then driven off the LCT onto the beach and then inland. The whole process was then done in reverse in order to return to the hards. From 31 July to 6 August, the composite regiment participated in Exercise HAMMER. It was designed to practice set-piece attacks on well-defended positions in cooperation with the infantry battalions of 6th Brigade. This would practice the battalion groups in the initial phase of an assault – the breaching of a defensive minefield. Each battalion of the brigade would spend three days with the regiment. While the tanks were committed to Exercise HAMMER, the Regimental Headquarters (RHQ) and the three squadron headquarters (SHQ) were employed in a series of administrative exercises. The first, Exercise ADAM, was held on 8–9 August. It was a signals and movement exercise designed to practice communications, the passing of orders, and the siting of the headquarters. On 10 August, Exercise PICKAXE got underway. The aim of this exercise was to practice commanders at all levels in breaking out of a beachhead and capturing an important tactical feature; in mounting a tank-infantry attack; in following up and defeating a retreating enemy; in protection against air and armoured fighting vehicles (AFV) attacks; in the reconnaissance of enemy defensive and rearguard positions; and in a river crossing. The scheme went well, but the attempted river crossing carried out on 13 August was deemed unsuccessful because too many of the tanks were deemed to have been lost to minefields and anti-tank guns. After a few days of rest, the composite regiment was tasked to participate in Exercise EVE I, beginning on 16 August and ending on 18 August. The objective of the exercise was to practice the RHQ and the three SHQ in giving orders and forming up with the infantry. This exercise was repeated on 24–25 August as Exercise EVE II.

For most of the month of September, the *Sherbrookes* were scheduled to move to Castle Toward, Scotland, to practice the loading and unloading of the tanks onto LST; in swimming the tanks in 9ft of water; and in evacuating from a tank when it was under water. Each squadron was to pass through in turn and follow the same training schedule. While the squadrons passed through Castle Toward, the regiment also had the use of Beachy Head Ranges. The squadrons not in Castle Toward got a chance to fire the 6-pdr main gun and the .303-cal Browning machine-gun from the Ram tanks. They engaged snapped and stationary targets.[9] Special attention was given to the rapid acquisition of targets and traversing off to divergent targets. Rather than return to Worthing on 21 September as planned, C Sqn was ordered to remain in Castle Toward to help train the infantry. For the remainder of the month, the squadron conducted both day and night schemes with the infantry battalions of 9th Brigade to assist the infantry in capturing a beachhead.

2nd Cdn Armd Bde had access to the Kirkcudbright AFV[10] Ranges in Scotland for the month of October. The *Sherbrookes* were the last regiment to pass through. Twenty Sherman tanks were signed out and sent forward over the course of the week from 17 to 24 September. On 12 October, the regiment finally entrained for the ranges and arrived the next day. The firing practice included individual firing on the armour piercing (AP) ranges, followed by individual firing on the high-explosive (HE) ranges. The troops then got the chance to do troop battle runs while the echelon personnel fired their rifles, the Bren guns, the Sten guns, PIATs[11] and grenades. The men also got the chance to fire the .50-cal Browning anti-aircraft gun mounted on the turret. To close off the practices, the squadrons conducted battle runs. On 23 October, the regiment left to return to Worthing. In the opinion of the men, the 75mm main gun of the Sherman was a vast improvement over the 6-pdr, which only fired a 37mm round; additionally, the Sherman tank was easier to handle than the Ram. The first stage of training in preparation for Operation OVERLORD was over.

October had been a month of changes within the regiment. On 7 October, Mobilisation Order No. 92 was issued. It specified that the regiments of 2nd Cdn Armd Bde were to mobilise to full War Establishment, excluding first reinforcements, as of 1 November. This meant that the *Sherbrookes*, hitherto tasked with the defence of the United Kingdom, were now definitely slated for a European campaign. Exercise CHASER was held on 29–31 October. It was a brigade-level exercise to practice the armoured regiments in an operational move by road followed by an attack against a well-defended enemy position. This was the third phase of an invasion of the European continent. At the end of the exercise, the regiment moved to a new location in New Milton. After a few days settling in, the regiment participated in Exercise ROUNDABOUT. The objective of the exercise was two-fold: first, to exercise 2nd Cdn Armd Bde in its operational role when under the command of an infantry division, and second, to cover the third phase of the invasion of the Continent – the enlargement of a beachhead. A week later, Lt-Col Gordon held an Orders Group (O Group) for Exercise PUSH, the upcoming brigade-level exercise.

However, instead of moving off as planned on 24 November, all the officers and NCOs left at 10.30 for 9th Brigade HQ in Chilworth Manor at Brockenhurst to attend a presentation by Major-General (Maj-Gen) Rodney Frederick Leopold Keller, the commander of 3rd Cdn Inf Div. He spilled the beans and revealed with breath-taking clarity just what was in store for the regiment. He stressed that what he was about to reveal was of a secret nature, but that he trusted all the men to remain quiet. 3rd Cdn Inf Div had been designated as an assault division for the invasion and had been scaled down accordingly, even to the point of dropping its recce unit. The armoured cooperation was to come from 2nd Cdn Armd Bde which was to be under the division's command. A normal division was made up of 19,000 men while this division had 31,000 men all told. He explained that the upcoming exercises were to be regarded as of an operational as well as a training nature. There would possibly be attacks from the air and by enemy E-boats. Because 3rd Cdn Inf Div and 2nd Cdn Armd Bde were chosen to participate in the invasion, they had to be worthy of the role. The exercises they conducted would be closely watched by the General Staff and the senior naval, military and air force officers. He stressed that they all had to prove themselves to these officers. The training conducted over the past summer had been a march up to the use of landing craft, while the training in Castle Toward had been company and squadron schemes. From now on, the training would concentrate on the assault phase. In the ensuing manoeuvres, the battle drill would be 7th Brigade right with the Hussars, 8th Brigade left with the Garrys, and 9th Brigade with the *Sherbrookes* for exploitation. 9th Brigade would also practice in the assault in case of a miscarriage of the plan.

Maj-Gen Keller then went on to stress the need for security. The men were to be cautioned not to discuss military secrets with others, above all women – desirable or undesirable. He stressed that he expected every officer and NCO to be able to handle the job two levels above his own. Changing over to the subject of the landing, he stressed the need of getting out of the landing craft quickly; of fire and movement; of taking up proper fire positions; and then digging in and consolidating. The assault was planned for daylight in order to be able to use the support weapons with effect, whereas at night the enemy would have the advantage of having his guns on a fixed line. Also, at night, the Navy had difficulty with the safe navigation of the LCT and it would be more dangerous to clear minefields in the dark. In closing, he stressed that success would be achieved through simplicity and speed.

The next morning, Lt-Col Gordon held another O Group for Exercise PUSH. He explained to the squadron commanders that the aim of the exercise was to practice 9th Brigade in breaking out of a beachhead already made by 8th Brigade during an initial landing during Exercise VIDI. Movement controls would be imposed to imitate those controls that would be imposed prior to a real landing. The vehicle markings had to be completed immediately and they would be checked and cleaned at every halt during the exercise. Each squadron would also have to prepare a list of the vehicles being taken on Exercise PUSH, showing the War Department numbers, the type of vehicle from tank to motorcycle, and the crew. Each vehicle was to carry a complete and proper load of ammunition and equipment and each man was to carry a full complement of personal ammunition. The assault group was composed of 9th Brigade and the *Sherbrookes*, and was to act as the reserve brigade group of an assault division.

The regiment learned a great deal from the exercise. The days at sea seemed endless; each LCT was cut off from the others in complete radio silence, waiting for the word to land. The crew commanders had to be 'mentally ambidextrous' when guiding their tanks from the turret using only the intercom system. They heartily appreciated the 'compo' rations which included meat, biscuits, chocolate bars, fruit puddings and salads with mayonnaise, and had to be guarded with one's life. They learned how to pitch their tents forward in the winch houses of the LCT and to laugh at the simplicity of the life belts which they quickly renamed 'Mae Wests'. They learned how the craft loads were calculated and how each man had to be tagged and recorded as he embarked on the LCT, and then the tags collected on disembarkation. Terms such as 'Bostic C' and 'Bostic A', 'asbestos compound' and 'grease waterproofing' or 'plastic cement' began to whirl around in everyone's brain and, finally, the issue of 'bags, vomit'. Exercise PUSH was the most strenuous experienced to date, and the men loved it.

No sooner was the regiment off Exercise PUSH than Lt-Col Gordon held an O Group on 5 December for Exercise FROST. The object of this exercise was to practice the armoured regiments in road movements and harbouring by day and by night, and to practice the intelligence personnel in the passage of information. Lt-Col Gordon said that he expected his orders in a sealed envelope at noon the next day. However, at 17.00 on 6 December, he informed the DCO and the squadron commanders that the exercise had been postponed for at least a month. Instead, a seven-day period of intense maintenance, followed by an inspection by the staff of 2nd Cdn Armd Bde, would be conducted. Periodic checks would be made by the brigade, picking any tank at random. The number of hards for tanks that could take an LST was small in England and so speed became an essential factor in embarking the invasion fleet. Exercise NUDGER II was designed to practice the Royal Navy in the rapid loading and turn-around at loading hards. C Sqn of the regiment and A Sqn of the Garrys were assigned to participate. Over a three-day period from 16 to 19 December, C Sqn practiced loading a complete squadron of eighteen tanks, two tracked ammunition (ammo) carriers, plus thirty-two wheeled vehicles onto an LST at the hards in Southampton. On the last day of the exercise, the squadron completed the loading in sixty minutes flat. The second stage of preparatory training was over, but every vehicle was to be 100 per cent ready and kept that way. The squadrons immediately got to work.

On 3 January, Exercise FROST began. Its aim had not changed from the briefing received on 6 December. The regiment crossed the start line at 09.00 with sixty-nine tanks from the three fighting squadrons and the RHQ; fifty-one vehicles from the A Ech; and fourteen vehicles from the B Ech. The convoy travelled 58 miles to a harbour in Stocton Wood near Salisbury. The next day, the convoy moved 57 miles to a new harbour in Heckfield Heath just south of Reading. En route, the umpires handed out envelopes containing documents supposedly taken from an enemy prisoner of war. The umpires then timed how long it took for the information to reach the RHQ. That night, the regiment travelled 19 miles to another harbour in the area of Nettlebed Wood north of Reading. At 02.00 on 7 January, the regiment made another night move of 45 miles to the outskirts of Oxford and then to a laager on a road near Chipping Norton. After a two-hour stop for maintenance and refuelling, the convoy moved another 80 miles to a harbour in Great Wood on the estate of Lord Lansdowne. The next day, another night move was carried out to a laager on the road at Lydlinch Common. There, the convoy stopped to conduct maintenance before making a second move to return to New Milton. Exercise FROST was a test of endurance for both the men and the machines.

At 14.00 on 9 January, Lt-Col Gordon announced that the regiment would move to Lyndhurst to practice the new 21st Army Group doctrine with regards to infantry cooperation with Sherman tanks. The regiment would work with 9th Brigade and spend three days with each of its battalions. The training schedule would consist of a firepower demonstration on the first morning by a troop of Shermans and a company of infantry. In the afternoon, there would be lectures and discussions on the new doctrine. The next day, there would be a company-squadron level scheme, followed up on the last day by a battalion-regiment level scheme and closing discussions. The training would take place over the period from 12 to 20 January. Between 15 and 19 February, the regiment sent ten tanks and their crews on Exercise POPLIN. The aim of this exercise was to measure the level of noise made by an LCT breaching, the tanks disembarking, and incidental noises aboard the LCT such as the starting of the tank engines, on landing and then the sound of them running off into the distance. Each morning, the tanks were loaded onto an LCT which then sailed out to disembark them at different points on the Isle of Wight.

Training with 9th Brigade became the focus for the regiment; 9th Brigade held Exercise PEDAL on 16–17 February. The brigade wanted to practice its battalions in the rapid movement to, and the seizure of, an objective; to test the Highland Light Infantry of Canada (HLI of C) and the Stormont, Dundas and Glengarry Highlanders (SD&GH) on bicycles, and the North Nova Scotia Highlanders (North Novas) on transports or the tanks; and for the tanks to consolidate after two hours in anticipation of an enemy counter-attack. On 28 February, 2nd Cdn Armd Bde was inspected at Bashley Lodge by General (Gen) Sir Bernard Law 'Monty' Montgomery, the General Commanding 21st Army Group. He ordered all the men to break ranks and to gather round his jeep. He spoke a few words of encouragement before moving off at 12.00.

Exercise PRANK was initially planned to begin on 10 March, but it was advanced to 2 March. Its aim was to practice the briefing procedure so that the troops might go into an operation with the full knowledge of their tasks. To add realism, the beach exits would be cratered and blocked; thereby creating a real need for the preparation of tracked and wheeled exits before the vehicles could leave the beaches. In addition, the umpires would create vehicle and personnel casualties to produce the problems inherent to such casualties occurring. The serials moved off on 8 March and immediately loaded onto LCT in Southampton. As expected, the beach exits had been cratered and blocked to create casualties. On being declared a casualty, the vehicle could not move until it was recovered and once removed would take no further part in the exercise. Some tanks bogged down in the craters and had to be left behind. The troop leaders and the squadron second-in-command (2i/c) were forced to change tanks in a hurry and leave their disabled tank for a beach recovery unit to deal with it. The tanks moved to the assembly area where the waterproofing hardware was removed. The North Novas then scrambled up onto the Shermans and the battlegroup advanced to the objective. On arrival, A Sqn and B Sqn dropped off the infantry and took up positions to support them by fire while they dug in and consolidated. With the infantry consolidated, the tanks withdrew to New Mills Heath near Swanage where they prepared for their counter-attack role.

PREPARATIONS FOR D-DAY

On 11 March, the exercise ended and the regiment returned to New Milton. The remainder of March was spent conducting maintenance and getting the tanks in tip-top shape. During the last two weeks of March, the number of the regiment's vehicles was brought up to full strength. In addition to the Shermans, the regiment received the new Firefly tank, similar to the Sherman but equipped with a 76mm 17-pdr main gun. The Firefly was the British answer to the German Tiger tank. The regiment had received a proportion of Fireflies when the Ram training tanks were turned in for Sherman operational tanks. It was a new addition to the regiment but no one had had an opportunity to fire the 17-pdr main gun. Therefore, 2nd Cdn Armd Bde sent a contingent of twelve officers and ninety-nine other ranks from all three armoured regiments to the Warcop Ranges in Cumbria. The *Sherbrookes* sent four officers and forty-seven other ranks on 4 April. They arrived the next day and followed an introductory course on the 17-pdr. The next day, they got their chance to fire the weapon with HE, and on 7 April they moved to the AP range. The men were quite enthusiastic and were greatly impressed by the new weapon. The war establishment for the armoured regiments was:

RHQ	4 Shermans	CO, DCO, 2i/c HQ Sqn and a spare
HQ Sqn	6 Shermans	Ack-Ack Troop (Lieut, Sgt and 4 Cpls)
	11 Stuarts	Recce Troop (Lieut, 4 Sgts and 6 Cpls)
A, B and C Sqns	3 Shermans	SHQ (OC, 2i/c and RLO[12])
	5 Fireflies	Troop leaders (5 Lieut)
	10 Shermans	2 per troop (Sgt and Cpl)

While some of the men were on the Warcop Ranges getting acquainted with the new tank, the rest of the regiment prepared for a move to West Walk Camp South near Wickham. The main body was to go with the North Novas to Camp A-15, one mile north-east of Wickham and 6 miles east of Southampton. The advance party moved off at 09.00 on 5 April. On its arrival, the regiment was confined to barracks. The troops were put in bell tents and the vehicles parked on standings on the main Wickham-Droxford road.[13] Censorship of outgoing mail came into force on 8 April. The North Novas were placed in West Walk Woods but the officers and sergeants of both units messed together and the men got to know each other on a first name basis. The North Novas chaffed the tankers for being 'grease monkeys', but the *Sherbrookes* hooted back at the infantry that they were 'peashooters' – in reference to their rifles and Bren guns.

On 12 April, the regiment began Exercise PEDAL II, a scheme designed to allow the regiment a chance to run-in its new tanks. The regiment left West Walk Camp South and travelled 9 miles north to a harbour on Bramdean Common. The convoy of 91 vehicles and 454 all ranks left the next day in serials for a new harbour 15 miles east and 6 miles south of its present position. On 14 April, the convoy moved from Singleton to an assembly area where the North Novas were loaded onto the tanks. The battlegroup then advanced on its objective on Wepham Downs. The attack on the enemy position was carried out using live ammunition. Once the position consolidated, the tanks were released and the regiment proceeded to Whiteways Lodge to harbour for the night. The next day, it returned to West Walk Camp South.

Exercise FABIUS III was scheduled as the last exercise prior to the invasion. It was the last series of exercises in stage four and aimed at practicing each of the forces in the invasion plan:

FABIUS I	Naval assault force 'O' for American forces landing on Omaha Beach
FABIUS II	Naval assault force 'G' for British forces landing on Gold Beach
FABIUS III	Naval assault force 'J' for Canadian forces landing on Juno Beach
FABIUS IV	Naval assault force 'S' for British forces landing on Sword Beach

FABIUS V and FABIUS VI were to exercise the machinery for loading personnel and equipment for the augmentation forces for the invasion.[14] Exercise FABIUS III was designed as a full-scale division exercise and a dress rehearsal, not only for the fighting troops, but for the administrative and supply groups under beachhead conditions. The objective was to establish a beachhead on the Selsey Peninsula and then penetrate inland to the northeast. The forward infantry brigade groups would first gain a toehold on the beaches before 9th Brigade and the *Sherbrookes* were allowed to land and exploit their success. While waiting for the exercise to begin, 3rd Cdn Inf Div was visited by King George VI and Lt-Gen Crerar on the Fareham Recreational Grounds.

PREPARATIONS FOR D-DAY

On 29 April, the regiment left West Walk Camp South and travelled through Fareham and Bursledon to the dispersal point at Fair Oaks and thence to Camp C-6 in the vicinity of Eastleigh. The men stayed in camp the whole of the next day before moving to the hards in Southampton and loading onto LST at the Southern Railway docks. Once loaded, the LST sailed down the Solent and anchored in Stokes Bay off the Isle of Wight. During the night of 3–4 May, the flotilla moved off from Stokes Bay and sailed all night. The next morning, the LST arrived in Bracklesham Bay and the first wave went ashore under the cover of a smoke screen. The tanks had difficulty getting off the beaches because the exits were blocked with vehicles. Therefore, the tanks were late in getting to the assembly area. Once they had married up with the North Novas, the assault group carried on beyond Chichester and rushed towards Petworth. Due to poor weather, however, the naval authorities put a stop to further disembarkation. Therefore, after dinner, the regiment received orders to return to the hards. The LST returned to Stokes Bay for the night before returning to Southampton on 5 May.

The regiment received the last of fifty-one new Sherman Mk III (M4A2) tanks on 9 May.[15] Over the following week, the regiment also received three armoured recovery vehicles (ARV) and twenty-one new Firefly tanks. The troops had half a month to get the tanks ready, a task that usually took a full month's hard work. The crews had to dissolve the preservative grease from all the gun parts; tune up the engines; change the rubber shod tracks for steel tracks; clean out the tanks; and stow the tanks with battle necessities such as rations, water cans, binoculars, ammunition, signal flares, etc. The tanks had to be waterproofed to enable them to wade through water up to 6ft deep. It was the dirtiest, messiest and gooiest job in the Armoured Corps, but, a tank 'drowned' in seawater was a useless piece of junk – the innumerable bearings, once touched by salt water, quickly corroded.

On 13 May, a parade was held for Gen Dwight David Eisenhower, the Supreme Allied Commander, and two days later the regiment moved from Camp C-6 to Camp A-15 in Brooklands, 6 miles southwest of West Walk Camp South. The vehicles were parked on standings on the Southampton-Portsmouth highway facing southwest. This tended to indicate that the embarkation point would be at Gosport or Portsmouth, and not Southampton. Preparations and waterproofing continued and the vehicles were finally ready on 25 May. That night, all the camps were sealed except for the drivers who stayed with their vehicle. Unfortunately, the regiment suffered a loss on 24 May when RSM Dufault unscrewed the wrong end of a No. 77 phosphorous grenade.[16] He had to throw it away when it ignited but there were buildings and vehicles all around and so he chose to throw it under a lorry to limit the blast. He badly burned his hands and face before he could take any actions to get out of the danger zone. He was taken to the hospital and SSM D.E. MacLeod was appointed as the acting RSM for the invasion. His appointment became permanent on 6 June.

For the remainder of the month, a series of briefings and conferences were held from 3rd Cdn Inf Div down to individual crews. The maps used were all labelled 'Bogus Op OVERLORD'. The land was identified accurately, but with false names for the communities, rivers and roads. By 29 May, all the men of the *Sherbrookes* had been thoroughly 'put in the picture'. Most had heard the operation outline at least five times. The regimental strength stood at 37 officers and 661 other ranks on 31 May – still short 1 officer and 14 other ranks. The assault vehicles moved out of Camp A-18 and travelled to Camp A-17 at Parks Gate. At 02.00 on 3 June, the craft serials moved off from the camp in small packets and proceeded to G-3 Hard in Gosport. There, forty-eight Porpoises were waiting to be chained between the tracks of the tanks.[17] Also known as Turtles, they could carry 110 rounds of 75mm or 76mm ammunition – HE, AP or smoke rounds. The tanks were loaded onto LCT which then sailed out into the Solent and anchored off Calshot Castle. However, stormy weather on 4 June forced a twenty-four-hour delay in the invasion. Finally, at 14.15 on 5 June, the anchors were drawn up and the flotilla moved off. At 17.30, the LCT of the regiment passed the boom of the outer harbour and surged into the choppy, grey waters of the English Channel.

Chapter 2

6 June: The D-Day Landings

In August 1941, during a secret meeting in Washington sanctioned by US President Franklin Delano Roosevelt and British Prime Minister Winston Spencer Churchill, the British and American Chiefs of Staff agreed that should the United States enter the war, the main effort would be devoted to the defeat of Germany first. Only after her defeat would the full might of the Allies be turned against Japan. This decision was confirmed in December 1941 at the Arcadia Conference in Washington. The initial operational plan, drafted by Gen George Catlett Marshall Jr., the American Chief of Staff, called for the invasion of France by 1 April 1943. Codenamed ROUNDUP, the plan called for an invasion using thirty American and eighteen British divisions. The invasion force would land somewhere between Le Havre and Boulogne with the aim of advancing on the large port of Antwerp. The officer assigned to plan the details of the invasion was Brigadier-General (Brig) Dwight David Eisenhower. The Imperial General Staff accepted the plan even though they had misgivings at the possibility of building on time the 7,000 landing craft of all types that would be required for the assault.[1]

Planning for the invasion was under the direction of a British officer, Lt-Gen Frederick Edgworth Morgan, the Chief of Staff to the Supreme Allied Commander (Designate) or COSSAC. Lt-Gen Morgan was appointed to the position in March 1943, even before a Supreme Commander had been decided upon. Because the appointment came so late, it virtually killed the possibility of executing Operation ROUNDUP in 1943 and COSSAC's planning target date was changed to 1 May 1944. The new plan called for five infantry divisions to land simultaneously on the beaches, two airborne divisions to drop on strategic sites inland, two divisions off the beaches in landing craft for follow-up and twenty further divisions to be used to build up the beachhead once established. However, when the question of obtaining the required number of landing craft again became an issue, the planning was dropped to three divisions in the initial invasion force.

Two sites were deemed to meet most of the criteria for the invasion: the Pas-de-Calais area and the Cotentin-Caen area. The Pas-de-Calais area was only 20 miles across the English Channel and the beaches were almost ideal. The downside was that the Germans had evaluated the same potential for the area and the defensive preparations were greater there. Furthermore, the Canadian raid on Dieppe in August 1942[2] had shown that it was extremely dangerous to try to seize a defended port. The Cotentin-Caen area, on the other hand, was at a greater distance and would require longer turn-around times for the naval and air sorties. However, the beach defences were relatively light and the beaches themselves were acceptable. In the end, the site for the Allied assault on Hitler's Atlantic Wall was chosen in the Normandy area between the Orne and Vire estuaries and along the eastern shore of the Cotentin Peninsula. The area contained many fine beaches and was sheltered in some degree from the prevailing westerly winds coming off the Atlantic Ocean. The area was favoured because it was suitable for the maintenance of an invading force and was within range of fighter aircraft stationed in the United Kingdom. Allied intelligence estimates had identified limited, and even weak, German forces and defences along that section of the French coast.

Lt-Gen Morgan's plan was submitted to the Combined Chiefs of Staff during the Quadrant Conference held in Quebec City, Canada, in August 1943. The plan was approved and its detailed planning was authorised. At the end of 1943, President Roosevelt named Gen Eisenhower as the Supreme Allied Commander.[3] In order to respect British pride and the British contribution to the projected invasion, a British officer was required to command the armies in Normandy. Gen Eisenhower's preference was Gen Sir Harold Alexander, but Prime Minister Churchill and the Chief of the Imperial General Staff opted to give responsibility for the assault to Gen Montgomery, Commander-in-Chief of 21st Army Group and the hero of El Alamein. As well, British officers would also command the air and sea elements of the invasion. 21st Army Group would be composed of First United States Army (First US Army), under the command of Lt-Gen Omar Nelson Bradley and Second British Army (Second Brit Army), under Lt-Gen Miles Christopher Dempsey.

Both Gen Eisenhower and Gen Montgomery considered the COSSAC plan of an invasion using only three divisions on a narrow front weak. The plan was reworked to allow for the simultaneous landing by five divisions spread over 50 miles. The new plan was to attack with both armies simultaneously. First US Army was to capture beachheads on the right or

6 JUNE: THE D-DAY LANDINGS

western flank between the Drôme and Vire Rivers and on the eastern shore of the Cotentin Peninsula near Saint-Martin-de-Varreville. In advance of the landings, paratroopers from 82nd US Airborne Division (82 Airborne) and 101st US Airborne Division (101 Airborne) would drop and capture crucial communications sites in-land and help isolate Cherbourg. Once the initial bridgehead established, First US Army would capture the great port of Cherbourg as quickly as possible. It would then develop operations southward towards Saint-Lô.

The task of Second Brit Army was to capture beachheads on the left or eastern flank in the region enclosing Port-en-Bessin, Bayeux, Caen and Cabourg, at the mouth of the Dives River. XXX British Corps (XXX Brit Corps) would land on Gold Beach, while First British Corps (First Brit Corps), to which the Canadian contribution would be attached, would land on Juno and Sword Beaches. In advance of these landings, 6th British Airborne Division (6th Brit Airborne Div), including 1st Canadian Parachute Battalion (1st Cdn Para Bn), was to drop east of the Orne River and seize crossings over the Caen Canal and protect the left flank. Once the beachheads established, Second Brit Army would develop the beachhead south of the Caen-Saint-Lô line and southeast of Caen in order to gain airfield sites and to protect the flank of First US Army while it was capturing Cherbourg. All preparations were to be completed by 31 May 1944. Two five-day periods in which tidal and lunar conditions were good had been identified: from 2 to 6 June inclusive, and from 17 to 21 June inclusive. On 8 May, the decision was taken to select D-Day as 5 June with alternative dates as 6 or 7 June.

Responsibility for the Canadian sector was given to 3rd Cdn Inf Div and its commander, Maj-Gen Keller. Under his command were three infantry brigades: 7th Brigade commanded by Brig Harry Wickwire Foster, 8th Brigade commanded by Brig Kenneth Gault Blackader, and 9th Brigade commanded by Brig Douglas Gordon Cunningham; with 2nd Cdn Armd Bde commanded by Brig Robert Andrew Wyman in support. The remaining elements of the First Cdn Army – its headquarters under Lt-Gen Crerar, and the remainder of Second Canadian Corps (Second Cdn Corps) under Lt-Gen Guy Granville Simonds and composed of 2nd Cdn Inf Div and 4th Cdn Armd Div – would then gradually establish themselves in Normandy over the next few weeks. Maj-Gen Keller's plan was to attack on a two-brigade front: MIKE Beach on the right and NAN Beach on the left. His task on D-Day was to seize an area extending 10 miles inland, including the high ground west of Caen and astride the main road to Bayeux. His plan would be conducted

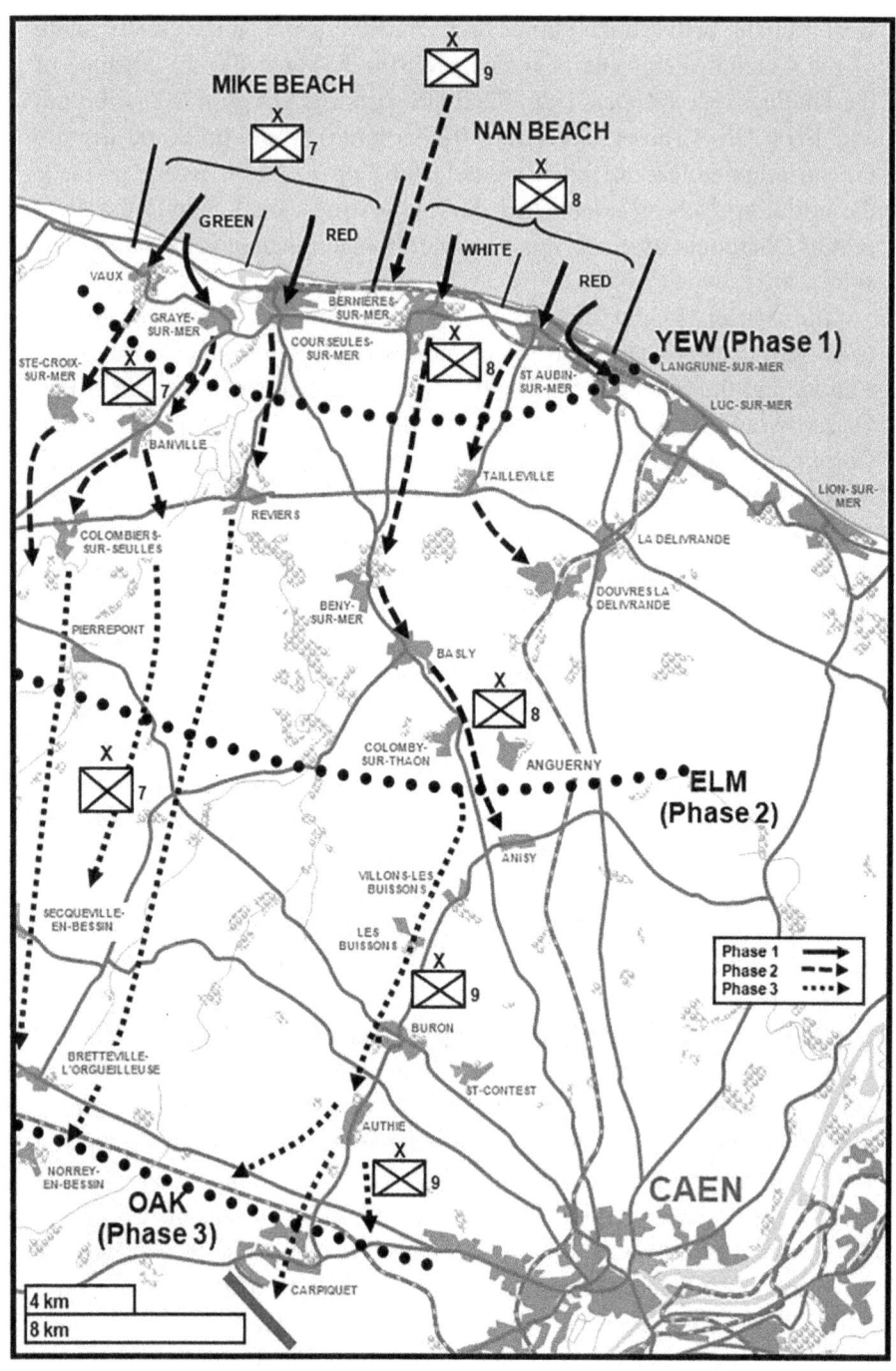

6 June 1944: The D-Day plan for 3rd Canadian Infantry Division.

6 JUNE: THE D-DAY LANDINGS

in five phases. Phase 1 of his plan was to land a brigade on either side of the mouth of the Seulles River, to mop up the coastal region and to capture a bridgehead along objective YEW (a line stretching behind the towns of Vaux, Graye-sur-Mer, Courseulles-sur-Mer, Bernières-sur-Mer and Saint-Aubin-sur-Mer). 7th Brigade, supported by the tanks of the Hussars, would land on MIKE Beach, the right flank of the Canadian sector. 8th Brigade, supported by the tanks of the Garrys, would land on NAN Beach.

Once consolidation completed, Phase 2 called for the division to seize the immediate division objective ELM, a line stretching from Creully through Pierrepont and ending near Colomby-sur-Thaon. The right assault brigade group was to secure crossings over the Seulles River and establish itself on the southern bank southeast of Creully. The left assault brigade group was to establish a firm base on the high ground Basly-Anguerny-Anisy. While this was happening, 9th Brigade was to land on either MIKE or NAN Beach and to move to its assigned assembly area near Bény-sur-Mer. When objective ELM was taken, 9th Brigade would take the lead and capture the final division objective OAK, the railway running parallel to and just south of the Caen-Bayeux road between Putot-en-Bessin and Carpiquet. The North Novas, supported by the tanks of the *Sherbrookes*, was to advance 9 miles and seize the town of Carpiquet and the airport situated there. During Phase 4, the division would reorganise on OAK and prepare to repulse the expected German counter-attack. Once OAK was taken, 2nd Cdn Armd Bde was to be prepared to exploit a further 6 miles to seize the high ground around the village of Évrecy as part of Phase 5.

D-Day was not a particularly exciting day for the Sherbrooke Fusilier Regiment. It was too much like 'just another scheme' for the men to get excited about it. They were at sea and out of sight of land, but they had been that way before. Even when they sighted the shores of France that morning, they remembered that some of them had blundered as close three months before. There was the noise of gunfire, but they had heard that before too. They could see landing craft and vehicles burning on the shores, but they had also seen Studland Bay pocked with craters to make things look more realistic. Most convincing of all were the 'mix-ups', for which old soldiers have their own name, and on which they pounced as perfectly valid excuses for not taking anything too seriously. When they finally did land, there was a big traffic jam in Bernières-sur-Mer, the seaside town through which they were expected to move; and it took nearly six hours just to drive the 3 miles to the first assembly area. Yes, it was all so like just another scheme that some of them felt that they might just as well get a little sleep, while the others propped shoulder to the gun or read action-packed yarns from *Dime Detective* and *Western Story* magazines.

Although the squadron commanders had received a briefing on the real D-Day objectives several days before leaving, none of the crews had been informed. The orders for each troop and crew had been sealed for security reasons with instructions to not distribute them until the LCT had passed the harbour boom and reached the open Channel. These had been placed in a Hessian bag and given for safekeeping to the commander of each LCT. The orders for the operation, maps of France and the various codes to be used were distributed among the crews. The maps were now fitted under talc traces that had been previously marked. However, no maps of the coast area itself of 1:50,000 scale were included and therefore half the traces

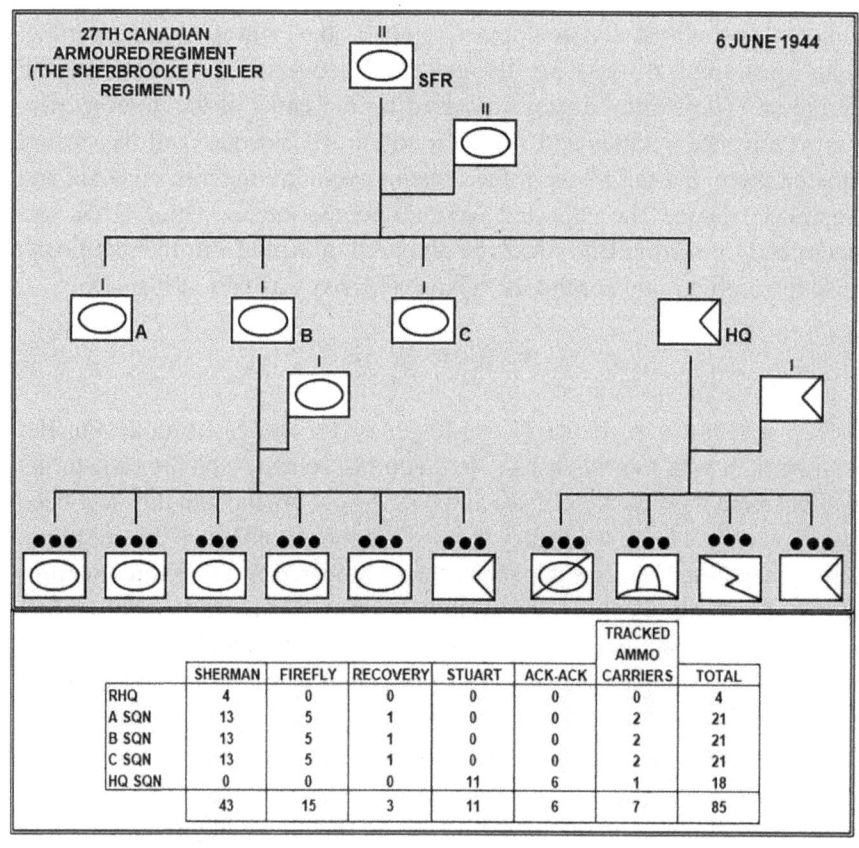

were useless. Only a few vehicles had maps showing the assembly area. After distribution, a briefing was given. Most of the men were seasick, so many did not look at the plan, merely content with storing the maps and data in their turret. They were too sick to care about where they were going.

The landing craft carrying the tanks of the *Sherbrookes* arrived off the coast of France and in view of the Normandy beaches at about 10.00 on 6 June. The crossing had been difficult with rough seas. Wet and cold, most everyone had suffered from some degree or other of nausea. All around were more landing craft. Maj Baldwin, the officer commanding of HQ Sqn, landed with two soldiers and a jeep with 8th Brigade. He was the tank unit landing officer (TULO) for the regiment. Unfortunately, his LCT hit a mine on its approach and a 15-cwt truck became jammed in the doorway. The landing craft had to back up into deep water where the truck was pushed off before the LCT could attempt another landing. Because of the congestion on the beach caused by an 88mm anti-tank gun positioned on the high ground inland, Maj Baldwin could not accomplish his role as TULO.

The landing craft of 9th Brigade had been circling patiently 15 miles off shore in 5ft seas since their arrival. All around, the soldiers could see every type of military craft afloat. Battleships were firing their big guns from 10 miles offshore while cruisers and destroyers moved closer to the landing beaches to give direct fire support. The crews could hear the shells going overhead, sounding like freight trains. Each ship had a barrage balloon and all were firing guns and rockets over their heads. Planes attacked the enemy strongpoints on the shore. The regiment's thirteen LCT had started to move forward at 08.00 and stayed 8 miles offshore waiting for their cue to land. At 10.30, a radio message was received that the Queen's Own Rifles of Canada (Queen's Own) and the North Shore (New Brunswick) Regiment (North Shore Regt) had reached YEW at 10.20. The LCT commenced making great circles as they moved in. Slowly, the circles got smaller and smaller, and when they reached 2 miles from the shore, the LCT spread out in a line formation. The troops had been sitting on the tops of their tanks watching the shore and waiting for their turn. The bombings and bombardment of the naval guns made quite a bit of smoke and only the red flashes of each explosion could be seen from a distance. As they approached the shore, they saw fires burning on the beach, heard small arms fire coming from isolated strong points, heard small scale naval shelling and saw German prisoners under guard. Trooper (Tpr) Arnold B. Boyd thought, 'Well, the war's just about won by now.' At 1.5 miles from shore, the crews stowed their gear and unchained their vehicles. They could now see the beach. Finally, they got the word at 11.30 to make their approach. They met sunken LCT and LCI, some sideways in the wash. Just before reaching the beach, the LCT let the barrage balloons go up. The beach was littered with German obstacles with Tellermines or artillery shells attached to them.

Because the beaches at Saint-Aubin-sur-Mer were still not secure, all the landing craft of 9th Brigade were directed towards NAN White Beach. At 12.15, all the LCT arrived without casualties and the first tanks landed just west of Bernières-sur-Mer. With about 30 yards to go, the ramps were let down and the tanks crossed shallow water, 3½ft deep, onto the beaches and removed their waterproofing, a steel frame with airplane fabric covers up to 5ft feet high placed over the gun muzzle and mantle, over ventilation ports and around the back deck and turrets. The beaches were already littered with waterproofing from the Duplex-drive tanks of the Hussars and the Garrys. The beach masters wanted the crews to keep going and take off the waterproofing later; it was becoming a nuisance to the landings. The crews took them off anyway because they wanted to be ready to fight if necessary. Inside the turret, the tank driver inserted an electrical connection into a socket, similar to a cigarette lighter in a car, and an electrical current detonated the Cordex explosive that blew all the paraphernalia free. Each tank seemed to explode with a loud bang as the fabric was blown off. The crew commander would then pull a trigger and the towering breathing tubes would clatter to the ground. The remainder of the crew would then use wrenches and crowbars to tear off the breathing tube mounting fixtures. The engine servicing compartment door was opened and the level of water that had infiltrated into the compartment was checked. The troops had done a good job at waterproofing and most compartments had hardly enough briny in there to make up a good gargle. At 12.26, 2nd Cdn Armd Bde HQ received the code word 'NUTS' from the *Sherbrookes* – the tanks were on the beach.[4]

B Sqn, however, had experienced a series of mishaps. When the ramp of the landing craft of Captain (Capt) Merritt Hayes Bateman, the squadron 2i/c, went down, his tank had to move forward slowly and balance on the ramp. It moved ahead and then fell into water 11ft deep. When he tried to fix himself to the radio net, the radio shorted out. Smoke filled the turret and all communications, both external and internal, were knocked out. Capt Bateman rigged up two strings from the shoulder straps of his driver's uniform and passed them back through the turret. He thereby steered the driver like a team of horses until repairs could be made. Troop 3 leader Lieutenant (Lieut) Lawrence Norman Davies's craft hit a mine that breached the bow but caused very little damage. The commander of the LCT carrying the tanks of Sgt Angus J. Parsons's troop let down the ramp too soon. When his tank came out it went right under water. They shipped a lot of water but kept on going. Lance-Corporal (L/Cpl) J.G. Slater landed on the beaches and stepped into a shell hole from an 88mm gun. As he was going down into the crater, he had his helmet shot off. He went through the rest of the war without a helmet.[5]

C Sqn's landing was completely uneventful; the LCT landed its tanks approximately at the point planned. The tanks were held up on the beaches by the usual congestion of vehicles experienced during training exercises. However, to differentiate this from an exercise was the presence of a 'few bundles of grey bags' which had been German soldiers. The sight of these came as a shock to most of the *Sherbrookes* as they were the only incongruous things in Exercises PUSH, PEDAL and FABIUS III. The landing craft carrying the fuel truck driven by Tpr George K. Mann of C Sqn, loaded with 225 jerry cans of fuel and a motorcycle, hit a sunken vehicle on its approach. When he drove off the craft he was still a good distance from the beach and was sitting in water up to his waist. When he finally made it to the beach, his truck fell into a shell crater that had filled with water. He was now up to his chin in water. An attempt was made to drag the truck onto the beach using a tank but the undercarriage of the truck ripped off. With nothing but the uniform on his back, Tpr Mann was told by Maj Baldwin that he was of no use to anybody without his weapon and gear. Tpr Mann was told to swim back out to the landing craft. Several hours later he came back, sitting on the roof of another truck and landed again on the beach.[6]

Before leaving England, Capt Theodore William Brokovski, the Regimental Medical Officer (Med O), had filled his jeep with medical supplies and equipment to evacuate the wounded. When his jeep rolled off its landing craft, it was behind a half-track. The half-track got stuck momentarily and the jeep lost its momentum and ploughed into a hole where it got stuck and the motor drowned. Not wanting to be left behind, he immediately grabbed a stretcher and threw as many shell dressings and medical supplies as he could save from the water onto it. He waded ashore with his driver/corpsman and began plodding up the road after the last disappearing tank. He made for a determined figure – wet, dusty, bedraggled and yet with an unfaltering step, stretcher over his shoulder and his corpsman trotting along beside him.

Before the regiment left England, each officer had been given a 40-oz bottle of Canadian Club rye whiskey. Capt Sydney Valpy Radley-Walters, the 2i/c of C Sqn, had promised his crew that if they were lucky enough to hit the beaches of France then they would all share a drink from the bottle. As they waited for their turn to go through the seawall, he passed the bottle down to his driver. Although Tpr Edward J. Herman had been very seasick on the crossing, when the bottle came back it was missing three fingers of rye. Capt Hector MacDonald Belton, the recce/liaison officer for C Sqn, was plastered with flowers, cigarettes and wine as he passed through Bernières-sur-Mer. An old fellow ran alongside his tank for two blocks holding up a glass of wine before he finally managed to reach it. An old lady cut every single rose off her rosebush and gave them to the men as they passed. Capt Belton found it comical to see tanks with flowers on them blasting away in battle. When asked where he went during the bombardment, a small boy pointed to a hole in his back yard.

The beach was a busy place. The artillery was firing down, the ships were firing over the heads of the troops, and planes were attacking targets of opportunity. All the men wanted to do was get off the beach. However, the engineers had only blown two holes through the 6- to 8.5-ft high concrete seawall and therefore the regiment was delayed for an hour before it got a chance to pass through Bernières-sur-Mer and move towards its assembly area in Bény-sur-Mer. At one point, Maj-Gen Keller, Brig Cunningham and Lt-Col Gordon took it upon themselves to help the military police in directing traffic in an effort to clear up the traffic jam that had been created in Bernières-sur-Mer. Finally, at 16.05 under clearing skies, the regiment left for the assembly area with the North Novas riding on the tanks. 4 Troop of C Sqn, under the command of Lieut Clarence Frederick Thompson, led the way for the *Sherbrookes*. As the regiment approached Bény-sur-Mer, someone got trigger happy and everyone started shooting at each other before a ceasefire was called. The regiment finally arrived at ELDER, the code name for the assembly area, at 16.45. The Porpoises were unchained from the tanks and pooled for future use.

In ELDER, both the *Sherbrookes* and the North Novas, under the command of Lt-Col Charles Petch, shook out and organised themselves. At 18.20, and behind schedule,[7] the recce troop under Lieut Gordon Alexander Kraus led the advance followed by C Coy, the vanguard of the North Novas. A Coy on the tanks of A Sqn took the right flank, while B Coy on the B Sqn tanks took the left flank. The Battalion HQ (BnHQ) and the RHQ stayed in the centre on the road towards Villons-les-Buissons, while D Coy on the

6 JUNE: THE D-DAY LANDINGS

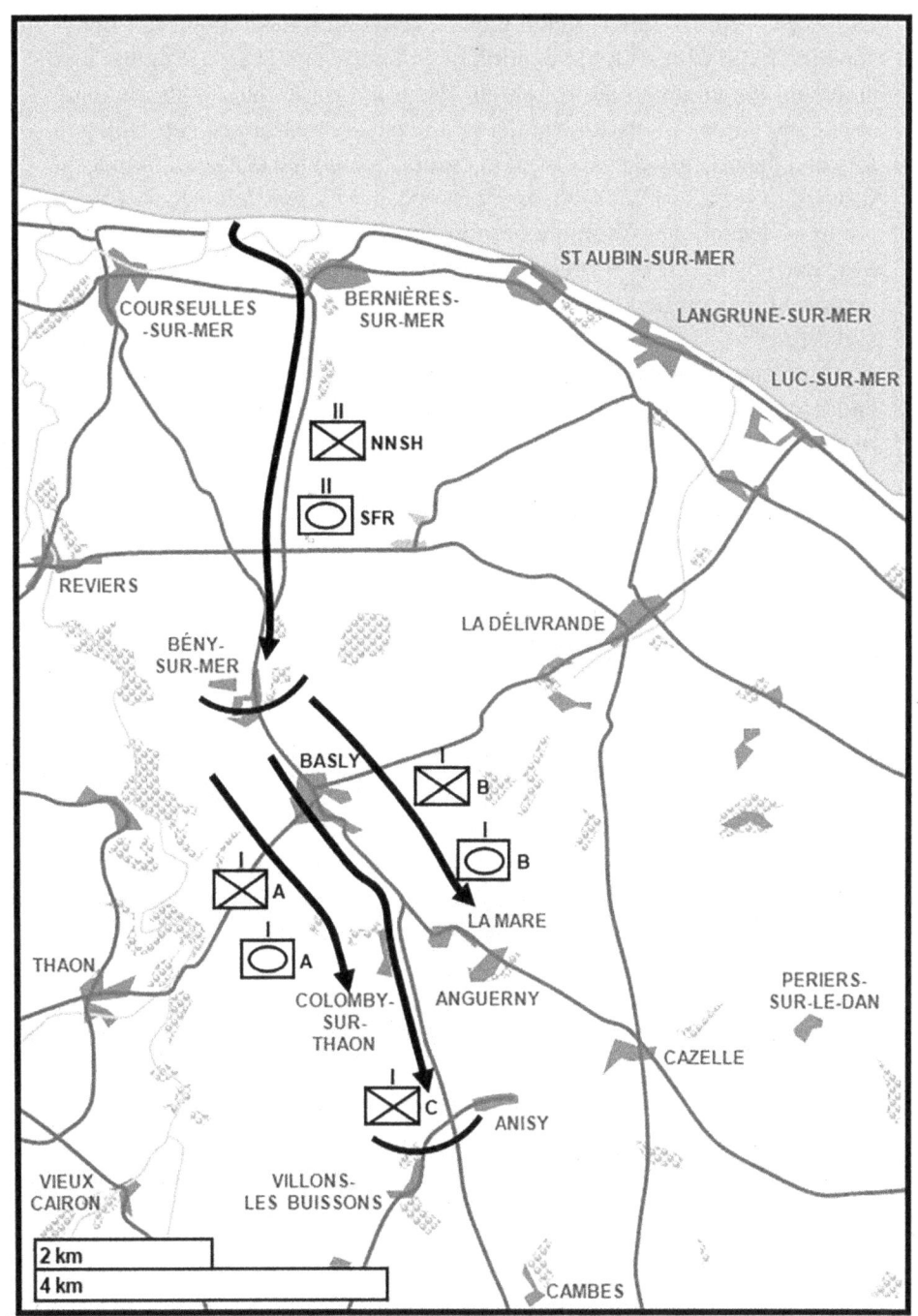

6 June 1944: The North Nova Scotia Highlanders battlegroup advance.

tanks of C Sqn followed behind them. The column moved through Bény-sur-Mer and Basly to La Mare, north of Colomby-sur-Thaon. Progress was slow and the column had to fight all the way up the route. After moving about 500 yards, A Sqn came under severe enemy mortar and anti-tank gun fire, and the infantry quickly went to ground behind the tanks. 1 Troop went forward to search for the German mortar position. Lieut John Henry Casey, the troop leader, was hit in the head by machine-gun fire and was quickly evacuated by his crew. Sergeant (Sgt) Ralph Robert Beardsley assumed the command of the troop and he and Corporal (Cpl) G.A. Leonard advanced and threw No. 36 fragmentation grenades into some trenches to silence the machine-guns. They then took out the four 122mm Howitzer mortars that had been harassing the column. At about 21.00, Cpl Dalmain C. Bailey of the recce troop encountered two 88mm anti-tank guns manned by ten soldiers. He fired his co-ax machine-gun at them and they immediately surrendered. He drove them back like a herd – at a run in front of his tank – to the main road where he met some men of the North Novas and turned the prisoners over to them.

After waiting all night and morning on 6 June for orders to repel the invasion, *Generalleutnant* Edgar Feuchtinger, the commander of *21.Panzerdivision* (21.Pzdiv), the *Panzer* division in support of *7.Armee* defending the coast in Normandy, finally received instructions from *Heeresgruppe B*[8] at 10.00 to prepare a counter-attack planned for that afternoon. Three battle groups were created. *Kampfgruppe* Rauch, based on *Panzergrenadier-Regiment 192* (Pzgren-Rgt 192), was to break through to the coast at Lion-sur-Mer, while *Kampfgruppe* Oppeln, based on *Panzer-Regiment 22* (Pz-Rgt 22), had the task of reaching the coast on the western edge of the Orne Estuary. Together, these two battle groups were tasked with preventing the Canadian and British divisions from linking up. The third battle group, *Kampfgruppe* Luck, was already located on the eastern side of the Orne River and it was tasked with reaching the coast near Franceville-Plage. The reorganisation of 21.Pzdiv took most of the afternoon and it wasn't until 16.20 before the counter-attack was finally ready to begin. *Kampfgruppe* Oppeln was launched from Lébisey but, after encountering anti-tank fire from Bienville and Périers-sur-le-Dan, the attack was broken off. *Kampfgruppe* Rauch launched its attack from the Anisy region and moved up between SWORD and JUNO Beaches. It reached the coast slightly west of Lion-sur-Mer at 20.00. There, when it came under fire from British tanks attacking from Cresserons, it was ordered to return to its line of departure for the night.

6 JUNE: THE D-DAY LANDINGS

Faced with a weak left flank, Lt-Gen Dempsey ordered all three of his divisions to halt their advances and to consolidate on their immediate objectives. At 21.15, 3rd Cdn Inf Div confirmed the order and at about 22.00, Brig Cunningham called off the advance and gave orders for 9th Brigade to form a fortress around the crossroads between Anisy and Villons-les-Buissons. After the infantry finished digging their weapon pits and slit trenches, siting their weapons and were secure in their fortress, the tanks of the *Sherbrookes* moved back to La Mare, just behind Anguerny. There, they harboured for what was left of the night. Few had been able to sleep since being loaded into the LCT and during the crossing. No one had a wink of sleep on either 4 or 5 June due to the tremendous excitement and the sense of responsibility that prevailed. Most had spent the night before the invasion sitting in their tanks, ready to go. The tanks were now put in a big circle. There was no time to sleep or eat. There was no time for anything but looking into the dark and wondering 'What's ahead?' The *Sherbrookes* seemed to be completely surrounded. At about 01.00, an enemy patrol composed of five half-tracks – *Sonderkraftfahrzeug 251* (Sd.Kfz.251) – and motorcycles from Pzgren-Rgt 192 tried to infiltrate the line of the *Sherbrookes* and the North Novas. At 02.00, things got uneasy as machine-gun fire opened up all around. The crews were nervous. Lieut Samuel William Wood, the troop leader of 4 Troop, B Sqn, let off a round from the main gun of his Firefly. The result was one dead cow. However, he continued to engage the enemy and his tank accounted for three half-tracks destroyed. The tanks remained in this spot until first light. Maj Walsh, the OC of C Sqn, viewed it as: 'No one was afraid and the usual exercise atmosphere prevailed. We had not yet learned to be afraid, but that lesson was not to be long in the learning.'[9]

At one point, the Med O's scout car drove up to the tank of Lieut Thompson. Capt Brokovski explained that two of their scout cars had run into trouble at the Colomby-sur-Thaon crossroads. Capt Gérard W. Côté, the Captain-Adjutant (Capt-Adjt), and Lieut Trevor Charles Stevens, the regimental signals officer (Sigs O) in the other scout car, were cut off by an enemy patrol in the regiment's rear while travelling back to 2nd Cdn Armd Bde HQ. Capt Brokovski had managed to escape. He stayed the night with Lieut Thompson for protection. The enemy patrol, it was later learned, was driven off by Le Régiment de la Chaudière (R de Chaud) and the second scout car was found abandoned, undamaged and with its contents intact. The body of Lieut Stevens was found beside it. Capt Côté and his driver, Sgt Norman H. Barter, had been taken prisoner. Unfortunately, Capt Côté had been carrying a copy of the Operations Order for the invasion with him. Thus, the Germans captured a copy of all the maps and code signs for one week as well. With the codes compromised, new codes would have to be issued on a daily basis.[10]

By the end of the day, 3rd Cdn Inf Div was well established on its intermediate objectives, though well short of the planned final D-Day objectives. Although only one Canadian unit had reached its D-Day objectives, the first line of German defence had been completely smashed. On either flank, Allied progress had been similar. On the left, 3rd British Infantry Division (3rd Brit Inf Div) had landed without too much difficulty but was still 3 miles from Caen due to heavy resistance inland.[11] On the right, 50th British Infantry Division (50th Brit Inf Div) got ashore easily and was only 2 miles from Bayeux. The Americans had landed with relative ease on UTAH Beach but the fighting on OMAHA Beach had extracted a heavy toll. By evening, Canadian troops had progressed further inland than any other Allied formation; the Canadian assault force had suffered 1,074 casualties, of which 359 were fatal.

Tank Comparisons: Technical data[12]

CANADA

	Stuart	Ram	Sherman	Firefly
Weight (combat load)	14,700 kg	29,484 kg	31,600 kg	32,700 kg
Crew	4	5	5	5
Main gun	37mm Gun M3	57mm 6pdr OQF	75mm Gun M3	76.2mm 17pdr ROQF
Muzzle velocity	2,900 ft/sec	2,150 ft/sec	2,300 ft/sec	2,900 ft/sec
Machine guns	3 X .30-06 M1919A	1 X .30-06 M1919A	1 X .50cal M2 MG 2 X .30-06 M1919A	1 X .50cal M2 MG 2 X .30-06 M1919A
Ammunition:				
Main gun	147	92	104	77
Machine guns				
.50cal	6,750	4,400	500	500
.30cal			6,750	6,750
Speed on road	58 kmh	40 kmh	42 kmh	40 kmh
Autonomy on road	217 km	232 km	210 km	161 km
Armour:				
Frontal	44mm	25mm	51mm	51mm
Turret	38mm	87mm	76mm	76mm
Dimensions:				
Height	8'1"	8'9"	9'8"	9'0"
Length	14'2"	19'0"	19'3"	25'9"
Width	7'6"	9'5"	8'9"	8'9"

GERMANY

	PzKw IV	Panther	Tiger I	Tiger II
Weight (combat load)	26,000 kg	45,400 kg	56,900 kg	60,800 kg
Crew	5	5	5	5
Main gun	75mm KwK 40 L/48	75mm KwK 42 L/70	88mm KwK 36 L/56	88mm KwK 43 L/71
Muzzle velocity	3,000 ft/sec	3,300 ft/sec	3,300 ft/sec	3,400 ft/sec
Machine guns	3 X 7.92mm MG34	3 X 7.92mm MG34	3 X 7.92mm MG34	3 X 7.92mm MG34
Ammunition:				
Main gun	87	92	92	84
Machine guns	3,150	4,800	4,800	5,850
Speed on road	38 kmh	55 knh	38 kmh	42 kmh
Autonomy on road	210 km	250 km	195 km	170 km
Armour:				
Frontal	80mm	60mm	100mm	100mm
Turret	50mm	110mm	100mm	180mm
Dimensions:				
Height	8'9"	9'9"	9'7"	10'1"
Length	23'0"	28'5"	27'8"	33'9"
Width	9'5"	11'5"	11'6"	12'4"

Chapter 3

7 June: The Battle for Carpiquet

In general, the terrain in Normandy is open and quite flat. To the north and extending inland to a depth varying from 10 to 40 miles was *bocage* country – 1 to 3 acre fields separated by hedgerows and small villages connected by roads no wider than an English lane and often cut 3 to 5ft below the surrounding fields. The Normandy countryside had deep, rich topsoil free of stones. The immediate terrain directly in front of the Canadian beaches was a large agricultural plain dotted with wheat fields and apple orchards, but with few hedgerows. Thus, for the first 12 miles inland to the Phase 3 objective OAK, the countryside was low-lying and featureless, consisting of gently-undulating cultivated land. There were few hedges and few isolated farms. The rural population was concentrated in many stone villages and hamlets. The plain was dominated in the south by the town of Caen and the Carpiquet aerodrome. It was cut from south to north by the Mue, a small river enclosed in a steep valley; and from west to east by *Route Nationale 13* (RN 13) joining Caen and Bayeux, and the Caen-Cherbourg railway line. The Abbaye d'Ardenne northwest of Caen offered a commanding view of the whole plain. South of the Odon River, the country began to rise gradually towards hills of slate and granite rock which attained heights of 1,100ft at about 45 miles from the coast. The fields tended to be smaller here and were separated by tree hedges based on thick earth banks. The river valleys were generally steep sided. The ridges were often topped by dense stands of oak, pine and beech. Cross-country movement by vehicle became more difficult the farther inland you went.

The general tactics used in Normandy were for the infantry to lead the advance, supported by massive artillery fire and tanks. The objectives were generally limited in size and distance. Once the infantry took an objective, they consolidated as quickly as possible on the objective with their anti-tank guns, the tanks and the artillery, and prepared for the expected immediate counter-attack. Tanks could not move through hedgerows without the help of the engineers who would have to use explosive demolitions to create a

7 JUNE: THE BATTLE FOR CARPIQUET

breach. This created a natural funnel affect and offered excellent fighting positions to the defenders. The tanks, restricted to movement along the few roads, made it easy for German anti-tank gunners to delay and hold up advances for hours at a time. To the southeast, the land was more pastoral with dominating ridges and hills. This terrain would allow the Germans to use the technical superiority of their tanks and anti-tank guns to engage the Canadians from long range.

The weather on the morning of 7 June was cool, cloudy and windy, but it would clear in the afternoon offering increased visibility. At 06.45, 9th Brigade ordered the North Novas battlegroup to continue its advance as soon as it was ready and to capture Carpiquet, its D-Day objective. The same formation was to be used but with a slight change in the axis of advance which would take it through Villons-les-Buissons. Once again the *Sherbrookes* were in support of the North Novas. In the plan, 14th Field Regiment, RCA (14 Fd Regt), the artillery support element, was supposed to provide four Forward Observation Officers (FOO), one to each company. Unfortunately, only two FOO were provided and so they were kept with the BnHQ. At 07.30, the advance began. The Stuart tanks of the regimental recce troop led the way followed ten minutes later by the North Novas vanguard composed of C Coy mounted in their carriers followed by a platoon of medium machine-guns from the Cameron Highlanders of Ottawa (CH of O) and a troop of M10 tank destroyers from the division anti-tank regiment. Two assault sections of pioneers, one section of the battalion mortars and the battalion's four towed 6-pdr anti-tank guns followed suit. The main body was next in line composed of A Coy riding on the tanks of A Sqn advancing 500 yards to the right of the axis of advance and B Sqn advancing 500 yards to the left of the axis with B Coy riding on its back decks. The combined headquarters of the RHQ tanks and the North Novas BnHQ moved down the centre line in front of C Sqn bringing up the rear, with D Coy on its back decks. The SD&GH would later follow in depth on the right with the HLI of C on the left.

Almost immediately, an anti-tank gun held up the advance of the vanguard on the outskirts of Villons-les-Buissons. Lieut Kraus, the troop leader of the recce troop, ordered Sgt H.R. Sauvé and L/Cpl P.W. Coveny to give supporting fire to the infantry. The North Novas mortar platoon engaged the position with twelve rounds while Sgt Sauvé and L/Cpl Coveny gave direct fire. C Coy made a quick dash and knocked out the German position with a flurry of grenades. Villons-les-Buissons was then cleared without difficulty. Once this was complete, the advance resumed. However, German

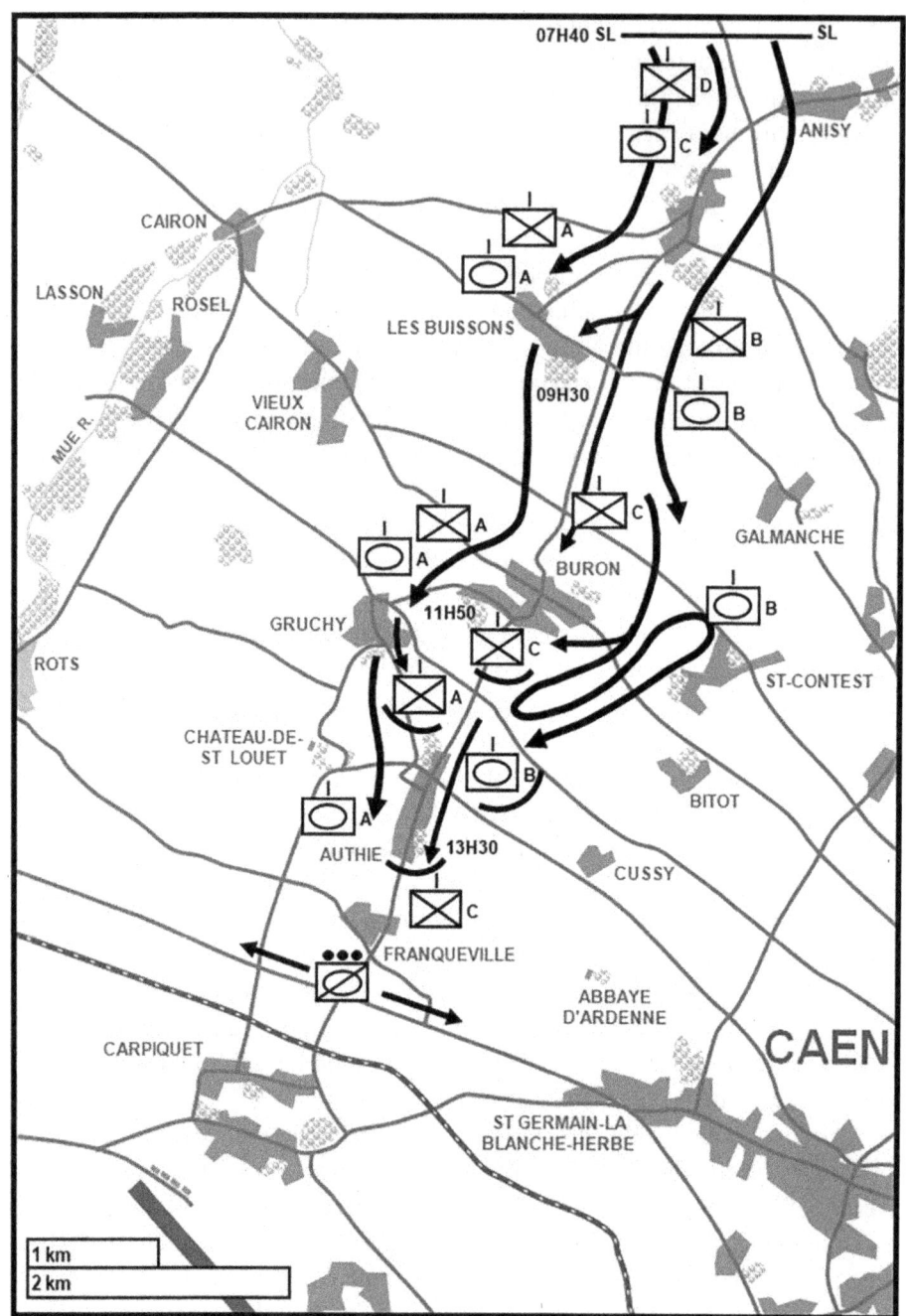

07.00 to 14.00 – 7 June 1944: The North Nova Scotia Highlanders battlegroup's movements and positions.

7 JUNE: THE BATTLE FOR CARPIQUET

resistance was once again encountered near les Buissons. A mobile 88mm anti-tank gun, supported by German infantry with machine-guns, was positioned just to the west of the village. Lieut Kraus tasked Sgt Frederick J. Allsop and Cpl Bailey to lay suppressing fire while Sgt Sauvé and L/Cpl Coveny made a flanking move. When Sgt Allsop tried to move into a better position, his tank was hit by a second 88mm gun concealed nearby. The tank started to burn so the crew bailed out. He gave his maps and codes to Cpl Bailey for safekeeping. Sgt Sauvé and L/Cpl Coveny arrived to lend a hand after taking out the first threat and fired on the second anti-tank gun using their co-ax machine-guns. The gun was finally put out of action by Cpl Joseph P. Fountain using a 37mm HE round. In the confusion, another 88mm gun was spotted moving up the road towards them, but it, two half-tracks, and a vehicle that looked like a self-propelled (SP) rocket carrier,[1] were captured along with two German soldiers. When Sgt Allsop moved forward to search the prisoners for intelligence documents and material, a German soldier hiding in a hedge behind him took aim. Tpr L.D. Flavelle spotted the German and shot him with his pistol before he could fire. Cross-fire from the Shermans opened up and so they had to evacuate the position. Unfortunately, Sgt Allsop was hit by shrapnel and died on the spot.

A Sqn and B Sqn finally got underway and advanced on either side of Villons-les-Buissons. As B Sqn passed to the left of the village, Lieut Davies, troop leader of 3 Troop (the lead troop for B Sqn) noticed a lot of movement in the orchard. He opened fire with his .50-cal Browning anti-aircraft machine-gun on a piece of camouflage. Tracer rounds started a fire which quickly uncovered a black cross, so he ordered his gunner to use the 17-pdr main gun and blew up another half-track with a *Reihenwerfer* mounted on it. It burned beautifully. The troops flanked the orchard about 600 yards to the east and moved into a hull-down position. Lieut Davies's gunner spotted a German on a motorcycle and took him out with very accurate co-ax fire. The troop continued south and spotted a well-camouflaged vehicle on the perimeter of an orchard. It was hit with the .50-cal Browning machine-gun and a huge explosion resulted. It turned out to be a lorry loaded with 150mm ammunition. Another 17-pdr shot finished the job. Lieut Ian Aldous MacLean's troop from C Sqn was ordered forward to assist C Coy in clearing les Buissons. Just as the troop got ready to leave, Lieut MacLean caught his wrist on the counter balance of his main gun; although the wrist swelled up and was probably broken, he continued on. Sgt Thomas C. Reid was put in the lead and the troop systematically blasted all the houses holding up the infantry in les Buissons by knocking down the houses of resistance story by story and took out the machine-gun positions there. The infantry reported les Buissons cleared at 09.30 and pushed on towards Buron. As the North Novas advanced, it came under fire from a machine-gun nest in a farm house in the southern outskirts of Saint-Contest. What remained of the recce troop moved up on the left flank, and Lieut Kraus and Sgt Sauvé silenced the position using their combined firepower. The infantry then signalled that they were closing in to finish mopping up. Sgt Sauvé fired on a half-track vehicle south of Saint-Contest. It caught fire and smoked for half an hour.

Buron was a larger town than either of the two preceding villages. Pre-war Buron was a small, picturesque hamlet of Saint-Contest. In its centre was a castle with a square tower surrounded by a wooded park, enclosed in large stone walls with a massive main door opening onto the road to Creully. The town square included a café-general store, a bakery and the Place de la Mare which included a water source at its centre. On the northern approach into the town from les Buissons, the entrance to the town had several small orchards surrounded by stone walls to both the left and the right of the main road. North of that position, the Germans had commandeered civilians to dig an anti-tank ditch on both sides of the road. On the south side of the town, a low stone wall ran along the left side of the road from Buron to Authie. On 6 June 1944, the town was unoccupied by the enemy. That night, however, infantry had come forward and occupied both the town and the anti-tank ditch to the north. At the start of the invasion, artillery and naval shelling, as well as bombardment from the air, had hit Buron and by now it was nothing more than a pile of rocks occupied by German troops.

While C Coy had been clearing les Buissons, the recce troop had advanced on the left flank to the southern edge of the town of Buron. Lieut Kraus tasked Sgt Sauvé and the tanks of L/Cpl Coveny and Cpl Bailey to hold the town while he went back to bring up the vanguard. The three tanks held the town for one and a half hours. They were subjected to very intense mortar fire and several small, disorganised counter-attacks by infantry. On the right flank, A Sqn had passed around Villons-les-Buissons with Lieut Ashbury Roland Truax's troop leading the way. Although C Coy had reported les Buissons cleared, when the lead troop passed through the village it encountered heavy sniper fire which caused a slight delay and forced the infantry to dismount from the tanks. Another SP, anti-tank gun was encountered on the northwest edge of the town with entrenched German infantry and machine-guns protecting it. A Sqn used its machine-guns and

7 JUNE: THE BATTLE FOR CARPIQUET

a short tank run over the position to remove the threat. A Coy of the North Novas then began the dangerous task of clearing the village. While it got on with the job at hand, the tanks moved forward to set up a defensive barrier in the area south of the village. When the job was completed, they could see that C Coy had already entered Buron some distance ahead of them.

As C Coy approached Buron, an 88mm gun at the edge of the main road opened fire. The tanks following in support knocked out the gun and its crew was taken prisoner. As Lieut MacLean's troop approached Buron, it was met with a hail of small arms fire. The tanks replied with co-ax fire and silenced the firing. The first house the troop got to in Buron again brought forth machine-gun fire. Sgt Reid lobbed HE rounds in through the windows. Any enemy infantry that then ran out towards the road got mowed down by Lieut Elliott A. Spafford, who had joined the troop along with his troop from B Sqn. Any enemy infantry that ran to the left were caught by Lieut MacLean, Sgt Raymond A. Cathcart and Cpl Thomas Quinn. C Coy sent out patrols to determine the enemy's strength and disposition. Buron seemed to be alive with snipers and machine-guns; there were too many gardens, alleyways, and nooks and crannies to make the going easy. Germans seemed to surrender from every attic, cellar and hole in the ground. Thirty Germans sheltering in the château surrendered without a fight. Other German prisoners were collected in the town square and were sent back under guard towards Villons-les-Buissons. During the hostilities, the inhabitants had taken refuge in a ditch near the main square or in their cellars and barns. They now emerged to greet their Canadian liberators with cigarettes, candies and canned goods, and to see the feared Hun being marched off to captivity.

While C Coy was fighting in Buron, the B Sqn advance on the left came under heavy shelling from Saint-Contest, 1,000 yards to its left. Saint-Contest was located on higher ground than Buron and offered the Germans great fields of fire and observation on the approaching Canadians. The tanks stopped and the soldiers from B Coy dismounted and scattered in an effort to find cover. When the shelling subsided, the infantry got back on the tanks and the advance continued. Almost immediately, the heavy shelling resumed. Once again, the infantry dismounted but this time moved off towards Buron on foot and took shelter behind the stone wall leading to Authie. Lt-Col Gordon determined that the shelling was coming from Gruchy and Saint-Contest. He therefore ordered B Sqn to send a troop to clear Saint-Contest, while A Sqn was ordered to do the same at Gruchy. B Sqn's Sherman tanks and the troop of M10s moved off to the right of

Galmanche and closed with Saint-Contest and Buron. Maj Mahon dispersed the troops and organised a squadron shoot. The tanks opened fire on a variety of targets spotted up to 3,000 yards to the south: tanks, half-tracks, 88mm anti-tank guns, motorcycles and infantry. The remaining high buildings, including the square tower of the château in Buron and the clock spire of the church in Saint-Contest, were engaged because they were deemed to be potential observation posts (OP) for German artillery spotters or snipers. The enemy retaliated with shell and mortar fire.

The German fire was deadly and Maj Mahon's tank was hit and put out of action. Maj Mahon had his arm smashed between the elbow and the shoulder, and his gunner, L/Cpl John Kachor, was killed. Sgt A.J. Parsons and Cpl Gordon M. Drodge received minor wounds. The squadron sat and waited awhile. Suddenly, Lieut William Henry Trenholme, the troop leader of 2 Troop, was killed when his tank took an HE round on the pistol port. Sgt Ernest B. McMillan's tank, also with 2 Troop, took grenade fire from infantry in some bushes and was also put out of action. Cpl Albert E. Sambrook was injured when his tank was hit in the track by an 88mm HE anti-tank round and blew a sprocket. Despite the heavy mortar fire, Lieut Wood got out of his tank and fastened a tow cable between the two tanks and pulled the disabled tank to safety. The tank was towed back to Bény-sur-Mer and Cpl Sambrook was evacuated to the rear. The remaining ten tanks were reorganised under the command of Capt Bateman while Maj Mahon was evacuated to the rear for medical attention. He reorganised the squadron into two troops: 2 Troop and 3 Troop, with their combined six tanks, were placed under the command of Lieut Davies and he was given the task of leading the assault on Authie in support of the North Novas. The remaining four tanks of 1 Troop and 4 Troop were taken over by Lieut Keith Lynn Steeves with the task of providing cover on Lieut Davies' left flank.

C Coy finally reported 'ALE', the codeword for the capture of Buron, at 11.50. The order was given to not waste time mopping up Buron but to push forward to Authie. A Coy had finally reached Buron and had taken up a defensive position to the south of the town and to the right of the road to Authie. It waited there for an hour while the town was cleared. From its position it could see Authie to the front and Gruchy to the right. B Coy had taken up a fire position in the orchard southeast of Buron while B Sqn tanks took up fire positions at the crossroads east of Gruchy, ready to engage targets in Authie. C Coy mounted its carriers and pushed through Buron, leaving the role of mopping up the remaining enemy to D Coy supported

7 JUNE: THE BATTLE FOR CARPIQUET

by five tanks from C Sqn. C Coy passed through B Coy and moved towards Authie, where it was held up on the outskirts by six machine-guns. Maj Arnold, the commander of A Sqn, ordered the troops of Lieut Thomas Alfred Lee Windsor and Lieut Murray Joseph Fitzpatrick to push forward and they rapidly dealt with the situation. As C Coy entered the town at 12.30, they once again came under artillery fire and were forced to dismount from their carriers which were sent under cover behind a hedgerow before being sent back to Buron for their safety. Lt-Col Petch requested artillery support on both Galmanche and Saint-Contest but was told by the FOO supplied by 14 Fd Regt that the guns were unavailable; half the regiment was in the process of moving up to a new firing position near Basly while the remainder of the regiment was still in Bény-sur-Mer, almost 13,000 yards from Authie. To make matters worse, when the artillery regiment arrived at Basly, the area was under continuous mortar fire. Lt-Col Petch then tried to get naval gunfire but failed to do so due to poor communications.[2]

B Sqn skirted Authie on the left and engaged the Germans as they tried to flee to their rear in front of the advancing infantry. Lieut MacLean and Cpl Quinn deployed to the left of the village and knocked off the fleeing enemy infantry. As they continued the advance, Lieut MacLean's troop was joined by a recce tank. Lieut Spafford was ordered to move forward and give additional support to Lieut MacLean but his troop was held up in Buron because the road was jammed and it was under heavy mortar fire. German infantry was seen running out onto the road but they were shot down by Lieut Spafford's machine-guns. Sgt Cathcart led the way out of the town and proceeded down the main road to Authie, where his troop met up with Lieut MacLean's troop. On the way, the troop did speculative fire[3] on haystacks and houses. Suddenly, an anti-tank gun opened up on the right. Both Sgt Cathcart and Lieut Spafford retaliated with HE and co-ax fire which forced the Germans to abandon their position. Therefore, Lieut MacLean instructed his troop to take out any abandoned guns as they were encountered.

After a sharp skirmish, Authie was taken and C Coy began to dig in on the south edge of Authie amid intense mortar and artillery fire. Authie was finally reported clear at 13.30. The infantry rested and ate rations while the BnHQ was moved forward to the road junction just back of Buron. The recce tanks had pushed forward of Authie to the outskirts of Franqueville and were within sight of the main objective: the airfield at Carpiquet. On the right, A Sqn had gotten as far as the Château-de-Saint Louet. One section of carriers was ordered to bypass Authie and to conduct a recce into

Franqueville. It encountered mortar fire and had to return north of Authie. A second section also tried but had to turn back. A Sqn was then ordered to push forward as fast as possible. The troops of Lieut Windsor and Lieut Fitzpatrick moved forward and reached the outskirts of Franqueville. Now, the tanks could easily see the hangars of Carpiquet Airfield and immediately began to engage the position. A Coy had dismounted between Buron and Authie and started towards Authie on foot. On the left, B Sqn was a little behind A Sqn and east of the road to Authie in an orchard just past Buron. The tanks of C Sqn and D Coy were in the centre of Buron. However, it was becoming apparent that the battlegroup was too far ahead with no one on their flanks and without artillery support. 3rd Brit Inf Div on the left was not keeping up with their pace and, while 7th Brigade was keeping abreast, it was so far to the right that it could not be seen by anyone in the battlegroup.[4] Therefore, at 14.00, Lt-Col Petch ordered A Coy and B Coy to close up on C Coy to form a battalion fortress on C Coy's position. However, the vanguard commander informed Lt-Col Petch that he wanted to come back to the high ground at the crossroads just north of Authie because he had limited visibility at his current position. Lt-Col Petch agreed and since A Coy had been unable to reach Authie, it was ordered to dig in on the right side of the main axis, to the southeast of Gruchy. C Coy was instructed to move back and dig in with A Coy while B Coy was ordered to dig in on the left. D Coy was instructed to bring up the rear. However, B Coy was pinned down in Buron by enemy shelling and could not move. Furthermore, before the platoons of C Coy could withdraw from Authie, all hell broke loose.

On 31 January 1943, the army of *Generalfeldmarschall* Friedrich von Paulus surrendered at Stalingrad. To that date, over one million casualties had been suffered by the German *Wehrmacht* on the Eastern Front, 300,000 at Stalingrad alone. Ten days later, Hitler sanctioned the creation of a division composed of members of the Hitler Youth. The Hitler Youth had been brought up on dreams of fighting glorious battles and dying for the *Führer* and the Fatherland if necessary. It was intended that this new division exemplify the brand of sacrifice and fighting spirit that Total War required. *1.SS-Panzerdivision (Leibstandarte SS Adolf Hitler)* (1.SS-Pzdiv) was tasked with providing the new division's cadre. On 30 October 1943, this new division was named *12.SS-Panzerdivision (Hitlerjugend)*

(12.SS-Pzdiv). Its organisation comprised one *Panzer* regiment *SS-Panzer-Regiment 12* (SS-Pz-Rgt 12) (composed of a battalion equipped with ninety-eight *Panzerkampfwagen IV* (*PzKpfw* IV) tanks and another battalion with sixty-six Panther tanks), one artillery regiment, two *Panzergrenadier* regiments (each composed of three battalions of *Panzergrenadiers*) and an engineer battalion. Each of these units had its own recce, anti-tank, anti-aircraft and signals section. Its training area was set-up near Beverlo, Belgium. 12.SS-Pzdiv was composed of tough and experienced officers and NCOs, most of which were veterans of the bitter Russian campaigns. However, almost two thirds of the 20,540 men of the division were 18 years old. All drill and ceremony was avoided. Instead, their training concentrated on combined-arms operations under the most realistic battle conditions possible. The young soldiers were trained to accept responsibility; to have a sense of community; to be prepared for self-sacrifice; not to be afraid to make decisions; to show self-discipline; and to be a team player. However, while very well trained, they had still not received their baptism of fire.

At around 10.30[5] on 6 June, *SS-Panzergrenadier-Regiment 25* (SS-Pzgren-Rgt 25) of 12.SS-Pzdiv received its marching orders and at 10.00 the main body of the regiment began its move from its billets near Vimoutiers, in the area of Verneuil-sur-Avre, towards a new assembly area around Lisieux. At 16.00, *Heeresgruppe B* ordered 12.SS-Pzdiv to assemble in the area east of Caen and to prepare a counter-attack. An hour later, SS-Pzgren-Rgt 25 received orders to attack the area from the western outskirts of Carpiquet-Verson-Louvigny, with *SS-Panzergrenadier-Regiment 26* (SS-Pzgren-Rgt 26) on their western flank. The lead element of the division was to be SS-Pzgren-Rgt 25 under the command of 34-year-old *SS-Standartenführer* Kurt Meyer, known affectionately to his SS comrades as *PanzerMeyer*.[6] He was an aggressive and determined officer who possessed supreme self-confidence, bordering on arrogance. SS-Pzgren-Rgt 25 was composed of three battalions of infantry supported by an independent company of engineers, reconnaissance, anti-aircraft and heavy guns. It had been allocated *II Bataillone SS-Panzer-Regiment 12* (II./SS-Pz-Rgt 12), equipped with ninety-eight *PzKpfw IV* tanks. At 15.30 on 6 June, when official orders were finally received to commit 12.SS-Pzdiv, its lead element had already reached a point only 80 kilometres away from Caen.

At last light, the lead elements of SS-Pzgren-Rgt 25 crossed the Caen–Villers-Bocage road and the remainder of the main body moved into the area during the night. On receiving their orders at 06.00 to conduct a reconnaissance in force, the regiment sent out a combat reconnaissance group. It now reported to Meyer that as at 14.00 that afternoon, Carpiquet, Rots and Buron were still in German hands. Buron was held by scattered elements of *716.Infanterie-Division* (716.Inf-Div). Les Buissons, however, was in Allied hands. The western outskirts of Caen and the airfield at Carpiquet were not defended; the *Luftwaffe* ground personnel from *16.Luftwaffe-Feld-Division* (16.Lw-Fd-Div) tasked with the airfield's defence had left in panic when the invasion began. Meyer arrived in the area of Caen at about midnight and attended a conference with *Generalleutnant* Edgar Feuchtinger, the commander of 21.Pzdiv, and *Generalleutnant* Wilhelm Richter, the commander of 716.Inf-Div. As he was leaving the conference, Meyer received a call from the commander of 12.SS-Pzdiv, *Brigadeführer* Fritz Witt. The situation demanded speedy action and *I.SS-Panzerkorps* (I.SS-Pzkorps) had ordered an attack against the bridgehead to be launched at 17.00 on 7 June. The enemy, he stressed, must be denied Caen and the Carpiquet airfield at all cost. 21.Pzdiv would advance to the east of Caen while *Panzer-Lehr-Division* (Pz-Lehr-Div) would take the western flank. The *Hitlerjugend* would advance towards the coast in the centre and push the British and Canadians off the beaches. However, petrol shortages and traffic chaos would mean that SS-Pzgren-Rgt 26 and *I Bataillone SS-Panzer-Regiment 12* (I./SS-Pz-Rgt 12), the Panther battalion, would not be in position to attack until 8 June at the earliest. Meyer went off and set up his headquarters in a small café in Saint-Germain-la-Blanche-Herbe. He spent the rest of the night looking over the terrain, going as far forward as the town of Buron itself, to recce the approaches to the town. There he planned the basis for his counter-attack the next day. At 04.00, he issued his verbal orders for the following day. *I Bataillone SS-Panzergrenadier-Regiment 25* (I./SS-Pzgren-Rgt 25) would be right forward and would maintain contact with the 21.Pzdiv. II./SS-Pzgren-Rgt 25 would be left forward, with III./SS-Pzgren-Rgt 25 in depth to its rear. At 10.00, he moved his forward command post into the Abbaye d'Ardenne. Most of the infantry had arrived during the night but his tanks only began to arrive an hour later. Meyer now deployed his three battalions and the fifty *PzKpfw IV* tanks at his disposal. All of his tanks and the 88mm anti-tank guns were placed in hull-down positions on a ridge near the Abbaye d'Ardenne. The *Panzergrenadier* companies were ordered to move quickly along the hedge-lined roads before taking up vantage fire positions on the flanks of the Canadian line of advance. His headquarters was established in the Abbaye d'Ardenne and one company of tanks was in the monastery grounds. Another company of tanks was set up on a reverse slope positions south of Franqueville.

7 JUNE: THE BATTLE FOR CARPIQUET

The Germans used the Abbaye d'Ardenne, the highest feature in the area, as a vantage point for observation and to direct artillery fire. From the church tower, the terrain as far as the coast was spread before Meyer like a sand table. He could see ship after ship bobbing in the water. He could see the flurry of activity on the beaches and the area just inland from the coastal towns. He could clearly make out enemy tank formations forming up west of Douvres. As he watched, a tank suddenly pushed through the orchards of Saint-Contest. The tank stopped and its crew commander opened his hatch and observed the terrain. Seeing no movement, he calmly lit a cigarette. Meyer thought: 'Was he blind? Didn't he realise he was only 200 meters from the *Panzergrenadiers* of II./SS-Pzgren-Rgt 25 and the barrels of its antitank guns?'⁷ Suddenly, Meyer understood what was happening. The tank was providing flank protection. He could see more tanks rolling forward from Buron towards Authie, right across the front of II./SS-Pzgren-Rgt 25; all the while showing their unprotected flank. The commander of the Canadian spearhead seemed only concerned with the airfield at Carpiquet directly to his front, not realising the danger around him. Meyer immediately issued orders to all the infantry, artillery and tanks units: 'Do not fire! Fire on my command only!'⁸

If the Canadian advance continued, Carpiquet and its airfield would be taken. Meyer had already sent the five tanks of *5.Panzerkompanie* (5.Pzkom) to reconnoitre the road between Franqueville and Authie and it had come upon the tanks of A Sqn of the *Sherbrookes*, losing three of its tanks in the process. The skirmish had put the Canadians on their guard. He concluded that although the planned counter-attack was scheduled for 17.00, if he waited then the advantage would be lost. Meyer's new plan was simple. As soon as the lead enemy tanks passed Franqueville, III./SS-Pzgren-Rgt 25 would attack supported by the tank company on the reverse slope. Once it reached Authie, the other battalions would join the fight. When the North Novas vanguard began to push past Franqueville and started to cross the Caen-Bayeux road, Meyer gave the signal for the attack to begin. The *Panzer* crews powered up their engines and rolled forward.

At 14.10, the first German tanks made their appearance on the left flank of the North Novas battlegroup advance. The recce troop had reached the southern edge of Franqueville when a group of four German *PzKpfw IV* tanks from 5.Pzkom suddenly moved over the crest of the hill to their front.

As Lieut Kraus reached the rise in the ground, he came over the radio saying, '88 at 2 o'clock. I'm going in.' He hesitated briefly before continuing. Suddenly, there was a flash on the left of the tank and some smoke came out on the right.[9] The Stuart then burst into flames, as did that of L/Cpl Coveny. Lieut Kraus jumped out as did his gunner L/Cpl H.W. Pépin. Unfortunately, the two other crew members were trapped in the tank. L/Cpl Pépin jumped back onto the tank and tried to traverse the gun from over the driver's hatch. He couldn't, so he transferred his attention to the co-driver's hatch and rescued Tpr Henry M. Jenkins who had suffered severe burns. All this was done despite continuous enemy tank fire. Lieut Kraus suffered a broken leg and his driver, Tpr James H. Davidson, was killed. Sgt Sauvé, the last remaining recce tank in operation, had lost the use of his main gun. He only had his ack-ack[10] gun and the co-ax machine-gun working. He therefore headed back north with the casualties from Lieut Kraus's tank on the rear deck. As Cpl Fountain approached Carpiquet on the right side of the main axis, leading a group of the last three tanks of the troop, he called out that he could see the windsock at the aerodrome. It seemed as if the aerodrome was undefended. He ordered Tpr Hugh W.M. Buckley, his gunner and wireless operator, to send the information to Lieut Kraus. When radio contact could not be established and all hell broke loose around them, he decided to take his group and return to the rear to report the situation. On the way back, he spotted an 88mm anti-tank gun behind Franqueville. He ordered Tpr Buckley to traverse left and load an HE round, and the gun was taken out of action.

With the recce eliminated the remnants of 5.Pzkom and *15.Panzergrenadierkompanie* (15.Pzgrenkom) swept around Franqueville. The German *Panzers* caught A Sqn by surprise. Lieut Windsor's tank was hit. Within minutes, Lieut Fitzpatrick lost two of his three tanks. Tpr William G. Hardy and Tpr Malcolm MacKenzie were killed, and Cpl Ernest Warnes was seriously wounded when a shell pierced their turret. Cpl Warnes was evacuated from the tank and the remaining crew gave him first aid. Lieut Fitzpatrick took up a position in the orchard just south of Authie and stayed there with about twelve men of the North Novas in an effort to stop the counter-attack. He discovered that his 17-pdr would not work due to a failure of the breech mechanism. The Germans advanced with two waves of infantry and then tanks moved forward slowly with determination. He observed the German attack and countered with machine-gun fire. He stayed in this position until the German *Panzergrenadiers* were almost upon them. When Cpl Warnes was fit to move, Lieut Fitzpatrick took

7 JUNE: THE BATTLE FOR CARPIQUET

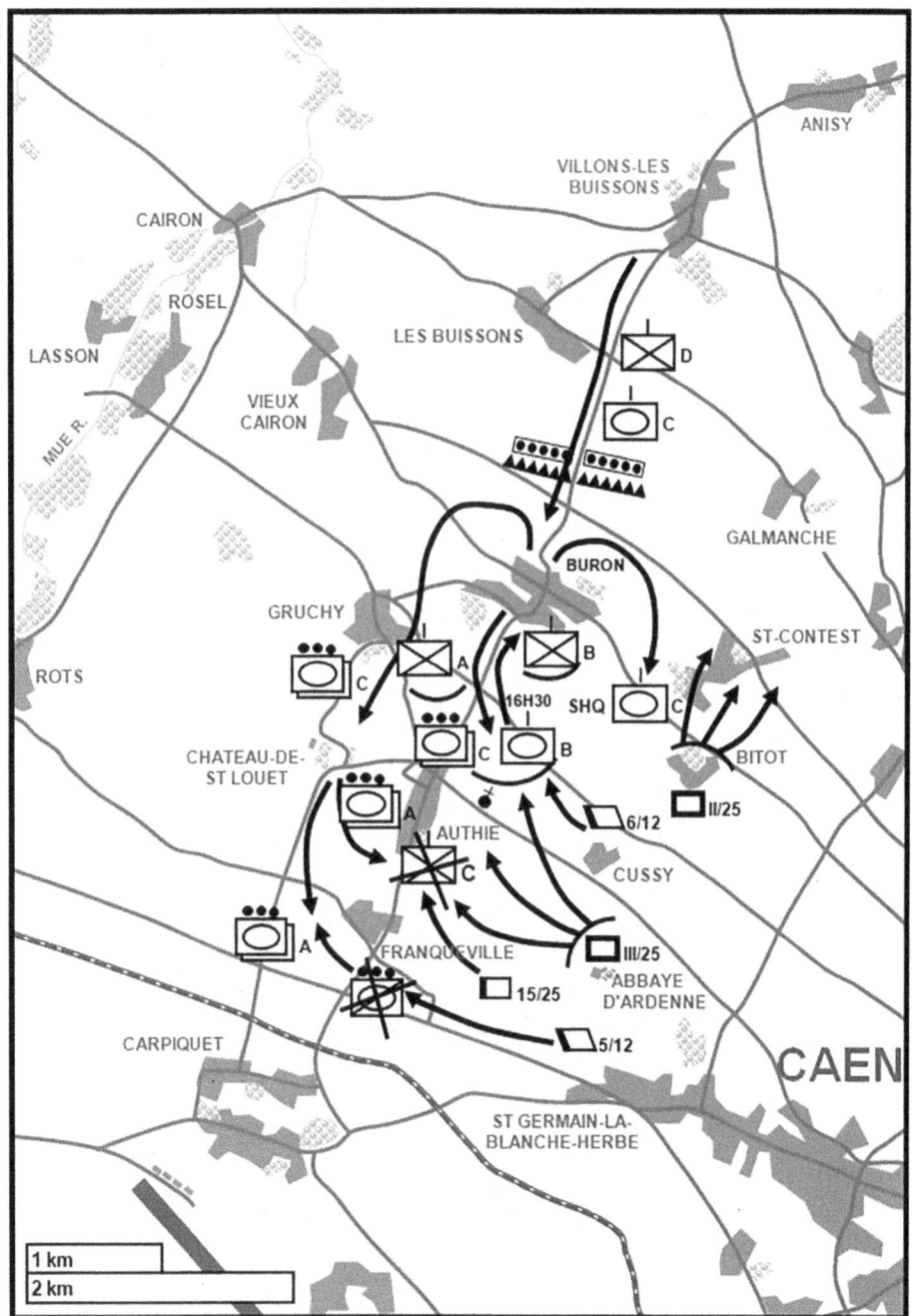

14.00 – 7 June 1944: The first German counter-attack by *12.SS-Panzerdivision (Hitlerjugend)*.

him back for medical assistance on his back deck. He was held there by four men while Sgt Arthur J. Cormier directed the driver back through the regiment. He returned to the rear with his crew, less one crew member who was taken prisoner. The Germans succeeded in knocking out more tanks before the first *Panzer* finally started to burn with flames shooting out of its hatches. All told, three *PzKpfw IV* tanks were knocked out. The German *Kampfgruppe* then moved towards Gruchy.

Lieut MacLean's troop was once again ordered to move forward and give assistance to A Sqn. He ordered Sgt Reid to advance and knock out an enemy tank about 800 to 900 yards to his front. Lieut MacLean ordered him to take out the tank on the left. Tpr H.J. Gilbert, his gunner, lifted the ring cupola on his first shot and it started to burn after the third round. Either Lieut MacLean or Sgt Cathcart managed to brew up the other tank. Suddenly, Sgt Reid's tank was hit. The round had shot right through the turret and hit the blanket box. The next shot unseated his loader-operator, Tpr W.A. Galley. At that point he realised that they were being fired upon by twelve tanks lined up in a hull-down position about 2,500 yards away. A third round went through the engine, permanently disabling the tank.

Suddenly, the vanguard was heavily attacked from the direction of Saint-Contest and Cussy by at least nine tanks and about two companies of infantry. It was becoming apparent that this was not an isolated incident but a well-planned, major counter-attack on the battlegroup. It was too late for the vanguard to withdraw to the battalion position, so C Coy decided to stand and fight in front of Authie. However, from its position in the orchard just south of Authie, C Coy had limited visibility. The fields seemed to dip and blend with the sky. The land fell gently beyond Franqueville and Carpiquet was not visible. The approaching German forces had ample cover from observation until they topped the rise a few hundred yards away. C Coy was taken by surprise as the attack moved on Authie accompanied by a renewed artillery barrage. Initially, the barrage failed to hit the C Coy positions, falling harmlessly behind them on the forward edge of the town. However, as the German infantry advanced, the artillery fire was adjusted onto the orchard. Lt-Col Petch ordered B Coy to move forward and to reinforce C Coy. Before B Coy could move, a new heavier artillery attack opened up. Canadian artillery support was still not available so Lt-Col Petch ordered B Coy to hold its prepared position just forward of Buron and to muster as many men as it could. B Coy dug in just to the right of the exit from Buron. C Coy succeeded in repulsing several German attacks and held on to its position for more than an hour. However, outnumbered and without artillery support, it was soon overrun.

7 JUNE: THE BATTLE FOR CARPIQUET

B Sqn had been advancing with little or no opposition when Capt Bateman received an order from Lt-Col Gordon to move forward and give support to C Coy. Lieut Davies started to advance in a two-up formation at the same time as III.SS-Pzgren-Rgt 25 – supported by the tanks of 6.Pzkom – launched its main attack towards Buron from Cussy, and II./SS-Pzgren-Rgt 25 – supported by 7.Pzkom – launched its attack towards Saint-Contest from Bitôt. Lieut Davies stopped two tanks with his 17-pdr. He then advanced, halted and scored another hit. A mass of German armour, followed by infantry on foot, now appeared out of the Abbaye d'Ardenne area. The German tank and anti-tank fire was devastating. Caught off guard, the Sherman tanks of B Sqn were hit broadside and another four tanks were lost without ever getting a chance to fire back. Sixteen German tanks were advancing at a range of between 1,000 and 1,200 yards. German tanks were everywhere. Anti-tank guns were blasting away from the left and rear. Tracer rounds and gun flashes were everywhere. Lieut Davies tried to get into an orchard but a huge log barred the way. Tanks were hit and burning all around him. One was hit directly in front of him and another was hit to his right. 88mm fire was cutting down trees all over the place. Tanks were burning everywhere and a tremendous confusion reigned. Lieut Trenholme, the troop leader for 2 Troop, and Sgt McMillan were both killed. Capt Bateman's tank was hit and the crew evacuated the tank, all except Tpr Norman E. Wilkinson. Tpr R.W. Munroe, on the ground beside the tank, tried to extinguish a fire that had broken out. When he succeeded, he jumped back on the tank to try to pull Tpr Wilkinson from it, but he was so badly burned that he was already dead. When Tpr Munroe pulled on Tpr Wilkinson's arms, the skin came off like gloves. Tpr Ernest J. Klose's tank had also taken a hit and had jumped a track. He fought from his position near Buron until the Germans finally captured the tank and took the crew prisoner.

When Tpr Junuis M. Severeid's tank was hit, it brewed up and the crew evacuated it. Unfortunately, the driver was stuck inside the tank because the main gun was traversed over his hatch. Tpr Severeid got back into the burning tank and successfully traversed the gun so that the driver could get out; unfortunately, the driver would later die from the burns he received. Sgt Joseph S. Savard's tank was also knocked out. All the crew but the gunner bailed out. They crawled away about 100 yards from the tank and waited for a chance to go back and get the gunner out of the tank. Sgt Savard had a broken arm and his loader-operator was badly wounded. Tpr J.A. Young, the co-driver, volunteered to go back despite the heavy mortar and machine-gun fire falling all around the tank. He dashed across the field and climbed into the tank. He stayed there for what seemed to be a very long time. He finally got out and returned to the others. He reported that the gunner was dead and that there was nothing they could do for him. Lance-Sergeant (L/Sgt) Douglas R. Lavallière, who had taken over Capt Bateman's old tank after his was knocked out near Saint-Contest, was successful in taking out three SP guns which were bordering the aerodrome. As his tank advanced towards the airfield, it hit a *PzKpfw IV* on their left on a small hill. Unfortunately, before he could get back under cover, his tank was hit by another tank on the hill. It took four shots to knock his tank out. L/Sgt Lavallière escaped without any serious injuries, but a crew member was killed and two were badly burned. He tried to get his gunner back to the rear and succeeded in getting back most of the way when he was himself wounded in the hand by a shell burst. He lost consciousness. When he came to again, he managed to get his gunner back to Buron.

C Sqn was with D Coy and its tanks were nose to tail on the main road through les Buissons. As soon as the first reports of German tanks came in, Lt-Col Gordon ordered Maj Walsh to send help to both A Sqn and B Sqn. Lieut Nairn Stewart Boyd with 3 Troop and Lieut Thompson with 4 Troop were sent forward on the left to give support to B Sqn. When the troops reached the area of B Sqn, they took up a position to cover the infantry now trying to get back to Buron. They too were engaged by the enemy. B Sqn had passed through a hedge as it advanced and Lieut Thompson tried to follow them. A heavy mortar round hit the deck at the left front of the tank. It jammed the turret, blew the hatches and knocked him unconscious. His crew evacuated him back to les Buissons. Sgt Charles R. Arsenault, the second tank, was following behind and saw Lieut Thompson get hit. He realised enemy fire was coming from off to the right; after being fired upon, he fired five rounds of HE in its direction and the gun was silenced. Lieut Boyd was recalled and Lieut Spafford, the troop leader of 1 Troop, was instructed to continue on the centreline as the protective troop for the RHQ. The remainder of the squadron was ordered to carry on, with 3 Troop leading followed by the SHQ and 2 Troop. Sgt Arsenault heard over the radio that Lieut MacLean was short tanks in his troop. Now the only remaining tank from his troop, he decided to move forward and join up with Lieut MacLean's troop. He advanced through Buron amid mortar and sniper fire. At the exit of the town, he stopped and fired a few rounds into the woods off to the right before advancing into the open field left of Authie. Straight to his front, he noticed some movement in the dust and after a few minutes he saw two tanks emerge. He fired at both and they brewed up.

7 JUNE: THE BATTLE FOR CARPIQUET

Initially, the only opposition facing Lieut MacLean was enemy infantry until an anti-tank gun suddenly opened up from the right. He quickly dispersed the troop and gave instructions to take the gun out. Then, both Lieut MacLean and Lieut Steeves were hit almost simultaneously. Both brewed up. Lieut MacLean felt a terrific shock and twanging in his ears. In a daze, he realised that he had been hit. He felt the heat luring up through the turret and so he ordered the crew to bail out. Lieut MacLean, Tpr Hubert Thistle and Tpr Alfred J. Steer hid in some tall grass about ten yards away from the burning tank. The ammunition started to explode so they decided to crawl back towards Buron, 1.5 miles to the north. After five minutes, they stopped for a breather while Lieut MacLean took stock of their position. They had no weapons and there was heavy small arms fire going on all around them. They continued forward and after crawling for about an hour, they stopped again. There seemed to be a lull in the shooting so Lieut MacLean risked sticking his head up to take a look around. Coming towards them from behind were hundreds of Germans sweeping through the fields to counter-attack Buron. A German spotted him and cried out. Realising that they were surrounded, the three were forced to surrender. Lieut MacLean and his crew were taken prisoner.

As 3 Troop of B Sqn advanced, the troop leader's tank was hit. Lieut Steeves and his gunner struggled frantically to get out of the turret – Lieut Steeves fell back in but his gunner managed to get out. Lieut Steeves finally succeeded in getting out but was badly burned. Unfortunately, his co-driver couldn't get out because the main gun was traversed over his hatch. The remaining tanks of the troop – Sgt Cathcart, Cpl Quinn, L/Sgt Hugh G. Fisher and a recce tank – all scooted behind a large barn. L/Sgt Fisher decided to make a run back and started down the road but was struck three times. The tank, as well as L/Sgt Fisher and his loader-operator, burned up. Lieut Spafford and Sgt Cathcart were caught in the open and were sitting ducks. Sgt Cathcart fired and hit one tank before reporting he had another group of five tanks to his front. Off to the left, Sgt Arsenault saw eight tanks coming towards him. As he traversed his gun on them, he tried to warn the other tanks but failed to do so because both his A and B aerials had been blown off by mortar fire. He fired two rounds and hit one tank but with no apparent damage. A German tank returned fire so he quickly used the cover of a small hedge to move his tank to woods on his right. As he moved, another tank came wildly out from behind a hedge and ran straight for him. His driver pulled a hard right and the tank ran up on a stump. Unable to move, the crew waited patiently for help. Lieut Spafford ordered everyone to fall back and move to rejoin C Sqn on the north side of Buron. On the way, he picked up three men from Sgt Reid's crew. Two of them were wounded and were dropped off at the North Novas advance Battalion Aid Station (BnAS). Once off the stump, Sgt Arsenault advanced to within 25 yards of the forward edge of Buron, firing all the way. As he was turning to return to les Buissons, he spotted a German tank hiding behind a wall. He fired, hit it and it brewed up. On his way back to the woods, he was ordered to move into the field to the east and shell Saint-Contest. An anti-tank gun was harassing the unit's position. As soon as he had stopped on the top of a small hill, his tank was hit. Although his co-driver was slightly wounded, he backed out to the rear. From this new position, he shelled Saint-Contest until he ran out of ammo. The gun was silenced and he then moved back to the orchard and rejoined his squadron. At about 14.30, Lt-Col Gordon reported back to the 2nd Cdn Armd Bde HQ that the *Sherbrookes* were heavily engaged with enemy tanks in the area of Buron and asked for reinforcements. Brig Wyman ordered the Hussars to standby to move in full strength to give assistance. He then moved forward to make a personal recce of the situation.

What was left of the recce moved back to Villons-les-Buissons and met up with the R de Chaud. For his part, Sgt Parsons arrived from the rear and rejoined B Sqn just as the action started. He was moving up a narrow field with hedgerows when he noticed two German tanks. He instructed his gunner to get the tank on the left when at the same time he saw that the tank on the right was taking aim. Its round went right over their heads. He ordered the tank into reverse but still took a shot in the turret ring. Radio communications were gone and the turret could no longer traverse. He pointed out the position to three other *Sherbrooke* tanks and then made his way back to the rear to get another tank. German infantry was now advancing towards B Sqn so Lieut Davies decided to withdraw what was left of 2 Troop and 3 Troop with the aim of consolidating what tanks remained on the ground immediately to the rear of the North Novas to await further orders. His radio had gone dead, but as he withdrew he waved to the other tanks he passed to follow him back; he was not sure of how many tanks followed him out.[11]

At 16.30, it was determined that it was impossible for the North Novas to push forward to Authie to relieve the pressure on C Coy. Lt-Col Petch decided to bring the forward troops back and form a fortress on the southern edge of Buron while the BnHQ moved back to the woods at les Buissons. A Coy had received orders to dig in to the west of Authie.

7 JUNE: THE BATTLE FOR CARPIQUET

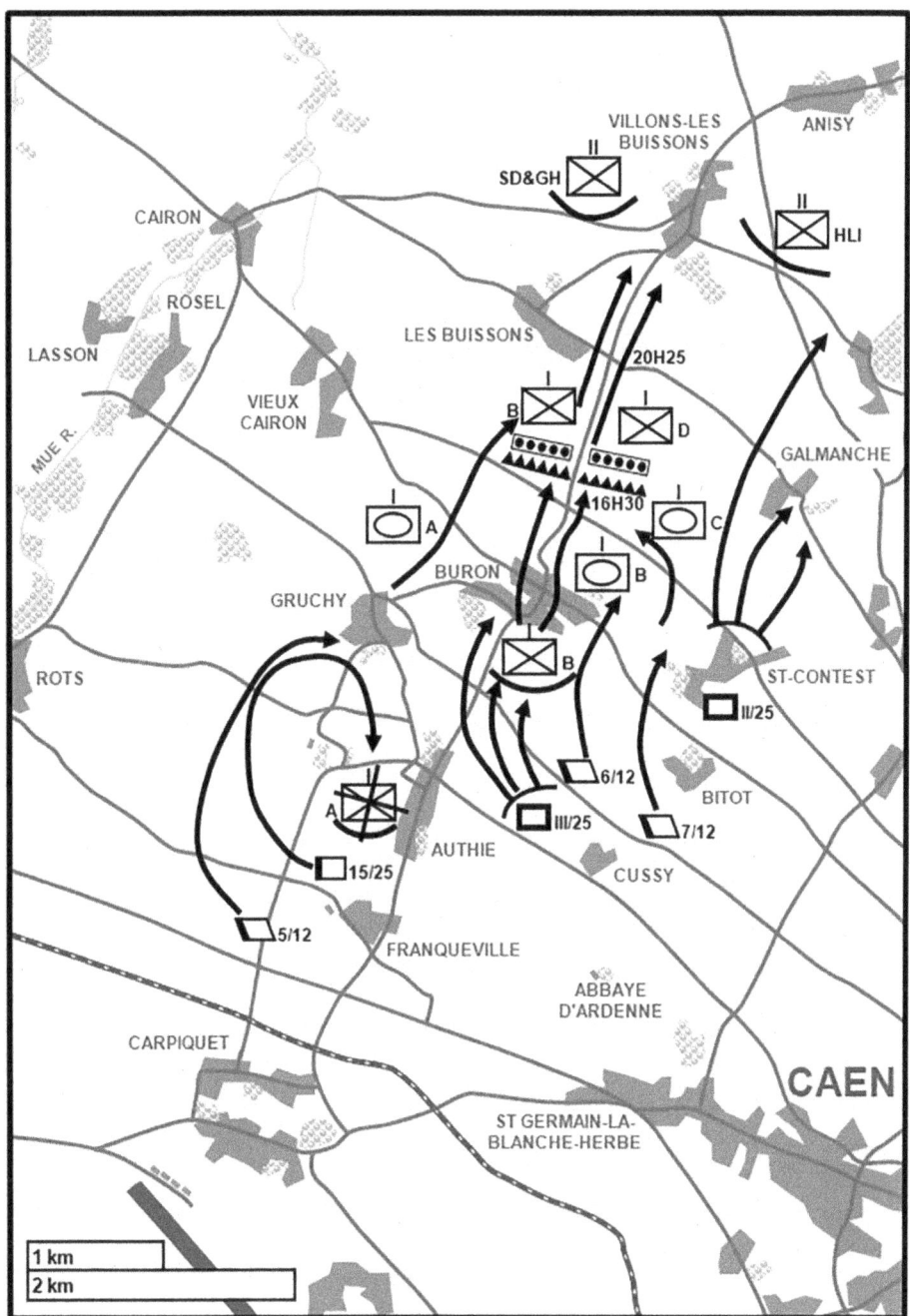

16.30 – 7 June 1944: The second German counter-attack by *12.SS-Panzerdivision (Hitlerjugend)*.

An area between Authie and the Château-de-Saint Louet was selected. The company was still digging in when it suddenly came under attack from the area of Gruchy by the *Kampfgruppe* that had hit A Sqn. German tanks and infantry appeared in the low ground on the right flank. Without tank or artillery support, the position was quickly surrounded and A Coy was taken prisoner. At the same time, with B Sqn taken out of action, III./SS-Pzgren-Rgt 25 closed in on Authie and C Coy was overrun. The battalion then pushed northward towards Buron. All hell broke loose in the fields between Authie, Gruchy and Buron. Bedlam was the result. Everyone was shouting. Villages, buildings and haystacks were burning. Tanks, both German and Canadian, were brewing up. B Coy on the left was forced to move back towards Buron.

Lieut MacLean's troop never arrived to help C Coy. When it was realised that the troop had been attacked, Maj Walsh sent Lieut Boyd's troop forward to complete the task assigned to Lieut MacLean. At this point, the only tanks of the *Sherbrookes* which were not yet committed to the battle were three tanks of C Sqn belonging to the OC, the 2i/c and Capt Belton, the rear liaison tank. Lt-Col Gordon was concerned that the enemy armour would break through on the left flank. At around 16.40, he ordered Maj Walsh to move C Sqn to Saint-Contest and to block the German advance. Maj Walsh asked: 'Can I have some of my sub-units sent back to me?' Lt-Col Gordon simply repeated his order: 'Enemy armour breaking through on the left. Take your squadron to meet them.'[12] Taking the three tanks available to him, he moved into a narrow field surrounded by poplars on some high ground to the west of Saint-Contest. Three German tanks were approaching with the intention of taking the same high ground. Capt Belton destroyed one, while Capt Radley-Walters got another. Once in position, German infantry supported by eight tanks were seen coming out from the area of the Abbaye d'Ardenne and moving across their front towards Buron. At that distance, 1,000 yards, the Sherman tanks could not knock out a tank, but they fired anyway as the tanks continued to advance. Finally the German tanks turned and went back. Capt Belton claimed two tanks hit while both Maj Walsh and Capt Radley-Walters each claimed one. The German infantry hesitated but then continued their advance. The tanks engaged them with their machine-guns until the infantry finally retreated.

From his position on the high ground astride the Abbaye d'Ardenne-Saint-Contest road, Maj Walsh could see tanks and infantry streaming back through Buron. It looked like a full retreat was in progress on the road from Buron to les Buissons. When no other enemy armour appeared and nothing else seemed to be moving back from Buron, he ordered his remaining tanks to move back to les Buissons. On the way back, he was confronted by another German tank. He manoeuvred and accidentally backed up into a bomb crater. The engines conked out. When two other German tanks were spotted approaching their position, he and his crew evacuated the tank and got into Capt Radley-Walters's tank. All of a sudden, a German tank was seen coming down the same hill they had just come along. The gunner couldn't see it so Maj Walsh had him lie down and he got into the gunner's seat and knocked out the German tank with a shot just under the mantle of the gun where the armour was thin. Another tank was seen coming down the road from Saint-Contest and it was also knocked out.

Tpr Robert E. Hutcheson's tank knocked out the two remaining German tanks in the 'horseshoe trap' on Carpiquet. After withdrawing to Villons-les-Buissons, he got ammunition and took it out to the North Novas who were trapped in Authie. When he got back to the rear, Lt-Col Gordon asked him to go back out again and he brought back three platoons. The remnants of C Sqn, six tanks in all, moved back to the southern edge of the woods at les Buissons and prepared to make another stand. Although A Sqn had managed to knock out seven German tanks, it was no longer a cohesive squadron. The German attack had come right through Authie and Gruchy and had overrun the two forward companies of the North Novas. The remnants of A Sqn were on the high ground to the right of Buron and C Sqn covered their return to the woods. C Sqn did the same thing for the B Sqn tanks that had been gathered by Sgt Cathcart. L/Sgt Lloyd G. Ride's tank was hit and although he was killed, his crew drove the tank back into the regimental area.

After applying two hours of continuous shell and mortar fire, Meyer ordered II./SS-Pzgren-Rgt 25, with three companies of *PzKpfw IV*, to attack from Saint-Contest towards Buron in a tight wedge formation. The Germans pushed into Buron, and the infantry penetrated the forward positions in the town and attacked D Coy using bayonets. The German counter-attack finally restored the situation and the Canadians were forced back. D Coy was forced to retreat but it dug in at the anti-tank ditch about 500 yards north of the town after its forward positions were overrun. B Coy withdrew through D Coy to previously dug slit trenches directly to their rear, and the battalion went to ground and prepared to hold to the last. A soldier from D Coy arrived at the BnHQ and reported that they had lost communications with everybody and that support was needed immediately. Artillery and naval gun fire was once again available and it helped slow down the German attack and to inflict heavy casualties. C Sqn continued to fight as it moved back to the edge of the woods at les Buissons; Lieut Spafford knocked out two tanks before being hit in turn by an AP round on the right sponson. Tpr W.M. Johnston, the gunner, was slightly wounded, but Tpr Chester M. Shannon was more seriously wounded and the crew applied first aid before sending him to the North Novas BnAS. The tank did not brew up but when Lieut Spafford and his gunner/driver returned to try to recover it, they saw that the right track had been smashed by another shell at the rear idler, the turret would not traverse properly and the 17-pdr would not fire. Sgt Cathcart's tank also received two hits which temporarily put his tank out of action. The crew was shaken up but okay.

It was found that only five men from C Coy and a few from A Coy had managed to move back. In the course of the afternoon, those remaining stumbled back in small groups with the support of the tanks. Word was passed to the SD&GH and the HLI of C to immediately start to dig in to create a brigade fortress in the area of Basly and Villons-les-Buissons. As soldiers arrived in two and threes, platoons were organised. The *Sherbrookes* did the same as the tanks worked their way to the rear. Late in the afternoon, the tanks of Capt Joseph Henry Gilbert and Lieut Bradley arrived in the assembly area in Bény-sur-Mer. After a short halt, both tanks moved forward to join the other tanks in battle. Many of the tanks in the battle were either out of ammunition or had run completely dry. Maj Baldwin organised the regimental B Ech and sent ammunition, petrol and diesel up to the fighting troops. Since no tanks could be released to come to the rear for refuelling during the tank battle, SSM C.L. Nicholson volunteered to refuel the tanks in the field. He brought his convoy through mortar, shell and small arms fire. During the refuelling, one of the tanks was hit and destroyed. Nonetheless, the troopers continued to fuel and replenish every tank they could get to. 85th Light Aid Detachment (85th LAD), which was permanently attached to the *Sherbrookes* as their level 1 maintenance workshop, had arrived off Mike Beach at about 16.00 the previous day and had been ordered to stay off shore for the night. They finally landed at about 16.00 on 7 June and immediately moved up to join the A Ech of the *Sherbrookes* at Bény-sur-Mer. As soon as they arrived in location, they were plunged into full scale activity on vehicle casualty repairs.

Lt-Col Petch asked the *Sherbrookes* to put in a hasty attack on Buron and rescue D Coy dug in to the north of the town. The task fell upon Capt Radley-Walters to support the move, Maj Walsh's tank had lost power and he was content to act as his gunner for the operation. At around 20.00, the group moved out with about twelve tanks, three or four of which came from C Sqn. The attack was put in just as the enemy was attacking D Coy for a second time. It caught the Germans flat-footed and arrived just as the Germans and North Novas were fighting hand to hand, with bayonets and close combat raging. A veritable massacre of the enemy took place. The attack succeeded in pushing the Germans out of Buron and into Authie, and gained time for D Coy to withdraw with most of its troops. Unfortunately, as D Coy withdrew from Buron, it left behind its dead and any wounded who could not be moved. Also left behind were the burnt-out remains of tanks, while others continued to burn giving off a bitter odour and thick black smoke. Although Buron was recaptured, the North Novas could only muster part of D Coy and the remnants of B Coy and C Coy.[13] It was getting dark and it would be impossible to consolidate the town and hold the position through the night. In view of this, Lt-Col Petch asked for permission from Brig Cunningham to withdraw to the high ground in the woods at les Buissons with the SD&GH and the remainder of the *Sherbrookes*. Permission was granted and a brigade fortress was established at about 21.45.

At 22.05, it was reported that the firing seemed to be dying down. When the Germans realised that the infantry had withdrawn from Buron, the German infantry quickly followed up and reoccupied the town. The attack by SS-Pzgren-Rgt 25 seemed to have achieved total surprise. Franqueville and Authie had fallen quickly. III./SS-Pzgren-Rgt 25 had advanced to Buron while II./SS-Pzgren-Rgt 25 had pushed through Saint-Contest before being engaged by tanks. However, Meyer realised that 21.Pzdiv was not supporting his attack. He could observe Canadian tanks with 7th Brigade moving forward on the west side of the Mue River towards Bretteville-l'Orgueilleuse. SS-Pzgren-Rgt 26 was responsible for that area but it had not yet arrived in position. Meyer concluded that he faced the risk of tanks on both sides of his formation and so he had no choice but to halt his attack or become vulnerable to encirclement.

At last light, the *Sherbrooke* tanks took up positions centered on the orchard just south of les Buissons and were subjected to heavy mortar and artillery fire. Nothing was seen in Saint-Contest or Gruchy but fire from there was observed. Most of the crews had not slept in several days and now, with the comfort of the infantry dug in around them, they organised themselves for a night's sleep. The fitters went to work as soon as the tanks established a laager for the night, as they would every night. They went out to bring back disabled tanks and then worked all night to get them back into fighting shape. They moved from hide to hide and repaired the tanks using small blackout lights that showed as little light as possible. They were able to fix almost anything – if they didn't have the part, they made it. During the night, the Germans conducted a search of the battlefields of Authie and Franqueville. A complete set of 3rd Cdn Inf Div signals instructions were recovered from the first Canadian tank that had been knocked out. Unbeknownst to the Canadians, the codenames and signals instructions remained in use by the Canadians for two more days. This allowed the German signals intelligence platoon of SS-Pzgren-Rgt 25 to monitor and evaluate Canadian signals traffic.

In its first action, 9th Brigade had gone up against a ruthless if equally inexperienced force. Essentially, the Germans had sent into battle the equivalent of a reinforced Canadian brigade: three battalions from SS-Pzgren-Rgt 25, supported by the tanks of an armoured battalion from SS-Pz-Rgt 12. Added to this force was an equivalent force composed of a battalion from 716.Inf-Div, supported by the armour and artillery of *Kampfgruppe* Rauch from 21.Pzdiv. The major difference was that while all four German battalions of *Panzergrenadiers* were used, 9th Brigade failed to send its two other battalions into the battle. Their employment might have been decisive in holding the gains made by the North Novas battlegroup, thus making possible the capture of Caen and the Carpiquet airfield much sooner than reality would have it. On the other hand, with so little reconnaissance information available, 9th Brigade could have been facing the entire German 12.SS-Pzdiv. Had all three battalions of the brigade been committed to the battle, the loss of the brigade's infantry battalions might have led to a German counter offensive that might have pushed the Canadian beachhead back into the sea.

The battle had lasted six hours. Company sized groups of Canadians were surrounded by Meyer's troops in the small Norman villages. Many fought to the last man, while others surrendered only when they ran out of ammunition. Heavy Canadian artillery and naval gun fire finally caused many German casualties and helped stop the German drive north. The outcome showed that the North Novas had suffered with 84 killed, 30 wounded and 128 captured. Out of the twenty officers of the original rifle companies, only eight remained.[14] The *Sherbrookes* had lost twenty-six killed, twenty-six wounded and nine taken as prisoners of war; along with twenty-eight tanks destroyed or damaged.[15] At 02.00 on 8 June, the *Sherbrookes* tank

7 JUNE: THE BATTLE FOR CARPIQUET

state sent to BdeHQ reported that only twenty-four tanks were fit for action with another seven to be ready within twenty-four hours. Twenty-one tanks had been knocked out. Enemy 88mm anti-tank guns had caused most of the casualties. In return, the regiment claimed it had knocked out thirty-one German tanks, four SP guns and eighteen anti-tank guns; as well as many half-tracks, light transport, infantry and other weapons. Although SS-Pzgren-Rgt 25 had been reduced as an effective fighting force, 12.SS-Pzdiv still had another uncommitted *Panzergrenadier* regiment and its Panther battalion. In return, 9th Brigade still maintained two fully effective battalions ready for battle, even though its armoured capability had been severely diminished. Although the German counter-attack was contained, 9th Brigade had paid dearly in its baptism of fire. While it is argued that the Germans had won the day, it is not truly clear as to who emerged the real winner – if there was one.

Appendix 1: German Attrocities

12.SS-Pzdiv murdered Allied prisoners both during and after the battle for Carpiquet, and then took pains to hide their actions. In Authie, the bodies of two murdered soldiers were placed in the street so that a tank could repeatedly run over them. The street has since been renamed as 'Rue des Canadiens' in their honour. More were killed in Buron. A total of thirty-seven Canadian prisoners of war were killed. During the night of 7 June, two frightful events happened which would be a forewarning of what was to come.

Ambush

At 23.30, the regimental Catholic padre, H/Capt Walter Leslie 'Friar Tuck' Brown, had to go forward to conduct a burial service and Lieut William Frederick Grainger decided to hitch a ride with him. The jeep, driven by the padre, took the wrong leg at a Y-intersection near Villons-les-Buissons, went past the last outposts and got lost in the area of Galmanche. There it encountered a patrol from I./SS-Pzgren-Rgt 25. Lieut Grainger and L/Cpl John H. Greenwood, a wireless tech who had come along to repair some tanks, decided to position themselves on a small rise and to engage the enemy patrol with grenades and small arms fire. Getting out of the jeep, they were hit with German fire from a *Schmeisser* submachine-gun. Both Lieut Grainger and L/Cpl Greenwood were wounded, but the patrol must have seen L/Cpl Greenwood move because they finished him off. Just before passing out, Lieut Grainger saw the padre, wearing his white clerical collar and a red cross on his arm to identify himself as a non-combatant, get out of the jeep and walk towards the German patrol with his arms raised in total surrender. When Lieut Grainger regained consciousness after about fifteen minutes, he saw that the Germans were gone and he confirmed that L/Cpl Greenwood was dead. He restarted the jeep and succeeded in getting back to the rear. Cpl R.A. Bryant's crew from 1 Troop A Sqn found the padre's body one month later on 11 July in about the same place where Lieut Grainger had last seen him. His body was surprisingly in a good state of preservation. His hands were tied behind his back and the only apparent wound was a knife or bayonet wound in the chest.[16]

7 JUNE: THE BATTLE FOR CARPIQUET

Abbaye d'Ardenne

The Abbaye d'Ardenne is a walled assortment of medieval buildings; principally an early Gothic church, a large stone barn supported by sixteen massive stone pillars, and several farm houses, buildings and gardens. The Vico family had lived there since the 1920s. Roland Vico was the mayor of Saint-Germain-la-Blanche-Herbe, the commune in which the Abbaye d'Ardenne is located. His services within the Resistance led to his arrest on 15 December 1943 and he was deported to the Mauthausen Concentration Camp in Germany. Francine, his wife, had also worked with the French Underground during the war. She was arrested by the Gestapo just before Christmas 1943 and was imprisoned in Caen until the end of March 1944. Their son, Jacques, was in charge of a stock of weapons dropped by parachute by the Allies and concealed in the Abbaye d'Ardenne grounds. When word of the impending arrests came, he and his younger brother, Jean-Marie, moved the weapons and Jacques went into hiding south of Caen. In August 1944, after the Allies seized Caen and started their pursuit of the retreating German forces, Madame Vico and her family moved back into their home at the Abbaye d'Ardenne. In January 1945, her youngest son, Michel, discovered what appeared to be a jawbone in the soft ground where he was playing. After further examination, it was confirmed that it was in fact a body in an unmarked grave. The excess earth from the grave had been hauled away as if to conceal it.

Civil Affairs in Caen were informed of the find and they immediately placed a temporary marker on the grave. On 8 February 1945, they returned to recover the body. When excavated, it was found that the grave contained the bodies of six Canadian soldiers stacked in two layers of three men. The bodies were identified as troopers George V. Gill, Thomas H. Henry and James Layton Bolt of the *Sherbrookes*, and privates Charles Doucette, Reginald Keeping and James Moss of the North Novas. All had been reported missing in action on 7 June 1944. A month later, Madame Vico noticed that her flowers were not growing where she had planted her bulbs in her garden the previous fall. Instead, they seemed to be scattered about. When the family dug in the garden, it discovered another unmarked grave containing five bodies. Over the next few months, five more shallow graves were found containing a total of nine additional bodies.

Pathologists who examined the bodies concluded that the men had died from shots to the back of the head or, in some cases, from being clubbed to death. A young Pole, who had been drafted into service with the SS but had deserted in 1944, reported that he had witnessed the murder of seven Canadian prisoners of war at the Abbaye d'Ardenne. It was clear that members of the SS-Pzgren-Rgt 25, which had established its headquarters there, had murdered the Canadian soldiers. Eighteen bodies were identified as soldiers who had been reported missing during the fighting on 7 June 1944:

Sherbrookes:	Lieut Thomas Windsor	Tpr James Bolt
	Tpr George Gill	Tpr Thomas Henry
	Tpr Roger Lockhead	Tpr Harold Philp
North Novas:	Cpl Joseph MacIntyre	Pte Ivan Crowe
	Pte Walter Doherty	Pte Charles Doucette
	Pte Reginald Keeping	Pte Hugh MacDonald
	Pte Hollis McKeil	Pte George McNaughton
	Pte George Millar	Pte Thomas Mont
	Pte Raymond Moore	Pte James Moss

During the fighting on 7 June, two platoons of C Coy of the North Novas had become encircled in Authie. Tanks of the *Sherbrookes* were ordered to counter-attack in order to relieve the infantry trapped there. One of the troops sent was under the command of Lieut Windsor. In the ensuing battle, his own tank was knocked out and he and his crew – Tpr Philp, Tpr Bolt, Tpr Lockhead and Tpr Marcel J.A. Dagenais – were captured. Tpr Dagenais was the only French-speaking member of the crew and, because his captors were able to question him, he was separated from the rest of the crew and sent to the rear.[17] At around the same time, Tpr Gill and Tpr Henry were also captured when C Coy surrendered.

Meyer had set up his regimental headquarters in the Abbaye d'Ardenne during this period and was arrested at the end of the war and charged with war crimes. He was transported to Aurich, Germany, to face charges for murder. The trial took place in December 1945. The evidence presented revealed that during the night of 7–8 June, Lieut Windsor had refused to answer any questions other than to give his name, rank and service number. He was slapped in the face for his impertinence and he and ten other prisoners were led into the garden and were either shot or clubbed to death. In the early hours of 8 June, seven more prisoners were brought to the Abbaye d'Ardenne for questioning. They too were led out of the chapel and into the garden where each was shot in the back of the head. Although throughout the trial Meyer denied knowledge of the specific events in question, he was found guilty on 28 December 1945 and sentenced to death. On 15 January 1946, it was learned that the Canadian general responsible for him, Maj-Gen Christopher Vokes, a past commander of 4th Cdn Armd Div, recognised that German prisoners of war had suffered the same consequences at the hands of Canadian soldiers, and so he commuted Meyer's sentence to life imprisonment. Meyer started to serve his sentence in Dorchester, New Brunswick, Canada. He was later transferred under British-German jurisdiction where the same sentence meant only fourteen years in prison. He was released for good behaviour on 7 September 1954 after serving only eight years. Meyer died in 1961 of a heart attack.[18] Over time, more war crimes would be attributed to the *Hitlerjugend*. For instance, during the fighting around Bretteville-l'Orgueilleuse on 8–9 June, another forty-five Canadian prisoners of war, mostly from the Royal Winnipeg Rifles (Winnipeg Rifles) of 7th Brigade, were murdered after their capture. After the battle for Putot-en-Bessin, officers of *SS-Panzergrenadiers-Regiment 26* (SS-Pzgren-Rgt 26) ordered the execution of twenty-six Canadian prisoners of war at the Château d'Audrieu.

Chapter 4

Operation CHARNWOOD
The Battle for Caen

During the afternoon of 8 June, *General der Panzertruppe* Geyr von Scheweppenburg, the commander of *Panzergruppe West*, visited the 12.SS-Pzdiv HQ. He outlined his plan to mount an offensive using 12.SS-Pzdiv, 21.Pzdiv and Pz-Lehr-Div. The plan was to take Norrey-en-Bessin, Bretteville-l'Orgueilleuse and Putot-en-Bessin; and then to proceed north along the Mue River and Seulles River valleys to the estuary at Courseulles. If successful, this offensive would effectively drive a wedge between 50th Brit Inf Div and 3rd Cdn Inf Div. The attack was planned for the night of 10–11 June. *SS-Standartenführer* Meyer believed that the attack was critical. If this counter-offensive failed, then the German forces would not have another chance to drive the Allies into the sea. He believed that after the planned attack came to an end, the three *Panzer* divisions would be burnt out and unable to repeat such an operation.

The *Sherbrookes* remained in the brigade fortress in the orchard just south of les Buissons for most of the day on 8 June. A Sqn took up a defensive position around the perimeter of the orchard and watched the right flank, while C Sqn guarded the left flank. At about 08.30, an OP reported that enemy infantry was approaching in half-tracks. When they were 100 yards away, the brigade fortress opened fire and forced the enemy to withdraw. A captured German half-track, complete with papers and equipment, was brought in by Lieut Harold Davis Spielman, the regimental intelligence officer (Int O), who turned it over to 2nd Cdn Armd Bde HQ to be searched for useful information.

At around 11.30, another OP reported that the enemy, 900 yards away and deployed in an extended line, was creeping forward through the tall grass towards their position. When they were 600 yards away, the German artillery opened up and at 200 yards the 88mm guns opened fire from Gruchy and Buron. At 100 yards, 3-in mortars joined in. The Canadian position was shelled and mortared for an hour by the combined fire of 155mm, 177mm and 88mm guns from the vicinities of Saint-Contest and Gruchy. In the barrage, Capt Radley-Walters's tank was knocked out by a near miss. Lieut Bradley's tank was struck in the front bogey wheel by an 88mm round which penetrated into the hull under the driver's seat, but without causing injury to the crew. Maj Arnold's tank suffered a direct hit on the turret from a mortar shell without suffering any damage other than shaking up the crew a bit. Once again the brigade fortress returned fire and, with the help of the co-ax machine-guns from the tanks, the enemy was forced to withdraw. SP artillery had moved forward into a position behind the fortress and now laid down supporting fire when called for through the FOO. What was left of C Sqn was ordered southwest of Villons-les-Buissons in order to make a show of force and to try to find out exactly where the Germans were located. However, each time C Sqn moved in the open, it immediately came under enemy artillery fire. It was forced to jockey back and forth for most of the day until it was finally determined that the church steeples in Saint-Contest and Gruchy were being used as OPs for directing the artillery and mortar fire. Therefore, the 17-pdrs of the Fireflies were ordered to return fire. Maj Walsh, in a borrowed tank, and the remainder of C Sqn spent most of the day chipping away at the Saint-Contest church tower.

Throughout the day, wounded and lost members of the regiment succeeded in making their way back to the safety of the brigade fortress. The severity of their wounds gave an indication of the savagery of the previous day's fighting. Sgt Savard had been knocked out and wounded the day before and didn't know where the enemy lines were. He had crawled around the villages on his hands and knees before finding his way back. Tpr Severeid came back with his jowls hanging down like melted wax and his hands completely burnt. All he asked for was a cigarette. He died later that day. Lieut Steeves made it back but he was also badly burned. He ears were burnt off, as well as most of his clothing.

Brig Wyman, the commander of 2nd Cdn Armd Bde, decided to reinforce the right flank of the Canadian advance. He ordered the Garrys to relieve the *Sherbrookes* in les Buissons and for the *Sherbrookes* to move to an area near Camilly to support 7th Brigade and defend against any subsequent German *Panzer* attacks. This move would also position his armour on the western approach in anticipation of an advance beyond the final Operation OVERLORD objectives and towards the high ground at Évrecy. At 17.30, the *Sherbrookes* were relieved by the Garrys and at 18.00 the regiment started its move via La Mare, Thaon and Camilly. Maj Cave, the DCO, stayed behind to exchange information with Lt-Col R.E.A. Morton, the CO of the Garrys, and his tank was struck by a shell. Sgt Gilbert E. Aulis was wounded and the tank had to be evacuated to the rear. The remainder of the regiment took up a defensive position for the night on the high ground just southwest of Camilly. Over the course of the night, the *Sherbrookes* received fifteen replacement tanks and crews. Lt-Col Gordon reorganised the regiment into two composite squadrons of fourteen tanks each. He also put four tanks in each troop since he didn't have enough troop leaders or tanks to create a third squadron. Maj Arnold retained the command of A Sqn; Maj Walsh was put in charge of B Sqn to replace Maj Mahon, who had been evacuated after losing an arm at Buron.

At first light on 9 June, the regiment moved south in support of the Regina Rifle Regiment (Regina Rifles). 7th Brigade had set up a defensive position around Bretteville-l'Orgueilleuse and the Germans were continually

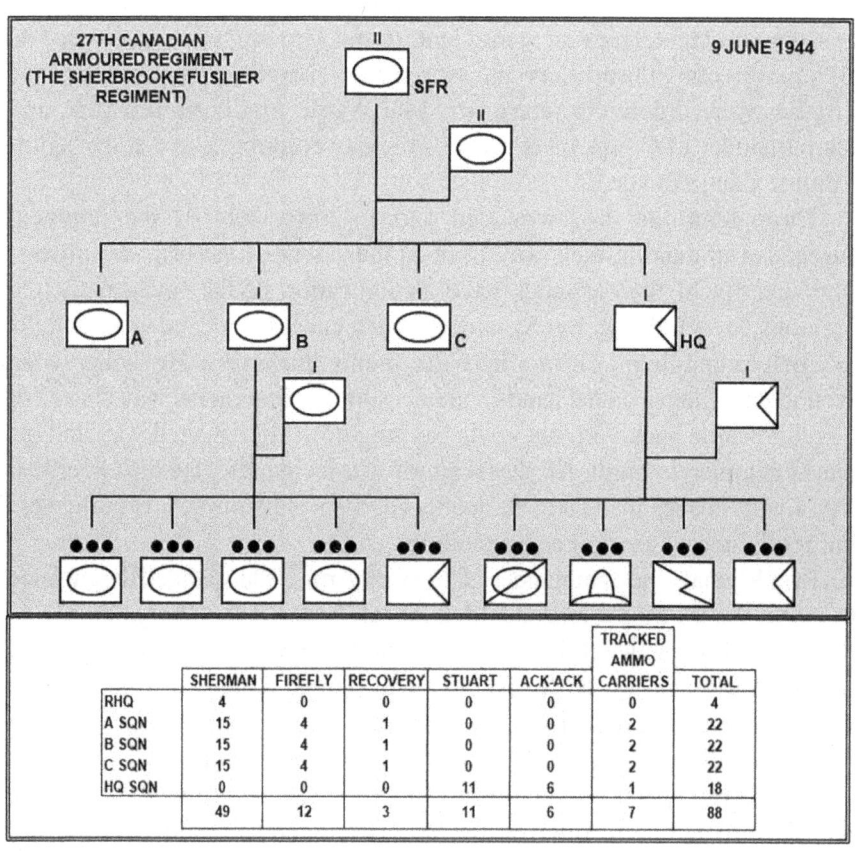

	SHERMAN	FIREFLY	RECOVERY	STUART	ACK-ACK	TRACKED AMMO CARRIERS	TOTAL
RHQ	4	0	0	0	0	0	4
A SQN	15	4	1	0	0	2	22
B SQN	15	4	1	0	0	2	22
C SQN	15	4	1	0	0	2	22
HQ SQN	0	0	0	11	6	1	18
	49	12	3	11	6	7	88

attacking in an effort to dislodge the Canadians. A Sqn entered a laager just south of the village of Secqueville-en-Bessin while the RHQ joined up with the 7th Brigade HQ just north of Bretteville-l'Orgueilleuse. B Sqn, under Maj Walsh, moved towards the high ground southeast of the town but north of RN 13. German armoured vehicles had been reported to be approaching Bray so the squadron was positioned to block their advance. However, the enemy failed to materialise. Lieut Bradley took over Lieut Thompson's troop; now down to only two tanks, his own and that belonging to Sgt Arsenault. As Lieut Bradley and Sgt Arsenault passed through the town, they were stopped by the Regina Rifles and told to go no further. Instead, they were asked to move back and help some men who were trapped to the left of the town. The troop, with another tank from 3 Troop, used co-ax fire into a field in support of the men. The main guns were also used to blow down two or three buildings in which German troops were hiding. More main gun fire was used to blow down a high stone wall behind which Germans were also hiding. When they returned to the village, the Regina Rifles thanked them and told them their men had managed to escape the trap. The tanks then moved back to rejoin the rest of the squadron.

In the early afternoon, Meyer decided to try another raid using the Panther battalion. The Canadian strong points in Norrey-en-Bessin and Putot-en-Bessin were jutting south between SS-Pzgren-Rgt 25 and SS-Pzgren-Rgt 26. Meyer decided to send a company of twelve tanks forward without infantry or artillery, expecting the surprise and shock effect to unnerve the defenders now dug-in in Norrey-en-Bessin. Once taken, the Canadians would be forced to withdraw from Putot-en-Bessin and the Germans would regain the initiative and push northward. The German force was composed of tanks belonging to 3.Pzkom.[1] It moved south from Rosel through Rots and then turned sharply towards the west at Villeneuve. The tanks formed a long line and headed out across the open fields towards their objective. They were driving for Bretteville-l'Orgueilleuse and Norrey-en-Bessin using the same route Meyer had used the day before.

During the early afternoon, the fourteen tanks of the composite B Sqn, augmented by the four tanks from Lieut. Fitzpatrick's troop from A Sqn, had moved to the high ground east of Bretteville-l'Orgueilleuse. The squadron now observed the German tanks moving forward from the orchard in Villeneuve towards Norrey-en-Bessin. Lieut Spafford led his troop in an attack on the enemy tank held wood. Although his tank was hit twice, it did not brew, nor was the main gun made unserviceable. He pushed his small attack home. Lieut Spafford was talking on the radio when three of the German tanks came across his front. Cpl J.G. Jones tried to interrupt him but was told to shut up. Therefore, he and the gunner took the initiative and opened fire. They immediately engaged a *PzKpfw IV* tank and it was knocked out but did not burn. A Panther was then engaged with similar results. In the end, the crew knocked out all three tanks. All across the line, one by one, the Panthers started to fall victim to the Canadian tanks in ambush positions. The Panthers caught fire and the crews who escaped were badly burned. The whole German attack was a dismal failure with seven Panthers knocked out, fifteen Germans dead and twenty badly wounded. The Queen's Own was detached and placed temporarily under the command of 7th Brigade, and they moved to Bray to secure the brigade's left flank.

Throughout the afternoon, several more reports were received of an enemy attack forming up in Putot-en-Bessin. With each report, a couple of troops were sent to break them up. A little infantry was encountered and the tanks were fired upon by a couple of anti-tank guns. These could not be pin-pointed but men were seen near Le Mesnil-Patry. Two pill boxes near Les Salles were silenced by the Fireflies. The composite squadron kept up continuous fire but received very little if any in return. Several likely targets were hit and a petrol dump or lorry was set ablaze. The Germans started to shell Bretteville-l'Orgueilleuse. It was thought an enemy OP had been set up in the church tower at Norrey-en-Bessin so the artillery FOO riding in Lieut Spafford's tank asked him to knock it down. They did so, including the church towers at Putot-en-Bessin and Rots. The shelling of the guns stopped immediately afterwards.

By early evening, B Sqn had run out of ammo and therefore moved back to the area west of Bretteville-l'Orgueilleuse where it was relieved at 18.00 by A Sqn, under the command of Maj Arnold. B Sqn had accounted for seven Panthers, three *PzKpfw IV* and one *PzKpfw III*; not counting numerous machine-gun positions and pill boxes. Other than Sgt Arsenault's tank, which was taken out by an Allied, or friendly, minefield, the squadron suffered no loses to enemy action. Late in the afternoon, A Ech was established in Camilly in order to be positioned closer to the fighting to help speed up the resupply. B Sqn now headed back to refuel and rearm its tanks at Camilly before setting up for the night at Secqueville-en-Bessin. Upon their arrival, A Sqn observed enemy movement towards the Carpiquet Airfield. Therefore, the FOO attached to A Sqn called down artillery fire on the woods 4,000 yards to the front. However, due to the intensity of the fire, the results could not be observed. At dusk, Maj Arnold ordered his squadron to move back to rejoin the remainder of the regiment at Secqueville-en-Bessin.

OPERATION CHARNWOOD: THE BATTLE FOR CAEN

The *Sherbrookes* continued to support 7th Brigade for the remainder of that day and the next. At one point, Maj Cave shot at a haystack using spec fire and was surprised to see the tracer rounds ricochet off the haystack. He followed up with a 75mm AP round which seemed to have no effect. His gunner was puzzled by the event. On later investigation, it was discovered that the haystack was a cover for a *PzKpfw IV* tank which had been knocked out by the AP shot. When the infantry attempted an attack, the Germans laid down the most accurate mortar fire the regiment had seen to date; the tanks even witnessed a German mortar round land right inside of an infantry Bren carrier. The tanks then carried out a troop shoot on the church in Norrey-en-Bessin which seemed to be a likely OP and proceeded to knock it down; the artillery had refused to engage the church as it was too fine a target for their guns.

The regiment moved back to the high ground southwest of Camilly on 11 June. The tanks remained there for six days with the RHQ in the middle and the two composite squadrons protecting the front and flanks and the recce troop protecting the rear. During this first lull in operations, Brig Wyman called a two-day conference for all the officers of the brigade to discuss the recent actions and the enemy tactics. General consensus was shared by the troop leaders of all three armoured regiments in their preference for a four-tank troop rather than a three-tank troop as provided by the war establishment. They also agreed that they preferred that the Fireflies be shared down to the smallest sub-unit – the troop – rather than to concentrate them in the same troop or squadron. Two of the troop leaders outlined a tactic that they found worked well for them: the three Sherman tanks of a troop would advance in line followed by a Firefly tank which gave them support with its superior range, hitting power and AP performance.

As a result of the conference, several deficiencies were identified and new strategies were adopted. It was recognised that tanks were not best suited for town or village fighting. Their field of manoeuvre was negligible and they became easy targets to sticky bombs, grenades or snipers. Therefore, they should support the infantry into built-up areas by using supporting fire from a commanding position outside the town or village. If it became necessary to go in, the infantry must definitely lead and not more than one troop should be employed in each thrust. The Stuart was too light and vulnerable for this type of work and the Firefly was unwieldy within a village because of the length of the barrel of the main gun. Therefore, it was determined that the Sherman was the best tank for village fighting. As a future policy, tanks would be in support and not under the command of the infantry below division level. Tank commanders were to cooperate with the infantry to their utmost, but were to also advise them on the proper employment of tanks. Each tank squadron would be organised on a four troop basis and each troop would have three Shermans and one Firefly.

In the course of the first week of operations, the *Sherbrookes* lost three of its five majors. When Maj Arnold's tank was hit near Bretteville-l'Orgueilleuse, he was evacuated for battle exhaustion. As the oldest of the squadron commanders, he did not have the physical reserves and just could not take any more. Maj Mahon had lost his arm during the action at Buron. Maj Cave was the only regimental officer from the PAM but, although he had displayed calm and assuredness while training in England, when his tank was hit and put out of action, he also ceased to function as a soldier and had to be evacuated to the rear. Capt Bateman, who had been acting as the OC of B Sqn after the loss of Maj Mahon, was admitted to the field hospital on 11 June. These circumstances forced Lt-Col Gordon to reorganise the squadrons. He promoted Capt Radley-Walters to the rank of acting major on 13 June and named him the OC of A Sqn. Capt Gilbert, the last senior officer in B Sqn, was appointed as its acting OC. Over the next days, replacement personnel arrived. H/Capt Cutler joined the regiment on 17 June to replace the padre, H/Capt Brown, who was still registered as missing. That same day, Lieut T.H. Hunter was taken on strength as the new Sigs O.

By mid-June, Second Brit Army was stalled in front of Caen while First US Army was progressing slowly through dense bocage country. Gen Montgomery was therefore forced to rethink his strategy in Normandy. His new intentions were to defeat the Germans by holding the maximum number of enemy divisions in the British sector between Caen and Villers-Bocage. The British and Canadian front faced seven-and-a-half of the eight *Panzer* divisions and six of the twelve *Panzergrenadier* divisions. At the same time, the Americans were to conduct a broad sweep on the right flank to threaten the withdrawal of those same divisions. On 18 June, Gen Montgomery ordered Lt-Gen Dempsey to capture Caen using a pincer movement from both flanks. During the first phase, 3rd Cdn Inf Div, supported by 2nd Cdn Armd Bde, was to capture Carpiquet and its airfield. During the second phase, a full-scale assault on Caen would be launched. 3rd Brit Inf Div would advance on the left while 3rd Cdn Inf Div attacked south from Vieux-Caron and east from Carpiquet on the right flank. The operation was scheduled for 22 June. On 19 June, however, a summer gale of extraordinary force hit the Normandy peninsula. The unloading of supplies was forced to stop for three-and-a-half days while the storm battered the coast. The American Mulberry was damaged and would have to be repaired. Gen Montgomery was forced to delay the attack and a new start date was set for 26 June under the codename Operation EPSOM. Unfortunately, that start date would again by postponed and on 30 June it was again delayed to early July.

The regiment's total strength on 22 June was still below its full complement of tanks. The RHQ had four Shermans and nine Stuart recce tanks. Each of the three squadrons had fifteen tanks organised with four tanks in each of its three troops and three tanks in the SHQ. However, each squadron had only two Fireflies. That same day, more replacement officers began to arrive. On 25 June, Maj Fred W.K. Bingham was taken on strength and posted as the OC of B Sqn. The next day, Maj William C. Weber, the OC of HQ Sqn of 2nd Cdn Armd Bde, was transferred to replace Maj Cave as the regimental DCO.

Gen Montgomery's original plan for the capture of Caen was postponed due to the storm of 19 June. A new assault was rescheduled for 26 June under the same codename, Operation EPSOM. Lt-Gen Sir Richard Nugent O'Connor's Eighth British Corps (Eighth Brit Corps) was ordered to seize crossings over the Odon River. Once the crossings secured, 11th British Armoured Division (11th Brit Armd Div) would lead the break out from the bridgehead. Its objective was Hill 112. Once the hill secured, Third British Corps (Third Brit Corps) was to advance south and seize Caen itself under the codename Operation ABERLOUR. As part of this operation, 3rd Cdn Inf Div was to attack south from Vieux Cairon and east from Carpiquet. On 25 June, the *Sherbrookes* were placed under command of 27th British Armoured Brigade (27th Brit Armd Bde) for Operation ABERLOUR and Lt-Col Gordon moved to 2nd Cdn Armd Bde HQ to plan and discuss the operation. The tanks, however, remained in their positions throughout the day. The regiment was to support the drive made by the British troops on the right flank as part of Operation EPSOM. That day and the next, heavy artillery fire fell just behind the unit's positions. It started early in the morning and continued all day. At 17.00 on 26 June, Lt-Col Gordon issued his orders at the RHQ. The assault was scheduled to begin on 28 June. The regiment would be in support of 9th Brigade and both would be under the command of 3rd Brit Inf Div. The plan was for the *Sherbrookes* to advance two squadrons up: A Sqn left towards Buron, B Sqn right towards Gruchy and C Sqn in depth. Flails, flame-throwing Crocodiles and AVRE[2] were to join the unit at Le Vey later in the afternoon. Wireless traffic was to be kept to a minimum and line communications were to be used where available. H-Hour would begin once 8th British Infantry Brigade (8th Brit Inf Bde) on the left flank had captured La Bijude and Épron.

At 05.00 on 28 June, A Sqn moved to the orchard at Les Buissons while B Sqn moved forward to Vieux Cairon with the task of being prepared to thrust on towards Carpiquet Airfield if and when the attacking British units succeeded in gaining their intermediate objectives. C Sqn moved forward and took over the old positions of A Sqn at Le Vey. Three recce tanks under Lieut Charles W. Bennett moved to an orchard on high ground in the vicinity of Bretteville-l'Orgueilleuse. From there, they were to observe the progress of the attacks towards the towns of Gruchy, Buron and Galmanche, and the Carpiquet Airfield. Only the occasional movement of German infantry from Buron towards Saint-Contest was reported. The troops remained in their positions all day waiting for the word to move. They suffered light mortar fire and shelling in the morning, and again in the afternoon.

On 17 June, Hitler had made a rare visit to the Western Front and met with *Generalfeldmarschall* Erwin Rommel and *Generalfeldmarschall* Gerd von Rundstedt near Soissons, France. Although the German commanders recommended a withdrawal to the general line of the Orne River, Hitler refused. Instead, he ordered the units to dig-in and establish a strong defensive line. He outlined his plan for a major offensive to recapture the port of Cherbourg and thereby split the Allied beachhead. The counter-attack on Cherbourg was planned for the next day. Spread out over a wide area, the *Hitlerjugend* were moved back to retrench on Caen with the arrival of *II.SS-Panzerkorps* (II.SS-Pzkorps).

The initial British advance succeeded in taking both its Odon crossings on 27 June and Hill 112 on 28 June. On 29 June, II.SS-Pzkorps, the largest German armoured formation, entered the battle with 79 Panthers, 79 *PzKpfw IV*, 76 *Sturmgeschütz III* (*StuG III*) and 30,000 men, and prepared to launch its counter-attack. Alerted by the ULTRA code-breaking operation[3] and fearful that the tanks of 11th Brit Armd Div would be cut off around Hill 112, Gen Montgomery decided to pull back his armour from the bridgeheads south of the Odon River. Instead, he unleashed his artillery and airpower against the Germans. The *Panzer* divisions were caught off guard in their assembly areas by huge artillery barrages and waves of Typhoon fighters and Lancaster bombers. The German *Panzers* managed to advance but met with fierce resistance from the British armoured brigades. Nonetheless, the Germans succeeded in pushing the British back across the Odon River. La Bijude and Épron were not taken, and in the confusion of the ensuing battle, word was received at 21.40 that German tanks supported by infantry from Grainville-sur-Odon had broken through the Canadian lines on the right flank and had reached Le Haut du Bosq. Word was received at 22.00 that Operation ABERLOUR was cancelled.

SS-Brigadeführer Meyer[4] knew that the *Hitlerjugend* were no longer fully operational. In fact, it only had the combat value of a weak battlegroup. SS-Pzgren-Rgt 25, reinforced with tanks from SS-Pz-Rgt 12, held the area north of Caen. The Germans had been in their positions for a month now and were well dug-in behind protective minefields. Two 300-yard long anti-tank ditches had been dug 300 yards northwest of Buron. Depleted as they were, the German defences were echeloned in depth. Instead of manning their main defensive positions, the defenders established forward outposts and lightly manned their main defensive line. A strong armoured reserve composed of tanks and SP assault guns were kept about 700 to 1,000 yards in depth in order to carry out immediate local counter-attacks.

Gen Montgomery set 8 July as the new date for the start of the assault on Caen. He issued his orders for Operation CHARNWOOD to Lt-Gen Dempsey and Lt-Gen Bradley on 30 June, stressing that the aim of his plan was to hold the maximum number of enemy divisions on the Eastern Front. A preliminary attack on Carpiquet was set for 4 July. Maj-Gen Keller gave the task of capturing the village and airfield to 8th Brigade with the Garrys in support. III./SS-Pzgren-Rgt 25 held the villages of Authie, Gruchy and Buron. Before 3rd Cdn Inf Div could take Caen, these villages would have to be cleared. Furthermore, it was feared that the German forces in that area could be withdrawn and sent to reinforce the defenders of Carpiquet. Therefore, orders were given to the *Sherbrookes* to conduct a diversionary, mobile operation aimed at confusing the enemy. The task was assigned to A Sqn. Late on 2 July, Maj Radley-Walters briefed his crew commanders on the upcoming operation, codenamed Operation WINDSOR. The objective was to force the enemy to react to the presence of the tanks, thereby disclosing the disposition of his weapon systems and troops on the ground. The squadron was to advance east for 600 yards from Villeneuve towards the high ground west of the Château-de-Saint Louet. After engaging the enemy there, the squadron would turn northeast and pass to the west of Gruchy.

Once the targets of opportunity found there were destroyed, it would then turn back west to exit in the area of Vieux Cairon. H-Hour was set at 05.15 on 4 July. 1 Troop under Lieut Fitzpatrick would be right front, while 2 Troop under Lieut Truax would be left front; 4 Troop under Lieut John D. Corless would be right rear while the SHQ remained in the centre rear.

At 04.45 on 4 July, the tanks moved up to the start line and, at 04.50, the guns of the artillery commenced the preliminary bombardment as per the fire plan. However, the heavy morning mist and the smoke caused by the barrage were so thick that no move forward was possible before 06.00. The squadron moved off cautiously. As A Sqn came over the rise, the Abbaye d'Ardenne came into view and, since SS.Pzgren-Rgt 25 was using it as its headquarters, the squadron immediately started to shell it and a workshop and a storage shed were set ablaze. Franqueville and Authie were also shelled. As the squadron veered north towards the Château-de-Saint Louet, 4 Troop lost two tanks when it bumped into a friendly minefield. Maj Radley-Walters moved up in his scout car and, despite the intense mortar and shell-fire,

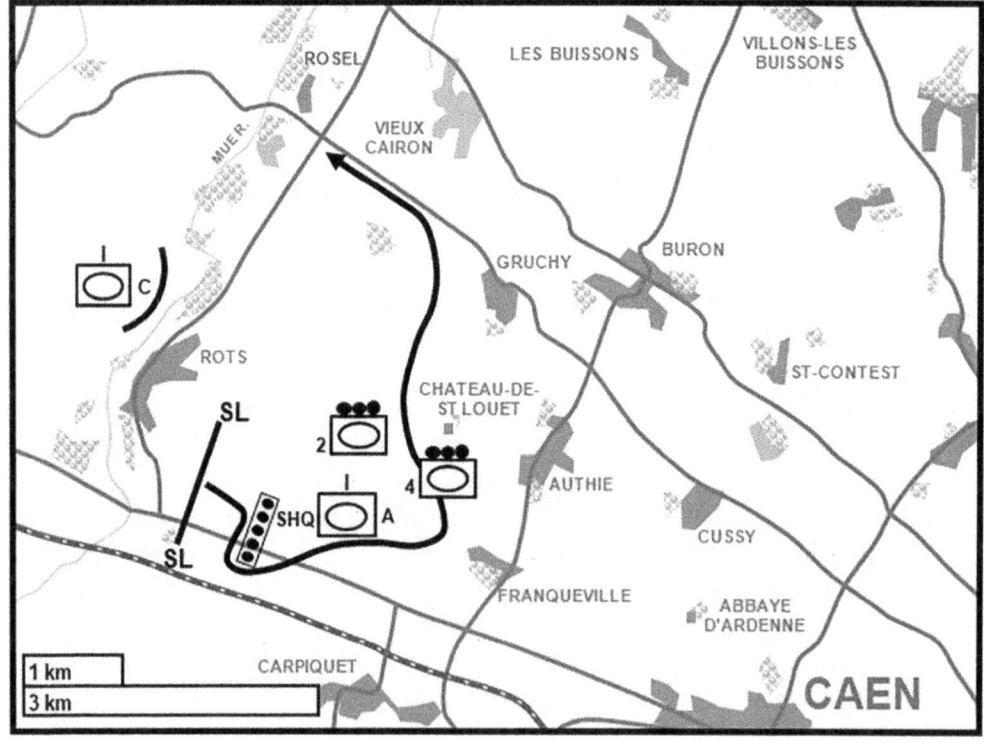

4 July 1944: Operation WINDSOR.

directed the remaining tanks around the obstacle. The tanks finally reached the château at about 10.00 and plastered it for forty-five minutes; 1 Troop knocked out a 37mm anti-tank gun and two machine-gun nests, German soldiers were observed to stagger out from around the château as if in a daze. No heavy opposition was encountered, although a little shell and mortar fire was experienced and a sniper was active but not located. The squadron then moved off towards Gruchy. On the way, the tanks used spec fire on likely enemy positions: hedges, trees, buildings and slit trenches. Heavier fire was coming from Gruchy. The tanks experienced fire from snipers, machine-guns, some 155mm mortars and an 88mm anti-tank gun. At 10.30, A Sqn reported that the trenches in the area of Gruchy were empty. Only slight resistance was being encountered and artillery fire was called down on some stragglers. A Sqn stayed in the area for about sixty minutes; 1 Troop and 2 Troop moved in very close and fired to their heart's content. A few tripwires were observed and the mortar fire was consistent but not heavy.

At 13.30, 2nd Cdn Armd Bde advised the *Sherbrookes* that 9th Brigade had been ordered to send strong patrols to Buron and Gruchy with the view of occupying them if possible. A Sqn was to give support to the move. Just before 14.00, 9th Brigade reported that its patrols had spotted four tanks in the vicinity of Buron. Forty-five minutes later, more tanks were reported southeast of Buron and the SD&GH reported fairly strong enemy resistance and withdrew. At 15.08, 9th Brigade cancelled the possible occupation of Buron and Gruchy and withdrew all its troops. Just before 16.00, A Sqn reported that there was only one machine-gun left active in Gruchy, that the commander of the German garrison in the Château-de-Saint Louet had been killed and that only one machine-gun had been encountered in Franqueville. The order was given and the squadron moved west. The 1st Battalion, Canadian Scottish Regiment (Cdn Scottish) held the line in this area and they put up a smoke screen to help cover the move back. The tanks exited between Rosel and Vieux Cairon using the marked lanes through the friendly minefield in front of Lasson.

On 5 July, Lt-Gen John Tredinnick Crocker, the commander of First Brit Corps, issued his orders for the assault on Caen. H-Hour was set for 04.20 on 8 July. The corps would attack with three divisions up: 3rd Brit Inf Div, supported by 33rd British Armoured Brigade would advance on the left from the northeast on a one-brigade front; 59th (Staffordshire) Infantry

Division, supported by 27th Brit Armd Bde, would advance in the centre on a two-brigade front; while 3rd Cdn Inf Div supported by 2nd Cdn Armd Bde would advance from the northwest on the right. A heavy aerial bombardment of Caen was planned for the evening of 7 July. On the morning of 8 July, both British divisions would attack at first light, while the Canadian division waited to move on orders from the corps commander. The Canadians were to capture Buron, Gruchy, the Château-de-Saint Louet , Authie and the high ground immediately south of Buron. During the final phase of the attack, 3rd Cdn Inf Div was to capture Cussy and the Abbaye d'Ardenne. During the exploitation phase of the operation, it would capture those parts of Carpiquet Airfield still in enemy hands, while the British divisions secured bridgeheads over the Orne River.

Maj-Gen Keller's plan was to capture the general line Franqueville-Abbaye d'Ardenne-Cussy, and to exploit to the line of the Bayeux-Caen railway. The operation would be conducted in three phases. In Phase 1, 9th Brigade would capture a general line from the Château-de-Saint Louet and the high ground north of Authie. In the process, the brigade would also clear the towns of Buron and Gruchy. H-Hour was not before 06.00 and one hour's notice to move would be given. In Phase 2, 9th Brigade would continue its advance and capture Franqueville, while 7th Brigade advanced on the left to take Bitôt, Cussy and the Abbaye d'Ardenne. During Phase 3, if ordered, 9th Brigade would send a strong, mobile, armoured and infantry force to mop up the open country towards the Mue River and link up with 8th Brigade already in control of Carpiquet. At the same time, 7th Brigade would be prepared to exploit up to the Bayeux-Caen railway on orders from Maj-Gen Keller.

9th Brigade's plan was to advance two battalions up with support from the *Sherbrookes*. A Sqn was to support the HLI of C, B Sqn was assigned to the SD&GH, and C Sqn was grouped with the North Novas. During Phase 1, the SD&GH would capture Gruchy while the HLI of C captured Buron and the high ground south of the village. The North Novas would remain in reserve and be prepared to move forward on orders from the BdeHQ. In Phase 2, the SD&GH would continue their advance and capture the Château-de-Saint Louet. The North Novas would pass through the HLI of C and capture Authie. The HLI of C would remain in Buron and become the brigade reserve. During the final phase, all the battalions would consolidate their positions and reorganise themselves with a battalion each at the Château-de-Saint Louet, Authie and the high ground south of Buron. One battalion would then be ordered to attack and capture Franqueville and exploit to the Bayeux-Caen railway. In addition, the SD&GH, with a squadron of tanks in support, would advance on order and mop up enemy pockets of resistance in the areas of Rosel, Le Bourg, the Château-de-Saint Louet and Gruchy.

At 04.30, First Brit Corps launched its attack. At 06.00, Buron was hit by bomber and fighter planes, followed by an artillery barrage. The initial reports from the lead elements of the British divisions were encouraging, so Lt-Gen Crocker ordered Phase 2 of his plan to begin at 07.30. The *Sherbrookes* were in support of 9th Brigade. A Sqn was with the HLI of

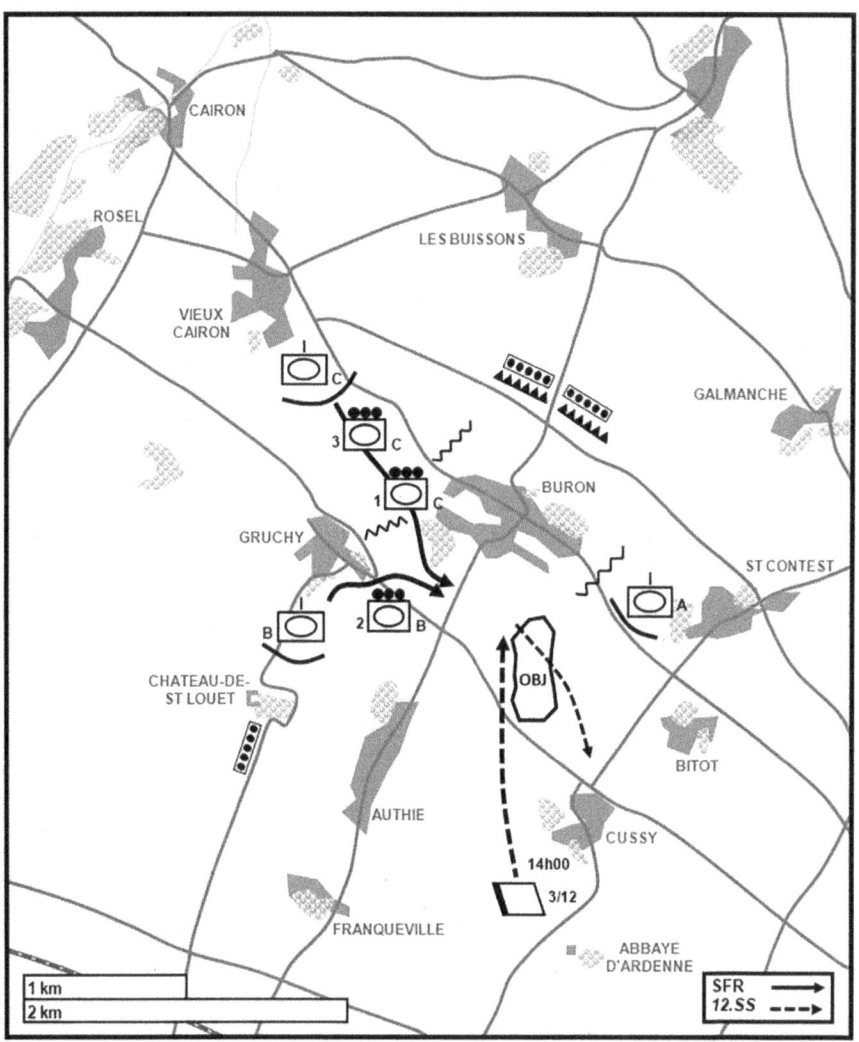

8 July 1944: Phase 1 of Operation CHARNWOOD.

C on the left with the capture of Buron as its immediate objective. B Sqn was on the right with the SD&GH with its sights set on Gruchy. C Sqn was in a position to give fire support to both squadrons from a hill on the outskirts of Vieux Cairon. With the Canadian attack on Carpiquet Airfield halted, the *Hitlerjugend* had moved reinforcements back north of Caen in anticipation of a renewed attack in that sector. Minefields and barbed wire had been added. Machine-gun positions, especially on the northwest side of Buron facing Villons-les Buissons and Vieux Cairon, had been sited to give protective fire. The stone wall that encircled the town was reinforced and the whole defence system was tied together using trenches and anti-tank ditches. The battalion was further reinforced by the presence of 7.Pzkom.

The HLI of C plan was to advance with D Coy, supported by 1 Troop, forward right and attack the western half of Buron after clearing out the two anti-tank ditches located in front of the village. B Coy, with 2 Troop in support, was to advance forward left and attack the eastern half of Buron. C Coy would follow in a close reserve role with the support of the tanks of 4 Troop. As soon as the infantry crossed the start line, they were hit with heavy artillery, mortar and machine-gun fire. However, they succeeded in reaching the anti-tank ditch without too much difficulty. The tanks on the right flank were fired upon from Authie and Gruchy, and Panthers were seen moving towards Gruchy. In response, the tanks began to build a smoke screen with the help of the artillery under the direction of their FOO. The two lead tank troops hit the anti-tank ditches at about 07.30. Although the *Sherbrookes* had hit them on D+1, the tankers had forgotten they existed and they were surprised when the first tanks were disabled. The ditches were heavily mined, with barbed wire strung along its entire length. A German company gave covering fire on the obstacle with anti-tank weapons and machine-guns. 1 Troop bumped into mines on the west side of the main road losing three tanks, including their Firefly. The tanks were then systematically destroyed by 88mm anti-tank guns firing from 1.5 miles to the southwest. The fourth tank was rescued by the Flail tanks and it joined up with the SHQ.

2 Troop advanced on the eastern side of the main road from Villons-les-Buissons. When it hit the ditch, two tanks were lost to German infantry defending the position with hand-held *Panzerschreck*[5] weapons. Sgt Denis E. Bégin's tank was then hit in the turret by a mortar bomb. Tpr Joe Neuman, the gunner, was wounded and had to be evacuated. Tanks and anti-tank guns from Saint-Contest joined their fire with that of the five *PzKpfw IV* tanks in Buron itself. The last tank, the troop's Firefly, was destroyed by

88mm anti-tank fire from southeast of Buron. The tank had been shooting up German soldiers in slit trenches, which the infantry couldn't get to. A German with a light anti-tank weapon opened up on it but the round glanced off the gun mantle. Just then, the crew spotted four Panthers coming up to take them on at about 800 yards. Lieut Truax's tank fired first but the round fell 100 yards short. The German tanks fired and hit the Canadian tank in its side but it continued to fire back. The second German shot hit the tank in the turret and the third shot hit the final drive. The tank started to brew up. Lieut Truax, injured in the action, ordered the crew to bale out. They took cover until the three injured crew members were evacuated.

Sgt Beardsley's tank was also destroyed but he succeeded in removing the .303-cal Browning machine-gun from the tank along with its available supply of ammunition. With his crew, he installed it in a ditch and from there continued to fight, killing many Germans and taking twelve prisoners including an officer. When all the ammunition was expended, he withdrew his crew under heavy mortar fire, taking his prisoners with him. Tpr D.D. Bartlett's tank was also hit. With the turret guns disabled and the three turret crewmen wounded, he directed the co-driver to fire his machine-gun at the anti-tank gun that had hit them. He then charged the enemy position and crushed the gun beyond serviceability. He followed that up by charging the infantry positions protecting it, and killed several machine-gun crews. He then returned to the safety of the rear.

Maj Radley-Walters moved the SHQ forward to support the left flank of the HLI of C as they finished clearing out the ditches and moved into Buron. At about 08.30, he called 4 Troop forward to replace 1 Troop. Using their co-ax machine-guns, the troop succeeded in pinning down the Germans but this was not enough to push B Coy through. He then decided to go around on the right side of the trenches and get into the village behind the German defences. Another smoke screen was laid between Gruchy and Buron to mask their move. At 11.00, the Flails and field engineers were called up to clear a path through the minefields to the southwest. The engineers cleared a path wide enough for a tank, and Maj Radley-Walters pushed eight tanks through – all the tanks that were still mobile. At the same time, the infantry cleared out the ditches. As he pushed the remnants of his squadron towards Buron, his tank came upon a *PzKpfw IV* in a hedgerow. He fired but missed. As he manoeuvred his tank, the German tank turned and fired in turn. It also missed. The German tank fired again two more times before hitting the water jerry cans strapped to the outside of the hull. It fired again and finally hit the right sponson of his Sherman. Maj Radley-Walters succeeded in finding shelter behind a stone wall. His gunner, Tpr Paul A. Paquette was slightly injured in the ankle. While this was going on, the rest of A Sqn moved to an orchard on the northeast side of Buron. From there, Maj Walsh's tank could be seen. It had stalled and been left behind on 7 June. It was now being used by the Germans as a machine-gun post. It was rapidly destroyed and the Germans killed.

The anti-tank ditch was 12ft wide and 15ft deep. With the tanks caught up on the minefield, the infantry got separated from the tanks and advanced into a kill zone between the ditch and the town. B Coy lost half its strength to well-camouflaged machine-gun posts. The attack began to lose its momentum and so Lt-Col Franklin McCallum Griffiths, the CO of the HLI of C, was forced to commit his reserve companies. Lieut Charles Campbell, the Int O of the battalion, tried to get tank support for B Coy but was unsuccessful. He therefore ran out over 300 yards of fire-swept ground to make physical contact with the tanks. He had to run out a second and third time before he was finally carried on the back of a tank to Maj Radley-Walters' position. He explained that B Coy was under heavy fire on the left flank. He also pointed out that there were no mines on the left. The remaining tanks then veered northeast and passed between the anti-tank ditch and the northern side of Buron. A German company of infantry was dug-in and it was impeding the advance of the HLI of C. The squadron managed to clear out the position and the tanks used their main guns to knock down openings in the stone walls to allow the infantry to gain access to the orchards and gardens, which turned the tide in favour of the HLI of C. The tanks succeeded in advancing as far as the orchard on the east side of the town. It was now approximately noon and the squadron strength was down to five or six tanks.

On the east side of Buron, a trench had been dug to intersect the road leading to Bitôt. A plan was devised whereby the tanks would drive down it with one track in the trench, while firing down its length with their co-ax machine-guns. The Flails would follow behind and flail the entire length of the trench. Lastly, the infantry would follow behind and clear the trench of any remaining Germans. The squadron went down the trench twice, but the Germans just lay down and the tanks drove over them without hitting them. The Germans then got back up and resumed fighting. The HLI of C fought hand to hand before finally managing to clear the trench, while the remaining tanks of A Sqn took up a defensive position on the high ground between Buron and Saint-Contest.

At about 13.30, the HLI of C reached their objective. D Coy on the right had cleared a path through the town and had crossed the Creully road, turned south and fought to their objective. B Coy on the left had met with heavy resistance on the north side of Buron and had taken heavy casualties. A Coy, following D Coy, fought its way into the northwest part of the town. Although the fight had lasted all morning, it wouldn't be until the next morning before the last German positions were taken. The cost was high. The HLI of C lost 262 men. Among the casualties were Lt-Col Griffiths and most of the company commanders. Due to the confusion, Lt-Col Griffiths had called an O Group in the centre of the town to get an update. A mortar shell exploded in their midst and he was killed, along with Maj Ray G. Hodgins, Maj David Durward, a lieutenant and three signallers.

B Sqn was in support of the SD&GH. The plan devised by Maj Bingham was to first move from the assembly area in Vieux Cairon to a position of fire about 600 yards south of the town. From there, they would shell Gruchy until the infantry was close to the town; the fire would then be directed towards the Château-de-Saint Louet. As part of Phase 3 of the 9th Brigade plan, the squadron was to move forward towards Franqueville to support the infantry when they attacked it. Initially, when the attack was launched at 07.30, the SD&GH advanced without drawing fire but at 07.45 the advance came under heavy mortar fire. Moreover, as the infantry reached Gruchy at 07.54, enemy machine-guns opened up. It soon became apparent that the whole squadron would be needed to give support to the SD&GH. The squadron advanced with two troops leading. 1 Troop under Lieut Hugh Derek Foster was on the right flank in support of B Coy, while 3 Troop held the left in support of A Coy; 2 Troop gave support to the advancing troops from a position on the right flank and the SHQ followed on the left. 1 Troop attacked around the west side of Gruchy, the tanks firing HE rounds into the houses and stone walls. The corners of the hedgerows were singled out and many turned out to be *PzKpfw IV* tanks under cover. However, they had been more or less smashed by the artillery bombardment that had preceded the assault. At 08.05, the B Sqn tanks entered Gruchy and several minutes later German tanks were observed leaving the far end of the village. Many Panther tanks were also observed crossing back and forth between the château and Authie. At about 09.00, one rushed out from behind a hedge 450 yards away and Sgt John W. Taylor brewed it up. It took three hits before one went through the top deck and set off the ammunition stowed behind the gunner's seat.

Lieut Foster fired at a 20mm anti-aircraft gun in the field, wounded the German gunner and smashed its power traverse. He then drove his tank into the gun while Sgt Taylor advanced in support to within 50 yards of the gun. A German popped up from one of the numerous foxholes and threw a grenade at Lieut Foster's turret. The explosion came very near to killing him. Instead, a pistol duel resulted and the German was killed. Lieut Foster then dropped No. 36 fragmentation grenades into the rest of the numerous foxholes dug in the field. Sgt Taylor killed another German trying to crawl away, but at one point a *Panzerfaust*[6] hit his tank. Luckily, only ration boxes were damaged – but his track was almost cut in two by the same shot. Meanwhile, Cpl H.O. Seigrist's tank was struck by an anti-tank gun and had to retire back to the assembly area. The remainder of the troop, including Cpl Donald M. Dundas's tank, started to shell the Château-de-Saint Louet from close range but had to retire to Gruchy a few minutes later when they were mistaken for being enemy tanks and friendly artillery fire came down on them.

On the north side, 3 Troop encountered very stiff resistance from entrenched German infantry. Cpl Hutcheson's tank was lost when a German soldier placed a magnetic bomb on it. The explosion killed both the gunner and the radio operator. The troop succeeded in taking out the enemy machine-gun position, but long range anti-tank fire took out the remaining tanks of 3 Troop. At 09.12, enemy soldiers were spotted trying to leave the far end of Gruchy, but they were also cut down by the tanks. The troop finished mopping up the area between Buron and Gruchy and silenced the German anti-tank gun that was giving them trouble. At 10.38, the SD&GH reported that Gruchy was in their hands. In fact, enemy resistance was light. The pioneer platoon of SS-Pzgren-Rgt 25 held the town and it was entirely wiped out in their positions. At 10.55, Maj-Gen Keller ordered 9th Brigade to attack south and capture the Château-de-Saint Louet and Authie.[7] At about 11.30, 2 Troop moved up beside Lieut Foster's troop on the south side of Gruchy. Both troops put down co-ax fire on enemy weapon pits in the field between Gruchy and the Château-de-Saint Louet. Immediately, two anti-tank guns opened up from the château grounds and two tanks were knocked out.

According to the 9th Brigade plan, C Sqn was to remain in reserve south of Vieux Cairon and cover the advance of the other two squadrons into Buron and Gruchy. C Sqn would then support the North Novas as they passed through Buron and took Authie. The plan was briefed to the crew commanders during the evening of 7 July. After the artillery barrage quieted down, the tanks engaged the Germans in Buron and Gruchy using speculative fire, but no definite results were noticed. When Brig Blackader ordered the North Novas to undertake Phase 2 of his plan, the tanks of the squadron moved forward towards their start line just south of Buron. As Lieut William James Charters's 1 Troop advanced to the right of Vieux Cairon, the lead tanks ran into the minefields and Cpl Quinn's tank ran into the anti-tank ditch.

At 14.00, the Germans launched their first counter-attack from the Abbaye d'Ardenne area supported by infantry. The First Brit Corps recce

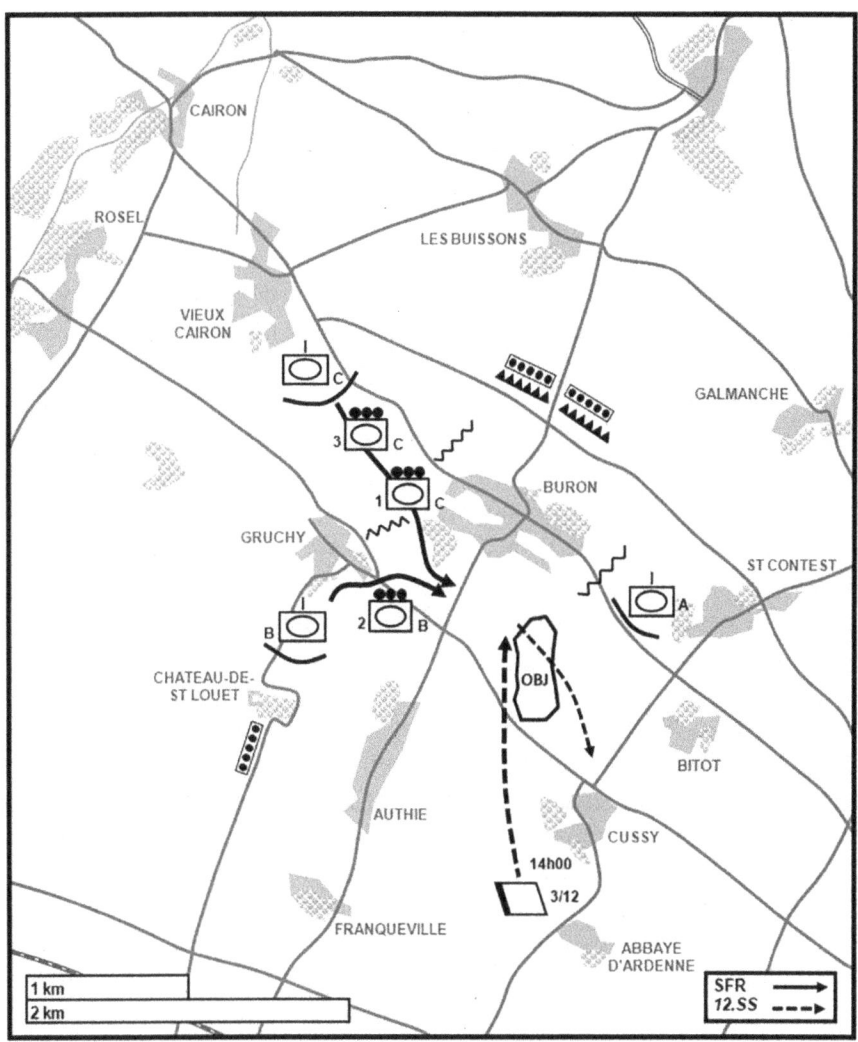

8 July 1944: The first German counter-attack.

regiment, the Inns of Court Regiment, had reported at 11.15 that eleven enemy tanks had been spotted moving northeast towards Buron about 500 yards east of the Château-de-Saint Louet. The information was passed on to the *Sherbrookes*. The *Kampfgruppe* was spotted by A Sqn as it passed to the west of Cussy. A Sqn was down to four tanks and the German Panthers were too far away for them to be engaged with tank fire. When the Germans got close enough to Buron, the *Sherbrookes* engaged them with their tanks and artillery. C Sqn had arrived at the orchard just as the German section farthest to the left crested the hill to their front. Two troops from C Sqn were sent in support of the A Sqn tanks on the high ground on the 80-contour ring. The infantry were still mopping up in Gruchy and were being hit by friendly artillery fire. Therefore, 1 Troop from B Sqn was ordered to remain on the southwest side of the town. Its presence seemed the only thing capable of stopping the German tanks from retaking Gruchy. Meanwhile, the two remaining tanks of 2 Troop under Lieut Charters were ordered to the orchard near Buron to give support to A Sqn. On the way, three enemy tanks moved across the skyline. The troop leader ordered the Firefly to fire on them but the results could not be accurately judged because the muzzle flash had thrown up a great deal of dust.

Lt-Col Gordon ordered C Sqn to move, at great risk, to occupy the dominating feature, the 80-contour ring, some 1,000 yards in front of the unit's foremost position. The squadron took a detour and arrived in Buron where they set up their position in the orchard southwest of the town. On their arrival, the squadron spotted several Panther tanks moving along the skyline to the south. As 4 Troop arrived in the orchard, Lieut Spafford spotted the tanks and saw that they would soon be in open view to the tanks on his left. He gave a warning and sent his Firefly to the left. He also fired two HE rounds to indicate their position. Sgt R.V. Olivier from 3 Troop could see three Panthers and immediately fired on one with the HE round already loaded in the breech. He hit the tank which stopped, and someone else hit it again and brewed it up. Cpl Leslie D. Williams of 1 Troop saw four tanks, fired on one and set it on fire. He fired three shots at another Panther but missed. Sgt Cathcart could only see three tanks but succeeded in knocking one out. Lieut Charters hit a third tank and it started to brew up.

Therefore, Lieut Boyd from C Sqn was sent with the three tanks of 3 Troop and Lieut Spafford arrived with the two tanks of 1 Troop. As the tanks came around the south side of Buron, between the town and the German counter-attack, the Germans opened up. Lieut Boyd's tank was hit, as was Sgt Martin Lefebvre's tank, and Lieut Boyd was killed. The remainder of the tanks stopped and took up a firing position. Sgt H. Fowlis's tank was fired on by the same Panther that had taken out the troop leader's tank. The tanks were more or less in the open so they manoeuvred around and took up a good position of observation. The gun was eventually taken out by another tank. Sgt Olivier had noticed infantry behind a hedge so he sprayed the position with co-ax fire and shelled it with HE. Unfortunately, his radio went dead and his co-ax machine-gun jammed. On the way back to the A Ech to get them repaired, Sgt Olivier spotted more infantry in trenches and threw grenades at them. At one point, a grenadier tried to climb onto the back of his tank and so Sgt Olivier killed him using his pistol.

By this time, Lieut Corless was out of ammunition. He recognised that the presence of a tank would help maintain good morale with the infantry and tell the enemy that there were tanks to be dealt with so he moved his tank into full view of the enemy. Meanwhile, Lieut Spafford moved 1 Troop out to the high ground on the 80-contour ring. They used machine-gun fire on hedges, slit trenches and infantry moving from right to left in front of Authie. Some tanks then threw HE rounds onto the town of Authie. Five Panthers were knocked out before the Germans turned back towards the safety of the Abbaye d'Ardenne. Lieut Charters observed an anti-tank gun in a hedge on the left in front of Authie and fired a round from his main gun; he missed so relayed his gun, but the 17-pdr wouldn't fire. Cpl Williams saw an AP round come close to Lieut Charters's tank. The troop leader returned to the orchard where he exchanged tanks with Cpl Williams. Once he returned to his former position, Lieut Charters once again fired on the anti-tank gun, scoring a direct hit with an AP round. The *Sherbrooke* tanks stayed in their positions for a short period of time before they started to receive harassing fire from enemy infantry as well as from German mortar fire. The infantry finally arrived on the high ground at 15.12, and by 16.00 their positions had been consolidated. The attack repulsed, A Sqn released the other tanks which returned to their respective squadrons.

As soon as the German attack was quashed, the North Novas began their attack on Authie. The plan was for D Coy to make a frontal attack with A Coy on the left and B Coy on the right. Once Authie was taken, C Coy would then go through and take Franqueville. The village was undefended, although the wheat fields around the Château-de-Saint Louet were manned by the remnants of a *Panzergrenadier* company. Lieut Thompson, the recce liaison tank crew commander, and Cpl Elmer L. Désilet were ordered forward to support A Coy into Authie, while the remaining three C Sqn tanks were kept in a supporting role in the orchard. The infantry was being hit with machine-gun fire from the area around Cussy. After laying down considerable fire on the machine-gun posts, the tanks advanced to the left of the village. Lieut Thompson's tank was immobilised by AP fire coming from an anti-tank gun located on the east side of the village. He could not locate it and so had to bail out. He took over Cpl Désilet's tank and moved to a better position of observation towards the front, while his crew moved off to find shelter in Authie. Lieut Thompson then noticed a FOO pass his position and as he moved towards him, he was hit by three rounds in rapid succession. Once again, the crew was forced to bail out, but this time Tpr Walter S. Stone was injured. Under heavy mortar and machine-gun fire, the crew took cover in Authie with Cpl Désilet. The FOO tried to escape to the rear of the village but he too was hit and his tank brewed up. His crew joined Lieut Thompson's group. The three crews were under tremendous mortar fire and could not locate any North Novas. They made their way to the rear of Authie by crawling through the buildings until they reached an orchard. They waited until the fire died down a little and then made their way back across the field to Buron where they reported back to Maj Walsh.

At the same time, the SD&GH pushed forward and took the Château-de-Saint Louet. 2 Troop of B Sqn gave them supporting fire until it was ordered to move down in front of Authie to take out some machine-guns that were holding up the advance of the North Novas. The machine-guns were engaged and silenced. By 15.30, both Authie and the Châteaude-Saint Louet were reported to be in Canadian hands and at 16.40, the château was reported clear. C Coy then pushed on towards the south and took Franqueville with the support of A Sqn and C Sqn. A Sqn was on the high ground southwest of Buron and was giving fire support to the North Novas as they entered Authie. B Sqn was giving fire support to the SD&GH from Gruchy, while C Sqn also gave fire support to the North Novas from the southwest side of Buron. The Royal Hamilton Light Infantry (RHLI) had moved up and was digging in on the 80-contour ring.

At about 17.00, a second German counter-attack to retake Buron was launched using the same route of attack. The remaining Panther tanks of 3.Pzkom had been reorganised and they advanced two sections up. On the Canadian side, the four remaining tanks of A Sqn, including a Firefly, were still deployed on the knoll to the east of the town. Maj Radley-Walters called Lt-Col Gordon and asked for reinforcements. A couple of 6-pdr anti-tank guns on the south end of Buron and a troop of eight M-10 Achilles SP anti-tank guns were positioned in the southwest corner of the town. When the German tanks came within range, the Canadian guns opened up and

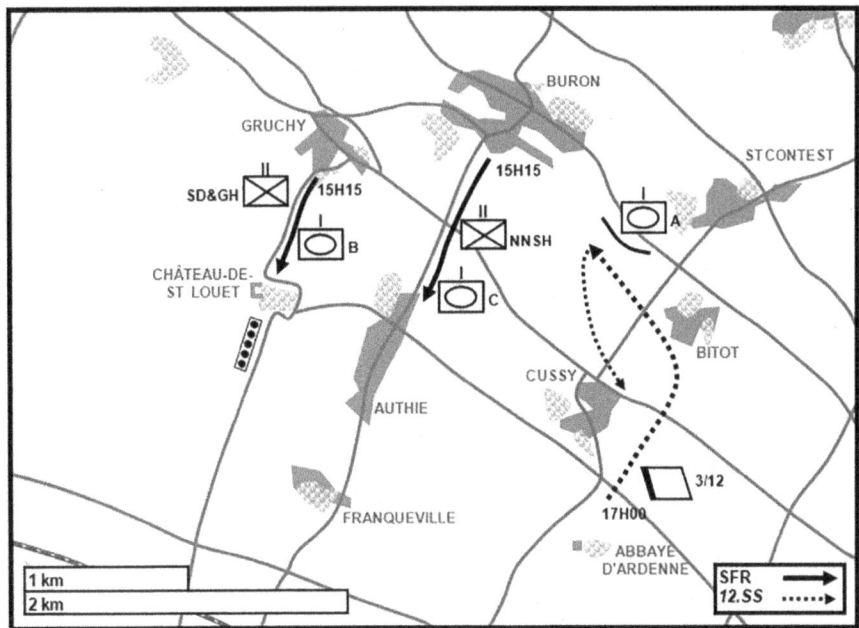

8 July 1944: Phase 2 of Operation CHARNWOOD and the second German counter-attack.

within a period of ten minutes, seven more Panthers had been destroyed. Two other tanks broke off their advance and returned to the safety of the Abbaye d'Ardenne. Allied artillery opened up on them as they retreated.

Meyer, who had been watching the counter attack from an Abbaye d'Ardenne OP, immediately returned to his DivHQ in Caen. No officers and only about 100 enlisted men and NCOs remained of III./SS-Pzgren-Rgt 25. It was evident to Meyer that he could no longer hold out against the advancing Canadian and British troops intent on taking Caen. Faced with a desperate situation, he asked for permission from the headquarters of *Panzergruppe West*, to withdraw his forces over the Orne River. Permission was refused. Hitler had given orders for 12.SS-Pzdiv to 'fight to the last man'. Meyer decided to ignore his *Führer*'s orders and at 19.15 issued his own orders for the evacuation of the remnants of III./SS-Pzgren-Rgt 25. The heavy weapons were to begin their withdrawal immediately, while the infantry was to cover the move before withdrawing themselves after darkness fell.

At 18.30, 7th Brigade launched Phase 3 of Maj-Gen Keller's plan. Although both German counter-attacks had been thrown back, the

Hitlerjugend were not beat. C Coy of the North Novas pushed forward with the remaining *Sherbrookes* tanks and took Franqueville. C Sqn had sent a troop south of Authie to support the North Novas into Franqueville while the remainder of the squadron, two tanks, remained in Authie. When the order was given at 18.30 to take Franqueville, all that remained of B Sqn was its SHQ and 1 Troop. The squadron 2i/c sent the troop forward with the task of wiping out a machine-gun nest that was holding up the North Novas advance. It moved forward and pushed into the ground south of the Château-de-Saint Louet, Firing at 1,200 yards, Lieut Foster disabled a *PzKpfw IV* tank in Franqueville, knocking it out after closing with the village. With the support of 1 Troop, the infantry took the village. The Cdn Scottish, supported by C Sqn of the Hussars, took Cussy at 00.30 but only after fierce fighting. The Regina Rifles, with B Sqn of the Hussars in support, met with heavy resistance before the Germans withdrew from the Abbaye d'Ardenne at midnight. Phase 4 of the 3rd Cdn Inf Div plan called for 9th Brigade to mop up the area north of Caen while 8th Brigade took Carpiquet Airfield and 7th Brigade pushed forward to quickly seize the Orne bridges before they could be destroyed. When darkness fell, the final phase of the plan was postponed until the next morning.

A Sqn had stayed in its position until 20.00 and had observed 7th Brigade's advance on Cussy and the Abbaye d'Ardenne. Although

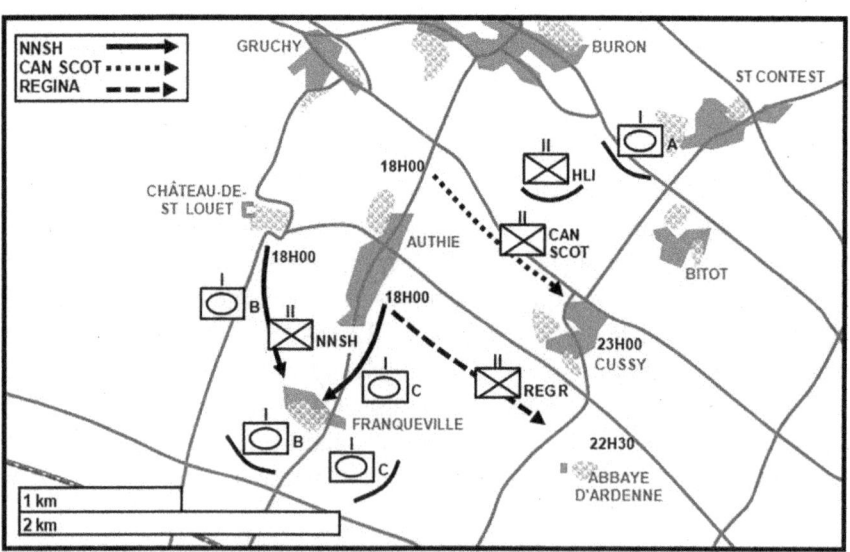

8 July 1944: Phase 3 of Operation CHARNWOOD.

C Sqn had received four fresh tanks, it remained in the orchard south of Buron until it was released at midnight; 2 Troop of B Sqn was joined by the remaining tank from the troop of the Hussars that had suffered two casualties from an anti-tank gun located in a hedgerow on the side of Authie. The troop knocked out the gun position before returning to the assembly area. As they were leaving, Cpl George S. Rice's tank was hit between the top of the track and the bottom of the sponson by an 88mm anti-tank gun. The round did not penetrate the tank but it knocked out his right engine. All three squadrons returned to the crossroads behind Vieux Cairon via Rosel and Cairon to replenish and harbour for the night. The *Sherbrookes* had lost eleven tanks, although seven were recoverable and four of them were already back in action. Three *Sherbrooke* soldiers had been killed and five were wounded. The regiment claimed seventeen enemy tanks knocked out and forty prisoners taken. The regiment also confirmed the presence of Tiger tanks in the battle. Later that night, the squadron was given first priority for replacements and it received seven replacement tanks with crews. Maj Radley-Walters reorganised his tanks into two troops of four tanks each and his SHQ. Five of the crew commanders were lieutenants, so he selected two to be troop leaders. A Sqn also lent a tank to B Sqn which was down to six tanks. Maj Bingham then organised his squadron into two troops of three tanks plus the OC's tank. C Sqn had a total of ten tanks, also organised into two troops. All the tanks refuelled, replenished their ammunition bins and rested in preparation for the move into Caen scheduled for the next morning.

Maj-Gen Keller decided to exploit the gains made that afternoon and to push the attack on Caen at the earliest possible hour; 2nd Cdn Armd Bde was ordered to provide support with the *Sherbrookes* and the Garrys. At around 03.00 the next morning, 9th Brigade was ordered to exploit the previous day's success and take Caen. The task was given to the SD&GH with the support of the *Sherbrookes* while the HLI of C provided a firm base. The objective was to maintain contact with the enemy, which was believed to be pulling out, but without becoming involved in a major action. The SD&GH were down to two companies with fifty-one men per company while the *Sherbrookes* were down to thirty-four tanks. C Sqn was already in Authie and so it was ordered to secure the start line for the offensive. B Sqn was in better shape than A Sqn so it was given the chore of supporting the infantry in their move forward through Authie and into Franqueville. From there, if the German opposition was light, they were to push down RN 13 into Saint-Germain-la-Blanche-Herbe and then into Caen itself. C Sqn was tasked with conducting a fighting recce as far as the northeast outskirts of Caen, while A Sqn was placed in reserve in a supporting role. The recovery team from 85th LAD was to move forward behind the tanks to quickly handle any vehicle battle casualties.

The SD&GH plan was to advance with two companies, each supported by a squadron of tanks. At 05.00, the battalion commander issued his orders. D Coy would lead the way supported by B Sqn of the *Sherbrookes*. C Coy would follow in depth with C Sqn, while A Coy and B Coy returned to Vieux Cairon. A delay in the H-Hour had been requested until 10.00 but the brigade commander had refused. Instead, at 09.00, he ordered the SD&GH to begin their advance immediately. At 09.38, they reported that they were on their start line. At 09.45, they reported Franqueville cleared. The advance now wheeled to the left and began to move down RN 13. B Sqn had been reorganised into two troops of three tanks each: two Shermans and a Firefly. 1 Troop was commanded by Lieut Davies while 2 Troop was commanded by Capt Gilbert; Maj Bingham's tank made up the SHQ. The plan he devised was for the squadron to move from Vieux Cairon to Franqueville and then to move on the north side of RN 13 towards Caen. The squadron moved off from its assembly area against little resistance at 08.45, with the infantry on foot. As Cpl Quinn was approaching the Abbaye d'Ardenne, he spotted a *PzKpfw IV* tank in a gap in the wall. He fired three shots at it and scored two hits. A little smoke came up but it didn't brew up, and there was no movement around it. At around 09.55, Capt Gilbert's tank struck a Teller mine on the outskirts of Saint-Germain-la-Blanche-Herbe and lost a track. Maj Bingham, who was following behind him, spotted another mine in front of his tank. He opened up on it using the .50-cal Browning machine-gun. The mine exploded and a piece of shrapnel hit Capt Gilbert in the shoulder. Maj Bingham moved forward to assist but he also hit a Teller mine and injured his back. He ordered two Flails to advance and clear the way for the other tanks. The minefield was only an anti-tank obstacle and so the SD&GH continued forward on foot.

Lt-Col Gordon ordered A Sqn to try to get through the minefield and for C Sqn to establish a fire base in the Abbaye d'Ardenne area. C Sqn moved forward and set itself up on the high ground immediately south of the Abbaye d'Ardenne, overlooking the main road into Caen. 4 Troop moved further forward to cover the Flails as they cleared a path through

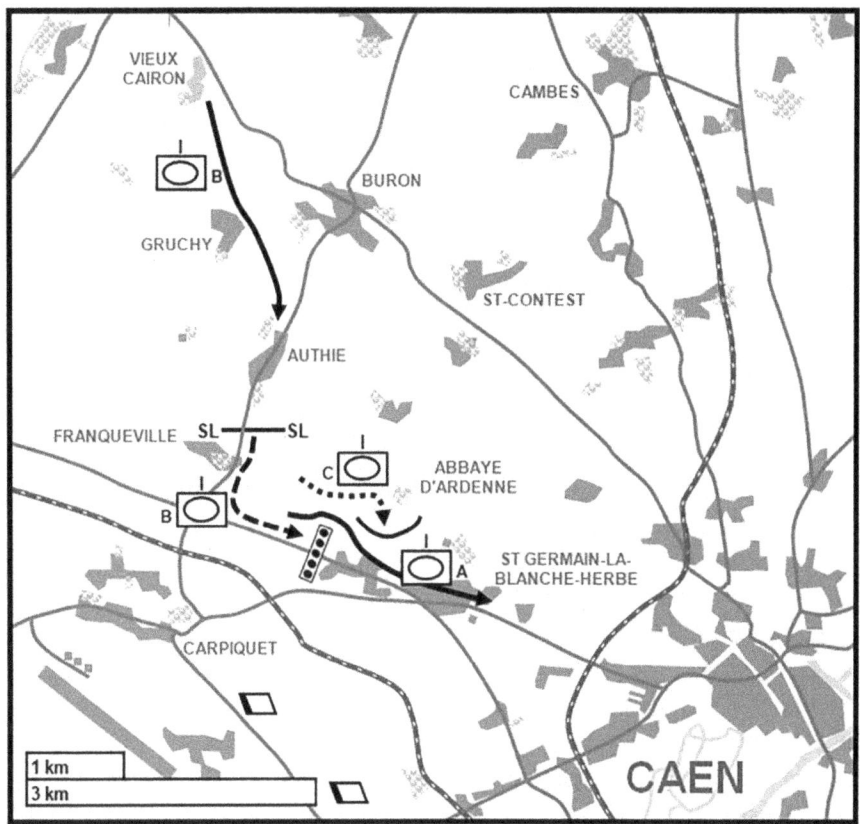

9 July 1944: Phase 4 of Operation CHARNWOOD.

the minefield. Two lanes were cleared through the minefield and marked with white tape. At 10.15, German tank fire erupted from positions east of Carpiquet. Five Panther tanks were spotted at a distance of about 2,000 yards on the right. Maj Bingham's tank was hit and set on fire. Lieut Foster rushed forward to get under cover but he also hit a mine about 150 yards in front of Maj Bingham's tank. It was disabled in an open space and on the skyline. Suddenly, two shots from the German tanks passed overhead. Lieut Foster began to turn his turret to engage the enemy when a third round bounced off his tank. As he continued to traverse, he spotted the Panther tanks and realised that his situation was desperate. He therefore ordered his crew to abandon the tank. At the same time, a fourth shot blew up the ammunition in the right rear sponson. The crew bailed out. A German 88mm anti-tank gun aimed an AP round at Sgt Harold A. Futter's tank 'Bomb', but the round only hit the breech of the .50-cal Browning anti-aircraft machine gun mounted on the turret. Fragments wounded Sgt Futter and Tpr James R. Fletcher, and cut the electrical leads to the wireless set.

Both A Sqn and C Sqn laid a protective smoke screen to obscure the German field of vision. The tanks were too far away to engage with AP rounds, so Lieut Charters engaged with seven rounds of delayed HE. Sgt Fowlis thought he spotted a Tiger tank and saw gun flashes from two more. When his gun failed to fire, however, he pulled back and returned to Vieux Cairon to get it fixed. Lieut Spafford, of C Sqn's 4 Troop, also spotted the tanks and engaged them with HE while he ordered his Firefly to engage with AP. The German tanks eventually withdrew but a hail of mortar- and shell-fire began to rain down on the C Sqn position. As soon as the situation was secure, A Sqn bypassed the minefield on the left. The tanks rapidly caught up with the SD&GH near Saint-Germain-la-Blanche-Herbe. At 11.15, the advancing Canadian infantry had reached the crossroads of the Bayeux and Carpiquet roads. At 12.00, they reached Beaulieu Prison meeting little resistance. However, they were hit by German machine-gun and mortar fire further up the Rue du Général Moulin. They succeeded in reaching the Place du Planître where they were met with machine-gun fire from a pill box. Two Sherman tanks countered and forced the gates of Les Pépinières. One of the Shermans hit a mine but the gunner managed to take out the pillbox on his first shot. About ten minutes later, at around 13.30, the SD&GH radioed back that they were in Caen. The North Novas and the HLI of C followed them in. As D Coy reached the railway on Boulevard Dunais, an infantry officer stopped a C Sqn tank coming down the Rue de Bayeux from Saint-Germain-la-Blanche-Herbe and ordered it to knock down the two towers on the Saint-Étienne-le-Vieux church. When questioned, he explained that enemy snipers were using the towers and were preventing the battalion from advancing further. Tpr Joseph Clare, the radio operator-loader for the crew, loaded a round while the gunner took aim. Just as the gunner was about to shoot, a message came over the radio that the intelligence people had reported the church was full of refugees. The order to fire was countermanded.[8]

At 12.35, the *Sherbrookes* sent word to the 2nd Cdn Armd Bde HQ that 'My Sunray[9] reports that he is in the centre of Caen.' Lt-Col Gordon had moved forward into the city to see for himself if the city was safe for his tanks. Virtually the whole of the central area had been destroyed by the Allied bombing on the night of 6–7 July. The northern area was badly damaged, but an island of refuge existed about the great church of Saint-Étienne-le-Vieux, the Abbaye des Hommes and the Hôpital du Bon Souvenir. C Coy and D Coy of the SD&GH reached the Place des Petites Boucheries by 13.00 and then proceeded by the Rue Guillaume-le-Conquérant and Place Fontette. A Coy and B Coy followed behind and turned up Rue Caponière and Rue du Carel. As A Sqn once more moved towards the city, four or five German tanks opened fire on them. Again, smoke was laid to obscure their vision while artillery fire engaged their position and A Sqn made a dash for it. C Sqn spotted three Tiger tanks across the valley about 3,000 yards away. The squadron's tanks immediately went into hull-down positions and opened fire. Sgt Reid engaged the tanks with his Firefly but his gun was not firing properly and so he withdrew to a position of observation. The German tanks withdrew under cover but the squadron was now down to five tanks and it came under constant mortar fire and occasional 88mm gun fire. Three tanks from A Sqn came up and joined C Sqn. On rounding a corner, A Sqn was amazed by the amount of rubble in the streets, at places as high as 10–15ft. The tanks could only move a few hundred yards up a street before it was blocked by rubble. The rule was to always swing right and so the squadron soon found itself in a suburb of Caen called Venoix. Maj Radley-Walters positioned his tanks on the high ground near the railway; 2 Troop was deployed on the left of the main road, exploiting to 500 yards, and 4 Troop was on the right, exploiting to 300 yards. Maj Radley-Walters decided to split the SHQ in two, sending two tanks with 2 Troop and the last tank with 4 Troop; 2 Troop took up a position overlooking the western approached to Venoix, while 4 Troop set itself up overlooking the south of the town. The SD&GH consolidated their position at the southwest corner of the town looking towards Venoix.

From its positions, A Sqn could oversee the villages on the Orne River and, when targets of opportunity were spotted, the tanks shot at German artillery and vehicles in and around Louvigny. Fleury-sur-Orne had high cliffs with caves that were being used by the Germans; at one point, an eight-barrelled *Nebelwerfer*[10] rocket launcher was seen to come out of a cave, fire and then return inside. Since the cave was too far away for tank fire, Maj Radley-Walters directed artillery fire onto the position and succeeded in destroying it. Almost immediately, however, a Red Cross flag was seen to emerge and it became apparent that the civilians from the city were also using the caves as protection against the previous day's bombardments.

Orders were received for C Sqn to move into Saint-Germain-la-Blanche-Herbe. As soon as the tanks started to move, the lead tank was fired upon by either an anti-tank gun or a Tiger tank as it reached the edge of the minefield. The tanks were forced to move back and retake positions of

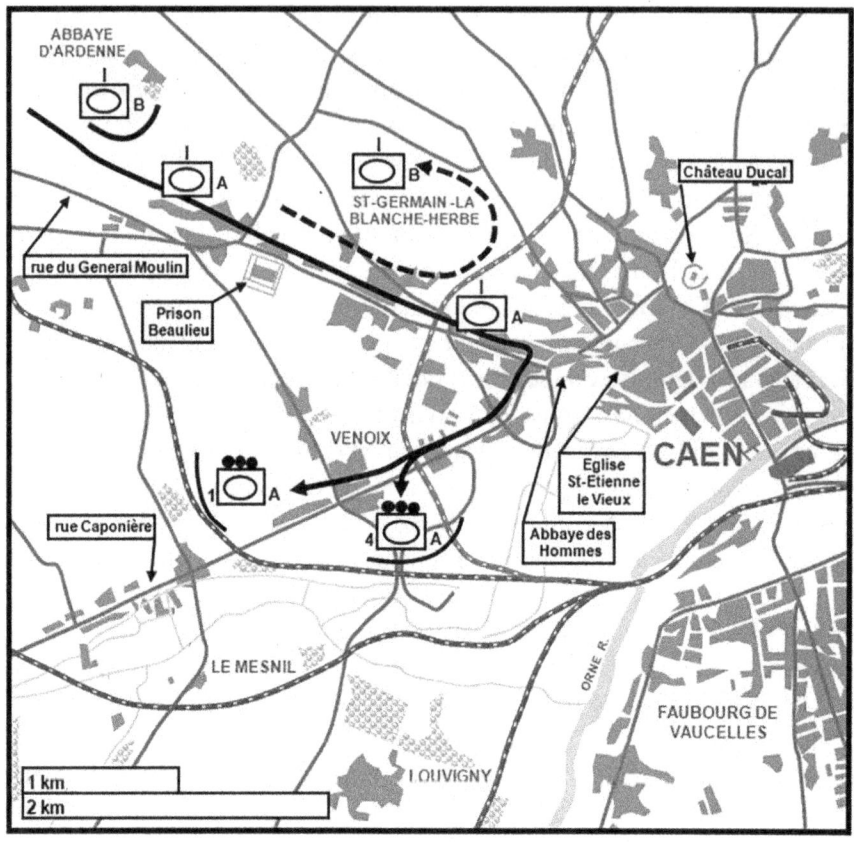

9 July 1944: The Sherbrooke Fusilier Regiment enters Caen.

observation. At dusk, the squadron finally succeeded in moving forward and it established a laager for the night in the orchard near Beaulieu Prison. The four remaining tanks of B Sqn, under the command of Lieut Davies, had taken up the rear behind A Sqn. Their original objective had been Saint-Étienne-le-Vieux church – it was supposed to have a red cross painted on its roof. The troop searched for it but failed to find it. Instead, they also found people hiding in caves near the Orne River. As they entered the town, they moved in a circling motion to the right and then moved back to the high ground north of Caen and overlooking the city. It would remain there until nightfall, at which time it rejoined the rest of the regiment in the town. They harboured about one mile east of Beaulieu Prison.

The population of Caen was surprised to hear French spoken by the Canadians. The town was in ruins but they were genuinely happy to see the *Sherbrookes*. The population almost killed them with affection. People came out of holes in the ground and threw their arms around the tankers. Everyone was crying and kissing them. The Canadians greeted them with cigarettes, chocolates and candy. An old man and a woman rushed out with a few flowers and threw them up at the tanks. Someone else came running out with a glass of water or wine, while another carried a tri-colour French flag. Two or three men hugged each other at the roadside and sang *La Marseillaise*, the French national anthem. A strange sight also greeted the men when they noticed several people wandering about who were clearly mentally and emotionally distressed. At first, they thought the bombings had snapped the mental equilibrium of the citizens, but it was discovered later that they came from a 'mental hospital' that had been hit. At 17.00, recce elements of 7th Canadian Reconnaissance Regiment (7th Cdn Recce Regt) finally reached the Orne River, only to discover that all the bridges had been destroyed by the Germans, save one. That bridge was found to be blocked by rubble and covered by enemy fire from the far bank. The bridges that were so desperately needed to continue the advance were missing, and the offensive ground to a halt. By 22.30, the Canadians were firmly established in Caen with only a few very small pockets of resistance remaining. The tri-colour flag flew once again from the town hall while, from houses, recordings of *La Marseillaise* could be heard with voices joining in.

With Caen in Allied hands, mine-clearance operations were launched, bulldozers were set to work to clear the streets and a convoy of trucks carrying supplies for the civilian population was brought in. The regiment spent 10 July in a counter-attack role as the infantry continued to mop up the city. The tanks were subjected to occasional long range shelling, but otherwise it was very quiet. C Sqn moved to an orchard covering the Venoix road and an area overlooking Bretteville-sur-Odon to the south; A Sqn remained in their same positions.

On 11 July, the regiment was pulled back and it withdrew to the ground southwest of Lébisey. There it was to repair, refit and re-equip to 100 per cent of its effective fighting strength.[11] The *Sherbrookes* pulled back to the area around Épron and Malon. The low ground selected for the RHQ and the echelons was soon affectionately nicknamed 'Happy Valley'. There, the troops got a shower and a change of clothes from the Mobile Laundry and Bath Unit. While A Sqn had still been in Venoix, one tank was positioned near a French restaurant. While digging slit trenches on 10 July, the crew hit a cache that held all the liquor from the bar – the owner had hidden it from the Germans. The crew covered it back up and dug their slit trenches elsewhere. When the squadron pulled back, Sgt Beardsley asked if he could have a truck to go back and get the liquor for the squadron. He came back that night with bottles of wine, Calvados and so on. A couple of bottles were distributed to each man and everyone passed out that night from the alcohol and fatigue.

On 18 July, the men spotted a German Storch, a light reconnaissance aircraft, flying at a very low altitude over the unit's location. About fifteen minutes later, Happy Valley came under a heavy concentration of mortar and artillery fire. The 210mm mortar shells wrought havoc, knocking out many soft-skinned fuel and ammunition trucks. More than twenty shells landed in and on the outskirts of the harbour area. The B Ech. took most of the brunt of the attack, with the regiment suffering twenty-six casualties. Four soldiers were killed or would die of their wounds in the days to come. Five officers, including Maj Weber, were wounded, as were seventeen other ranks. Luckily, the fighting squadrons were located a short distance away and did not suffer any vehicle or personnel casualties. There would be no time to recover morally. That same night, C Sqn moved off in preparation for a crossing of the Orne River and the remainder of the regiment moved off the next day.

Chapter 5

Operation ATLANTIC
The Battle for Verrières Ridge

With the loss of Caen, the Germans began to dig-in on the south shore of the Orne River and on the Verrières-Bourguébus Ridge, high ground 5 miles south of the city. Since the Allied landing had begun, the Germans had suffered over 100,000 battle casualties, but had received only 9,000 weak replacements; 2,360 officers had been lost, including 9 commanding generals, 7 staff officer generals and 137 COs. On 8 July, Hitler issued his 'Directive for the Conduct of Operations in the West'. In his assessment of the situation, Hitler was convinced that the Allies would attempt a second landing between the Somme and Seine rivers with the aim of capturing one of the large ports of Brittany. Therefore, he ordered his generals to avoid any major offensive that aimed at the destruction of the enemy in the beachhead. Instead, the German forces were ordered to fight a strictly defensive battle until additional forces arrived in Normandy. However, the German *Wehrmacht* had been bled on the Eastern Front and few reinforcements would become available to move west. A rare exception, Pz-Lehr-Div, with its 250 tanks, was sent to reinforce the 70 infantry battalions in the American sector.

The land south of Caen is a vast plain of open fields rising gently to the Verrières–Bourguébus Ridge. While the British and Canadian forces had been battling for Caen, elements of I.SS-Pzkorps had turned the ridge into their main defensive position. The ridge dominated the topography and was ideal as an armoured fire base. The villages were used to form strongpoints. Two railways cut a path from north to south and formed an obstacle that impeded the movement of armour. The Germans set up three lines of defence in anticipation of a British attempt to seize the high feature. The first line of defence, held by 16.Lw-Fd-Div, a division of mediocre quality, extended from Cuverville to Démouville. Directly behind them, two *Panzergrenadier* battalions from 21.Pzdiv provided depth. The second line of defence stretched from Démouville along the Caen-Paris railway and was centered on the strongpoint of Le Mesnil-Frémentel. The last line of defence formed the arc of a circle along the Bourguébus Ridge.

The ridge was not particularly high, just 27 meters, but its commanding height ensured that advancing forces would be exposed to German fire from the ridge itself, from the nearby industrial hamlet of Saint-Martin-de-Fontenay, and from positions to the west of the Orne River, including from Hill 112. Two armoured formations held the ridge: 12.SS-Pzdiv and 1.SS-Pzdiv. The *Panzer* formations were supported by artillery, dug-in Tiger tanks and mortar emplacements. *9.SS-Panzerdivision (Hohenstaufen)* (9.SS-Pzdiv) was held in reserve. Further support in depth was provided by *272.Infanterie-Division* (272.Inf-Div), *116. Panzerdivision* (116.Pzdiv) and a battalion of Tiger tanks. 1.SS-Pzdiv was positioned directly opposite Caen on the Verrières portion of the ridge and it had around 200 tanks including 59 *PzKpfw IV* and 46 Panthers. Additionally, the division's assault gun battalions provided thirty-five *StuG III* and twenty-five Tiger tanks. In addition, the division could count on 4,800 infantrymen, 35 75mm anti-tank guns, 72 88mm *Flak* anti-aircraft guns deployed in an anti-tank role, 194 field guns as well as 17 *Nebelwerfer* rocket launchers. For the upcoming battle, I.SS-Pzkorps had only 150 *PzKpfw IV* or Panther tanks and 15 Tiger tanks available; 12.SS-Pzdiv was positioned on the eastern flank on the Bourguébus Ridge proper, which was heavily reinforced with anti-tank guns along its southern and eastern edges. In order to allow the *Panzer* units free movement, it was decided not to establish anti-tank minefields behind the front line or between each defensive line.

On 10 July, Gen Montgomery called a planning conference with his two army commanders. Lt-Gen Bradley wanted to launch a second American breakout attempt on 18 July. Montgomery approved the American plan and ordered Lt-Gen Dempsey to use his armoured might to draw the German armour into the British sector so as to ease the way for the Americans; Second Brit Army had 2,250 medium tanks and 400 light tanks. On 13 July, Dempsey held a meeting with his corps commanders and outlined his plan for a breakout attempt. Operation GOODWOOD would see Eighth Brit Corps, with its three armoured divisions, strike south from the east side of the Orne bridgehead and seize the Bourguébus Ridge. Its objective was to seize Bretteville-sur-Laize and dominate the general Bretteville-sur-Laize-Vimont-Argences-Falaise area. First Brit Corps was to provide protection on the eastern flank while Second Cdn Corps, newly arrived in the order of battle, would clear Faubourg de Vaucelles and be prepared to exploit southward towards Falaise; Third Brit Corps would be held in reserve and be prepared to exploit the initial successes of the operation.

On 11 July, Second Cdn Corps under the command of Lt-Gen Simonds had entered the line. Composed of 3rd Cdn Inf Div and 2nd Cdn Armd Bde, both of whom had landed in Normandy on D-Day, the corps had become operational with the arrival of 2nd Cdn Inf Div which had previously seen action during the Dieppe Raid in August 1942. The last corps component, 4th Cdn Armd Div, was still in transit from England and would not be available for the upcoming operation. The corps had taken over an 8,000-yard stretch of the front including Caen from Third Brit Corps. Initially, its role in Operation GOODWOOD was to establish bridging sites across the Orne River and capture the Caen suburb of Faubourg de Vaucelles. It was

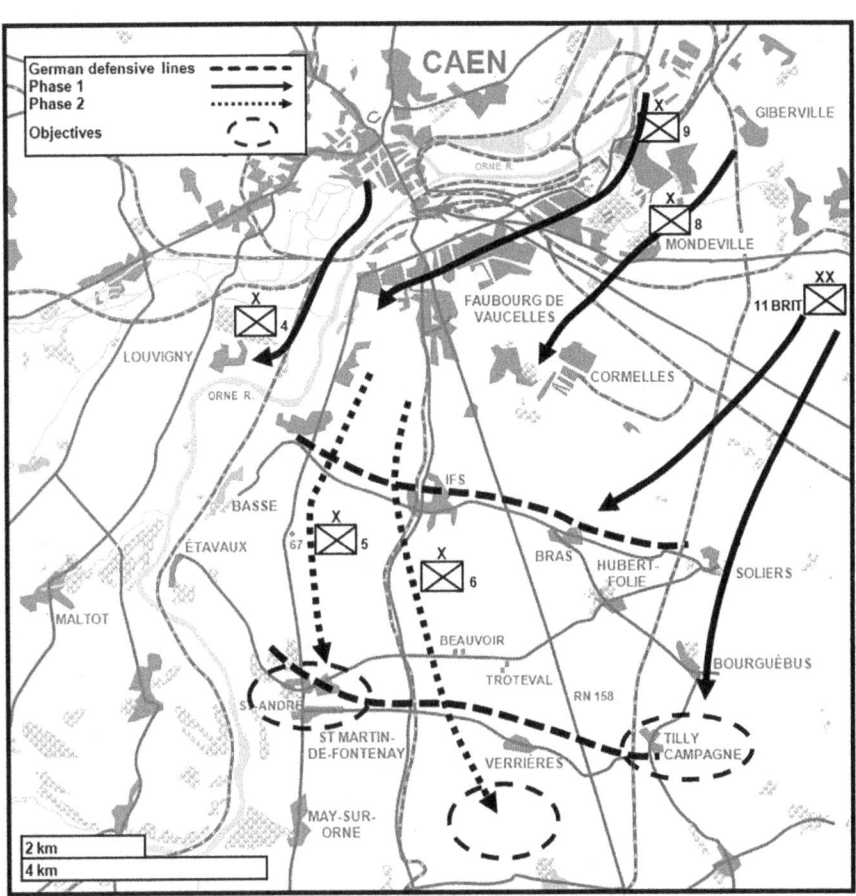

Operation ATLANTIC – The Second Canadian Corps plan.

to be prepared to exploit its successes and capture the high ground north of Saint-André-sur-Orne, to secure the high ground in the area of Verrières and to continue to advance in a southeast deviation towards Falaise. On 16 July, Lt-Gen Simonds welcomed all the COs of both 3rd Cdn Inf Div and 2nd Cdn Armd Bde into Second Cdn Corps. The main aim of the meeting was to issue his orders for Operation ATLANTIC, the Canadian contribution to Operation GOODWOOD.

For Operation ATLANTIC, Lt-Gen Simonds planned for engineers from 3rd Cdn Inf Div and 51st (Highland) British Infantry Division (51st Brit Inf Div) to breach the German minefields on the eastern side of Caen in the Bénouville area; 3rd Cdn Inf Div was to then pass two brigades across the river and attack southwestwardly from the Ranville area through Colombelles and Faubourg de Vaucelles. The tasks were given to 8th Brigade, who with the support of a squadron of tanks from the Hussars, was to lead the advance and capture Colombelles, Giberville and Mandeville; 9th Brigade would clear Faubourg de Vaucelles with the support of the Garrys and the remaining squadrons of the Hussars; 7th Brigade was to remain in reserve west of the Orne River and to be ready to put a battalion across the river through Caen; 2nd Cdn Inf Div was given the task of exploiting southward; 4th Brigade was to reconnoitre up to the Orne River and, if practicable, cross the river and seize the high ground north of Saint-André-sur-Orne – the brigade was then to capture Louvigny and prevent any interference from the west; 5th Brigade was to cross the Orne River at Caen and, if 4th Brigade had failed to do so, take Saint-André-sur-Orne. Subsequently, 4th Brigade and 6th Brigade would advance southward to exploit to the top of Verrières Ridge and capture the village of Verrières itself.

2nd Cdn Inf Div's plan called for a three-phase operation. In Phase 1, on completion of the planned air bombardment, 4th Brigade was to recce in strength to the Orne River and find suitable positions to ford the river. Once the crossings were established, 5th Brigade would have priority getting across and would assemble in the Caen area. If the Saint-André-sur-Orne position was not held by the enemy, then 4th Brigade was to advance and secure the feature on orders from the DivHQ. During Phase 2, 5th Brigade would capture the Saint-André-sur-Orne feature if it had not already been seized by 4th Brigade. It would have one armoured squadron under command and the division engineers in support; 4th Brigade was to attack and capture Louvigny and prevent enemy interference from the west of the Orne River. Phase 3 would be carried out using one of three methods: either

OPERATION ATLANTIC: THE BATTLE FOR VERRIÈRES RIDGE

6th Brigade would pass through the 5th Brigade area at Saint-André-sur-Orne and capture the Verrières feature; or 6th Brigade would move through 4th Brigade and advance across the Orne River and capture the Verrières feature; or 4th Brigade would capture the Verrières feature. Given an anti-tank battery and an armoured squadron, 6th Brigade would be placed on a two-hour notice to move from noon on D-Day. The *Sherbrookes* were put in support of 5th Brigade while the Hussars supported 4th Brigade and the Garrys remained under divisional command. 5th Brigade also received a machine-gun company in support and a battery of anti-tank guns under command.

At 07.45 on 18 July, the three British armoured divisions crossed their start lines after the German positions had been bombarded by the 2nd British Tactical Air Force (2nd BTAF) and the 8th US Army Air Force (8th USAAF). Unfortunately, the tanks entered what would later be known as 'Tank Alley'. The German *Panzer* units on Bourguébus Ridge could see the British tanks spread out before them, but held their fire. At 12.00, the lead tanks reached Hubert-Folie. Thirty minutes later, the 88mm Flak guns and the German tanks opened fire. The results were devastating. By 14.00, the British tanks were forced to retreat. The tanks regrouped and pushed forward again. However, at 18.30, German reinforcements from 1.SS-Pzdiv counter-attacked into the mass of British tanks – once again, the British were forced to withdraw; the battlefield was littered with burning hulks. Eighth Brit Corps had lost 197 tanks. In return, it accounted for only six Panthers, two *PzKpfw IV*, five *StuG III* assault guns and three 88mm Flak guns.

Earlier that morning, 8th Brigade of 3rd Cdn Inf Div also crossed its start line and entered Faubourg de Vaucelles. By dawn the next day, Faubourg de Vaucelles had been secured despite a delay in clearing the château grounds. On the right flank, 2nd Cdn Inf Div saw action for the first time since Dieppe; 4th Brigade attacked Louvigny, but the resistance was stiff and the attack had to be called off at last light. Meanwhile, 5th Brigade began to cross the Orne River at 22.15. During the night, the troops linked up with the Regina Rifles of 8th Brigade. With the consolidation of Faubourg de Vaucelles, the engineers could safely begin building bridges and a tank ferry on the western side of Caen. Lt-Col Gordon issued his orders for Operation ATLANTIC on 18 July. The *Sherbrookes* had been placed under the command of 2nd Cdn Inf Div. C Sqn was detached in support of 5th Brigade for the initial assault while the rest of the regiment was held under division command. At the same time, the regiment had been

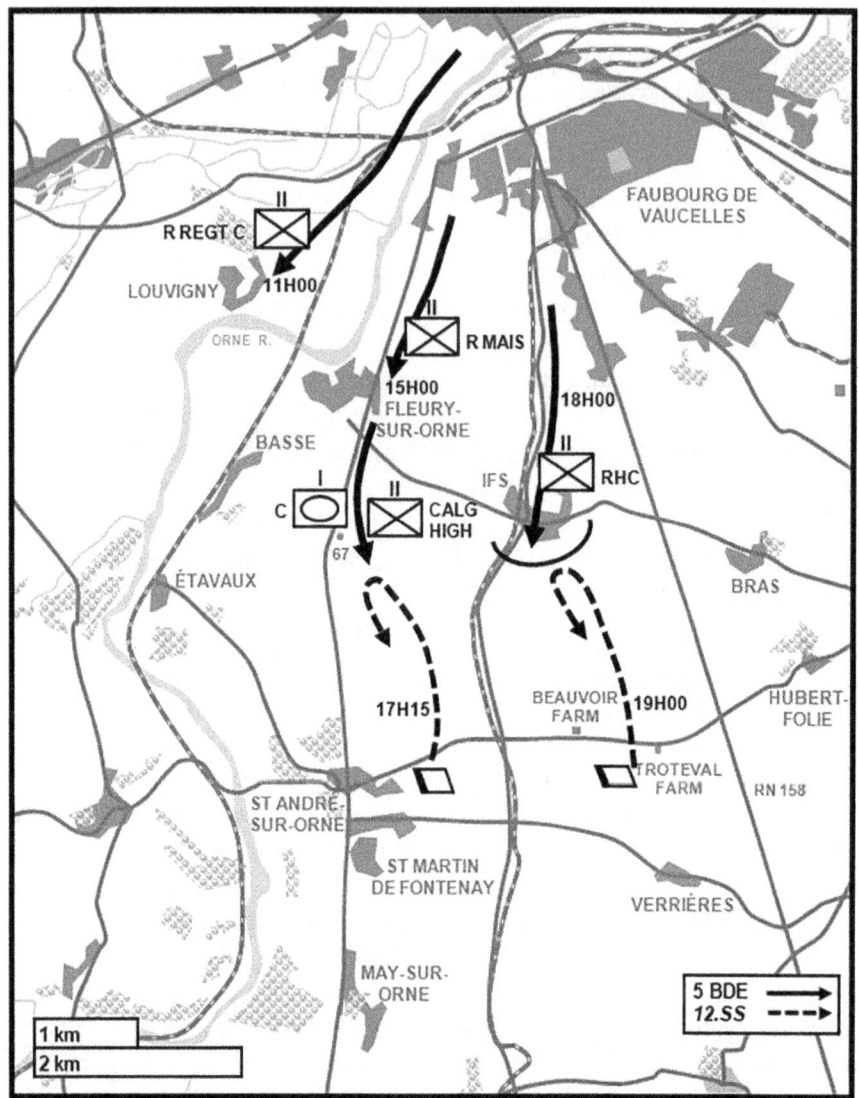

19 July 1944: Operation ATLANTIC.

ordered to be prepared to send at least one squadron to support 6th Brigade. Through a series of successive attacks, with each battalion passing through the previous, 5th Brigade was to capture the Saint-André-sur-Orne feature. The Régiment de Maisonneuve (R de Mais) was to lead off the advance and capture Fleury-sur-Orne. The Calgary Highlanders were then to push forward and take the high feature, commonly known as Point 67, just north of the final objective. Finally, the Black Watch (Royal Highland Regiment) of Canada (Black Watch) was to capture Saint-André-sur-Orne.

At 18.30 on 19 July, C Sqn moved from the Abbaye d'Ardenne to a position south of Beaulieu Prison to await its turn to cross the Orne River. As soon as 3rd Cdn Inf Div had consolidated the crossing site, the squadron began to move across. Starting at 09.20, the tanks began to be ferried across individually using a C40 raft pulled by two M14 half-tracks, one on each side of the river. The operation took approximately fifteen to twenty minutes for each tank. After the last troop finished crossing over at 13.30, the squadron assembled in the assembly area with the exception of Lieut Thompson's tank which had hit a soft shoulder. After making two complete rollovers, the tank came to rest beside the river bank. The crew was uninjured but the tank, although recoverable, was useless for the operation. Lieut Thompson got out and took command of another tank and proceeded with the operation.

C Sqn married up with the R de Mais. Unfortunately, the later mistakenly identified the start line of the creeping artillery barrage as the battalion start line and after the lead companies advanced 200 yards they came under friendly fire. After the initial confusion, the reserve companies were ordered to take over the advance. Opposition was light, apart from some snipers, and the squadron's tanks quickly supported the advancing infantry into Fleury-sur-Orne. At 17.15, after a quick tie-up with the Calgary Highlanders, C Sqn pushed forward and again, little opposition was encountered. Machine-gun nests and snipers were cleaned up and considerable speculative shooting was done. Artillery fire was called down onto the objective. The tanks moved into a position of fire and covered the advance of the infantry onto Point 67 at 18.30. The squadron came under fire from a medium calibre anti-tank gun firing from the area of Saint-André-sur-Orne. Cpl William's tank brewed up immediately but all the crew got out safely. Lieut R.E. Pinning's tank was hit through the final drive and was therefore unable to move. At about the same time, the Germans launched a small counter-attack. C Coy took the brunt of the attack but, with the help of B Coy managed to hold its position. When more anti-tank fire came from the south at 21.35, the tanks of C Sqn and the infantry teamed up to remove the threat. Dusk was fast approaching so Maj-Gen Charles Howard Foulkes, the commander of 2nd Cdn Inf Div, decided to halt the advance; 6th Brigade was given the task of pushing through 5th Brigade and of taking Saint-André-sur-Orne the next day.

At 21.00 on 19 July, Lt-Gen Simonds held an O Group to outline the tasks for the next day. His aim was to capture the Verrières feature; 3rd Cdn Inf Div was ordered to take over Bras and Hubert-Folie from 11th Brit Armd Div; 2nd Cdn Inf Div was ordered to complete the consolidation of the bridgehead along the Point 67-Ifs-Cormelles line. Maj-Gen Foulkes's plan was for 6th Brigade to cross the Orne River and advance with fire to capture Saint-André-sur-Orne and the reverse slope of the Verrières feature; 4th Brigade was to leave Louvigny and circle through Caen to provide depth. Brig Hugh Andrew Young, the commander of 6th Brigade, issued orders for his own plan. The Beauvoir and Troteval farms were located half-way between Ifs and Verrières village. The farms dominated the approaches to the ridge and had to be cleared in the early stages of the attack. Brig Young gave that task to Les Fusiliers Mont-Royal (FMR). Once the farms were cleared, the FMR was to continue its advance and capture Verrières village, while the South Saskatchewan Regiment (South Sask) took the ridge itself. On the right flank, the Queen's Own Cameron Highlanders of Canada (Camerons) were to take Saint-André-sur-Orne. A Sqn was to support the Camerons while C Sqn was ordered to support the FMR. At 23.00, A Sqn crossed the Orne River using the same ferry C Sqn had used that morning. It took up a position beside C Sqn in the area between Ifs and Fleury-sur-Orne. At 23.30, B Sqn moved to the orchard east of Beaulieu Prison.

The plan for the Camerons was to advance towards Saint-André-sur-Orne with two companies forward. A Coy was to seize and hold the orchards on the right side of the road from Fleury-sur-Orne. B Coy would advance on the left and seize the perimeter immediately east of the town and clear Saint-André-sur-Orne up to the Saint-Martin-de Fontenay-Verrières road. H-Hour was set for 12.00 but would later be postponed to 15.00. At 13.00 on 20 July, A Sqn and C Sqn moved into their assembly areas directly behind their start lines. Maj Radley-Walters and the CO of the Camerons agreed that A Sqn should shoot the infantry onto their objective from a position on Point 67. After the enemy positions were hammered by artillery fire and Typhoons fired on targets of opportunity, the tanks began to move forward across the open fields at 15.00 while the Camerons advanced on either side of the main road between Fleury-sur-Orne and Saint-André-sur-Orne. On crossing the start line, A Coy was held up by machine-gun fire from the right flank. The town was defended by three companies of *Panzergrenadiers* supported by several anti-tank guns and medium machine-guns. The A Sqn tanks came up and reached their intermediate position on the high ground at Point 67 about one hour after H-Hour. Few targets were observed and

OPERATION ATLANTIC: THE BATTLE FOR VERRIÈRES RIDGE

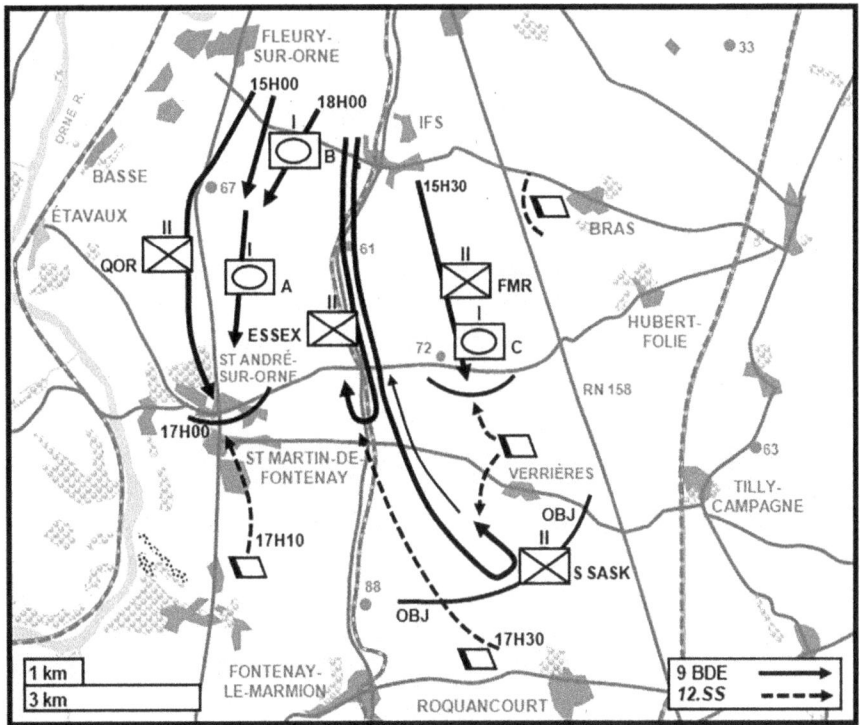

20 July 1944: Operation ATLANTIC.

so the squadron used spec fire along the forward edge of the town until the infantry arrived on the hill. The Camerons fought hard to enter the town and forced the enemy to make a hasty retreat. By evening, it controlled most of the town. When B Coy reached its final objective, no enemy resistance was encountered.

At 17.00, A Sqn moved up to the orchard to the left of the town to give fire support. Maj Radley-Walters positioned the troops in the orchard. 1 Troop and 2 Troop were ordered into hull-down positions of observation about 100 yards to the left of the orchard. The SHQ was in the forward edge of the orchard, while 3 Troop and 4 Troop were held in reserve to the rear of the orchard. Ten minutes after getting into position, the Germans launched an attack on Saint-André-sur-Orne, followed at 17.30 with a major attack on the South Sask. Two Panther tanks appeared on the horizon and were engaged by the SHQ. One was hit in the air louvers for the engine and the crew bailed out. The second Panther was hit by the Firefly and it brewed up. Soon after, a company of tanks and a battalion of infantry were seen advancing from the southeast. There followed an exchange of co-ax and bow gun fire with the enemy. Maj Radley-Walters coordinated with the anti-tank troop of 6th Brigade and on his order all the tanks fired at once. The attack was over in about ten minutes. At 18.00, Lt-Col Gordon ordered B Sqn to move up behind A Sqn as additional support to counter a reported armour threat. A Sqn had expended most of its ammunition and so the tanks were ordered to withdraw to a laager to replenish. On the way back, Sgt D.J. Miller in a Firefly was the last tank in the column; Maj Radley-Walters counted off his fifteen tanks as they passed by. Sgt Miller, however, reported that there was still a tank behind him. Maj Radley-Walters tried to communicate with it but it soon became apparent that it must be a German tank. Sgt Miller had been returning to the laager with his main gun pointing backwards over his back deck in order to allow freer movement through the trees, so when Maj Radley-Walters told him to shoot, the German tank was destroyed without any warning.

C Sqn started the day in support of the FMR. During the morning, 1 Troop under Lieut Charters, gave fire support to the Black Watch as it continued to clear Ifs; 3 Troop, under Lieut Ian James McCrimmon, was ordered to a position of observation to watch for enemy activity in the area of Basse and Étavaux. However, the weather was too misty and prevented the tanks from seeing much. The two troops were recalled at noon and moved back to the squadron assembly area to wait for the FMR to launch their operation. 2 Troop, under Lieut Thompson, was detached to support the South Sask on the right flank. When Lieut Pinning of 4 Troop lost the last two tanks of his troop to mechanical breakdowns, he joined up with 1 Troop. B Coy of the FMR was to lead on the right and capture Beauvoir Farm. C Coy on the left was to seize Troteval Farm. D Coy, following behind B Coy, was to push through and take Verrières village. The FMR advance was rapid, with B Coy consolidating on the south side of Beauvoir Farm at 16.30. Therefore, D Coy was ordered to push on to Verrières. Suddenly, a terrific concentration of mortar and gun fire opened up on the whole battalion front. D Coy was forced to halt its advance and it took up a position to the right of B Coy. The intense fire lasted for an hour-and-a-half, after which D Coy was ordered to withdraw and establish a position on the reverse slope on the north side of the farm.

Initially, 1 Troop had given support to the FMR to get to Beauvoir Farm. When Lieut Charters was injured by a mortar fragment, Lieut Pinning took over the command of the troop; 3 Troop supported C Coy safely into Troteval Farm, then moved up in preparation for the continued advance into Verrières. The infantry cleared the top stories of the farm buildings and declared the farm clear. One platoon was left in place while the advance continued. As soon as the advance was well started, approximately one company of German infantry came out of the cellars and opened up on the FMR from the rear, causing much confusion and numerous casualties. The FMR turned back but very few of those who went forward of the farms were heard from again. The remnants of the battalion dug in about 300 yards north of the farm. When the farm had been declared clear, 3 Troop had moved up to give support for the attack on Verrières. As Lieut McCrimmon's tank crossed the east-west road, it was hit by a 75mm round from the area of Verrières. The first shot hit the turret but was deflected by the extra Churchill tank treads that had been welded onto the turret. The next shot hit the left final drive and immobilised the tank. The crew bailed out and returned to the orchard at Ifs. The remaining two tanks of the troop began to back up when Sgt Lefebvre's tank was hit in the turret. He and Tpr Arthur Jelly, his gunner, were killed, but the remainder of the crew got out safely. The third tank moved back without incident. The Germans continued to fire on both immobile tanks until they brewed up.

The South Sask also began its advance at 15.00 behind a creeping barrage and with the support of 2 Troop of C Sqn under the command of Lieut Thompson. When it reached the crossroads to the west of Beauvoir Farm, the barrage lifted and moved forward. A German platoon of infantry came to life in the wheat field but was quickly disposed of in close fighting. Unfortunately, the delay caused the South Sask to lose the artillery barrage. Nonetheless, at 17.32, it informed 6th Brigade HQ that its two lead companies were on their objectives. But, as it reached the top of the crest of the ridge, the battalion came into the full view by the Germans in Fontenay-le-Marmion, Rocquancourt and Tilly-la-Campaign. A German battalion of *Panzergrenadiers* from 1.SS-Pzdiv counter-attacked and their tanks got right in among the South Sask, shooting infantry who moved, or crushing under their tracks those men who could not or would not move. The men of the South Sask were only able to escape through the grain fields by running as fast as possible back down the hill.

When the South Sask reported their objectives reached, the Essex Scottish Regiment (Essex Scottish), on loan from 4th Brigade, was ordered to move forward and occupy the area between Saint-André-sur-Orne and Beauvoir Farm. Before reaching their new position, the Essex Scottish met the men of the South Sask retreating. The forward companies saw the South Sask retreat as a rout. As they saw men retreating through their positions in a state bordering on panic, the men of the two forward companies of the Essex Scottish also began to withdraw as enemy tanks approached. Their CO, Lt-Col Macdonald, ordered the two forward companies to retire behind the reserve companies and dig in. Once started, however, the retreat collapsed into a race for safety. The lead companies followed the men of the South Sask back beyond the start line to safety, although the two reserve companies stood their ground and fought off the German attack. They spent the remainder of the night in their wet slit-trenches.

At around 20.30, some Panther tanks were observed to be advancing towards the two farms from beyond Verrières. Sgt Olivier of 2 Troop engaged the Panthers with his Firefly but could not see the outcome of his shots due to the poor visibility. When the enemy returned fire, he fired smoke rounds and withdrew behind the crest of the hill. After the smoke cleared, he moved forward again and spotted eight Panther tanks to his front; Lieut Thompson saw that he was out-gunned and in a precarious position, and so decided to withdraw the troop. The tanks fired smoke rounds to create a screen and then made a dash for cover. When half-way over the hill, the smoke screen cleared but the tanks had no more smoke rounds left. Two tanks were hit and put out of action. Lieut Thompson's tank was hit in the copula ring of the turret and he was wounded; Sgt Fowlis's tank was also hit. The first round knocked out his aerials, while a second round pierced his 75mm main gun. Both tanks, however, made it back to the rear.

At day's end, the Camerons still held Saint-André-sur-Orne despite numerous German counter-attacks. The FMR was well established in the Beauvoir and Troteval farms. However, at 22.00, German tanks attacked the FMR positions and surrounded B Coy and C Coy. Heavy casualties resulted and Beauvoir Farm had to be abandoned. The South Sask had been routed but the Essex Scottish held onto a tenuous position just north of the Beauvoir Farm-Saint-André-sur-Orne road. Operation ATLANTIC was proving to be a failure; 3rd Cdn Inf Div had suffered 386 casualties, of which 89 were fatal; 2nd Cdn Inf Div had suffered 1,149 casualties, of which 244 were fatal: the Essex Scottish had 37 soldiers killed out of 244 casualties; the South Sask had 215 casualties of which 62 were killed, including the acting CO, Maj G.R. Matthews; and the Camerons had 81 casualties of which 29 were killed. The *Sherbrookes* had suffered seven casualties of which three were killed, and two others would die of the wounds they received.

OPERATION ATLANTIC: THE BATTLE FOR VERRIÈRES RIDGE

At daybreak on 21 July, the tanks of the *Sherbrookes* once again moved up to support 6th Brigade. A Sqn moved up in support of the Camerons in Saint-André-sur-Orne while B Sqn was assigned to the Black Watch in Ifs. C Sqn, now down to six tanks, remained in reserve southwest of Ifs. The weather remained cloudy, foggy and warm. As A Sqn reached the high ground at Point 67 at about 08.00, tanks were immediately spotted in the valley to their front but because of poor visibility, the squadron was unsure if they were enemy or friendly tanks. As the morning fog cleared, it became obvious that there were two groups of German tanks supported by infantry moving towards Saint-André-sur-Orne in a flanking move. The first group of eight Panthers was 600 yards directly in front of A Sqn while the second group of six Panthers was about 300 yards to the left of the squadron. An hour long exchange of fire took place, but with no discernible results. One Sherman was knocked out before the Germans retreated. The tank had received two direct hits, one of which severely wounded the crew commander. The crew evacuated the tank and took the injured NCO back to the rear. Afterwards, Tpr Bartlett returned on foot and repaired the broken track in the midst of heavy mortar and machine-gun fire. He then drove the tank back to the RHQ for further repairs. The Camerons reported at 09.00 that it had repelled another German attack on its left flank. Maj Radley-Walters decided to move the majority of the troops to an orchard on the west side of the town; 3 Troop was ordered to remain on Point 67, while 1 Troop, 4 Troop and 2 Troop moved up under the cover of a smoke screen. As the smoke screen thinned, Lieut Corless exposed his tank in order to obtain the exact locations of the hidden enemy armour and anti-tank guns. His tank was hit twice in half an hour. Nonetheless, he continued to expose his tank until all the enemy positions were pin-pointed and destroyed by the other tanks of the squadron. His tank was finally knocked out; he was injured and had to be evacuated.

At 09.45, it looked as if the fight for Saint-André-sur-Orne was over. Suddenly, a German tank fired from the left flank and hit Cpl Rice's tank. Cpl Rice was killed and Tpr Raymond P. Norris and Tpr Frederick J. Wood were seriously wounded. Tpr W. Allen put both injured crewmen on the back deck of Sgt Taylor's tank and they were taken back to Fleury-sur-Orne for medical treatment. Tpr Allen returned to the tank on foot, started it and drove it back to the rear. Under the cover of heavy rain, a new German attack began, and for two hours A Sqn was engaged by the Germans from three sides. When the battle ceased at 14.30, the squadron, with the help of M10s from 3rd Anti-Tank Regt, had knocked out eight Panthers while losing five Shermans; 3 Troop was ordered to move up to the orchard to reinforce the

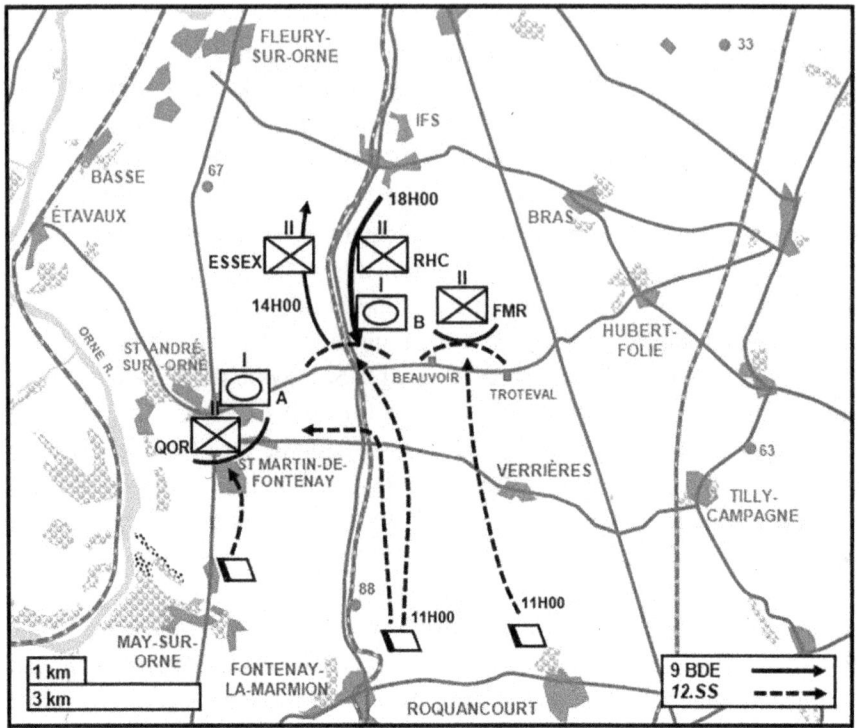

21 July 1944: Operation ATLANTIC.

remainder of the squadron. C Sqn therefore advanced to Point 67 to take over the position. As eight Panthers tried to escape from Saint-André-sur-Orne towards Hubert-Folie along the road between Saint-Martin-de-Fontenay and Verrières, the squadron engaged them for about thirty minutes. Sgt Cathcart and Sgt Reid each brewed up a Panther; Lieut Spafford engaged two Panthers with HE rounds, his hits were observed on both tanks and their crews were seen to evacuate. A Firefly was called up from B Sqn and the Panthers were brewed up. The rain started again and the remaining four Panthers sneaked off. A short time later, Lieut Spafford's tank was hit by AP fire from the direction of Verrières; the tank brewed up but the crew escaped unharmed.

Saint-André-sur-Orne had been attacked by at least three *Kampfgruppen*, each consisting of a battalion of infantry supported by a company of tanks. The assaults were led by five tanks abreast spaced 100 yards apart. The defenders could not destroy the tanks until they were within 800 yards of their position. The German long-barrelled 75mm gun, however, could engage and destroy the Shermans from twice that range. Only the Firefly could engage the Panthers at that distance, and then only with limited success. The two companies of the Essex Scottish that had retreated the previous evening were reorganised and sent back up to the front during the early hours of 21 July. The battalion held the crossroad east of Saint-André-sur-Orne but suffered further heavy casualties when an enemy *Kampfgruppe* broke into their position. At the same time, friendly artillery fire fell onto their trenches. Lt-Col Macdonald asked for permission to withdraw to a better position, but his request was denied. At 14.00, another well-organised attack shattered the frail defences and the Essex Scottish retreated in disorder. The Germans had now created a deep salient between the Camerons and the FMR. At the same time, lead companies of the FMR were overrun by eight enemy tanks and an infantry company. Beauvoir and Troteval farms were lost.

At 17.15, another German attack from the southwest and the southeast was broken up by artillery fire. Thirteen German tanks were destroyed along with two probables. During the attack, Capt Joseph Edward Fuger's tank was knocked out; Sgt Beardsley's tank was drilled twice in the fighting, wounding his driver and putting the main gun out of action. Tpr Edward Fidler's tank had also been hit and the crew commander killed, but the tank was still serviceable. Tpr Fidler got back into the tank and, even without a crew commander, he broke through the German lines and joined up with the rest of the squadron in Saint-André-sur-Orne. Sgt Lloyd W. Cuddie, in a Firefly, was isolated on the south side of the town – he was refused permission to return to the orchard. When the enemy began an encircling movement which, if successful, would have enabled them to destroy all the squadron tanks, Sgt Cuddie knocked out the lead Panther. The other Panther tanks tried to knock out his tank in turn, but he managed to contain the whole enemy force while four other squadron tanks moved into fire positions. Together, the five tanks proceeded to destroy the seven enemy tanks without further incident.

Maj-Gen Foulkes gave the Black Watch the task of retaking the Essex Scottish position. Lt-Col Gordon ordered B Sqn at 13.00 to liaise with the Black Watch in Ifs for their next operation. The infantry was to attack and hold a position at the crossroads east of Saint-André-sur-Orne. The H-Hour was set for 18.00 with a preliminary artillery barrage before the battalion moved off. Maj Ross Melville Houston, the squadron OC, decided to send two troops forward with the infantry while the SHQ and the remaining troop watched the flanks. The attack advanced behind a creeping barrage and was a success. B Sqn stayed in a position of support until the battalion anti-tank platoon was moved up into place. The tanks were engaged from the right by heavy anti-tank fire; one Sherman was lost with one trooper killed and two wounded. The regiment was informed that it had reverted to the command of 2nd Cdn Armd Bde and so, at 22.00, Lt-Col Gordon ordered the withdrawal of all the fighting squadrons and moved them into a laager east of Fleury-sur-Orne.

Only thirty-three tanks of the regiment, including those of the RHQ and HQ Sqn, were still fit to fight. A Sqn was down to six tanks. Cpl Kenneth Hill's tank had been hit in the copula by a shell that creased the top of the tank; Cpl Hill had been killed and the crew had bailed out. The tank was still serviceable and had run on for half a day before it ran out of fuel. That night, Maj Radley-Walters asked one of the drivers, Tpr Fidler, to go with him to see if they could retrieve the body of Cpl Hill and return with the badly needed tank. Cpl Hill lay in a doughnut position at the bottom of the turret, his legs were touching his head. They got a rope around him but couldn't get him out through the turret because rigor mortis had set in. Unfortunately, A Sqn needed the tank so badly, that they had to cut Cpl Hill in two with a machete to remove him. They succeeded in getting the tank out and sent it back to the echelon to get it washed out and cleaned.¹

At first light, A Sqn and B Sqn once again moved up to fire positions in support of the infantry, while C Sqn remained in reserve. The day was cloudy and warm with somewhat limited visibility. A Sqn was down to six tanks and it was again deployed in Saint-André-sur-Orne. At about 05.45, it moved up to the same orchard it had occupied on the previous days. The Germans launched a weak attack at 06.30 using infantry and tanks, but it was easily driven off. At around 10.00, the Germans launched another attack from the high ground southeast of the town using only tanks. The company of fourteen tanks was first spotted when it was 1,500 yards away – too far away for A Sqn to engage. The German tanks advanced using spec fire in an effort to draw out the A Sqn tanks, thereby getting them to give away their positions. When the Panthers were close enough, A Sqn finally opened up and within an hour five German tanks were burning. B Sqn had moved up in the centre in support of the Black Watch but the German tanks were too far away to successfully engage them.

Maj-Gen Foulkes was ordered to assist 43rd British Infantry Division (43rd Brit Inf Div) as it attacked south on the west side of the Orne River. He therefore decided to stage an attack on Évataux. The R de Mais was ordered to take the hamlet with the help of B Sqn. For their part, the Germans had orders to hold the position at all costs as the *SS Panzer* divisions were

Above: Several sergeants, as well as Lieut R. Codère and Lieut G.W. Côté, enroling new recruits under the attentive eye of Maj P. Camirand of Les Fusiliers de Sherbrooke, autumn 1940. (Photo from the Fusiliers de Sherbrooke collection / www.fusiliersdesherbrooke.ca / Public domain)

Below: The Sherbrooke Fusilier Regiment parades through Sherbrooke, Quebec, 15 February 1941. (*The Sherbrooke Daily Record*, 16 February 1941 / Public domain)

Above: Watching training in Canada (left to right: Lieut H.M. Belton, H/Capt (Padre) C.E. Beaudry, Lieut R.S.S. Grier, Lt-Col M.W. McA'Nulty, Capt J.H. Gilbert and Lieut K.T. Paton). (Library and Archives Canada / Department of National Defence fonds / File No. 1044)

Left: Unidentified personnel of the Sherbrooke Fusilier Regiment with Ram tanks, England, 18 July 1943. (Photo by Lieut C.E. Nye / Library and Archives Canada / Department of National Defence fonds / MIKAN 3514100)

Capt S.V. Radley-Walters (far right), Lieut N. Boyd (second from left) and fellow officers enjoying a culinary delight while training in England. (Photo from S.V. Radley-Warlters collection / Public domain)

A Ram tank of the Sherbrooke Fusilier Regiment hauls an anti-tank gun of the Perth Regiment out of the mud during a training exercise, 7 January 1944. (Photo by R.J. Elliott / www.canadaatwar.ca / Public domain)

Men of the North Nova Scotia Highlanders on an exercise with Sherman tanks of the Sherbrooke Fusilier Regiment at Wepham Downs, Sussex, 14 April 1944. (Library and Archives Canada / Department of National Defence fonds / File No. 1044)

Left: Sergeant J.E. Reynolds (left) and Bombardier W.S. Edgar (right) in the turret of a Sherman tank taking part in Exercise PEDAL II, England, 13-14 April 1944. (Photo by Lieut Donald I. Grant / Library and Archives Canada / Department of National Defence fonds / MIKAN 3514111)

Below: Waterproofing Sherman tanks of the Sherbrooke Fusilier Regiment, England, 20 April 1944. (Photo by Lieut Donald I. Grant / Library and Archives Canada / Department of National Defence fonds / MIKAN 3514116)

Above: Unidentified personnel of the Sherbrooke Fusilier Regiment in a Humber Mk I scout car, England, 20 April 1944. (Photo by Lieut Donald I. Grant / Library and Archives Canada / Department of National Defence fonds / MIKAN 3514121)

Below: An unidentified member of the Sherbrooke Fusilier Regiment with his unit's canine mascot, England, 20 April 1944. (Photo by Lieut Strathy E.E. Smith / Library and Archives Canada / Department of National Defence fonds / MIKAN 3514126)

Above: Soldiers of the 9th Canadian Infantry Brigade landing in Normandy from LCI 125 on Nan White Beach on D-Day. Tanks of the Sherbrooke Fusilier Regiment can be seen in the background. (Photo by Lieut Gilbert A. Milne / Library and Archives Canada / Department of National Defence fonds / File No. 1044)

Below: A Sherman tank of the Sherbrooke Fusilier Regiment, supporting 9th Canadian Infantry Brigade, comes ashore on Nan White Beach near Bernières-sur-Mer, 6 June 1944. (Library and Archives Canada / Department of National Defence fonds / File No. 1044)

Right: Trooper George Mann beside the new vehicle he would drive throughout the remainder of the war. This truck also served as an ambulance. (Library and Archives Canada / Department of National Defence fonds / File No. 1044)

Below: An observation post of *12.SS-Panzerdivision (Hitlerjugend)* in a parapet of the Abbaye d'Ardenne, June 1944. (*Bundesarchiv* / Public domain)

Above: Firefly "Chaser" of C Sqn being inspected by an SS officer outside Authie, 8 June 1944. The crew commander was most likely Lieut Ian MacLean, the troop leader of 2 Troop, who was taken prisoner on 7 June 1944. (*Bundesarchiv* / Public domain)

Below left: Firefly "Blondie" of B Sqn knocked out on 7 June 1944 near Authie. The soldiers standing on the tank were from *12.SS-Panzerdivision (Hitlerjugend)*. (*Bundesarchiv* / Public domain)

Below right: SS-Brigadeführer Kurt Meyer standing in court with escorts Maj A. Russel (left) and Capt E.D. McPhail (right). (Photo by Barney J. Gloster / Library and Archives Canada / Department of National Defence fonds / PA-141890)

Above: Members of C Sqn of the Sherbrooke Fusilier Regiment with a captured PzKpfw IV north of Caen, June 1944 (note the German truck with SS plates). (Photo by Jim Jones / Maple Leaf Up collection / Public domain)

Below: A tank from A Sqn of the Sherbrooke Fusilier Regiment, in support of the Highland Light Infantry of Canada, advances towards Buron, 8 July 1944. (Imperial War Museum / Public domain)

A tank from A Sqn of the Sherbrooke Fusilier Regiment and a Universal Carrier move forward in the area of Buron, 8 July 1944. (Imperial War Museum / Public domain)

A Sherman tank advancing through Buron, 8 July 1944. (Library and Archives Canada / Department of National Defence fonds / PA-129034)

A tank of the Sherbrooke Fusilier Regiment in Buron. (Library and Archives Canada / Department of National Defence fonds / PA-136846)

Above: A Firefly tank of the Sherbrooke Fusilier Regiment making a breakthrough for the infantry in the early dawn. (Library and Archives Canada / Department of National Defence fonds / PA-131391)

Below: A Sherman tank in Place des Petites-Boucheries, Caen, 9 July 1944. (Imperial War Museum / Public domain)

Above: A Sherman tank in Place des Petites-Boucheries, Caen, 9 July 1944. (Imperial War Museum / Public domain)

Left: A Sherman tank of the Sherbrooke Fusilier Regiment in front of a road block at Place du Planitre, Caen, 9 July 1944. (Imperial War Museum / Public domain)

Two Sherman tanks of the Sherbrooke Fusilier Regiment in Place Villers, direction Venoix. (Archives Départementales du Calvados / Public domain)

Right: A column of tanks of the Sherbrooke Fusilier Regiment leaving Caen. (Photo by Jim Jones / Maple Leaf Up collection / Public domain)

Below: This was the first and only bottle of beer issued to Trooper George Skinner from C Sqn of the Sherbrooke Fusilier Regiment. His tank driver, Trooper Roly Pilon, naps beside the tank while another crew prepares in the deep background. (Photo by Jim Jones / Maple Leaf Up collection / Public domain)

Infantrymen of the 4th Canadian Infantry Brigade prepare to ride into battle in Priest Kangaroos behind the Sherman tanks of the Sherbrooke Fusilier Regiment, 7 August 1944. (Library and Archives Canada / Department of National Defence fonds / PA-129172)

A shattered Sherman tank of the Sherbrooke Fusilier Regiment; it was hit by alternating armour-piercing (AP) and high-explosive (HE) shells. The turret of the tank was blown straight up and off the body. (www.i.igmur.com / 95BXoNx.jpg)

The only photograph taken of Michael Wittmann's destroyed late production model Tiger I (No. 007) still in the fields near Gaumesnil was taken by French civilian Serge Varin in 1945 when he was cycling down the Caen-Falaise highway (Route Nationale 158). This is the only photograph which he took that has survived.

Above: A tank from A Sqn of the Sherbrooke Fusilier Regiment protects the advance of soldiers of the Fusiliers Mont-Royal along rue des Prémontrés, Falaise, 17 August 1944. The gun fire is coming from the *École supérieure de jeunes filles* on the right where a dozen *panzergrenadiers* from the *12.SS-Panzerdivision (Hitlerjugend)* were barricaded. (Library and Archives Canada / Department of National Defence fonds / File No. 1044)

Below: Soldiers from the Fusiliers Mont-Royal work with an A Sqn tank of the Sherbrooke Fusilier Regiment to hunt snipers in Falaise, 17 August 1944. (Library and Archives Canada / Department of National Defence fonds / File No. 1044)

Above: Two Sherman tanks (14 on the left and 21 on the right) of the Sherbrooke Fusilier Regiment support the Fusiliers Mont-Royal during their attack on the *École supérieure de jeunes filles* where a dozen *Panzergrenadiers* of the *12.SS-Panzerdivision (Hitlerjugend)* still held out, 17 August 1944. (US National Archives / Public domain)

Below: Lieutenant-Colonel M.B.K. Gordon discusses the situation with Paratrooper D. Sharp (in civilian clothing); he had been captured on D-Day but later escaped. He was hidden by the inhabitants of the region of Falaise and rejoined the Allies on 19 August 1944 at St Lambert-sur-Dives. (Normandie / www.flickr.com)

OPERATION ATLANTIC: THE BATTLE FOR VERRIÈRES RIDGE

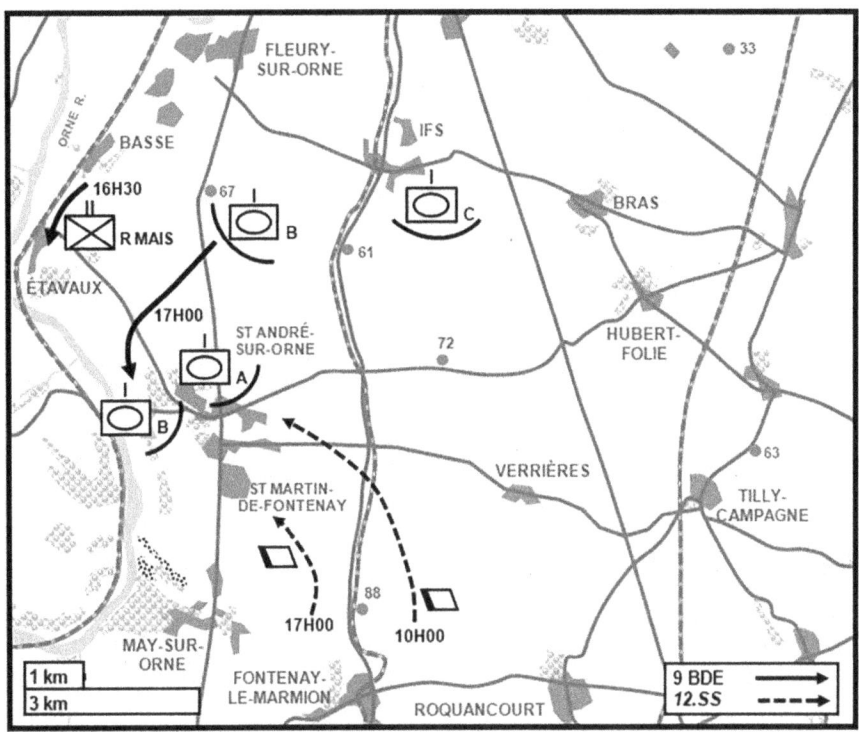

22 July 1944: Operation ATLANTIC.

expected to recapture Saint-André-sur-Orne soon. The plan devised was for the R de Mais to advance behind a creeping barrage while the tanks of B Sqn gave fire support from the high ground of Point 67. As the infantry moved forward, the tanks gave support using spec fire from their main guns and engaged targets of opportunity. Despite the barrage, the infantry was met by machine-gun fire from the forward edge of the hamlet. Heavy hand-to-hand fighting ensued. The R de Mais soon gained the upper hand and reported at 16.30 that Étavaux had been secured.

In order to relieve the pressure on Étavaux, the Germans moved forward in preparation for another attack on Saint-André-sur-Orne. At 16.00, German tanks appeared on the ridgeline but they were out of range for the tanks. They moved off and disappeared out of view. Lt-Col Gordon ordered B Sqn to move up to Saint-André-sur-Orne to strengthen A Sqn. Maj Houston left one troop with the R de Mais and the remainder of the squadron moved up the hill. However, before it could get into position, the Germans attacked at 17.00 with tanks and infantry. Two Panthers succeeded in getting to within

100 yards before they were spotted. A Coy of the Camerons was forced to withdraw from its forward position back into the town. A counter-attack was immediately teed up and the enemy was driven off and A Coy returned to its original positions. B Sqn took up fire positions on the right flank in an orchard just south of the town. At 17.20, the enemy launched a new attack by infantry supported by six tanks. A quick exchange of fire took place in which two German tanks were destroyed. A German tank, about 800 yards from Saint-André-sur-Orne, fired a round that hit an A Sqn tank and went right through it. The round continued on and went through a second tank before finally hitting Maj Radley-Walter's tank on the right side. The top of the track and the bogie wheel were blown off. Remarkably, one round had disabled three A Sqn tanks. The battle lasted thirty minutes and the *Sherbrookes* accounted for a further thirteen tank kills between the two squadrons and another two probables. At 18.40, a renewed German attack was repulsed and B Sqn reported that its tanks were having a field day shooting up the enemy infantry in the field. At 19.20, the Germans were reported to be withdrawing towards May-sur-Orne. At about 22.00, the squadrons were called back to Fleury-sur-Orne to replenish and harbour for the night. The squadrons were deployed in the early hours of 23 July to the same positions they had occupied the day before. However, the enemy was relatively quiet all day. In the early morning hours, the Black Watch repelled an attack by about fifty *Panzergrenadiers*. At 08.30, A Sqn spotted eighteen German tanks east of May-sur-Orne; they were 2,200 yards away and were engaged with HE rounds, but with little to no effect. Air support was requested but was unavailable.

With the successful attack by the Black Watch, the 6th Brigade front was once again stabilised along the road connecting Saint-André-sur-Orne to Troteval Farm. The Camerons had repulsed attack after attack on their positions and held firm. Although the two farms had been lost to the Germans, the FMR had stopped the German advance and their reserve companies had succeeded in digging in just below the crest. The British held onto Hubert-Folie and Bourguébus village. The Germans, however, still held the final objective: the Bourguébus-Verrières Ridge. Although skirmishes with the German defenders on the ridge would continue for several days more, Operation GOODWOOD in the British sector and Operation ATLANTIC in the Canadian sector were essentially over. The Allies had lost 314 tanks, of which only 174 were recoverable. The German losses were over 100 tanks, but unlike the British, who had more reinforcements of men and materiel, the Germans had committed their last reserves. They would no longer be able to put up a spirited defence against the next offensive.

Chapter 6

Operation TOTALIZE
The Drive towards Falaise

Operation GOODWOOD had failed. The British armour had suffered heavy tank losses – Eighth Brit Corps had lost 197 tanks against only 30 German tanks destroyed – and had failed to take Bourguébus Ridge. Likewise, the Canadians had failed to take Verrières Ridge. Nonetheless, Gen Montgomery still considered that his overall strategy was working. The Americans were sallying forth from the base of the Cherbourg Peninsula. Their nineteen divisions faced only nine German divisions and most of the German *Panzer* forces were committed to the British sector. Second Brit Army faced fourteen German divisions. Directly opposite the Canadians was the elite I.SS-Pzkorps. On 21 July, Gen Montgomery issued a new directive to his four army commanders. Lt-Gen Bradley's First US Army was to secure the whole of the Cherbourg Peninsula, while the newly deployed Third US Army, commanded by Lt-Gen George Smith Patton, was to be prepared to clear the whole Brittany Peninsula on the extreme western flank. First Cdn Army under Lt-Gen Crerar was to take over the sector held by First Brit Corps at noon on 23 July. Its task was to push the enemy back to the east side of the Dives River and to occupy such positions as to ensure that all territory on the west side of the river was dominated by Allied troops. Second Brit Army under Lt-Gen Dempsey was to stay in action in the sector east of the Orne River and to conduct a major advance towards Falaise and Argentan using two armoured divisions.

Lt-Gen Crerar ordered Lt-Gen Simonds to plan a breakout offensive along Verrières Ridge, to be launched in conjunction with Operation COBRA, the American breakout in the west. The plan for Second Cdn Corps – codenamed Operation SPRING – was to be executed in three phases. In Phase 1, two infantry divisions supported by an armoured brigade would attack and seize the ground around Point 122, the Cramesnil Spur; 2nd Cdn Inf Div would advance and capture May-sur-Orne and Verrières village on the right, while 3rd Cdn Inf Div captured Tilly-la-Campaign on the left. During Phase 2, an armoured division would advance, followed by an infantry division, with the task of widening the occupied area; 2nd Cdn Inf Div would take Fontenay-le-Marmion and attack Verrières Ridge; 3rd Cdn Inf Div was to capture Garcelles-Secqueville while 7th British Armoured Division (7th Brit Armd Div) thrust through the centre and took the Cramesnil Spur. In the final phase, two armoured divisions would seize the heights south of the Laison River. The start date was set for 23 July, but it would be postponed for forty-eight hours due to inclement weather.

In the meantime, I.SS-Pzkorps reinforced the ridge with an additional 4 battalions, 480 tanks and 500 guns. On 9 July, 12.SS-Pzdiv had evacuated Caen in the face of the strong Canadian push on the town. It had only thirty-two *PzKpfw IV* tanks and seventeen Panthers remaining, the equivalent of three companies. The next day, *schwere.SS-Panzerabteilung 102* (s.SS-Pzabt 102) was ordered to move forward and take up a holding position at the northern exit of Saint-Martin-de-Fontenay. It was allotted to II.SS-Pzkorps and was composed of Tiger tanks (*PzKpfw VI*). At the same time, *schwere.Panzerabteilung 503* (s.SS-Pzabt 503), composed of *Königtiger* tanks (*PzKpfw VIB*),[1] was attached to *SS-Panzergrenadier-Regiment 22* (SS-Pzgren-Rgt 22) of *10.SS-Panzerdivision (Frundsberg)* (10.SS-Pzdiv) and ordered into the Colombelles area. When Operation SPRING was launched on 24–25 July, four German *Panzer* divisions held the front line south of Caen – 21.Pzdiv, 12.SS-Pzdiv, 1.SS-Pzdiv and 10.SS-Pzdiv. Three additional divisions were held in reserve – 116.Pzdiv, *2.Panzerdivision* (2.Pzdiv) and 9.SS-Pzdiv.

Meanwhile, 3rd Cdn Inf Div assigned the task of capturing Tilly-la-Campaign to 9th Brigade. If successful, it would then take Garcelles-Secqueville, while 7th Brit Armd Div advanced and took the Cramesnil Spur; 6th Brigade of 2nd Cdn Inf Div was given the task of clearing the start line, the Saint-André-sur-Orne-Hubert-Folie road, on the night of 24–25 July; 5th Brigade would then move forward from Saint-André-sur-Orne to capture May-sur-Orne and Fontenay-le-Marmion, and 4th Brigade would first capture Verrières and Rocquancourt. The *Sherbrookes* were assigned to support 6th Brigade in the initial stages of the operation. At 20.00 on 24 July, the FMR, with the support of B Sqn, moved up to recapture and hold the Troteval Farm. At 20.52, the squadron reported that the infantry was in positions of observation. After the positions were secured and the infantry dug in, B Sqn was released at 22.30 and its tanks withdrew for the night. The Camerons attacked Saint-Martin-de-Fontenay

OPERATION TOTALIZE: THE DRIVE TOWARDS FALAISE

with the assistance of A Sqn. H-Hour had been set for 20.45. The Camerons encountered stiff resistance and reported only partial success at midnight. However, it maintained the pressure and the battalion reported the start line secured at 03.30 and Saint-Martin-de-Fontenay cleared at 06.30. At twilight, the Germans launched a small attack with infantry on the woods east of the main road at Saint-André-sur-Orne. A Sqn moved up to give support and the attack was quickly dispersed.

At 03.30, the North Novas of 9th Brigade began its attack on Tilly-la-Campaign. Searchlights were reflected off the clouds to indicate lanes and the direction of advance. They illuminated the German positions, but unfortunately also let the Germans see the Canadian infantry as it advanced. Machine-guns raked the advancing troops. Nonetheless, at 05.25, the lead companies fired flares to indicate that the town had been taken. At 06.14, the battalion asked for support against an expected enemy counter-attack and a squadron of tanks from the Garrys was dispatched to help defend the position. As it advanced, it encountered Panther tanks and 88mm anti-tank guns. Soon, eleven of the fifteen tanks of the squadron were burning, as were the carriers and SP anti-tank guns attached to the

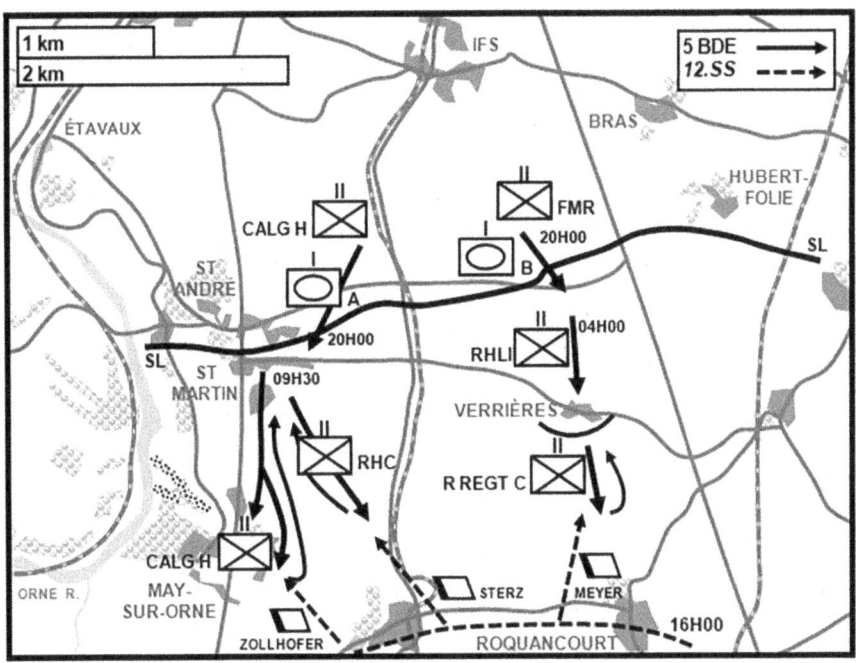

24-25 July 1944: The 5th Canadian Infantry Brigade's attack in Operation SPRING.

North Novas. That evening, the North Novas were ordered to move back when darkness fell.

The RHLI advance towards Verrières also met stiff opposition. It began its attack at 04.10 but soon lost the creeping artillery barrage when they had to clear enemy tanks from its start line. As the battalion advanced, it came under heavy machine-gun fire. Nevertheless, it reported the village secure at 05.30. The Germans launched a counter-attack with thirty tanks lined up in a row on the ridgeline and they pulverised the battalion's positions. But, at 07.50, the RHLI reported that it was firmly entrenched on its objective. Therefore, the Royal Regiment of Canada (R Regt C) launched its attack on Rocquancourt at 09.30. Its advance got as far as 400 yards before it was halted by exceptionally fierce fire from 88mm anti-tank guns, mortars and machine-guns positioned on the ridge. The lead company was almost annihilated with the majority of the troops either wiped out or taken prisoner of war.

With the success of Phase 1, the Calgary Highlanders were ordered to launch Phase 2 of the operation. However, when they reached Saint-Martin-de-Fontenay, they discovered that the village was still crawling with Germans. The two lead companies were ordered to bypass the town and continue the advance, while the two reserve companies were ordered to clear the town of the enemy. At 05.30, A Coy reported that it was in May-sur-Orne. However, the lead companies became pinned down by terrific mortar- and shell-fire, and took extremely heavy casualties. By late morning, Saint-Martin-de-Fontenay had been secured and the attack on Bourguébus Ridge was launched. H-Hour for Phase 3 had been planned for 05.30, however, the Black Watch encountered heavy resistance on the Saint-Martin-de-Fontenay road and had to clear the village in darkness. In the fighting, Lt-Col Stuart Stephen Tuffnel Cantlie was killed, as well as the senior company commander. Therefore, command of the battalion fell upon the shoulders of 24-year-old Maj Frederick Philip Griffin. It was 08.00 and the battalion had lost the armour and artillery support promised, and the element of surprise. Regardless, Brig William Jemmett Megill, the commander of 5th Brigade, decided to proceed with the attack and issued the order at 08.30. An hour later, the advance began towards Fontenay-le-Marmion. The Black Watch soon came under fire from all sides. The advance had run directly into a counter-attack by *Kampfgruppe* Sterz from 272.Inf-Div. The Black Watch had started the attack with 325 men, of which 310 would be killed, wounded or captured. Two entire companies were annihilated and the battalion lost all its senior commanders.

OPERATION TOTALIZE: THE DRIVE TOWARDS FALAISE

With the initial successes of the Canadians, *Generalfeldmarschall* von Kluge, the supreme commander in the west, released his operational reserve, 9.SS-Pzdiv. Two *Kampfgruppen* were formed. The first, the armoured-heavy *Kampfgruppe* Meyer, advanced east of Fontenay-le-Marmion towards Point 88 at the centre of Verrières Ridge. *Kampfgruppe* Zollhofer, an infantry-heavy battlegroup, advanced from the west of Fontenay-le-Marmion and headed for Saint-Martin-de-Fontenay; both attacks were launched at 16.00. The German counter-attacks succeeded in pushing the Calgary Highlanders out of May-sur-Orne and the North Novas out of Tilly-la-Campaign. The Germans launched another attack against the RHLI in Verrières at 18.00, but it was repulsed. At last light, it was the only unit to have seized and held its objectives. Second Cdn Corps consolidated its position along a front stretching through Saint-Martin-de-Fontenay to Verrières to Hubert-Folie to Bourguébus. The initial objectives of Operation ATLANTIC had been secured, but Second Cdn Corps was not in an immediate position to resume the offensive.

At 18.00, B Sqn was ordered forward to support the R Regt C, which was being attacked by enemy infantry and tanks in Verrières village. The squadron moved up through Hubert-Folie but was advised by British armoured officers against proceeding further up the road. Instead, Maj Houston deployed his troops to cover a gap on the left flank from the area of Hubert-Folie. At last light, the squadron was withdrawn for replenishment. At first light on 26 July, the squadron returned to the town in its role as flank guard. It received some AP fire in the morning but no tanks were hit. At 15.00, orders were received for B Sqn to return to a rest area north of Fleury-sur-Orne. The rest of the regiment joined them. The regiment stayed there in relative security over the next few days. On 28 July, Maj Radley-Walters and Sgt Beardsley made an audacious personal recce. A Sqn had previously destroyed a Panther recovery vehicle and together they retrieved a 75mm anti-tank gun, several machine-guns, the complete technical data on the Panther tank and the enemy's wireless code signals. They returned to hand over their booty to the intelligence section of the regiment.

On 27 July, Gen Montgomery issued a new directive to his army commanders. It was becoming evident that the American operation was making a breakthrough, so he decided to abandon another 'Operation GOODWOOD' launched towards Falaise, and replace it with an offensive

west of the Orne River. The bulk of Second Brit Army was to shift west to deliver the main blow on the eastern flank of the Americans. First Cdn Army was ordered to make additional, limited holding attacks in the sector south of Caen. Gen Montgomery stressed the importance of holding in place, for as long as possible, the strong enemy forces south of Caen. Lt-Gen Crerar instructed Lt-Gen Simonds that Second Cdn Corps was to draw up plans for an attack along the Caen-Falaise axis, with Falaise as the final objective. At the same time, First Brit Corps was to conduct a limited advance on Vimont to protect the Canadian left flank. Initially, Lt-Gen Simonds saw the attack carried out in three phases. In the first phase, 2nd Cdn Inf Div, supported by 2nd Cdn Armd Bde, would break through the German Fontenay-le-Marmion-La Hogue line of defence. In the next phase, the Haut Mesnil-Saint-Sylvain line would be breached. Finally, two armoured divisions would exploit the successes of the previous phases and seize the high ground dominating Falaise. On 30 July, Lt-Gen Simonds asked for another infantry division, another armoured division and total air support for forty-eight hours. However, that same day, Gen Montgomery ordered that all preparations for a new operation be put on hold.

By 1 August, First US Army had broken clear through the German left wing and was beginning to exploit its success. Gen Bradley handed over his command to Lt-Gen Courtney Hicks Hodges and took command of the newly formed 12th Army Group. At the same time, Third US Army under Lt-Gen Patton entered the battle on the right flank and was responsible for the main exploitation task. In retaliation, Hitler ordered *Generalfeldmarschall* von Kluge to mount a major armoured counter-offensive through Avranches against the American lines of communications. Operation LÜTTICH would push *8.SS-Cavalry-Division (Florian Geyer)* and 9.SS-Pzdiv forward in the hopes of splitting First US Army and Third US Army. Informed of the German intentions through ULTRA, Gen Montgomery and Gen Bradley decided to take advantage of the information and shape the German forces into a narrow, vulnerable pocket. That pocket would then be closed between Alençon and Falaise. On 1 August, Gen Montgomery ordered First Cdn Army to attack towards Falaise with the object of capturing as much terrain as possible and cutting off the German forces opposing Second Brit Army across the Orne River.

In presenting his plan to his division commanders, Lt-Gen Simonds stressed that although the Germans were well entrenched to their front, tactical surprise was still possible in respect to the time and method used. The main question was how to get the armour through the enemy's gun

OPERATION TOTALIZE: THE DRIVE TOWARDS FALAISE

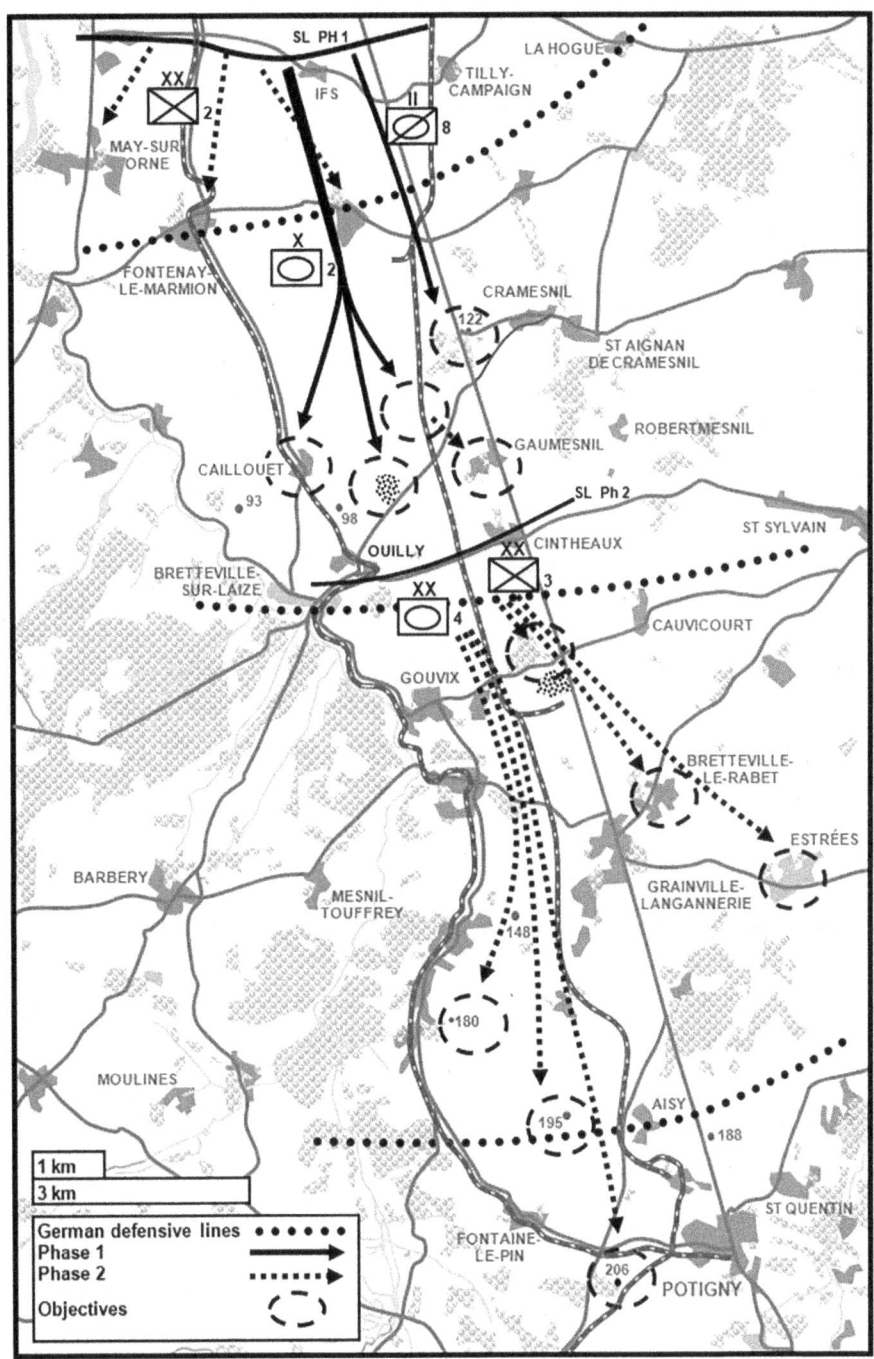

Operation TOTALIZE – The Second Canadian Corps plan.

screen to sufficient depth to disrupt the German anti-tank gun and mortar defence. His plan would use the cover of night to initiate the attack. During the first phase, 2nd Cdn Inf Div, led by 2nd Cdn Armd Bde, would launch a night attack without preliminary bombardment and break through the Fontenay-le-Marmion-La Hogue position. During the second phase, 3rd Cdn Inf Div, supported by an armoured brigade and heavy air support, would breach the Haut Mesnil-Saint-Sylvain position. Two armoured divisions, 4th Cdn Armd Div and 1st Polish Armoured Division (1 Pol Armd Div), would then exploit southward and seize the high ground at Point 195 and other high ground immediately dominating Falaise. Gen Montgomery gave his blessing to the plan on 3 August. It became known as Operation TOTALIZE. D-Day was set for 7 August with the H-Hour for Phase 1 set for 23.00. The H-Hour for Phase 2 was set at 14.00 on 8 August.

Lt-Gen Simonds' plan required originality and innovation. First, he would use heavy bombers in the ground battle in darkness. To do this, special procedures for marking the targets would have to be developed and tested. Second, every previous attack on Verrières Ridge had come at a heavy cost in human sacrifice, particularly with regards to the infantry. Therefore, he proposed to convert Priest SP guns into armoured personnel carriers. Each infantry division would be given thirty of the stripped Priest chassis, known as Kangaroos.[2] Several other aspects of the plan would require practice and coordination between the armour and the infantry. To assist in navigation at night, 40mm Bofors guns would fire on each battalion's objective. Search lights would also be used to reflect light off the cloud cover. Another innovation would be the use of a radio beam that would guide each column as it advanced. The signaller in the troop leader's tank would hear a series of dots and dashes. As long as the tank was within the beam, the signaller would hear nothing. However, if they veered too far left, the signal would be 'dot–dot–dot', and if too far right it would change to 'dash–dash–dash'.

During Operation SPRING, the Calgary Highlanders were surprised to find that the German defenders were using the mine tunnels just south of Saint-Martin-de-Fontenay to move from position to position. The decision was taken for 6th Brigade to mount an assault on the position. A Coy from the Camerons, supported by a detachment of twenty sappers from 11th Field Engineer Company and a troop from the *Sherbrookes*, was ordered to move forward and capture the Saint-Martin-de-Fontenay church. From there, they would seize the lofty mineshaft towers which provided the Germans with excellent observation of the Canadians. Once the sappers reached the mineshaft towers, they were to climb about 20ft up the towers to place demolition charges. The demolished towers were to create rubble which would block the mine entrances, thus preventing the Germans from using the tunnel system. H-Hour was planned for midnight 3–4 August; C Sqn was to supply one troop which would cover the withdrawal of the assault party should daylight overtake it before it finished its work.

Maj Walsh, who had returned to command C Sqn on 1 August, tasked Lieut Peter Edward Gannaw with the job of supporting the Camerons. He conducted a recce of Saint-André-sur-Orne to find a good fire position for his troop. He selected a small orchard about 500 yards from the objective which covered the left flank, the most likely approach by the enemy. At 23.00, the troop moved up under the cover of an artillery barrage. The troop had one Firefly and it was placed on a small ridge. The CO of the Camerons had marked Lieut Gannaw's map with the location of his defensive minefield. Unfortunately, the minefield was poorly marked on the ground and on his map. Two tanks were lost simultaneously as they attempted to skirt the minefield. The troop leader had to get out of his tank and guide it on foot through the minefield to its position. At 03.00, Maj Walsh ordered Lieut A.N. Cloutier and another tank to move forward to replace the two disabled tanks.

Lieut Gannaw sent a guide back to meet the two replacement tanks. Because of the fog, he decided to go right through Saint-André-sur-Orne rather than around it. He went through the village unchallenged and exited on the south side. The second tank was out of radio contact with Lieut Cloutier and, unsure of where to go, it stopped on the north edge of the town. Alone, Lieut Cloutier reached the area of the mine buildings. At the same time as he realised he had gone too far, he was hit by a 75mm anti-tank round fired at very close range from his left; the round entered the tank just behind the driver. The crew bailed out into a ditch; Tpr O.C.J. Litchfield, the gunner, saw that the tank had not brewed up so he got back in and tried, but failed, to restart it. However, he saw someone crawling forward in the ditch and warned Lieut Cloutier. When challenged, the intruder replied something in German and so Tpr Litchfield fired at him. A German machine-gun fired on the tank in retaliation. The anti-tank gun fired again and holed the tank in the turret. When two German half-tracks appeared about 100 yards south of their position from May-sur-Orne, the crew abandoned the tank and crawled up the ditch towards Saint-André-sur-Orne. They found shelter in an orchard on the west side of the village. When the assault party got to the mine area, it was hit by machine-gun and mortar fire. The company was rapidly reorganised down to platoon strength and the advance resumed. When it reached the mine, A Coy surrounded the mine and the sappers started to climb the scaffolding on the mineshaft towers. However, they were outlined by the bright moonlight and became easy targets for German snipers and machine-gun fire. The sappers failed to place their charges and the raiding party was ordered to withdraw when it became apparent they wouldn't succeed. The company returned to the rear at 03.55 with thirty-nine casualties, nine of which were engineers. Maj Walsh was informed of the loss of Lieut Cloutier's tank, and at 05.00 the tanks were ordered back from their positions.

At 11.30 on 5 August, Brig Wyman held a preliminary conference at Louvigny. He stressed that the brigade had only forty-eight hours to assemble, organise and train the assault force for Operation TOTALIZE. Every effort must be made to get as many tanks as possible ready before the operation started. Intelligence had been received that 1.SS-Pzdiv was withdrawing to Bretteville-sur-Laize to form a mobile reserve. Therefore, Lt-Gen Simonds modified his original plan. During Phase 1, the two armoured divisions would move up to their start lines. During the second phase, the two armoured divisions were to be launched directly through to the final objective; 4th Cdn Armd Div was to seize the areas around Points 180, 195 and 206; 1 Pol Armd Div, recently arrived on the Continent, would take the areas around Points 179 and 159; 51th Brit Inf Div would follow up behind 1 Pol Armd Div, and 2nd Cdn Inf Div was to secure Bretteville-sur-Laize on the right flank and the wooded area north of Cauvicourt on the left. Maj-Gen Foulkes wanted to concentrate his armour in order to punch a hole in the German defences. He divided his forces into four columns, each led by a gapping force composed of two troops under the squadron 2i/c, two troops of Flails and two troops of AVREs to mark the safe lanes through the minefields. The first troop of tanks was to advance with 3ft between each of the four tanks. The second troop would be deployed 4ft directly behind the first troop. Each subsequent troop would be 4ft directly behind the previous troop. Lt-Col Gordon would command the four gapping forces. One hundred yards behind the gapping forces would be the assault forces, composed of the remaining two troops under the squadron commander and deployed using the same spacing. An infantry battalion mounted in Kangaroos would follow behind the tanks. Behind the battalion would be machine-guns in carriers, towed anti-tank guns and engineer bulldozers. H-Hour for the operation was set for 23.30 on 7 August.

At 15.45, Lt-Col Gordon held his own O Group. The *Sherbrookes* were to be attached to 4th Brigade for the operation. Two troops from each

OPERATION TOTALIZE: THE DRIVE TOWARDS FALAISE

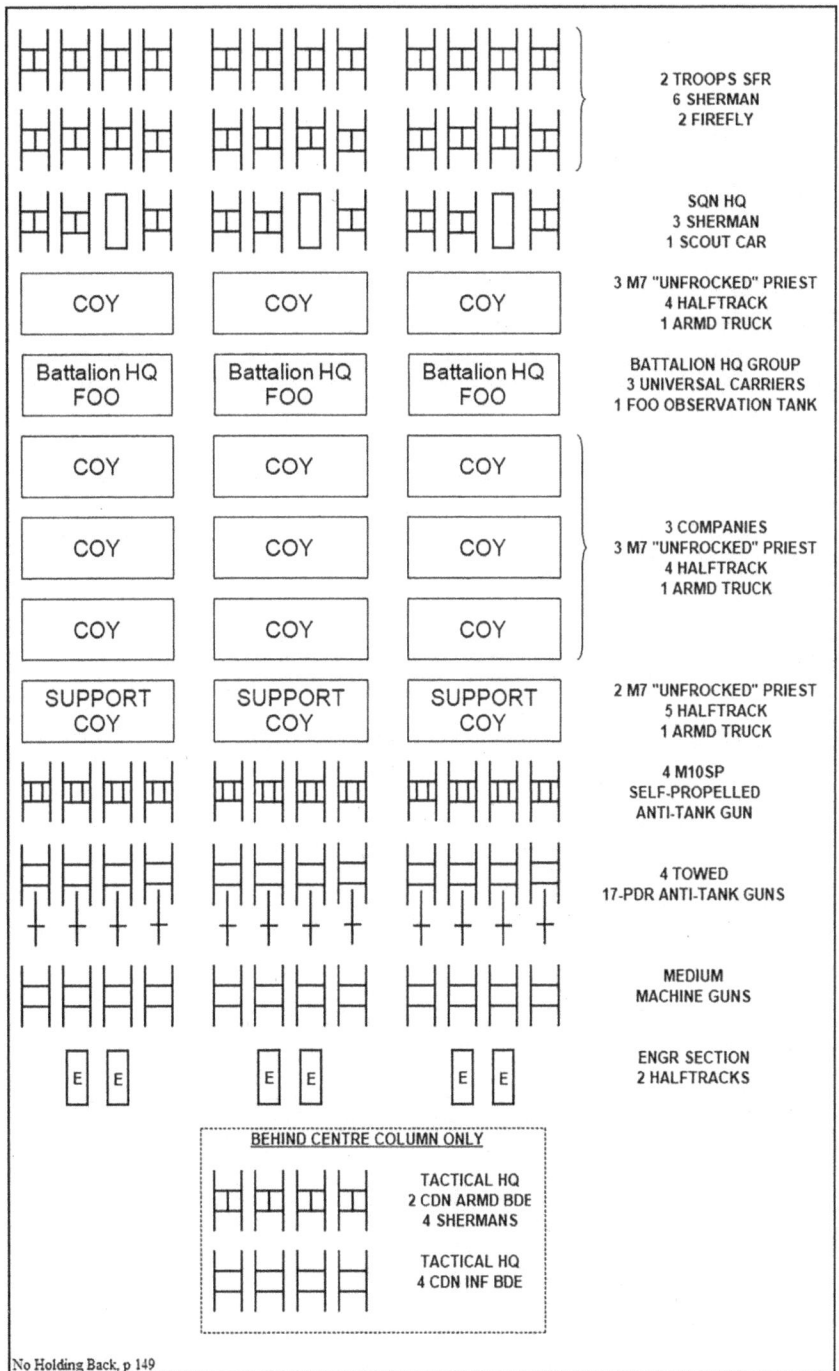

ASSAULT FORCE

ARMOURED THUNDER

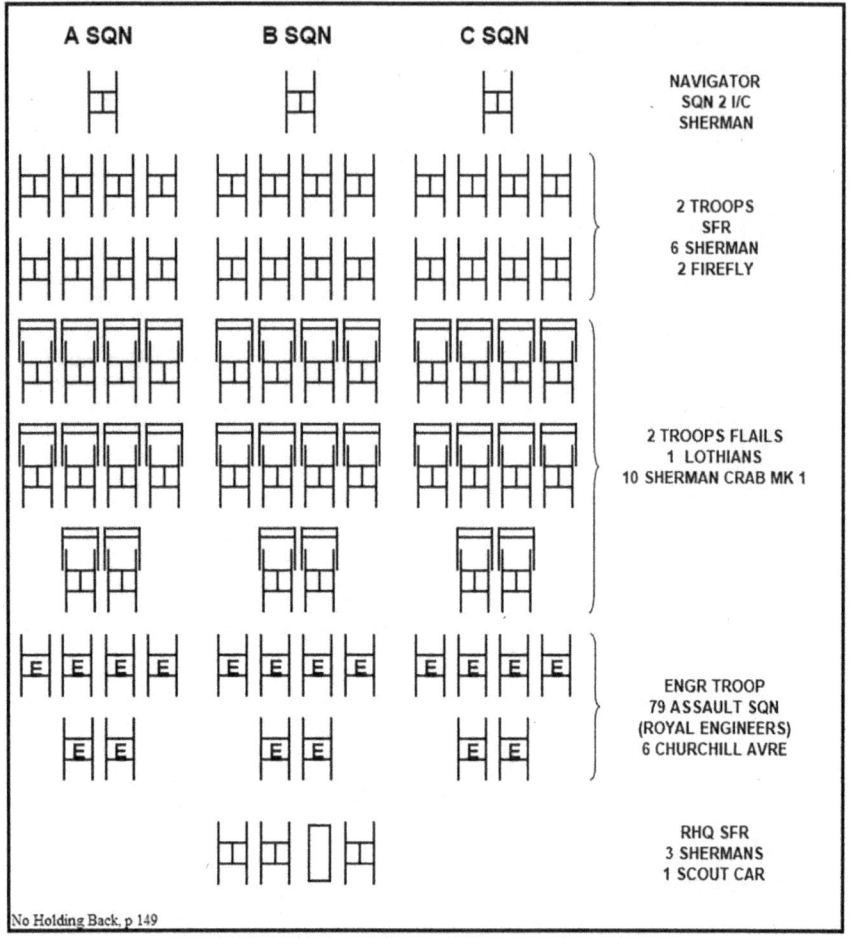

GAPPING FORCE - SHERBROOKE FUSILIER REGIMENT

squadron, under the command of their squadron 2i/c, were to be attached to the gapping force. They were to be in position by 18.30 that evening to practice the move with the AVREs and Flails. These troops were to practice with using the radio directional beam guidance system. The remaining two troops from each squadron, under the command of the squadron commanders, were to conduct rehearsals with the infantry mounted in Kangaroos and M14 half-tracks. Each squadron was to also receive a troop of SP anti-tank guns. The penetration force was to be divided into four columns and it was to seize a line from Bretteville-sur-Laize to Gaumesnil. The farthest column on the left would advance between Rocquancourt and the *Route Nationale 158* (RN 158) and was based on 8th Cdn Recce Regt.

Its objective was Lorguichon. The *Sherbrookes* would form three tight columns which would pass to the west of Rocquancourt. A Sqn would be in support of the R Regt C on the left flank – its objective would be to secure Point 122, the high ground northwest of Gaumesnil known as the Cramesnil Spur, and to then exploit to the village during Phase 2. B Sqn, attached to the RHLI, would be in the centre and would secure the quarry astride the Bretteville-sur-Laize-Saint-Aignan-de-Cramesnil road. C Sqn, in support of the Essex Scottish, would form the right flank and its objective was to secure Caillouet. Lt-Col Gordon would command the penetration force while Brig James Edwin Ganong, the commander of 4th Brigade, was to command the assault force. 6th Brigade would follow the penetration force on foot to take objectives closer to the start line that would be initially bypassed. The South Sask would take Rocquancourt, the FMR would take May-sur-Orne and the Camerons would take Fontenay-le-Marmion. 5th Brigade would be in reserve during the first phase but would help seize the Phase 2 objectives. All recovery, except for road clearances, was to cease forthwith.

For the next two days, the tanks and the infantry trained together, while the gapping force experimented with the radio directional equipment operating on the tank's No. 19 set. On 6 August, the tank squadrons married up with their assigned infantry battalions and the infantry practiced in elementary tank tactics. After supper, both brigades practiced forming up in the formation proposed for the next night's advance. Before last light, both brigades moved back to their original harbour areas. The next morning, the squadrons resumed their preparations and training for the upcoming operation. At 11.00, C Sqn moved into a preliminary assembly area just north of Beauvoir Farm and formed up in a similar formation as was practiced the previous night. B Sqn started its move at 13.00, while A Sqn moved to its assembly area near Fleury-sur-Orne and Ifs at 14.00. The assembly area for the regiment was just below the crest of the ridge, safe from enemy observation and direct fire. Although the vehicles threw up great clouds of dust, the Germans luckily did not take any air or artillery action against the force's concentration. The regiment's move was completed by 16.00. A Navy, Army and Air Force Institute (NAAFI) beer ration was issued and a hot supper with fresh bread was served. At 21.30, the four columns began to move forward to a position just north of the start line. By last light, 22.00, all the troops were in the assembly area awaiting the order to move.

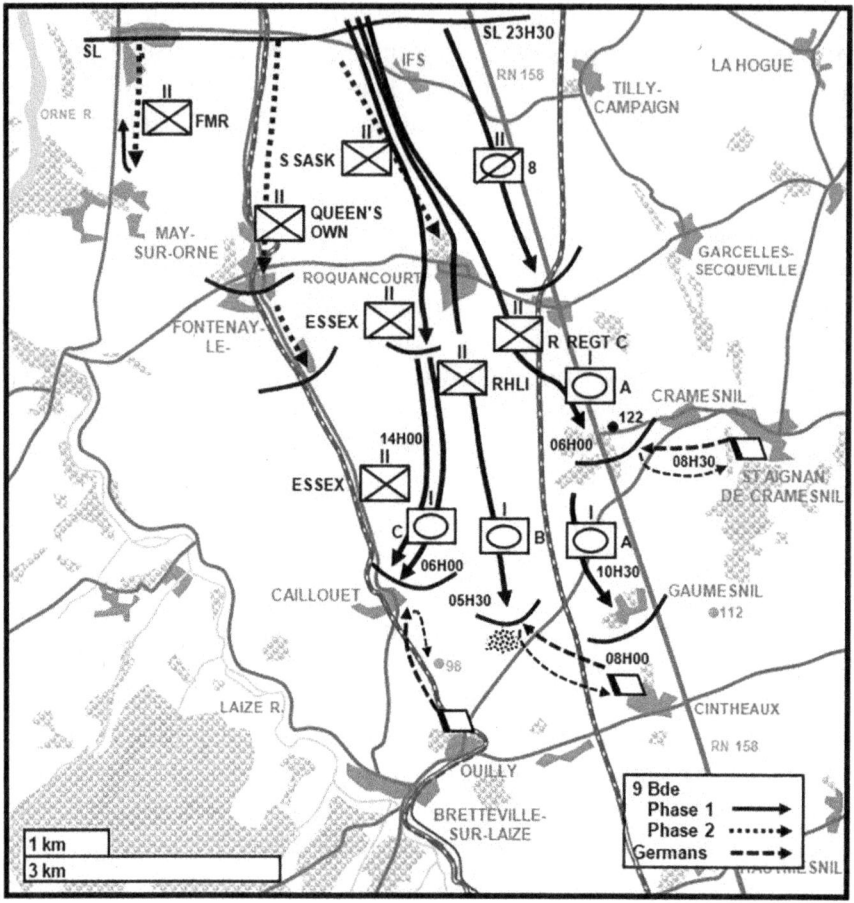

The night of 7-8 August 1944: Phase 1 of Operation TOTALIZE.

Just before 23.00, the artillery fired red and green illumination marker shells to identify the German positions. There followed a faint buzz that grew progressively into a roar as 1,020 Halifax and Lancaster heavy bombers dropped 3,462 tons of bombs on the identified targets. At 23.30, the order finally came and the columns began their advance. Fifteen minutes later, a rolling artillery barrage opened up. Sixteen searchlights were turned on to try to reflect light off the clouds ahead of the columns. Bofors guns opened up with tracer rounds; one gun for the left axis and two for the right. The Germans were taken by surprise and, other than enemy mortar- and shell-fire, gave no immediate reaction to the threat heading their way. The tank columns advanced at an average speed of 9 mph. After fifteen minutes, the lead tanks ran into the creeping artillery barrage which was not advancing fast enough. The night was quite dark and the dust, smoke, exhaust and ground mist made the advance very difficult. There were many collisions and even the report of Flails trying to climb onto the back of Sherman tanks. At 00.15, the Germans retaliated and laid a very dense smoke screen across the entire front. At the same time, the Bofors guns which had been firing tracer rounds to mark the lanes of advance ceased to do so as detailed in their orders. The lead troops found it almost impossible to keep their direction; the columns started to disintegrate and scatter with no guide to lead them. On short notice, the Bofors were ordered to resume firing but their tracers could not be seen because of the German smoke screen. However, when the smoke cleared, the tracers could once again be seen and the advance continued slowly; 8th Cdn Recce Regt moved up with RN 158 on its left flank. It encountered little resistance and soon occupied Lorguichon.

In the case of the *Sherbrookes*, the columns got considerably off course due to poor visibility and obstacles in the form of sunken roads and shell and bomb craters which prevented the columns from pursuing the geometrically straight course that was intended. The artillery fired their rounds for two minutes, and then lifted their fire as they advanced their line of fire 200 yards. Then, the guns would shoot again for two minutes. The tanks were supposed to advance when the fire lifted. Unfortunately, this method created difficulties because it caused a lot of dust and smoke directly ahead of the tanks. Rather than pass west of Rocquancourt, A Sqn passed to the left of the village at around 02.30. Lieut Charles Mecum Williams's troop led the way for the A Sqn gapping force. The other troop got lost and ended up with B Sqn. When the assault force passed the village, Maj Radley-Walters ordered the lead troop to position itself with the RN 158 as its left flank and the railway track as its right flank and to follow them up to Point 122. Total surprise was achieved and only Sgt Harry A. Milne's tank was disabled on a mine. At one point during the move, Lieut Williams came over the wireless and reported 'I've just hit a mine...' He cancelled the call on realising that when their tank had hit an anti-tank ditch, his gunner had been thrown forward in the dark and his foot had hit the main gun's solenoid switch, firing a HE round into the other side of the ditch wall about 10ft in front of Lieut Williams's face. The R Regt C following behind them failed to keep up and became confused; B Coy became entirely separated from the remainder of the column and the company headquarters and a platoon attached themselves to the RHLI column and would find themselves in the RHLI position at first light. The remainder of the company went astray near Rocquancourt and decided to dig in there.

The R Regt C objective was to capture Point 122 and take up a position astride the Caen-Falaise highway. The plan was for A Sqn to lead them to their dispersal point. Approximately two hours before daylight, the battalion crossed some higher ground but had doubts about whether it had reached its objective or not; if it kept on, it might possibly overshoot the objective. The column stopped until daylight finally arrived when it confirmed it was still 300 yards short of its objective. At 05.00, the battalion finally put in its attack, moving forward and taking its objective without much opposition at 06.00. A Sqn then took up a defensive position in preparation for the counter-attack expected at first light. At about 08.30, the Germans attacked from the area of Cramesnil with infantry supported by two Tigers, two Panthers and a couple of *Jagdpanzers*.[3] The German tanks fired on the battalion positions from the far side of Cramesnil. One Panther succeeded in penetrating the R Regt C positions and got to within 70 yards of the BnHQ. The attack lasted for an hour before it was beaten off. The battalion lost four carriers loaded with ammunition destined for the mortar platoon and an M10 SP anti-tank gun was brewed. A Sqn lost two tanks knocked out: Capt R. Raites's tank was hit in the back deck and Sgt Reid's tank was hit by an 88mm anti-tank shell which went right through the back of the tank, through both motors and out the other side. In return, all four German tanks were destroyed, as well as six other armoured vehicles.

At first, all went well for B Sqn, whose role was to help the RHLI seize Point 46, the high ground at the quarry astride the Bretteville-Saint-Aignan-de-Cramesnil road; Capt Bateman was the 2i/c and navigator for his column. Visibility was bad due to the air bombing, the artillery and the German smoke screen. The Bofors were useless, as were the searchlights. The radio detection method allowed him to keep his column on track, however the radio signals ceased or were hard to distinguish after the lead tanks got over the first hill. Sgt Parsons was the point tank followed immediately by a Flail to clear any mines should the point tank blow up. Fortunately he did not, but the point tank in C Sqn hit a mine and the explosion lit up the whole countryside. After the smoke screen laid down by the Germans lifted and the Bofors started to fire again, it was realised that the column had strayed off course some distance west and hit Rocquancourt straight on. As the RHLI approached the village, two Kangaroos ran into bomb craters and became casualties. B Sqn drove down the main street of the village, but the infantry got lost within Rocquancourt itself. 88mm anti-tank guns began to fire at point blank range and, fortunately for the tanks, concentrated their fire on C Sqn and the Essex Scottish. However, the delay caused the column to lose the protection of the heavy artillery barrage. The Germans were caught, literally, 'with their pants down', and were running around in their underwear as the squadron drove right through their camp. They didn't fire at the column and the tanks didn't fire at them. They surrendered to the infantry following behind.

The lead tanks continued to stray and got lost; Lt-Col Gordon personally took over the lead of the column and directed it back towards its objective. The column got back under way and proceeded south. It reached the open ground of the abandoned airfield and crossed it amid machine-gun and small arms fire and the occasional anti-tank fire and mortaring. At 05.00, the armoured personnel carriers reached their dispersal point and the troops unloaded. The objective, Point 46, was recognised ahead. The order of march of the assault force had become considerably mixed up and it took some time to reorganise the infantry in preparation for an assault on the objective. However, it was discovered that the objective had been abandoned and the companies quickly moved into their positions. At 05.30, the tanks reached the quarry. The RHLI sent its companies forward and, finding the enemy established in it with four tanks and a *Jagdpanzer*, they established themselves about 200 yards north of the objective. The infantry dug in as close as possible to the enemy while B Sqn took up a defensive position. At around 08.00, the ground mist lifted and almost at once a German force composed of tanks and SP guns attacked the RHLI. They got close enough to engage the carriers of the battalion motor platoon and the mobile machine-guns of the Toronto Scottish Regiment. The FOO attached to the RHLI got a troop of tanks from B Sqn to engage the tanks and four German armoured vehicles were destroyed and the attacking force driven off. One Sherman was knocked out, as was one M10.

For the first 2,000 yards after crossing the start line, the gapping force of C Sqn encountered little resistance and made good progress. The assault force, however, was engulfed by the German smoke screen, causing confusion among the lead tanks which became scattered and converged on the centre column. The advance was halted while the situation was sorted out. When the smoke cleared, the tanks were still west of Rocquancourt but very close to the village. The advance continued for another 2,000 yards before it encountered an 88mm anti-tank gun. A Flail tank to the rear was hit but the crew was unhurt. The gapping force carried on while the assault force halted close to an enemy strong point where it encountered three anti-tank guns and suffered the loss of a half-track, some personnel and an M10 SP anti-tank gun. A platoon was sent to deal with the 88mm gun but was driven off by machine-gun fire. With the delay, the Essex Scottish got separated from the gapping force and the infantry underestimated the distance to the objective. Confusion reigned. When the CO, Lt-Col C.E.F. Jones, was reported missing at 03.27, Maj Jack Burgess, the acting battalion 2i/c, took over and ordered the battalion to deploy and dig-in. The tanks of C Sqn had continued to move forward to the objective and reported very little enemy resistance when they reached Caillouet at about 06.00. When the tanks reached the dispersal point, the squadron formed a close laager to wait for the infantry until first light, at which time the tanks spread out under cover in anticipation of a German counter-attack. It finally materialised in the form of an infantry assault supported by one anti-tank gun. The gun hit Lieut Gannaw's tank which brewed up immediately. The ammunition in the tank was exploding out of the turret hatch and fire was also coming out. His driver was still inside in serious pain and screaming for help. Lieut Gannaw finally succeeded in getting him out. Unfortunately, he later died of the burns he received. Lieut John Douglas Craig was wounded by flying shrapnel and also had to be evacuated. The squadron spent the remainder of the morning laying spec fire on suspected mortar positions.

Maj Burgess had returned to Rocquancourt during the night and had found his wounded CO. At first light the Essex Scottish realised that it was still 3,500 yards from its objective. It had lost fourteen half-tracks, two M10 SP guns and a FOO observation tank. It was finally reorganised and ordered southward at 08.45. The advance came to a halt 1,000 yards from Caillouet when it encountered four Tiger tanks in a hull-down position in the town at 10.25. Tank support was sent forward and at 14.00 the Tigers finally moved out. The Essex Scottish pushed forward the final distance and Caillouet was taken. At 09.10, A Sqn and 8th Cdn Recce Regt were ordered to move across to support the infantry in taking the quarry while the remainder of the *Sherbrooke* tanks moved back to Point 122 to form a fortress with the R Regt C. The troops of Lieut John Elmo Murray Logan and Lieut Thomas Garfield Gould led the way, with Maj Radley-Walters in support. In the open field just north of the quarry, a *Jagdpanzer* knocked out Cpl Peter J. Hart's tank. Although Lieut Gould was wounded in the head and arms by shrapnel, the attack continued. The *Jagdpanzer* was knocked out and the infantry moved into the quarry at around 10.00. After the quarry was taken, A Sqn was released at 10.30. It skirted the woods to the west of Point 122 until it reached the railway. The aim was to move into a position from which it could give support to the R Regt C for their planned attack on Gaumesnil. The tanks turned south past La Jalousie until they reached the rear of the town. There was a large château with a tall stone and cement wall which completely enclosed the property. It offered good firing positions to the east and southeast. A Sqn had only ten to twelve tanks, of which two were Fireflies. The tanks took up defensive positions around the château and made holes in the stone walls so that the tanks could observe and engage any targets coming north on the Caen-Falaise road or in the fields to the east of it. By 11.15, the squadron was all set up.

By 06.00, all three squadrons had reached their objectives and had taken defensive positions in anticipation of an expected enemy counter-attack. All the battalions, with the exception of the Essex Scottish, were fully consolidated on their objectives. At 06.15, Brig Wyman reported that the area was secure and that the situation appeared to be entirely suitable for further operations to begin. As Lt-Col Gordon looked over the battlefield from his position just south of Rocquancourt, he came to the conclusion that the enemy defensive line had been broken. No enemy, except for the odd infantry stragglers, could be seen to the front. He asked for permission to seize the opportunity and to continue the advance on Falaise. He had six troops of tanks, two squadrons of Flails and a squadron of AVREs; the remainders of A Sqn and B Sqn would also soon become available. In anticipation of a positive reply, he issued orders to reorganise the squadrons. Brig Wyman moved forward to Lt-Col Gordon's position to better assess the situation for himself. The timetable for the aerial bombardment planned to begin Phase 2 of the operation could not be changed, although it was moved up by forty-five minutes to 13.00. Previous intelligence reports had placed 1.SS-Pzdiv astride the second defensive line stretching from Bretteville-sur-Laize to Saint-Sylvain. Lt-Gen Simond's headquarters believed that there would be an additional risk of the lead troops being marked as targets by the bombers; it was also thought that 4th Cdn Armd Div would be passing through 2nd Cdn Armd Bde's positions in a few minutes.[4] Therefore, permission was denied. At 06.30, a German straggler shot and wounded Brig Wyman. He managed to stay in command until Col J.F. Bingham, the brigade 2i/c, moved up and relieved him at 09.30. The Canadian advance, however, ground to a halt while 6th Brigade consolidated its positions and waited for the air bombardment.

By noon, most of the Canadian and British battalions had made, or were making, their objectives. The result was a broken and demoralised *89.Infanterie-Division* (89.Inf-Div) and a gap of approximately 3.5 miles in the German lines. Just after 13.00, the anticipated American air strike was launched; 678 Fortress bombers from 8th USAAF hit the towns of Bretteville-sur-Laize, Saint-Sylvain, Haut Mesnil, Cauvicourt and Gouvix. However, due to navigation errors, several bombers dropped their sticks short and hit 1st Pol Armd Div and 3rd Cdn Inf Div. Maj-Gen Keller was wounded in the left hand and the right leg and had to be evacuated; he was replaced by Brig Blackader. Two companies of the North Shore Regt were wiped out and 4th Medium Artillery lost half its guns. The intelligence office of the *Sherbrookes*, a M14 half-track, was located with the Main HQ of 2nd Cdn Armd Bde and it was also hit by the American bombers. It was destroyed along with all the regiment's records on hand. L/Sgt Lloyd M. Jenne was killed and five other ranks were wounded. All told, the Canadians suffered 65 killed and 250 wounded; and 55 vehicles destroyed.

At 01.45, 12.SS-Pzdiv had been ordered to cancel its move west to block Second Brit Army and was put at the disposal of *5.Panzerarmee* (5.Pzarmee).⁵ The division still had a battalion of *PzKpfw IV* tanks, three companies of Tigers from s.SS-Pzabt 101, a company of *Jagdpanzers*, a battalion of *Panzergrenadiers*, three divisional artillery battalions and a *Nebelwerfer* battalion. Early in the attack, *SS-Brigadeführer* Meyer had moved forward to see for himself what was happening. He was met by the remnants of 89.Inf-Div stumbling past him and rapidly concluded that he needed to stabilise the front north of Potigny. In his mind, Potigny was the key terrain and if it fell to the Canadians, then 5.Pzarmee and 7.Armee would be lost. The division had only forty-eight tanks remaining, but it had nineteen Tiger tanks from s.SS-Pzabt 101, two flame-throwing Tigers and a large number of 88mm anti-aircraft and anti-tank guns from *III.Flak-Korps* attached to it. He decided to stabilise the front. He approached the fleeing soldiers and organised them into a defensive position around Cintheaux. Meyer wondered why the Allies had not resumed their advance. He could see tanks to his front but they weren't doing anything. Most of his own troops were in Bretteville-le-Rabet and Estrées-la-Campagne. The only armour he had in Cintheaux was eight Tiger tanks of s.SS-Pzabt 101 and a platoon of three *Jagdpanzers* from *Kampfgruppe* Waldmüller.

Meyer had met earlier with *General der Panzertruppe* Eberbach, the commander of 5.Pzarmee, and had been given full freedom of action. He saw two possible routes of advance for the Canadians: the first down RN 158 to Falaise, and the second from Saint-Aignan-de-Cramesnil to

Estrées-la-Campagne, then southwest across the Laison River through Olendon and Épaney to Falaise. He considered the second route as the better of the two, but decided to try to block both possibilities at the same time. He therefore centered his defence on Cintheaux and planned to launch an attack east of the road with lightning speed. The objective would be the woods southeast of Garcelles-Secqueville and the H-Hour would be 12.30. He ordered *Kampfgruppe* Krause to occupy the high ground west of Potigny and defend the area between the Laison and Laize rivers. He also ordered *Kampfgruppe* Waldmüller to counter-attack and seize the high ground south of Saint-Aignan-de-Cramesnil. He met with *SS-Hauptsturmführer* Michael Wittmann,[6] the acting battalion commander of the heavy tank battalion of s.SS-Pzabt 101, at about 12.00 in Cintheaux and ordered him to begin a counter-attack no later than 12.30 in support of *Kampfgruppe* Waldmüller in an attempt to regain the initiative and thwart the impending Canadian attack. As the German tanks began to roll northward at 12.30, Meyer stood on the northern outskirts of Cintheaux. The land is flat with a slight rise to the east. Artillery fire was falling but the tanks pushed through the steely inferno. *Kampfgruppe* Waldmüller followed the tanks with its *Panzergrenadiers*. All of a sudden, American bombers appeared overhead. Meyer was convinced that the *Kampfgruppe* would be wiped out before the counter-attack started; instead, the bombers flew right over it without dropping a single bomb. Wittmann led the spearhead accompanied by four other Tiger tanks and moved northward on the east side of RN 158 between Gaumesnil and Saint-Aignan-de-Cramesnil. Two other Tigers were in support on the west side of the road. Behind them, a number of *PzKpfw IV* tanks, half-tracks and *Jagdpanzers* followed. Wittmann's small unit advanced in an echelon formation with Wittmann tracking the road.

A Sqn of the *Sherbrookes* had established a blocking position in the château grounds just north of Gaumesnil by 11.15. The squadron had the task of assisting the R Regt C in taking Gaumesnil at the start of Phase 2 of the operation and so Maj Radley-Walters had moved forward to the château grounds to the rear of the hamlet. The eastern edge of the hamlet was near RN 158 and the château had a tall stone and cement wall completely surrounding the property. He ordered the tanks to make holes in the wall to provide observation south along RN 158 and east onto the open fields, and to create firing positions, while still maintaining excellent protection for the tanks. At around 12.15, A Sqn spotted five advancing Tiger tanks followed by two *Jagdpanzers*, some *PzKpfw IV* and a number of halftracks. Four Tigers were in front, of which one was running close to the east side

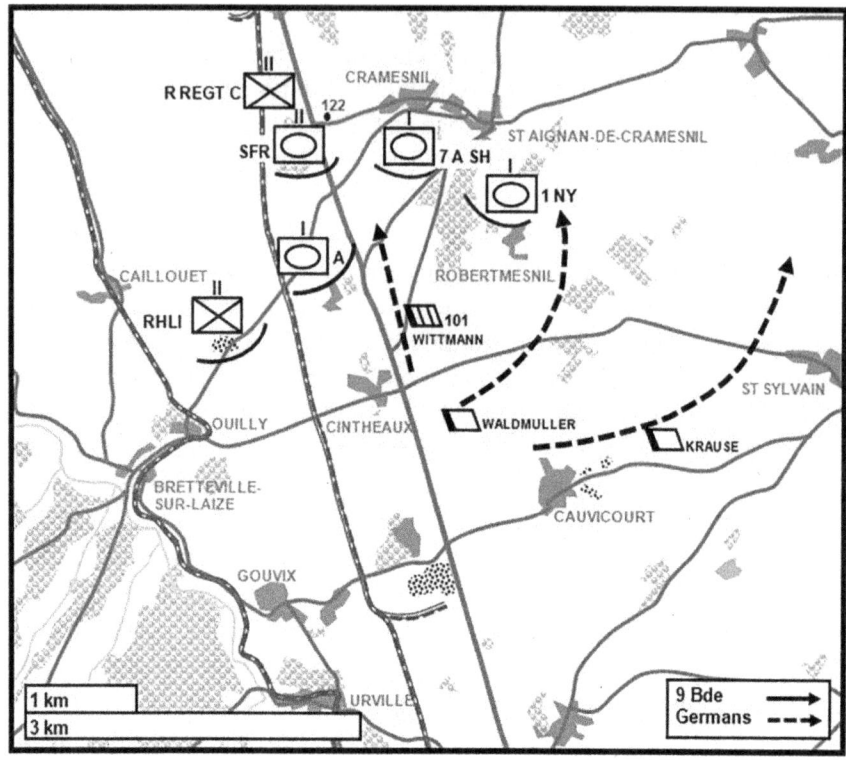

12.30 – 8 August 1944: The counter-attack by *Kampfgruppe* Waldmüller.

the highway. The fifth Tiger was following the lead elements along the west side of the RN 158, followed by a *Jagdpanzer* driving on the highway itself. The German attack was supported by mortars and artillery, and the area was thick with smoke. Maj Radley-Walters issued orders for the squadron to hold its fire until the tanks got close enough. When the tanks got to about 500 yards, the squadron's tanks opened up and knocked out the lead Tiger moving on the west side of the road. Maj Radley-Walters then hit one of the *Jagdpanzer*. Then all the squadron tanks opened up and the German force veered east towards the wooded area south of Saint-Aignan-de-Cramesnil. Two Firefly tanks belonging to B Sqn joined the battle from their position in the La Jalousie area. Another Tiger, advancing along the east side of the road, was reported hit along with two *PzKpfw IV* and two *Jagdpanzers*.[7] Several other Tigers were brewed up by British forces in position just south of Saint-Aignan-de-Cramesnil. The left prong of the German attack failed, with the destruction of Wittmann's force. On the right, however, the attack by *Kampfgruppe* Krause advanced into a small wood midway between Saint-Sylvain and Robertmesnil. From this position, it would be able to effectively block any Allied advance east of Saint-Aignan-de-Cramesnil. In the centre, however, *Kampfgruppe* Waldmüller's attack on Saint-Aignan-de-Cramesnil lasted until about 15.00. At that time, the attack petered out and the *Kampfgruppe* retired back to its start line.

A Sqn of the *Sherbrookes* remained in its position to give support to the R Regt C which was ordered to occupy Gaumesnil at 14.00. The attack on the village was launched by two companies at 15.30 and the village was reported occupied and the battalion's consolidation on the position completed at 17.00. In fact, when conducting his recce, the CO of the R Regt C was surprised to find A Sqn already there. Once the infantry entered the village, the tanks of A Sqn were ordered to Caillouet to give support to the Essex Scottish as it drove into the town. C Sqn had already taken positions to give supporting fire. Together, the two squadrons formed a firm base for the advancing infantry. At the same time, 2nd Cdn Inf Div launched an attack on Bretteville-sur-Laize with the Calgary Highlanders at 16.00. The town was captured while the R de Mais took Quilly, both operations carried out with the support of tanks from the Hussars. The FMR attacked May-sur-Orne at 15.45. When the Germans spotted the flame-throwing Churchill tanks which were giving support to the infantry battalion, they evacuated the village.

As soon as the towns were reported clear, 4th Cdn Armd Div started to bypass them in their attempt to drive to Falaise. The division had concentrated its forces during the night between Fleury-sur-Orne and the Caen-Falaise road, while 1st Pol Armd Div had assembled south-east of Cormelles. H-Hour for Phase 2 was to start immediately after the air bombardment planned for between 12.26 and 13.55; the start line was a line running just north of Robertmesnil and Gaumesnil to just south of the quarry east of Caillouet. The plan was for 4th Cdn Armd Div to advance with 10th Brigade on the right and 4th Cdn Armd Bde on the left. The tanks were to bypass Cintheaux and Haut Mesnil to the east and capture Bretteville-le-Rabet. In a second push, they would then capture the Fontaine-le-Pin feature which included Points 195 and 206. For its part, the infantry was to capture Cintheaux and Haut Mesnil, to mop up the general area and to take over the control of Bretteville-le-Rabet from the tanks. The infantry would then relieve the tanks on Points 180, 195 and 206 in order to allow them freedom of movement for exploitation south towards Falaise.

At 13.55, 1st Pol Armd Div crossed its start line. Within five minutes of launching its advance around the east side of Saint-Aignan-de-Cramesnil, the Poles ran into a battalion of 88mm anti-tank guns positioned only 200 yards away. The 24th Polish Uhlan Regiment rapidly lost forty of their fifty-two Shermans. At 14.25, the lead elements reported that they had been halted by tanks from *Kampfgruppe* Krause set up in the woods between Saint-Sylvain and Robertmesnil. At 15.00, they were again hit by anti-tank fire. A solid attempt was made to capture Point 140 but the Poles were driven off by the ferocious firepower of the German armour located there. At 16.10, they reported twenty Tiger tanks in the area south-east of Saint-Aignan-de-Cramesnil. The situation soon turned into a stalemate with 1st Pol Armd Div losing fifty-seven tanks – nearly a third of their tank strength. For their part, 4th Cdn Armd Div crossed the Bretteville-sur-Laize-Saint-Aignan-de-Cramesnil road at 13.55; its advance was slow due to resistance from Gaumesnil, but things improved with its capture by the R Regt C. The Canadian Grenadier Guards (CGG) crossed the start line at 14.26, its advance delayed while they helped secure Gaumesnil and again when they encountered a battery of 88mm anti-tank guns at Cintheaux. The force finally reached the outskirts of Bretteville-le-Rabet as darkness fell. The CO of the CGG decided that it was too dark to attack and so retired his tanks back to Cintheaux to harbour for the night.

At 16.00, Eberbach ordered a withdrawal to a new defensive line running from Moult through Saint-Sylvain to Les Moutiers. 12.SS-Pzdiv was ordered to move to a line running roughly between Saint-Sylvain and Bretteville-sur-Laize. Meyer took advantage of the lull and immediately ordered both his *Kampfgruppen* to disengage from the advancing enemy and to return to the Laison sector under the cover of darkness, a move which was accomplished without difficulty. There, he issued new division orders. *Kampfgruppe* Krause was ordered to defend the high ground north of Mazières and Rouses, including Point 132; *Kampfgruppe* Waldmüller was to defend the sector from Point 140 to Point 183 on the Caen-Falaise road; III./SS-Pzgren-Rgt 26 was to defend Point 195, and all the remaining tanks of SS-Pz-Rgt 12 were to be staged in the woods at Quesnay. At the same time, *Kampfgruppe* Wünsche was withdrawn from the Grimbosq area and ordered to return to the Falaise area and prepare a new defensive position north of Potigny along RN 158. Later that night, a *Panzer* battalion from

OPERATION TOTALIZE: THE DRIVE TOWARDS FALAISE

9.SS-Pzdiv was ordered to move east to support the defence, but it was later reported that the battalion was committed to battle and could not be sent. Instead, s.SS-Pzabt 102 was sent east; unfortunately for the defenders, it only had thirteen serviceable Tigers.

This was their first engagement for both 4th Cdn Armd Div and 1st Pol Armd Div and they fell back to the habits borne of training back in England. Both divisions stopped to resupply and rest for the night when darkness fell. Lt-Gen Simonds's plan was getting behind schedule so he ordered the two armoured divisions to press on through the night; 1st Pol Armd Div was ordered to recce forward and to be prepared to seize Cauvicourt at first light, while 4th Cdn Armd Div was ordered to push down the Caen-Falaise road using searchlights. Maj-Gen George Kitching, the commander of 4th Cdn Armd Div, held an O Group at 20.00 and ordered his brigade to continue its advance during the night and to secure Point 195. It would first capture Bretteville-le-Rabet before securing Point 195; 10th Brigade was to follow the armour and assist in the capture of Bretteville-le-Rabet by taking the villages of Langannerie and Grainville-Langannerie. At midnight, Brig Eric Leslie Booth, the commander of 4th Cdn Armd Bde, ordered the British Columbia Regiment (BCR) to loop east around Bretteville-le-Rabet and occupy Point 195; Worthington Force[8] crossed its start line at 02.00. No navigational aids were available this time and during the night the force got lost as it moved forward and veered towards the east. At first light, the force reported that it had reached Point 195 and had started to consolidate on the position; no enemy was found on the position. In reality, the force was at Point 132, 6 kilometres southeast of its intended position. When Worthington Force was spotted at first light, tanks from *Kampfgruppe* Wünsche were ordered to engage the position; Worthington Force was rapidly surrounded and came under fire from Tigers from the west and Panthers from the east. Throughout the day of 9 August, it suffered severe casualties to men and equipment. Although it was finally realised that they were not on Point 195, they were ordered to hold on 'come what may'. When Worthington Force radioed for help, the Governor General's Foot Guard (GGFG) was ordered to move to Point 195 to give support to the BCR; H-Hour was set for 13.30. The regiment soon met with stiff resistance from *Kampfgruppe* Krause, which was deployed in Quesnay Woods. The GGFG was pushed back with twenty-six Shermans destroyed, about half its fighting strength. After fourteen hours, the Germans mounted a major attack and Worthington Force was pushed back. Eight Sherman tanks succeeded in getting back to friendly lines and the remaining infantry crawled away to escape the attacking German infantry.

Brig Booth ordered Halfpenny Force,[9] a combined force of the CGG and the Lake Superior Regiment, to advance along RN 158 and capture Bretteville-le-Rabet. Its H-Hour was set for 03.15. The tanks reached the low ground west of the village at 06.00 and supported D Coy of the Algonquin Regiment (Algonquins) as it cleared the village. The village was reported cleared at 15.00. Even while fighting was still going on in Bretteville-le-Rabet, the Argyll and Sutherland Highlanders of Canada (Princess Louise's) (Argyll & Sutherland) advanced and took Langannerie while the Lincoln and Welland Regiment (Lincoln & Welland) took Grainville-Langannerie. Both villages were reported secure by 18.00 with the support of a squadron of tanks from the 29th Canadian Reconnaissance Regiment (The South Alberta Regiment) (29th Cdn Recce Regt). Halfpenny Force advanced around Langannerie with orders to move to Point 195, but was halted near Point 151. During the evening, the Lincoln & Welland continued its advance and secured Saint-Germain-le-Vasson. The Poles also moved forward during the day and seized Cauvicourt and Saint-Sylvain before taking Estrées-la-Campagne. Lt-Gen Simonds was still intent on seizing the high ground around Points 195 and 206, so ordered 4th Cdn Armd Div to renew its attempts to seize the high ground west of the Caen-Falaise road and then to exploit towards Falaise. The task fell again onto the shoulders of 10th Brigade. That night, the Argyll & Sutherland marched single file up the hill and dug in on Point 195 without arousing the Germans. The next morning, however, the Germans launched a series of counter-attacks which were all beaten off. On 10 August, the Lincoln & Welland moved forward from Saint-Germain-le-Vasson to a spur beside Point 195. The CGG were ordered forward to reinforce Point 195 and then to attack Point 206. While the CO of the CGG was giving his orders on Point 195 for the attack on Point 206, the Germans launched another fierce counter-attack. The attack was of such strength that the attack on Point 206 was temporarily called off; the CGG remained on the position for the rest of the day.

At 10.00 on the morning of 10 August, Lt-Gen Simonds held another O Group. He wanted to restore the lost momentum of the attack. He had at his disposal 3rd Cdn Inf Div which, with the support of 2nd Cdn Armd Bde, was to secure crossings over the Laison River east of Potigny and then push across the river and seize the commanding ridge west of Épaney. 1st Pol Armd Div would then follow behind and advance on Sassy. The first obstacle for 3rd Cdn Inf Div was to clear Quesnay Woods where *Kampfgruppe* Krause was still holed up with many 88mm anti-tank guns. The task was given to 8th Brigade. However, for all practical purposes,

OPERATION TOTALIZE: THE DRIVE TOWARDS FALAISE

Operation TOTALIZE was over; Second Cdn Corps had advanced 9 miles, but the Germans had managed to once again stabilise the front. On the morning of 11 August, Lt-Gen Simonds finalised the situation; he cancelled all planned attacks and issued new orders. The infantry divisions were to relieve the armoured divisions in the line: 3rd Cdn Inf Div on the left and 2nd Cdn Inf Div on the right; 4th Cdn Armd Div was to return to the area of Saint-Sylvain while 1st Pol Armd Div was to patrol forward towards the Laison Valley. Lt-Gen Simonds attended a conference at Gen Montgomery's headquarters later in the afternoon and modified his plan as a consequence. He ordered an infantry brigade from 2nd Cdn Inf Div, supported by an armoured regiment from 2nd Cdn Armd Bde, to cross the Laize River at Bretteville-sur-Laize with the object of seizing the high ground west and south of Falaise. The task was given to 4th Brigade with the *Sherbrookes* in support. The route of advance would pass from Barbery through Moulines towards Clair Tizon. That night, 4th Brigade began to cross the Laize River.

Early on 9 August, the *Sherbrookes* had been put in support of 4th Brigade in a role of observation. Little activity could be seen and the assessment made by the troops was that the front appeared to have jelled. The regiment spent all day on the high ground just north of Caillouet. That evening, the tanks moved back to an area of relative protection and settled down to a good rest. The next day, the squadrons remained in the same position and continued to clean and maintain their vehicles. A Sqn was placed in support of 5th Brigade and returned to the high ground north of Caillouet. However, no activity was noted. On 11 August, the *Sherbrookes* were placed in support of 4th Brigade and ordered to prepare for a new drive south towards Falaise, after crossing the Laize River at Bretteville-sur-Laize.

Appendix 1: The Death of Michael Wittmann

When the Tigers of *s.SS-Pzabt 101* were hit as they approached Saint-Aignan-de-Cramesnil on 8 August 1944, no one knew at the time that one of the German casualties was *SS-Hauptsturmführer* Michael Wittmann. Since then, several hypotheses have been advanced into who delivered the fatal blow to Tiger '007', which he commanded. The list of possible candidates includes:

1. **A rocket from either 2nd BTAF or 8th USAAF**. This idea was the product of German propaganda which wanted to preserve the image that the Tiger tank was impervious to Allied tanks. The possibility that Wittmann's tank was hit by a rocket has been discredited. Neither the Canadian, British nor German sources mention the presence of Typhoons during the battle. No pilot from either of the two air forces laid claim to having destroyed a German Tiger tank in that sector that day. In fact, the After Action Report by 2nd Cdn Armd Bde mentioned that 'because of limited visibility from the objective [probably a reference to the Cramesnil Spur], full use could NOT be made of the air support that was available'. Furthermore, Meyer wrote in his memoirs that 'the feared fighter-bombers were absent'. Therefore, although Typhoons may have been present in the area, they can most likely be ruled out.
2. **A lucky British artillery strike with a 5.5 in round**. The damage visible in the only available photograph of Wittmann's tank does not support this.
3. **A tank or tanks from 1st Pol Armd Div**. They were not yet in the immediate vicinity. In reality, they were moving towards an assembly area east of Saint-Aignan-de-Cramesnil in preparation for a drive south as part of Phase 2 of Operation TOTALIZE. The error may stem from the fact that A Sqn of 1st Northamptonshire Yeomanry (1st Yeomanry) named their tanks after Soviet towns. Tpr Joe Ekins's Firefly tank had been christened as '*Velikye Luki*' which may have given the impression that the tank was Polish.
4. **A tank or tanks from 4th Cdn Armd Div**. Again, they were not in the immediate vicinity. The lead armoured elements of the division were those of the CGG, who were still in the area of Rocquancourt. In fact, the South Sask only reported the town cleared at 12.24.

5. **A Firefly tank from 1st Yeomanry.** In 1985, Les Taylor published an article in the magazine *After the Battle*, which credited Tpr Ekins and 1st Yeomanry with the destruction of Wittmann's Tiger. At the same time as A Sqn of the *Sherbrookes* was establishing itself in a blocking position near the château at Gaumesnil, A Sqn of 1st Yeomanry had established a similar position in an orchard just south of Saint-Aignan-de-Cramesnil. At about 12.20, three Tiger tanks came into view moving north in line. Troop 3 of A Sqn of 1st Yeomanry engaged the Tigers with their Sherman tanks, but they were too far away to have any effect. The squadron commander, Capt T. Boardman, promptly ordered a ceasefire and called up the only Firefly in his sector. When Sgt Gordon's 17-pdr arrived in the orchard, Tpr Ekins, the gunner, could see three Tiger tanks moving across his front at a distance of about 1,200 yards. When they got to a distance of about 800 yards, he shot at the rear tank in the column. At 12.40, he fired twice, hit it and set it ablaze. The other Tiger tanks retaliated and the Firefly was hit by either a round or a falling tree branch. The commander's hatch was hit and the crew commander was injured when the hatch fell on his head. Therefore, the tank moved back and Sgt Gordon got out to walk it off. As he was getting out of the tank, he was hit by shrapnel and had to be replaced by the troop leader, Lieut James, before the Firefly repositioned itself. At 12.47, Tpr Ekins fired at the second tank in the column. He hit it with his first round and the Tiger exploded. In the meantime, the remainder of the squadron had succeeded in immobilising the lead Tiger using 75mm fire and the Firefly destroyed it at 12.52 using two rounds. A remarkable exploit, Tpr Ekins had destroyed three Tiger tanks in about twelve minutes.[10]
6. **Tanks from A Sqn of the Sherbrooke Fusilier Regiment.** The *Sherbrookes* claimed to have destroyed two Tigers during the battle. The lead tank on the west side of the road was commanded by SS-*Hauptsturmführer* Hans Höfflinger, the operations officer of s.SS-Pzabt 101, and it was definitely hit by the *Sherbrookes*. The second tank claimed by A Sqn was located on the east side of the road and could be either Wittmann's or that of *SS-Untersturmführer* Ihrion, the third tank in the echelon formation, which had reportedly been hit by a shell that penetrated the left side of the turret.

The only two hypotheses which should be examined more critically are numbers 5 and 6. 1st Yeomanry claimed to have killed three Tigers and if their war diary is accurate, Wittmann's tank would have had to have been the first tank hit. The reasoning behind this is that from their point of view, 1st Yeomanry should have been able to see four tanks from right to left: Dollinger, Kisters, Wittmann and Ihrion, in that order. The third tank was the first tank hit and that would mean that Wittmann's tank would have been destroyed at 12.40. Höfflinger declared that the advancing tanks started taking heavy fire from anti-tank guns in the woods on the right and Wittmann called over the air 'Achtung! Achtung! Attack from the right! Attack from the right!' As Wittmann was talking on the radio, his transmission was suddenly cut off in mid-sentence. Höfflinger saw that the tank had stopped moving and that the turret was turned towards the right and the main gun was fully depressed. After his own tank was hit, Höfflinger and his crew moved back towards Cintheaux. Höfflinger got into von Westernhagen's tank and, together with Heurich's tank, tried to get to Wittmann's tank. Before the group could get to him, they saw Wittmann's tank explode sending its turret high in the air. He looked at his watch and saw that it was 12.55. If the explosion was the result of a direct hit at that same instance, then 1st Yeomanry couldn't have delivered the blow because their last kill was registered at 12.52. Also plausible is that the lay of the land offered a small depression. If so, then the three tanks visible to Tpr Ekins would most likely have been the echelon formation at 800 yards from his position: Dollinger, Kisters and Ihrion; 1st Yeomanry wouldn't have seen Wittmann's tank from their position and therefore the third tank would have been that of *SS-Untersturmführer* Ihrion.[11]

To add to the confusion, *SS-Hauptsturmführer Doktor* Rabe, the Med O of s.SS-Pzabt 101, who was following 500 metres behind the tanks in a *Kübelwagen*,[12] wrote to Wittmann's widow that he left his vehicle on foot to go to Wittmann's tank. When he got to within 250 to 300 yards of the tank, he suddenly saw the tank explode and the turret fly off. As historian Brian A. Reid, the author of *No Holding Back*, argues: Why did *Doktor* Rabe want to reach Wittmann's tank? Was it to give medical assistance to the crew because the tank had already been hit and disabled before the ammunition exploded? Or was it to get instructions from Wittmann on the tactical situation? Rabe's declaration did not specify his reasons for moving forward. However, it is unlikely that a Med O required instructions on the tactical situation. Therefore, it can be surmised that Rabe may have seen Wittmann's tank take a hit and was moving forward to give medical assistance to the crew. When the radio transmission from Wittmann stopped in mid-sentence, Höfflinger looked and saw that the turret of Wittmann's tank was turned to its right and the main gun was fully depressed. Unfortunately, the exact time that the transmission stopped was not recorded and it was only after this that Höfflinger's tank was hit. The delay between the stop in transmission and the explosion is unknown. The possibility exists that 1st Northamptonshire Yeomanry may have succeeded in getting a lucky shot that took out the Tiger.

Another major factor which comes into debate is that of the distance from A Sqn of 1st Yeomanry to Wittmann's tank. The distance was beyond the killing distance for the Firefly. A Firefly could engage tanks up to 800 yards with lethal accuracy; at 1,000 yards and more it remained lethal but lost its accuracy. Therefore, beyond 800 yards, the chances of knocking out a Tiger tank depended on where the round struck. A round that struck the bottom of the turret could deflect down through the thin roof of the tank and detonate inside the tank. Otherwise, at that distance, the round risked deflecting off the Tiger's superior armour protection without penetrating the tank. Tpr Ekins himself stated that he waited until the tanks were about 800 yards away before firing. It would seem improbable that he would have wasted his first shot on a target over 1,000 yards away when he presumably had three other targets much nearer and which presented a more immediate danger to the British position in Saint-Aignan-de-Cramesnil and La Bruyère. Doctrine dictated that the first target to be hit would be the one closest to your own tank and therefore the greatest risk to you, followed by the target posing the greatest threat to your own defensive positions, and lastly any other target of opportunity. It also goes without saying that the closer the target, the greater the chance of success in knocking it out.

An aerial photo, taken just days after the battle took place, shows the position of Wittmann's tank in conjunction with the blocking position established by A Sqn of the *Sherbrookes*. Maj Radley-Walters set up his tanks in the farm-château complex and punched holes in the stone walls surrounding it to give good fields of observation towards the east and southeast. The direction towards Wittmann's Tiger is slightly northeast of this position. The only visible damage to the tank, as observed on the photograph taken by Serge Varin, was a ragged hole in the left side engine air intake grating above the fuel tank. Monsieur Varin had stated to Monsieur Theffo, an amateur historian from the region, that there were no other perforations in the tank. This just happens to be the corner of the tank pointing directly towards the *Sherbrooke* position.

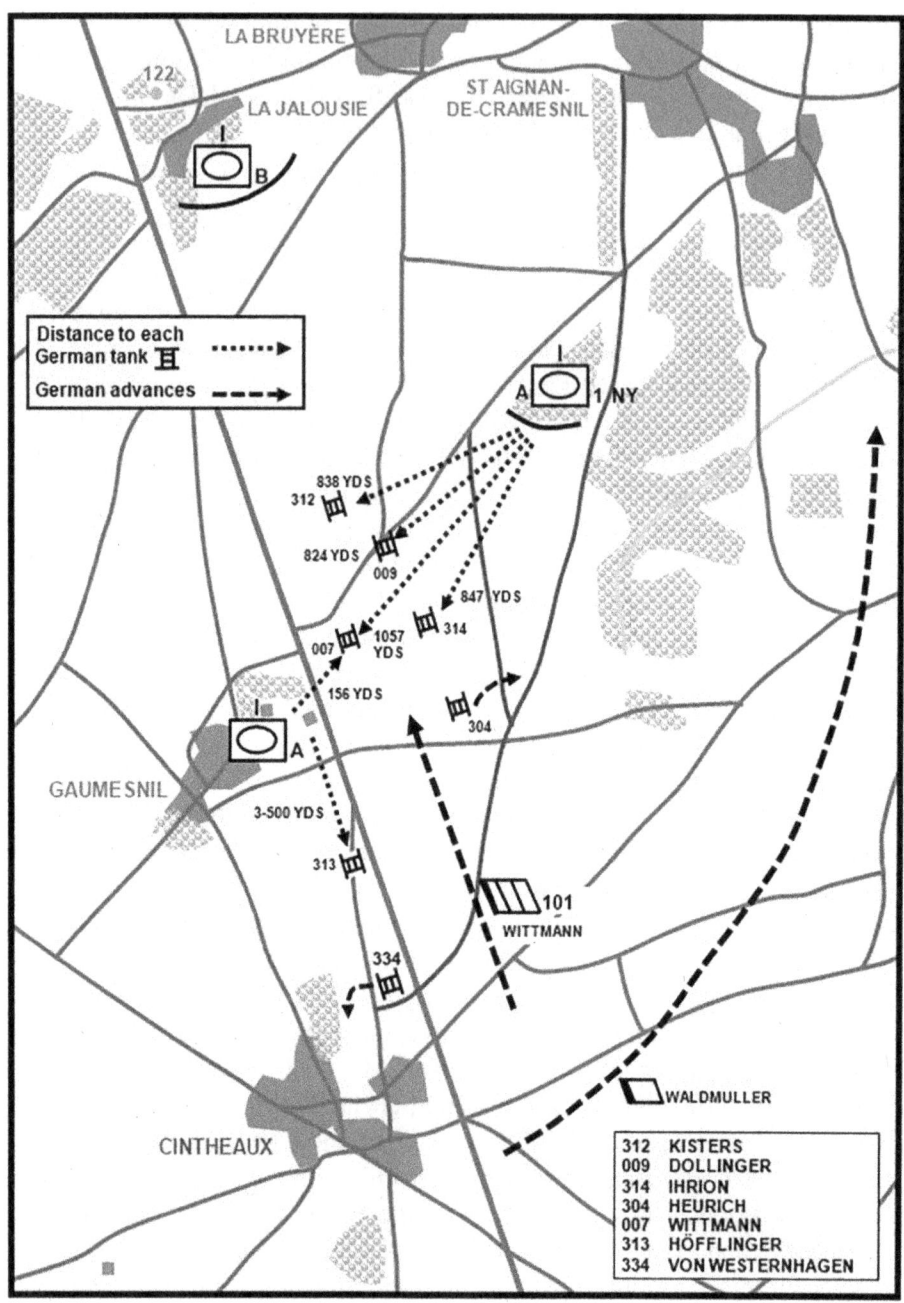

8 August 1944: The German counter-attack led by *SS-Hauptsturmführer* Michael Wittmann (the distance shown to each tank is as measured in *Battlefield Mysteries* 'Michael Wittmann's Last Battle').

OPERATION TOTALIZE: THE DRIVE TOWARDS FALAISE

Historian Norm Christie conducted scientific research on the battle using modern GPS[13] technology for a television episode of the *Battlefield Mysteries* series on the Canadian History Channel. Entitled 'Michael Wittmann's Last Battle', the show established that the distance from 1st Yeomanry to Wittmann's tank was around 1,050 yards, the maximum range of a Firefly, while the other Tigers were only at distances varying from 825 to 850 yards. On the other hand, the *Sherbrooke* tanks were only about 150 yards from Wittmann's tank. He concluded that the most likely unit to have killed Wittmann was A Sqn of the *Sherbrookes*. Historian Rod Michelburgh, in his book *Rare Courage*, quotes then Lieut Gould of A Sqn as stating that the troop leader who got Wittmann was killed four days later on 12 August. That was the day on which Lieut 'Bill' Logan was killed at Barbery.[14]

Although the most likely candidate for the destruction of Wittmann's tank is A Sqn of the *Sherbrookes*, the debate on who killed Michael Wittmann will never find a definitive answer. The reality of any battle can only be told by those who fought it, and it will probably never be told with absolute certainty. Most of its direct participants have long since taken the story with them to their graves. But in the minds of the soldiers of the *Sherbrookes* at the time, a Tiger was a Tiger and a Tiger was a threat. Therefore, one less Tiger was a good thing, no matter who did the shooting.

Chapter 7

Operation TRACTABLE
Closing the Falaise Gap

Operation TOTALIZE had succeeded in breaching the first two German lines of defence. The night move had achieved surprise and resulted in fewer casualties than Operation SPRING or Operation GOODWOOD and the attack had advanced almost 10 miles towards Falaise. The concept of an armoured personnel carrier to protect the infantry had proven its worth. However, Phase 2 of the operation had failed to produce the decisive breakout that Gen Montgomery had hoped for. The Germans still held the high ground north of the Laison River. The German positions had been breached but Second Cdn Corps had halted its advance in order to adhere to the air bombardment timetable set up for the beginning of Phase 2. *SS-Brigadeführer* Meyer recognised that a strong armoured thrust on the morning of 8 August would have taken the Allies all the way to Falaise. Instead, the halt gave time for him to strengthen his defences and stop the Canadian attack when Phase 2 was launched. From his perspective, Meyer laid the blame for the failure of the operation on the leadership of the two armoured divisions. To a certain degree, Lt-Gen Simonds also laid the blame on the tank units. For both division commanders, this was their baptism of fire and their inexperience was apparent. Both used their tanks piecemeal and with indecision. On 11 August, he berated his armoured regiment commanders on their indecisiveness and lack of aggressiveness. He demanded more drive then had been shown in recent operations. He stressed the necessity for pushing the armour to its very limits of endurance. The armour had to also be able to move at night in darkness and he would accept no excuse for failure. The final objective had not been taken and a new effort would have to be made. Regardless of the reason for the operation's failure, Second Cdn Corps now needed time to reorganise itself and prepare for another attack towards Falaise.

Even before Operation TOTALIZE had begun, Gen Montgomery had issued a new directive on 6 August for the next phase of the battle. His aim

OPERATION TRACTABLE: CLOSING THE FALAISE GAP

was to destroy the German forces in that part of France. To accomplish this, he planned to use the Allied forces to drive the enemy up against the Seine River. The left, or northern, flank was to pivot east while the right, or southern, flank was to push towards Paris. The failure of the German Operation LÜTTICH changed everything and, over the next two days, the plan was modified to exploit the situation. On 10 August, Gen Bradley ordered Lt-Gen Patton's Third US Army to spearhead north from the Le Mans area through Alençon to Argentan with a view to making contact with First Cdn Army driving south towards Falaise. Gen Eisenhower was at Gen Bradley's HQ at the time and he concurred with the order.

That same afternoon, Gen Montgomery instructed Lt-Gen Crerar to swing east around Falaise and then south towards Argentan. The next day, he confirmed the plan already hatched by Gen Bradley to attempt a pincer movement. The German salient that had developed because of Operation LÜTTICH contained 5.Pzarmee, 7.Armee and *Panzergruppe* Eberbach.[1] Gen Montgomery's aim was to trap and destroy the German forces in the salient. First Cdn Army was to drive south and capture Falaise, while Third US Army was to take Argentan and then drive north to meet up with the Canadians. While planning got underway, Second Cdn Corps was ordered to undertake a subsidiary operation on the western flank of the Laize River using a brigade and an armoured regiment. The intention was to threaten the enemy's position astride the Caen-Falaise road and thereby force him to weaken it before the main operation went in.

On 11 August, the evacuation of the German forces in the Falaise salient began. I.SS-Pzkorps was still the main enemy force in front of the Canadian army. I.SS-Pzkorps had to defend Falaise at all costs as the town was the only route with a good road for the encircled German forces to use. Therefore, it was given the task of fighting a rearguard action in order to slow down the Canadians and to keep open the Falaise Gap; 12.SS-Pzdiv had lost 414 men during Operation TOTALIZE, and most of its remaining men were centered about *Kampfgruppe* Krause. It was down to only thirty-five tanks – seventeen *Pzkpfw IV* and eighteen Panthers – but it could count on an additional seventeen Tiger tanks from s.SS-Pzabt 101 and s.SS-Pzabt 102 together. Meyer would incorporate the remaining elements of *Kampfgruppe* Waldmüller with those of *Kampfgruppe* Krause on 13 August. This would give a fighting force of about 20 AFV, an armoured recce section, 1 platoon of *Panzergrenadiers*, 300 dismounted *Panzergrenadiers*, 13 anti-tank guns and 4 batteries of field artillery. I.SS-Pzkorps was established on two lines of defence: the first consisted of a light screen of infantry with a second line 2 miles behind, the second line was made up of support points backed up by the *Hitlerjugend* and 88mm anti-tank guns. To facilitate the rearguard action, extensive use was made of mines and booby-traps, which included everything from souvenirs, buildings and even the corpses of dead Canadian soldiers.

Second Cdn Corps HQ started preparing its plan for the next operation on 11 August under the nickname Operation TULLULAH. The front line was still some 10 miles from Falaise and it faced a strong enemy 'gun screen' about 1,000 to 1,500 yards north of the Laison. The banks of the river were very marshy, thereby making the river a good anti-tank obstacle. The Laison River was held by three battalions of *Flak* troops backed by the two *Kampfgruppen* from the 12.SS-Pzdiv. Meyer established a new defensive line on the heights before Potigny, backed by the Laison River. *Kampfgruppe* Krause fell back to Point 195 while *Kampfgruppe* Waldmüller set up on a line from Point 134 to Point 140 to Mazières. The *Panzers* assembled in Quesnay Woods and were joined by *Kampfgruppe* Wünsche with its thirty-nine Panthers. For its part, Second Cdn Corps could count on 480 tanks, 1,500 vehicles of all sorts and over 12,000 men. In his estimate of the situation, Lt-Gen Simonds concluded that since his divisions had been unable to seize the position, the assault would require a corps attack. In preparation for the main effort, 2nd Cdn Inf Div was instructed to task a brigade, supported by an armoured regiment from 2nd Cdn Armd Bde, with a 'reconnaissance in force' on the western side of the Laize River. This feint was to be executed immediately that night. Its objective would be the capture of Clair Tizon.

On 12 August, Lt-Gen Simonds held a conference with his division commanders where he outlined his plan, which was basically the same as Operation TOTALIZE with the exception that it would be a day attack. First Cdn Army was to push southwards and seize the cliffs that dominated Falaise in order to prevent the enemy from escaping by road either through or near to Falaise. Second Brit Corps was to capture Falaise, while the Canadians were to establish themselves on the high ground north and east of Falaise. When Second Brit. Army had captured Falaise, Second Cdn Corps was to exploit in a south-easterly direction and either capture or dominate Trun; Lt-Gen Simonds rapidly modified his original plan, which now became known as Operation TRACTABLE, and issued his formal orders later in the day. The intention was to dominate and control the roads running east out of Falaise in order to prevent the further escape of German troops caught in the salient. Second Cdn Corps would attack with two divisions up. 3rd Cdn Inf Div would advance on the right with 2nd Cdn

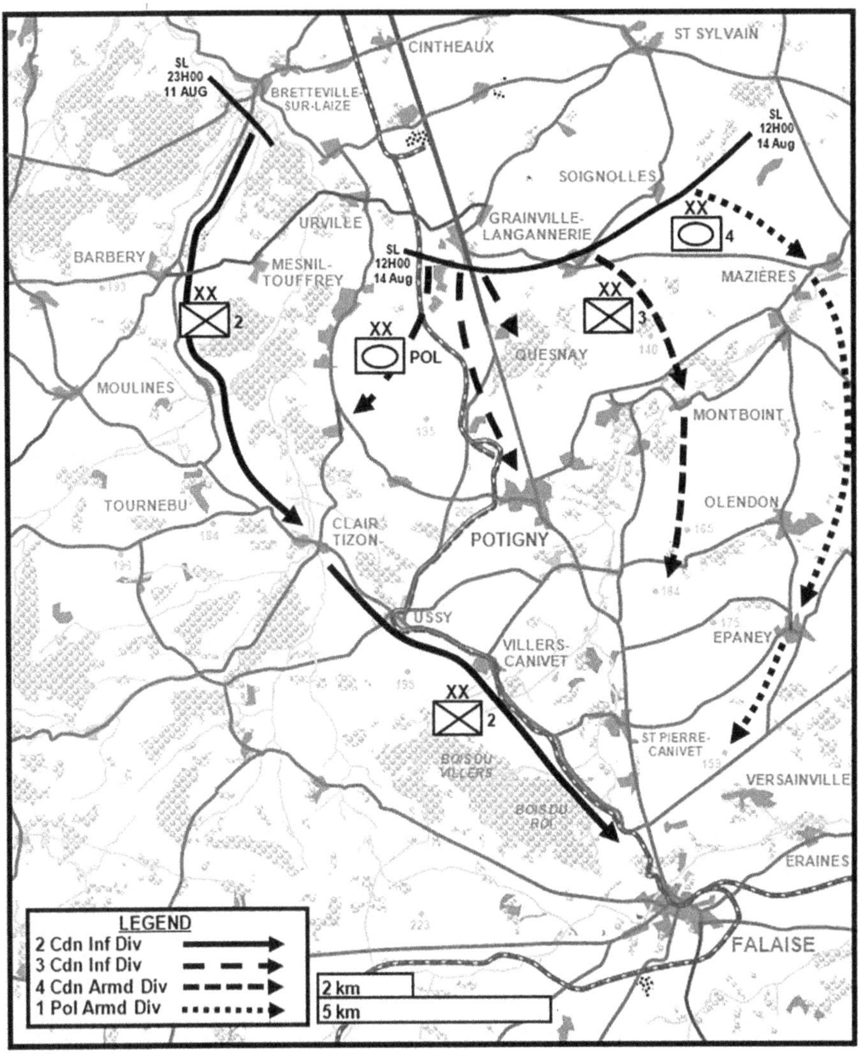

OPERATION TRACTABLE: CLOSING THE FALAISE GAP

Operation TRACTABLE – The Second Canadian Corps plan.

Armd Bde, less the *Sherbrookes*, under command. On the left, 4th Cdn Armd Div would advance with 8th Brigade under command. 2nd Cdn Inf Div and the *Sherbrookes* were to continue their efforts to reach Falaise from the northwest. H-Hour was set for 12.00 on 14 August. The planned start line was the road connecting Cauvicourt and Saint-Sylvain.

★ ★ ★ ★ ★

Maj-Gen Foulkes gave the task of the reconnaissance in force to 4th Brigade, and the *Sherbrookes* were placed in support of the brigade. The main objective was to capture Clair Tizon and establish crossings over the Laize River at that point. The brigade's plan was to maintain momentum once the start line was crossed by leap-frogging the battalions, each supported by a squadron of tanks. The RHLI was to lead off and capture Barbery and the high ground beyond the village. The R Regt C would take the second bound to Moulines, while the Essex Scottish would then seize and hold Point 184. The RHLI would then retake the lead and capture Clair Tizon and the R Regt C would pass through them and take Ussy. The move would begin in the early hours that night with the crossing of the Laize River at Bretteville-sur-Laize. Unfortunately, the terrain west of the Laize was hilly and dotted with many small woods; ground ideally suited to the 'shoot and scoot' tactics of a rearguard force. This tactic consisted of a small, but well-sited, force of tanks and mounted infantry engaging the advancing Canadian troops, thereby forcing them to deploy and prepare an attack on the enemy position. At the last minute, the defenders would move back rapidly to a new, possibly already prepared, position. Meanwhile, the attackers would have to reorganise before resuming their advance. All of this took time.

Since the end of Operation TOTALIZE, the *Sherbrookes* had spent most of their time cleaning and maintaining all of their tanks and vehicles in an intense effort to bring the regiment back to full fighting strength. At 18.06, the *Sherbrookes* were put on one hour's notice to move in support of 2nd Cdn Inf Div, and at 20.30, the regiment was officially placed under command of the division. When he received orders for the regiment to support 4th Brigade, Lt-Col Gordon decided to place A Sqn in support of the RHLI in the vanguard, B Sqn in support of the R Regt C, while C Sqn was tasked with supporting the Essex Scottish. Shortly after midnight, A Sqn moved off for the night approach through Bretteville-sur-Laize towards Barbery. The move through the town was extremely difficult for the tanks owing to cratering, but by 02.40 the RHLI had crossed the Laize River and were pushing south. Point 137 was reached at 03.50 without incident. The RHLI advance continued towards Barbery, but machine-gun fire from outposts set up in the area of Favrolle held up the battalion. The resistance pocket was eliminated and Barbery was cleared by first light. A Sqn reported at 04.36 that it was at Barbery plus 400 yards.

The Germans had set up a defensive position with an estimated two companies of *Panzergrenadiers* in the apple orchards that surrounded Cingal. The position dominated the ground and the Germans had registered

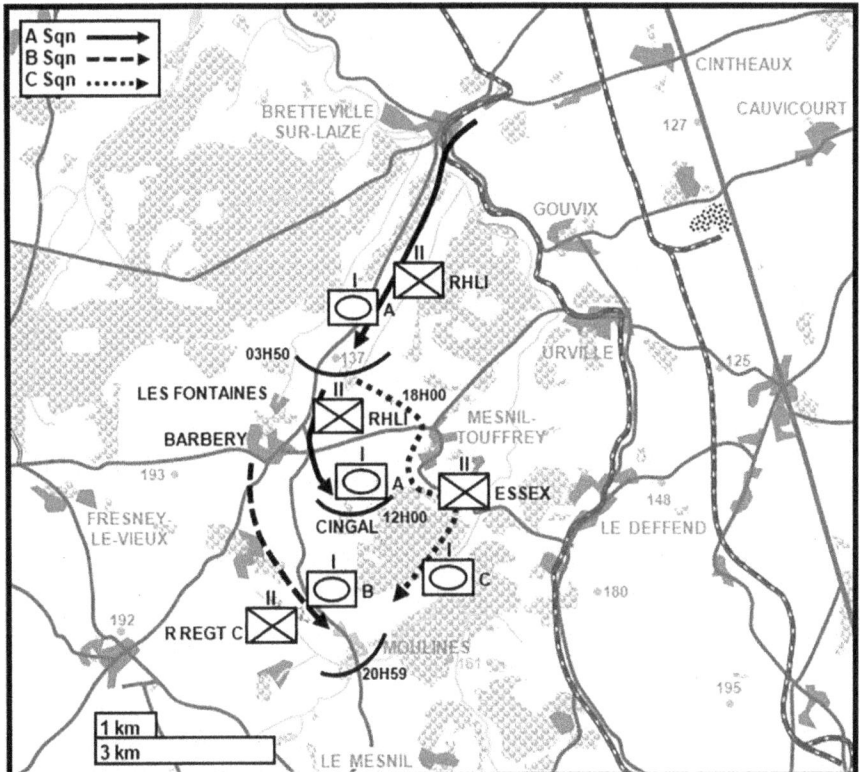

11-12 August 1944: Barbery.

all their artillery, mortars and *Nebelwerfers* on the obvious approach routes. At 07.30, the RHLI resumed their advance south from Barbery. The infantry advanced in the tall unharvested grain in an effort to avoid the mines that had been left on the roads. When the advance had gone a couple of hundred yards, the Germans suddenly opened up on the two lead companies from the area of Cingal where the woods closed in on both sides of the road. *Panzergrenadiers* then rose up and attacked the helpless Canadians. The advance bogged down and the RHLI dug in. The A Sqn tanks moved up to support the RHLI but soon four Tigers and several Panthers emerged out of the woods. The Tigers took on the A Sqn tanks while the Panthers concentrated their fire on the infantry who were madly trying to dig in.

The battle raged all morning. Maj Radley-Walters was called back for an O Group so Capt Kenneth Young Dick took over command of the squadron. He got the tanks into fire positions. Cpl Bryant put his tank about 30 yards behind Capt Dick's tank. Suddenly, two Panthers appeared out of nowhere just 200 yards from them. The Panthers began to machine-gun the RHLI before they could take cover. Capt Dick's tank was suddenly hit by an anti-tank gun and knocked out. His driver, Tpr Arthur McLean, was wounded and his co-driver was killed. Cpl Bryant's tank was hit as it advanced across an open field towards a wood for protection, an 88mm gun hidden in a hedgerow hit it in the engine. The tank succeeded in making it to the woods but was cut off from the rest of the squadron for a few days; Cpl Bryant was too far away and couldn't move his tank. Realising the situation, Tpr Fidler decided to get out and offer assistance. As he was preparing to leave, Cpl Leonard told him to be careful, and Tpr Fidler replied, 'Gord, if your time has come, you go', and left with the first aid kit. Both of Tpr McLean's legs had been mangled by the 88mm round. Nonetheless, he had succeeded, through sheer strength alone, to pull himself out of the tank and onto the turret. Tpr Fidler succeeded in getting him off the tank, carried him about 30–40ft away from the tank and began to give him first aid, while all the time under machine-gun fire. Two HE rounds landed almost together – the first hit a branch of a tree and the branch fell on Capt Dick's head, he would require evacuation. The other landed right where Tpr Fidler was taking care of Tpr McLean. Tpr Fidler was killed instantly but Tpr McLean was spared. He was evacuated to an aid station but would later die of his wounds. Lieut Logan was also wounded when his tank was knocked out; trying to get out of his tank, he fell back in before finally making it out and flopping to the ground. He was evacuated but unfortunately died on the way back to the casualty clearing station. Sgt Milton E. Thwaites's tank was also hit and he was slightly wounded. He suffered a very narrow escape when a burst of machine-gun fire grazed his throat. When it was realised that the Germans had moved out of Cingal, the RHLI moved forward and occupied the area. At last light, the German tanks moved in for the *coup de grâce*. After a final sweep with their machine-guns, they left the battlefield of smoking hulks, dead and wounded. The RHLI suffered 120 casualties. A Sqn had succeeded in knocking out one Tiger, but for a loss of four Shermans. That night, the squadron returned to Point 137 to refuel and replenish its ammunition.

While this battle was taking place, the R Regt C was ordered to take over the lead and capture Moulines. The battalion moved around the RHLI and fought its way forward across 2 miles of wheat fields studded with woods. Mortar-fire, shell-fire and sniping caused heavy casualties. Sgt Taylor's tank, the lead Sherman tank from B Sqn, was knocked out and the remainder of the troop was forced back to find cover. The gunner was killed while having never fired a shot in action. Sgt Taylor was severely injured and the remaining crew members, L/Cpl Raymond W.W. Tanner, Tpr Roy V. Harris and Tpr Laurie G. McClure, were forced to stay under the tank for six hours while waiting for the other squadron tanks to get to them. That morning, Maj-Gen Foulkes was told that 4th Brigade's advance was now the corps' main effort. The 'reconnaissance in force' had now become a division operation. At 18.00, the R Regt C launched its attack on Moulines with B Sqn in support. At 20.59, B Sqn reported that the town had been taken. The R Regt C had suffered ten killed and fifty-seven wounded.

C Sqn and the Essex Scottish were last in the order of march. By noon, they had advanced as far as the crossroads near Point 137. The infantry remained there while C Sqn moved off through Barbery to the high ground southeast of the town. It remained in that position all day while waiting for the forward elements to advance. At 18.00, the squadron withdrew from the position and returned to Point 137. On arriving, it was immediately dispatched to support the Essex Scottish, which was ordered to make a left flanking movement on Moulines through extremely heavy brush in very low ground. 2 Troop, composed of only two tanks, was lost, but both crews were safely evacuated; 1 Troop was ordered to continue the advance with the infantry while the remainder of the squadron, which consisted of only the three tanks from the Sqn HQ, returned to spend the night at the brigade strong point; 5th Brigade had followed behind and made a long, dry and dusty march to Mesnil Touffray.

The regiment had lost a large number of tanks in the day's battle. At 03.20 on 13 August, 2nd Cdn Armd Bde HQ advised the *Sherbrookes* that they would receive eight tanks at 07.30 the next morning. These, however, arrived at 10.15 but without crew commanders. Lt-Col Gordon reorganised the regiment into two columns of ten tanks each. Two troops of A Sqn formed the first column under the command of Capt Belton and it was attached to the R Regt C. The second column was based on C Sqn and was placed in support of the Calgary Highlanders. At 01.45 that morning, 5th Brigade had begun to move south. The Calgary Highlanders led the way, followed closely by the R de Mais. The formation advanced on the west bank of the Laize River towards Claire Tizon by way of Moulines, Le Becquet and Les Houles. The trails were no wider than a carrier with high banks on either side. The Germans had set up roadblocks and the Calgary Highlanders were victim to occasional shell-fire. Despite the resistance, the battalion pushed forward through the woods along the river valley and reached and cleared Le Mesnil by 05.45. Approximately seventy-five prisoners were taken. The fighting was not fierce despite well-placed machine-guns and infantry anti-tank weapons. There, the battalion was ordered to dig in while 4th Brigade captured Point 184. Around 100 German soldiers poured in to surrender. As the prisoners passed into the prisoner cage, it looked like a queue going up to the ticket box at a theatre with the Int O acting as the doorman. They all had an Allied leaflet entitled 'Safe Conduct' that assured them good treatment if taken prisoner. All were from *271.Infanterie-Division* (271.Inf-Div).

R Regt C with A Sqn was given the task of securing Point 184 just south of Tournebu. The column advanced against little opposition until it reached Point 151. This crossroads had been reported as clear, but on arrival there the column met with stiff opposition. It was engaged by well-hidden German machine-guns, and mortar- and shell-fire, which clearly had excellent observation. Lieut Haggitt Garth Mulock Colbeck's tank was knocked out by an 88mm anti-tank gun. He and two other crew members were wounded and had to be evacuated. The other tanks were forced to move back and look for cover. Even though the tanks managed to get in some good shooting against the infantry, the attack faltered. At 13.00, another attack was launched, during which Lieut Arthur J. Archibald's tank was hit and he was wounded. With the help of artillery support, the attack continued and the intermediate objective, the crossroads east of Tournebu,

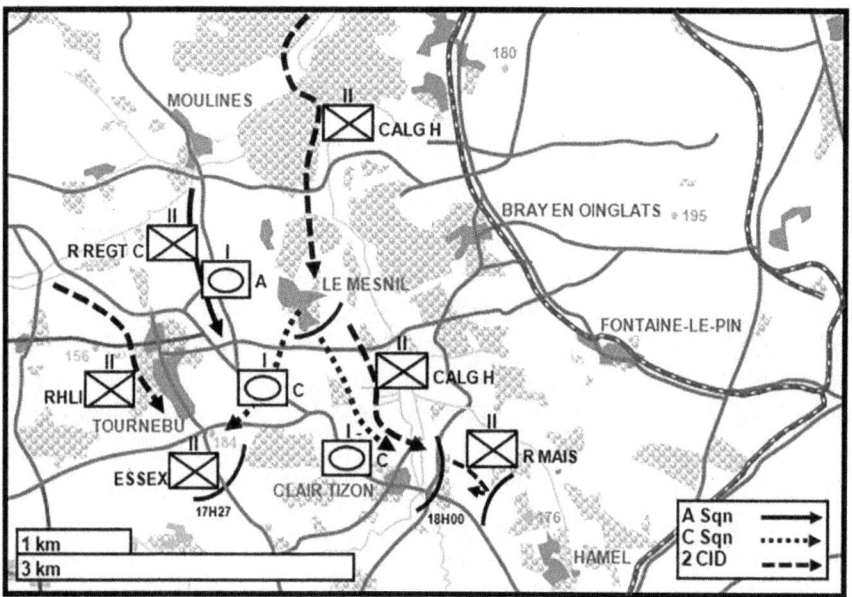

13 August 1944: Clair Tizon.

was reached and consolidated. At 16.00, the RHLI advanced on the right flank around the R Regt C. The battalion was moving via Le Becquet and Le Mesnil with C Coy and D Coy forward when it came under 88mm shellfire. The battalion was ordered to halt its advance and return via Le Mesnil and Point 151 to capture Tournebu. An enemy withdrawal was believed to be taking place but it was unknown if the enemy still held the village or not. The battalion moved off at 18.30 and found the town occupied by forty Germans who offered no resistance. The town was cleared in less than an hour and the Canadians found twelve 81mm mortars with a large supply of bombs, one Renault tank and dozens of machine-guns.

1 Troop of C Sqn had returned to the squadron harbour at 08.00 from the night move with the Essex Scottish. At about the same time, the squadron, which now included a composite group of tanks, moved off. The squadron moved forward to the area of Le Mesnil to support the drive by the Calgary Highlanders towards Clair Tizon. The village consisted of a few stone farmhouses lying mostly on the north side of a narrow east-west blacktop road. Located in a valley with high ground to both the east and the west, the Laize River flowed through the town, irrigating the orchards and farmlands that surrounded the small hamlet. At 14.32, orders were received for C Sqn to support the Essex Scottish with their task of capturing the area of Point 184. Therefore, half the squadron stayed in position to support the Calgary Highlanders while the remainder of the squadron joined up with the Essex Scottish. At 16.00, the squadron reported enemy anti-tank defences and infantry holding the high ground. The advance slowed. Finally, at 17.27, Point 184 was taken. One German officer and over one hundred other ranks from 89.Inf-Div were taken prisoner.

At 14.00, the Calgary Highlanders resumed their advance. They kept to the river valley and advanced by leap-frogging the companies. Each company held firm after each move while the next company moved forward. Progress was slow. In an orchard just south of Le Mesnil, Cpl Eric M. Hammond's tank was knocked out by an 88mm anti-tank gun firing from an open flank. Friendly artillery was called down on the position and the gun was destroyed. By mid-afternoon, one of the troops had reached Clair Tizon. At 18.00, the Calgary Highlanders, supported by artillery, crossed the narrow, shallow Laize River and established a small bridgehead on the east bank. A Coy and B Coy then crossed the river while C Coy and D Coy took up positions on the west bank. A subsequent shelling, however, forced the tanks to withdraw from Clair Tizon, leaving two knocked-out tanks. During the evening, the R de Mais, now composed of only two companies, tried to expand the bridgehead by seizing Point 176 above the village. The Germans held the commanding heights east of the river and repelled the attack. 271.Inf-Div launched a counter-attack with the support of Tiger tanks. Although the German attack was beaten off, the R de Mais was forced back across the Laize River with heavy losses. 271.Inf-Div was ordered to withdraw during the night to the Martainville-Combray line south of route D6. With the fall of Claire Tizon, the German defensive lines across the Caen-Falaise road were also threatened. The *Sherbrookes* had faced heavy fighting throughout the day and suffered numerous tank losses. At last light, both A Sqn and C Sqn moved back to refuel and replenish their ammunition at the regimental harbour just north of Le Mesnil. A Sqn had received some of the new tanks that morning, but C Sqn received some only that evening. Both squadrons were brought up to about ten tanks each.

During the early hours of the morning of 14 August, Brig Young, the commander of 6th Brigade, ordered each of his battalions to seize a new bridgehead over the Laize River. At 04.00, the battalions began to wade across the river behind a creeping artillery barrage. The Camerons were ordered to advance on the right flank and to take La Cressonnière. The enemy offered only token resistance up to the Laize River crossing, but it strengthened as the battalion pushed on towards its objective. At 09.10, the objective was taken and many prisoners of Russian and Polish origin, mostly deserters who gave themselves up at the first opportunity, were taken. In the centre, the South Sask made for the high ground southeast of Clair Tizon, Point 176, on which La Chesnaie stood. The FMR, for their part, was down to two under-strength companies. They were directed to seize a wood and orchard to the north of the South Sask objective. Unfortunately, the *Sherbrooke* tanks could not follow; two burnt-out Sherman tanks, which had been knocked out the day before in support of the Calgary Highlanders attack on Clair Tizon, blocked the bridge. An alternative crossing had to be found first.

A ford was finally identified to the north of the town and the regiment started to cross at 06.43. A Sqn led the way and moved forward to take up a position on Point 176 in support of the South Sask. As the squadron moved up, Maj Radley-Walters spotted three German tanks on his right – two Panthers and a *Jagdpanzer*. His gunner fired and put four rounds into the first Panther before it brewed up. He now turned his gun onto the second Panther and also set it on fire. Maj Radley-Walters moved his tank up towards the second Panther with the intention of using it as a shield. When he got to within 50 yards, the Panther suddenly came back to life. It fired and quickly put four rounds into the Sherman, causing it to brew

OPERATION TRACTABLE: CLOSING THE FALAISE GAP

up. The crew jumped out among a whole section of German infantry in a hedgerow. Both sides were equally surprised and refrained from shooting. Maj Radley-Walters and his crew ran back about 100 yards and flopped down. When the German infantry opened up with gun fire, they crawled away and, on the way back, came upon a 17-pdr anti-tank gun. The crew had been killed but Maj Radley-Walters managed to get it into action with the help of a soldier from the South Sask. With the soldier's assistance, he got off five rounds and finally took out the second Panther tank.

With the tanks of the *Sherbrookes* finally across the river, the Camerons and the South Sask moved onto their objectives with their help. At 07.43, the South Sask reported their objectives seized. Unfortunately, the FMR went astray in the dark and failed to take their objectives at daylight – they were rescued by some *Sherbrooke* tanks and brought back to the river. On reaching their objectives, both the Camerons and the South Sask deployed and started to dig-in in anticipation of the inevitable German counter-attack. *Kampfgruppe* Krause, composed of half a battalion of infantry from SS-Pzgren-Rgt 26, a few tanks and SP guns, some armoured cars and mortars, attacked in the early afternoon; 6th Brigade easily repelled the attack until it was ordered to withdraw its forward companies, now less than a mile from Ussy – an identified target for bombers on the launch of Phase 1 of Operation TRACTABLE. At 15.00, the FMR withdrew back over the river to reorganise.

The tanks of the *Sherbrookes* remained in their positions all day. Between 15.00 and 16.00, RAF bomber formations bombed the river valley immediately to their front. Target markers were seen to be dropped behind C Sqn's location so yellow smoke was used to mark their position as friendly. Unfortunately, the squadron and the South Sask took a hit. Two 1,000-lb bombs were dropped on the tanks: one behind and one directly in front of their position. No casualties were taken and the tanks were spared. Unfortunately, the South Sask was hit harder, suffering over 100 casualties. B Sqn also got hit by the Lancaster and Halifax bombers. A bomb dropped short and was a near miss for the tank 'Bomb'. It was shaken by the blast but suffered only a mechanical failure. The terrain was now filled with bomb craters 20–30ft deep and 30–40ft across. The squadron moved back to Point 184, the high ground immediately west of Clair Tizon, to refuel and rest. A Sqn followed under heavy mortar fire.

During the morning of 14 August, the men and vehicles of the Second Cdn Corps moved up towards the start line for Operation TRACTABLE. A couple of minutes after 11.40, radio silence was broken with the order

'Move now!' The leading armoured brigades began to roll forward towards the start line. At 11.55, the artillery began to lay tremendous smoke screens to mask the attack, and Operation TRACTABLE began at noon, as per orders. The initial objectives for both divisions were to seize bridgeheads over the Laison River, then seize the ridge due south of the river. During the day, Gen Montgomery once again modified his plan. Lt-Gen Crerar was told that it would be up to the First Cdn Army to take Falaise, not Second Brit Army as originally planned. He was instructed to do it as quickly as possible but without interfering with the larger task of driving southeast to capture Trun, and of linking up with Lt-Gen Patton's forces coming up from the south.

During the night of 14–15 August, 6th Brigade continued its advance southeast from the bridgehead east of the Laize River towards Ussy and Villers-Canivet; 4th Brigade and 5th Brigade took over from 1st Pol Armd

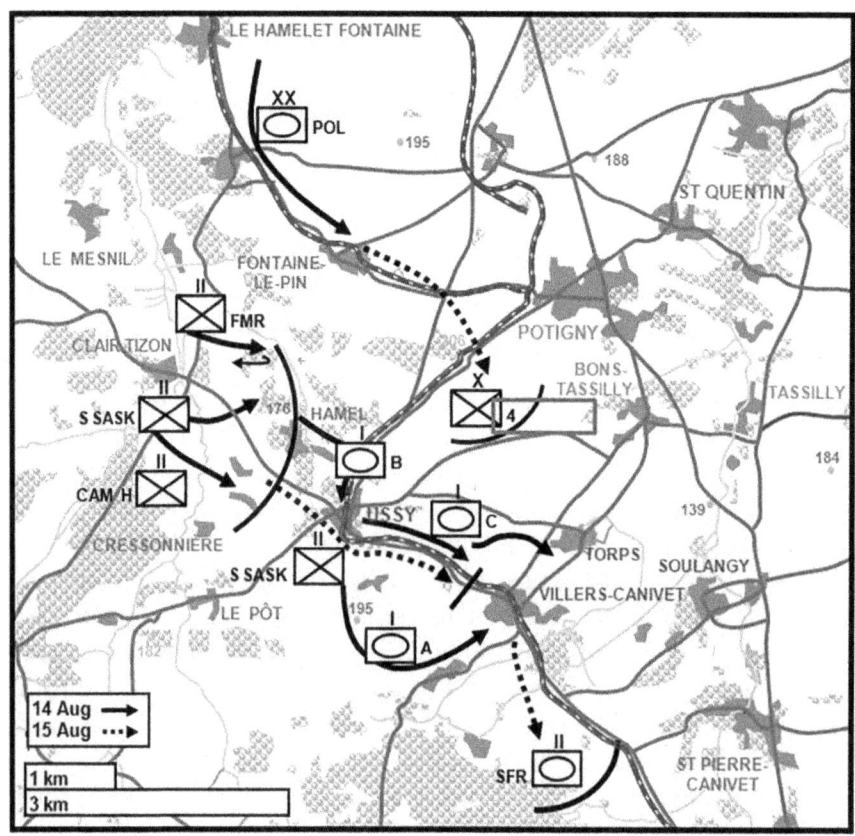

14-15 August 1944: Villers-Canivet.

Div, which proceeded to take over the left flank of Second Cdn Corps in a push towards Chambois. The night was dark and rainy and radio communications were bad; 4th Brigade's advance was difficult and the rain had washed the marking off the maps of the R Regt C, who subsequently got lost. By the next morning however, all three battalions of the brigade were on the high ground west of the town. On 15 August, Lt-Gen Crerar informed Lt-Gen Simonds that the objective for Second Cdn Corps had been changed and that, as soon as Falaise was taken and handed over to a Canadian infantry division, the two armoured divisions were to veer east and seize Trun.

At first light, the tanks of the *Sherbrookes* moved up in support of 6th Brigade's advance. C Sqn moved back to the same position where it had been bombed the previous day and stayed there until about 15.00. A Sqn moved stealthily back to Point 176 and took up defensive positions. The morning passed without incident. It seemed as if the Germans had withdrawn from the area, but in fact, the previous day's aerial bombing had hit the positions of *85.Infanterie-Division* (85.Inf-Div) hard and had broken the backbone of the German defence. With the Laison River breached, I.SS-Pzkorps requested permission to withdraw to the 5.Pzarmee sector. The request was denied. Instead, they were ordered to hold the line at Soulangy at all costs; Hitler would order another counter-attack to divide the Allied armies on 15 August.

At 12.40, B Sqn was teamed up with the South Sask to take Ussy through Hamel. Little opposition was met and at 16.22 B Sqn reported the village cleared. At 15.00, news was received that the Germans were using the road northeast of Villers-Canivet as an escape route. C Sqn was ordered forward through Ussy towards the village; no resistance was encountered except for a minefield on the approaches. A Sqn then swung out to the right and entered the village from the southwest. It pushed through the village and took up a position to the southeast. C Sqn took up positions to block the escape route until ordered to take up defensive positions in the same area as A Sqn at around 20.00. By 21.44, all the *Sherbrooke* tanks were in the same location to refuel and rearm.

Falaise was held by approximately sixty soldiers from 12.SS-Pzdiv supported by two Tiger tanks. Aircraft of RAF Bomber Command had attacked Falaise on 12–13 August with the view of blocking the German escape routes through the town. The town had also been subjected to harassing fire from Canadian medium artillery. The destruction was appalling. In some parts, it was difficult to tell where streets had run; it was little more than a shambles. Surprisingly, the castle where William the Conqueror was born sustained little damage and his statue in the square below was untouched. The task of taking the town was left to 4th Brigade; C Sqn was to move forward to dominate the approaches from the high ground immediately west of the main entrance to the historic city. The South Sask, with the tanks of A Sqn in support, was to advance from the north and clear the northern main road going east-west through the town. The Camerons with the support of B Sqn were to pass around the Bois du Roi and enter the town from the west and clear the southern main east-west road through the town. From the high ground, C Sqn would be in a position to support both battalions as they made their assault and to repulse any counter-attack by tanks.

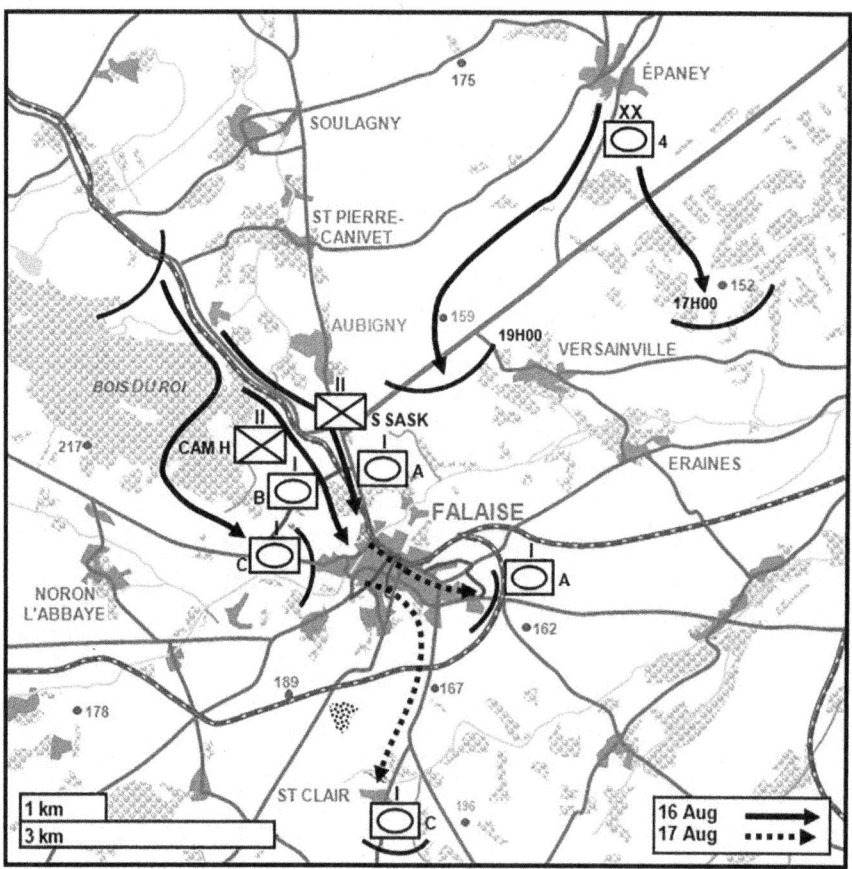

16-17 August 1944: Falaise.

OPERATION TRACTABLE: CLOSING THE FALAISE GAP

C Sqn moved down the Villers-Canivet-Falaise road and then cut southwest through the Bois du Roi. Coming out of the wood, the squadron moved into a position on the high ground overlooking the southern entrance to the historic town. The SHQ and a troop took up defensive positions on the high spur to assist the infantry with direct fire on suspected enemy positions. A Sqn moved behind C Sqn and then advanced on the northern approach with the South Sask. B Sqn advanced behind A Sqn on the south side of the Villers-Canivet-Falaise road with the Camerons. A Sqn was composed of two troops and the SHQ. It advanced down the main road and then into woods to the west of the main road. Just beyond the woods were the gates to the old city. This was the only way into the town from the north because of a moat on either side of the road and the very high cliffs to the west which gave the town its name. At 16.00, the attack went in. As the A Sqn tanks advanced, they came under fire from a German anti-tank gun positioned right at the entrance to the city. Two Sherman tanks were reported knocked out at 16.10; Lieut Williams's tank was knocked out just before reaching the river valley, but the crew escaped without injury. A little shaken, Lieut Williams sat down under a tree; when asked by Maj Radley-Walters what had happened, he reported that he didn't know. Maj Radley-Walters set off on foot down the road to see what the infantry were doing; Lieut Williams thought he should have someone to give him protection and so followed him. They spotted the anti-tank gun and returned to the tanks to direct their fire. Lieut Williams went back to retrieve his map case from the tree under which he had been sitting – but the tree had disintegrated. It had been destroyed by shell-fire, and had he stayed there instead of following his squadron commander, he would most likely have been killed in the explosion.

All the while, mortar and artillery fire came down on the infantry. The advance came to a standstill and the lead companies of the battalion hesitated. The other half of C Sqn moved down the spur in an attempt to support A Sqn. The craters caused by the RAF bombardment blocked many of the approaches to the main entrance and made movement difficult. Two tanks were knocked out. Lt-Col Frederick Alexander Clift, the CO of the South Sask, seeing that the battalion's momentum would be lost, moved forward through his two lead companies and, firing his own rifle, killed a couple of the anti-tank gun crew. Seeing such a vivid display of personal heroism, the rest of the battalion stood as one and started to move forward without waiting for orders. The South Sask crossed the Ante River, entered the town and established themselves in buildings along the east bank of the river. Lieut William Rex Martin then led his troop into town, but unfortunately his tank hit a mine on the bridge and was knocked out. Both Lieut Williams and Lieut Martin transferred to other tanks and entered the town. At 16.30, A Sqn reported that they were in Falaise and had destroyed two Panther tanks. The Camerons advance was greatly hindered by huge craters that prevented the tanks of B Sqn getting forward. B Sqn was down to four Shermans and one Firefly. Early in its advance, it suddenly came under AP and HE fire. Capt Norman Henry Welsh, the squadron 2i/c, set off on a foot recce with the FOO in search of the three SP guns and two Panthers suspected to be in the area. Both of them could be seen crawling over the crest of the hill towards the enemy position. In fact, the FOO captain actually succeeded in getting to within 75 yards of the German position. When they got back, the FOO got Cpl Hubert Birch's Firefly to move across the open ground to a hull-down position. He then directed the gunner, and two SP guns and a Panther were knocked out. Faced with a losing situation, the remaining German tanks started to move off. The battalion moved forward slowly amid house-to-house fighting.

1 Troop of A Sqn, under the command of Lieut Williams, was the first troop into Falaise and moved up the main street. Some opposition was encountered from snipers and, unfortunately, Lieut Williams's machine-gun jammed so all he could fire was his main gun. Suddenly, three Germans popped up from behind a hedgerow and fired a *Panzerfaust* at him. The round was close but went over his head; he used a HE round to take it out. He reported the incident to Maj Radley-Walters, who replied 'Never mind the Bazooka.[2] Get Going!' Lieut Williams tried to shoot at the Germans with his Sten gun and then his pistol as he went down the main street. The Camerons, the South Sask and the FMR continued to fight all night long. As it got dark, the tanks followed the infantry through the town. The city was burning and their path was dotted with burning or fallen buildings and rubble was everywhere. Two or three different approaches were tried without too much luck; B Sqn was held up by shell holes and bomb craters. When Lieut John Wesley Neill arrived in Falaise, he was met by Capt Welsh, the 2i/c for B Sqn. He was told that he was to replace Lieut Paul Wilfred Ayriss, who was being promoted to the rank of captain and moved to SHQ. Lieut Neill took over command of tank 'Bomb'. At 23.00, the South Sask reached the château square. At last light, the *Sherbrookes* moved back to a harbour area for the night, while the infantry consolidated their positions in the town. A Sqn, however, kept on pushing farther and farther through Falaise.

OPERATION TRACTABLE: CLOSING THE FALAISE GAP

The loss of Falaise deprived the Germans of their best remaining east-west road. All they had left was a lesser road running northeast from Argentan to Trun, and various secondary roads. It also closed the neck of the Falaise Gap to about 12 miles. At noon on 16 August, *Generalfeldmarschall* von Kluge told *Generaloberst* Alfred Jodl that Hitler's order for another counter-attack to split the Allies could not be executed. He again asked for permission to withdraw to the Seine River. Later that day, Hitler authorised a withdrawal of German forces but only to behind the Orne and the Dives rivers. Von Kluge issued orders for the withdrawal movement to begin that night. 5.Pzarmee and 7.Armee were to withdraw to the sector of the Dives River and the line Morteaux-Couliboeuf-Trun-Gacé-Laigue, while *Panzergruppe* Eberbach was to cover their withdrawal in the area of Argentan-Gacé and then disband. Daylight road movement was authorised for the first time, a move of which the Allied tactical air force would take full advantage. The next day, *Generalfeldmarschall* Walter Model appeared at the headquarters of *Heeresgruppe B* and relieved von Kluge, but nonetheless confirmed von Kluge's directive on 18 August. While 7.Armee and *Panzergruppe* Eberbach were to withdraw as quickly as possible, II.SS-Pzkorps was to hold the north wall and *47.Panzerkorps* (47.Pzkorps) was to hold the south wall.

At first light on 17 August, A Sqn moved through Falaise in support of the South Sask and reached the high ground at the railway junction with the road that lead to Damblainville. They had the task of preventing any withdrawals or counter-attacks. Just east of Falaise, the position gave a fine panoramic view of the 1st Pol Armd Div and 4th Cdn Armd Div attacks 2 miles to the east. A few prisoners and a German jeep were taken. At about 10.00, the squadron's position was buzzed by eight *Luftewaffe Messerschmitt* ME 109 fighters. Although the aircraft did not attack, the tanks fired at them using their .50-cal Browning machine-guns, but to no effect. The Camerons were given the task of clearing the eastern part of the town with the support of C Sqn. They started off at 06.00 amid cheering and waving civilians. The job was slow as the infantry was tired and in need of reinforcements. C Sqn made a recce in strength to the south and southwest, but no enemy movement was seen and so the squadron returned to the vicinity of the town square. C Sqn moved out of town onto the main road leading south and southeast and carried on down the road as far as the village of Saint Clair which it captured without firing a shot. It took up a defensive position in and to the south of the village; where it remained until 18.30, at which time it withdrew to the area of Aubigny and joined the remainder of the regiment.

B Sqn moved into Falaise with the Camerons and the FMR. The FMR had been given the task of clearing out the last snipers from the remaining strong points in Falaise. In particular, an estimated fifty to sixty soldiers of 12.SS-Pzdiv were holed up in the walled complex of the *École supérieure de jeunes filles* in the centre of town. Although orders were given for the division to evacuate the town, they had not been received. The FMR were ordered to clear them out. The building was surrounded by a heavy stone wall and it commanded the southern main east-west street through Falaise. The FMR used mortar fire to batter away at the ancient walls. Eventually, the mortar fire set the school ablaze. Tank 'Bomb' was in support of the FMR and was hit by a *Panzerfaust*. Fortunately, it hit a track welded to the turret and, aside from scarring the armour, did no other damage. All resistance finally ended at about 02.00 that night when the FMR assaulted the position in the midst of an enemy air attack. None of the enemy surrendered, but four Germans were reported to have escaped the inferno.

At 16.37, the *Sherbrookes* reverted to being under command of 2nd Cdn Armd Bde. The regiment moved back to the area of Aubigny where it was told to take forty-eight hours to rest and refit the tanks before rejoining the remainder of the brigade at Camembert. It was put on one-hour notice to move to any part of the front where the remnants of 7.Armee might possibly attempt a counter-attack. This resulted in about five quick moves in which no enemy were met but during which enemy vehicles were heard moving about in the darkness looking for possible soft spots in the Canadian defence through which they might possibly escape. The next day, 19 August, Lt-Gen Crerar issued new orders to First Cdn Army. First Brit Corps was to continue its advance along the Lisieux-Pont-Audemer axis. Second Cdn Corps was to follow the general line of Trun-Vimoutiers-Orbec-Bernay-Elbeuf. However, only active reconnaissance in the direction indicated could be carried out until Gen Montgomery 'removed the cork from the bottle'. At 11.00, Lt-Gen Simonds passed on these instructions to his division commanders. He emphasized that the encirclement of the enemy must be complete before the move could be undertaken. He instructed 10th Brigade to hold Trun; 4th Cdn Armd Bde was to set up on the highway north of Hordouseaux; 7th Brigade was to dominate the river line between Magny and Mandeville; 2nd Cdn Armd Bde and 9th Brigade were placed under command of 4th Cdn Armd Div; 9th Brigade was to hold Cantepie and Beaumais. The tanks were immediately dispatched to thicken up the infantry between Saint-Lambert-sur-Dive and Trun; 2nd Cdn Inf Div took over from 3rd Cdn Inf Div at Morteaux-Couliboeuf, Damblainville and the high ground to the north of the latter.

OPERATION TRACTABLE: CLOSING THE FALAISE GAP

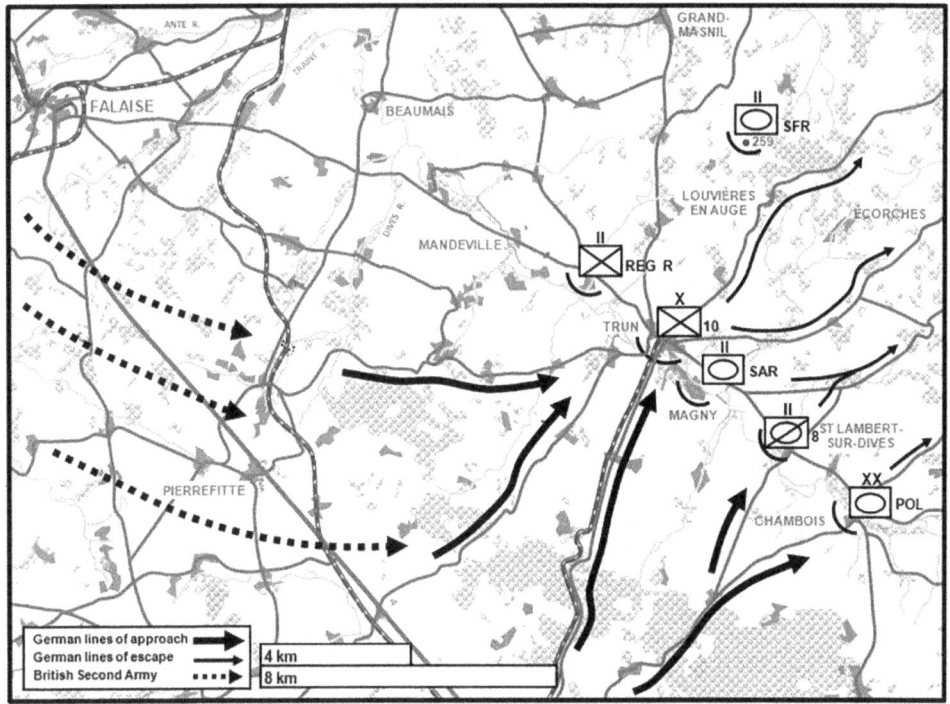

Closing the Falaise Gap.

The Poles were short on ammunition and supplies. By early evening, they had captured Chambois after hard hand-to-hand fighting. They linked up with Fifth US Corps which held the high ground east of the road to Mont Ormel. By last light, the forward elements of 1st Pol Armd Div had reached the outskirts of Chambois. Some of its positions were overrun by the sheer weight of the Germans descending on them. The Germans had swung north in the search of escape routes as the Americans advanced northward. With the Falaise Gap now all but closed, the Germans attacked east in an attempt to break through the Canadian positions between Chambois and Saint-Lambert-sur-Dive. Here they were compressed to roads and routes and tracks between the two villages. The Canadians developed a tactic to deal with the threat. The infantry and tank positions would cut off the German attack. Typhoons would wait nearby until a suitable and sizeable target had accumulated. Then, one after another, they would strafe, rocket or bomb the helpless surge below. When all their ammunition had been expended, they would return to their base while the artillery took over and continued the massacre.

The Germans were trapped in the Falaise Gap. Second Brit Army was pushing east and applying pressure on the Germans, while Third US Army was doing likewise from the south. The trapped remnants of 7.Armee decided to make a last furious attempt to break out at Saint-Lambert-sur-Dive. In a desperate attempt to help in the breakout, elements of II.SS-Pzkorps attacked westward from Camembert on 20 August. A five-hour battle ensued with 4th Cdn Armd Div and 1st Pol Armd Div, in an effort to prevent the German forces from breaching the Allied line. *General der Panzertruppe* Dietrich von Saucken would later claim that 150 German tanks were extricated from the Falaise Gap, most during the final attack. At the same time, the attack enlarged the remaining gap between Chambois and Saint-Lambert-sur-Dive by the sheer weight of numbers. 4th Cdn Armd Bde was then ordered to attack southeast from Hordouseaux in an effort to restore the situation. The Canadian and Polish positions held firm and the German attempt failed.

Gen Montgomery ordered the destruction of all the German forces in northwest France. The Americans were already in the suburbs of Paris. First Cdn Army was now ordered to advance as quickly as possible towards Rouen with the intention of crossing the Seine River and eventually clearing Le Havre Peninsula. On 20 August, Gen Montgomery issued a new directive that stressed the 'need for speed in getting on with the business' of destroying the Germans. The aim of the new offensive was for Second Brit Army to push on to the Seine River and then to the Somme River. It was to then push to Antwerp, thus liberating a deep water port and encircling the German forces still on the coast in the Pas-de-Calais area. First Cdn Army was to clean up the coast. First, they were to keep the battle securely corked at Trun; second, develop a strong thrust towards Lisieux and eastward towards Rouen; and third, when the battle was over in the Falaise Gap, move and cross the Seine River and clear the whole Le Havre Peninsula.

Initially, the *Sherbrookes* had remained in the vicinity of Aubigny on 18 and 19 August. At 13.30 on 19 August, the regiment was placed on a two-hour notice to move. Later in the day, it received orders to move to the area east of the Bois de Courcy. The *Sherbrookes* arrived there at about 22.00 and stayed there for only an hour before moving to Réveillon. The regiment spent the next morning there. At 12.00, 2nd Cdn Armd Bde came under command of 4th Cdn Armd Div, and at 12.45 the *Sherbrookes* were put on a one-hour notice to move. At 14.13, they were told to be ready to move as soon as possible. The regiment moved off shortly after that and arrived in the area of Montpinçon at around 18.00. That evening, it was placed under the command of 4th Cdn Armd Bde. Over the next few days, their task would be to cover the flank of the Trun Gap and to prevent enemy equipment and personnel from escaping. After supper, the tanks of A Sqn were on the road again towards Point 259, arriving there at about 23.00. They met up with the R de Chaud in their positions. C Sqn moved to the area of Écorches where its task was to set up a defensive position on Point 240. It arrived on the position at about 03.00. The infantry had already consolidated on the position so the squadron moved off the position to harbour for the night.

C Sqn remained in its harbour for the remainder of 21 August. It came under occasional shell-fire, and small infantry counter-attacks in the morning were beaten off. One troop with an additional Firefly left the harbour during the day and moved to a position from which it hoped to get a shot at enemy tanks. None were sighted and so the troop returned to the squadron area. At last light, the squadron moved to a more advantageous position at the extreme northeast of the Trun Pocket in order to cover a reported counter-attack from the northeast. A Sqn had taken up a defensive position when it had reached Point 259, and remained there all morning. At about 11.00, it moved off past the town of Les Champeaux with the Algonquins on their back decks. On the way, they passed several columns of bombed-out vehicles. The RAF had already taken its toll on German transport, animals, equipment and personnel. The sight of dead horses, destroyed equipment and dead German soldiers was frightful and the stench was terrible.

For the three day period from 17 to 19 August, aircraft from No. 84 Group had a field day against the retreating Germans. The Germans were attempting large-scale road movements in daylight and the weather was fairly good for flying. The Allied Expeditionary Air Force managed to complete 7,621 sorties over the period and destroyed or damaged nearly 400 tanks and 5,100 other vehicles of all sorts. With nowhere to go without facing immediate destruction, the Germans were surrendering in massive troves, either voluntarily or after stiff resistance. First Cdn Army processed 208 officers and 13,475 other ranks as prisoners of war, this not taking into account those taken by the other Allied armies. The carnage continued for another three days until all resistance in the Trun Pocket had disintegrated into small bands of disorganised, fleeing soldiers. After the battle, the Allies found over 4,000 destroyed or abandoned vehicles and equipment.

When the *Sherbrookes* arrived at Les Champeaux at 13.45, they found enemy on foot swarming all over them. A request was sent up to 2nd Cdn

Armd Bde HQ for infantry support. However, at 14.30 they reported that they were still waiting for infantry support. Later that night, a group of about 300 enemy prisoners in the RHQ area, under guard of a small Polish force, were reported trying to escape in the darkness. A patrol was sent out to bring them back. At first light on 22 August, Maj Radley-Walters and Lieut Williams went off in search of some SS troops said to be in the area. They came back with seven prisoners and some probable undisclosed loot. At 12.37, the regiment was ordered to move back towards Trun and was placed on immediate notice to move, but it was only at 13.30 that the squadrons actually started to move. Progress was slow. The route soon became an obstacle course and the tanks had to zigzag around destroyed enemy equipment and vehicles – the wreckage was phenomenal. At 16.00, the regiment finally arrived in the area of Écorches where the squadrons deployed on the high plateau east of the village in order to dominate one of the potential exits through the Trun Gap. C Sqn was placed in depth on Point 240. It received orders to send a troop to assist some Polish infantry. The troop arrived at the Polish position but was recalled immediately.

Hitler finally realised the seriousness of the plight of the German armies still caught in the salient and issued a new directive on 20 August. The Commander-in-Chief West was ordered to hold a bridgehead west of Paris and to prevent a breakthrough between the Seine and Loire rivers in the direction of Dijon. The battered remnants of 5.Pzarmee and 7.Armee were to reform behind the Touques River with the armour on the southern flank. The directive stressed that if the area forward of the Seine could not be held, they were to fall back to and defend the line Seine River-Yonne River-Canal de Bourgogne-Dijon-Dôle to the Swiss border. The bridgehead south of the Seine River at Paris was to be held at all costs: 'If necessary, the battle in and around Paris must be conducted regardless of the (possible) destruction of the city.'[3]

On 23 August, 2nd Cdn Armd Bde reverted to under command of Second Cdn Corps. At 14.40, the *Sherbrookes* were placed under command of 2nd Cdn Inf Div in preparation for crossing the Seine River. The division was to cross the Risle River near Brionne; 5th Brigade would then move across the Seine in the region of the Forêt de la Londe on the night of 25 August. Another move was conducted that evening. The regiment moved 15 miles to the northeast and harboured in a patch of woods just west of Orbec. The *Sherbrookes* moved through Vimoutiers on 23 August, where they picked up a young French Resistance boy named René Delaunay. He guided the recce troop to several woods and copses where large numbers of enemy infantry were hiding. The infantry followed up behind the recce and took them all prisoner.

With the collapse of the Falaise Pocket, the Normandy Campaign came to an end. Gen Montgomery estimated the German losses in Normandy as 210,000 taken prisoner, 240,000 either killed or wounded, 3,500 guns and 1,500 tanks either captured or destroyed, as well as vast amounts of mechanical transport, horse-drawn transport and equipment of all kinds. Forty-three divisions had been eliminated or severely mauled. Twenty army, corps or division commanders had been killed or captured, with another two wounded. As well, the Commander-in-Chief West had changed twice. 12.SS-Pzdiv went from 21,000 soldiers to only 60, which escaped on foot from the Gap; 2.Pzdiv escaped with 5 tanks, 3 guns and about 2,000 soldiers all told; 272.Inf-Div went from 14,000 soldiers to 300; 21.Pzdiv lost all of its 233 tanks and 350 officers and 12,000 men; 1.SS-Pzdiv fared better and managed to extract 40 tanks and 1,000 fighting men. A new phase of the war, the pursuit of the retreating and decimated German forces in the west, began.

Chapter 8

The Pursuit to the Seine

With the Canadians holding the backstop to the Falaise Pocket, the British and Americans collapsed the bag and captured or destroyed 7.Armee and 5.Pzarmee trapped there. While this was going on, Gen Montgomery issued a new directive for the pursuit phase of the war. For him, speed was of the essence. He wanted to ensure that a wider encirclement along the Seine was achieved with the maximum possible speed. For him, it was essential to cut off survivors from the Falaise Pocket and to drive across the Pas-de-Calais and capture the coastal ports; this in order to facilitate his maintenance requirements and to capture the flying bomb sites. 21st Army Group was to push along the Channel coast towards the Belgian border while 12th Army Group under Gen Bradley was to advance on the right flank of the British and drive north towards Bourgtheroulde.[1] Gen Montgomery ordered First Cdn Army to hold the Trun-Chamois line until the Falaise Pocket was eliminated. Once the Falaise Pocket was eliminated, First Brit Corps was to advance towards Lisieux and Rouen, while Second Cdn Corps advanced to the Seine and crossed it between Louviers and the sea. The whole Le Havre Peninsula would be cleared, with stress placed on securing the port facilities. Gen Montgomery suggested that 51st Brit Inf Div be allowed to take the small port of Saint-Valery-en-Caux, the same place where the division had made a gallant stand in 1940. Also, he proposed that 2nd Cdn Inf Div be allowed to take Dieppe after its disastrous raid there on 19 August 1942.

The terrain west of the Seine is well-suited for mobile warfare. Except for the traversing rivers, it is made up of broad open fields with few hedges to break the monotony of the landscape. The area between the Dives and Touques rivers is broken by narrow valleys of tributary streams and consists mainly of pastures and orchards. The Campagne de Neubourg area between Rouen and Évreux is a fairly level, cultivated plateau averaging 450ft in height. It slopes gently down towards the northeast, but steep escarpments on the edge of this feature overlook the Seine and Risle river valleys. The Seine is the most formidable water obstacle. Between Elbeuf

THE PURSUIT TO THE SEINE

and Le Havre, eight meanders cross its wide, flat valley. Each meander varies from 1 to 2 miles. On the inner bank, the ground is low and marshy near the river and wooded as it rises to the plateau. On the outer bank, the valley slope drops abruptly to the river in a steep escarpment. Several have heavily wooded areas, the largest being the Forêt de la Londe. The width of the Seine River varies from 490ft at Elbeuf to 1,000ft at Duclair and 1,600ft at Quillebeuf. Crossing the river were three bridges at Rouen and a couple more below the town. All the bridges had been severely damaged by Allied bombing.

On 20 August, Lt-Gen Crerar ordered Second Cdn Corps to cross the Seine River in the area of the Elbeuf bend. To accomplish this, he allocated 150 Duplex-drive tanks (left over from the Normandy landings), 300 DUKW (a six-wheel amphibious truck used to transport goods and troops over land and water), 115 LVT (landing vehicle tracked, nicknamed by the British as 'Water Buffalo') and 130 Terrapins (a British-manufactured amphibious armoured transport). It was felt that the Canadian crossing would most likely not meet any enemy resistance. Lt-Gen Simonds issued his own orders the next day. The Second Cdn Corps advance would be conducted on a two-division front: 4th Cdn Armd Div would advance on the right, while 2nd Cdn Inf Div advanced on the left; 2nd Cdn Inf Div would move east from Falaise, cross the Dives River and advance along an axis from Thiberville to Point 179, Brionne and then Bourgtheroulde; 4th Cdn Armd Div was to advance along an axis from Les Champeaux to Le Sap through Monnaie to Broglie then Le Neubourg and finally to Surtauville. 3rd Cdn Inf Div would follow behind the armoured division and then take up a position between the two lead divisions. It would then advance along an axis from Orbec to Thiboutière, through Valailles to Boisney then Harcourt, and finally through Saint-Pierre-des-Fleurs to the area of Elbeuf. Second Cdn Corps would then continue its advance with three divisions up. It was to be prepared to move to the Seine River, but not before 27 August. On 22 August, Gen Montgomery telephoned First Cdn Army HQ and asked if it was ready to remove the cork from the bottle. Lt-Gen Crerar replied that all organised resistance in the area Coudehard-Saint-Lambert-sur-Dive-Trun had ceased. Gen Montgomery therefore removed the restrictions he had imposed a few days before and ordered the Canadians to commence their advance towards the Seine River as soon as possible.

The enemy had lost a huge number of armoured vehicles, equipment and troops in the Falaise Pocket, which could not be readily replaced. The best it could expect to do would be to temporarily delay the Allied advance. This would be best accomplished if the German forces had sufficient numbers available to patrol and hold the Seine's many bends. On 20 August, Hitler ordered the German forces to hold a line along the Seine-Yonne-Dijon rivers. *Generalfeldmarschall* Model, who had replaced von Kluge, recognised that he did not have the personnel required, and those he had were in utter confusion. Furthermore, the catastrophic loss of war materiel further hindered his situation. Instead, he suggested on 24 August that he make a stand on a Somme-Marne line. Three days later, the German High Command would concur with Model, but he would also be ordered to hold the Seine-Yonne-Dijon line as long as possible to gain time to prepare his proposed defensive line. Elements and remnants of many formations and units of the shattered 7.Armee and 5.Pzarmee were found everywhere along the Allied front. No coherent order of battle existed. However, over the course of the next few days, three sectors would emerge. On the right, *86.Korps* was established in front of First Cdn Army. This was the best organised and equipped of the three sectors.

With the cork removed, Lt-Gen Simonds ordered Second Cdn Corps to race east with three divisions up on 22 August; 5th Brigade had already begun a reconnaissance in force through Vimoutiers, Orbec and Thiberville. The advance had started at 16.20 on 21 August. Now, the balance of 2nd Cdn Inf Div was to follow suit and advance on the left flank through Brionne towards Bourgtheroulde. Second Cdn Corps moved off at first light on 23 August. On 22 August, the *Sherbrookes*, still under the command of 4th Cdn Armd Div, was ordered to move up with the Lincoln & Welland on their back decks. At 12.37, the regiment was placed on immediate notice to move, but the move only began at 13.30. The terrain from Caen to Falaise had been a gently undulating, dusty, treeless area. However, south of Falaise, the terrain was made up of grain fields, pastureland, wooded areas and hedges. There was less evidence of war, it having been less subjected to shelling in the villages and towns. As the regiment moved eastward, its progress was slowed due to road conditions. The tanks had to zigzag around destroyed vehicles; the wreckage was phenomenal. The tanks were told to prepare for a long move; in all probability, the B Ech would not be seen for a period up to three weeks. At 21.00, a new move got under way with the Lincoln & Welland still on the regiment's tanks. En route, new orders were received that the tanks were to support the infantry in a right-flanking attack in an

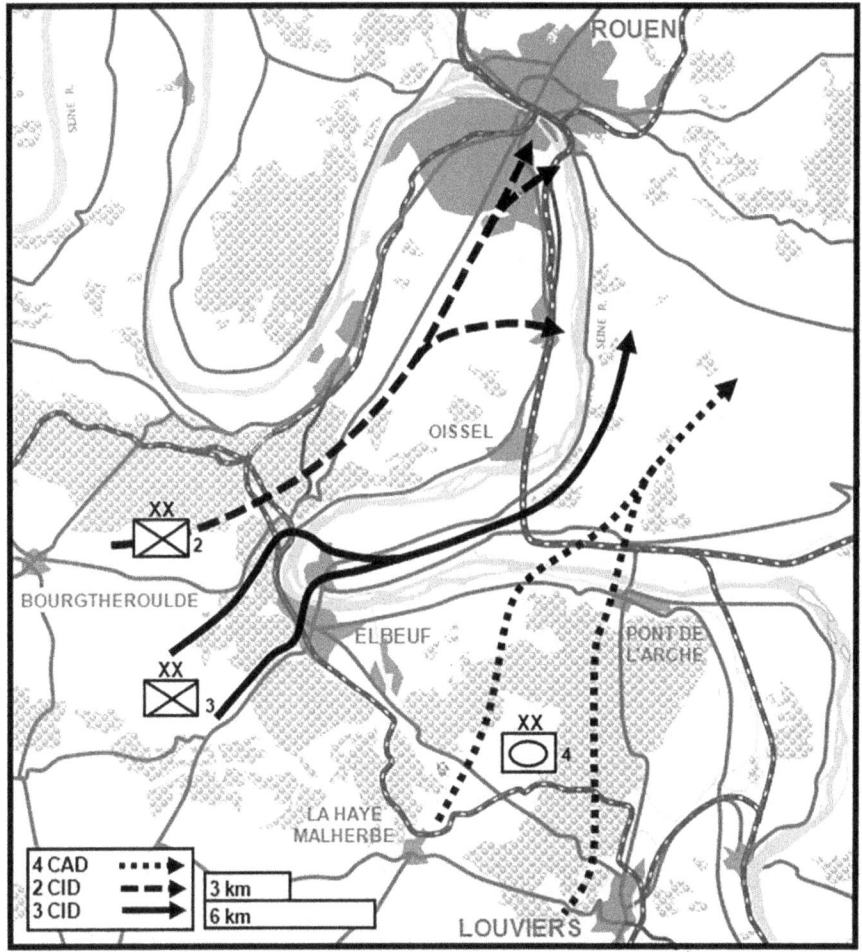

Crossing the Seine River – The Second Canadian Corps plan.

effort to gain the east banks of the Seine River. Because of the change in orders, the regiment would have to move all night. The tanks finally halted near Le Val Bequet at 04.00. The next morning Russian and Polish civilians, labour personnel who were hiding out in the area, reported when questioned that SS troops had left the area the previous evening in the direction of Le Sap. The move over the last few days was to be remembered as the most eerie march ever done by the tanks. Everyone was tired and on edge. Small pockets of enemy appeared in the most unexpected places. Sometimes they surrendered, sometimes they fought. Mines were a continuous hazard. Thick blasts of rain would obscure the entire sky for a couple of hours and then a blazing sun would dry up everything in twenty to thirty minutes. Moreover, the tanks were ordered to only travel cross country or along back roads.

The rule for the vanguard was that no tracked vehicle of the weight of a tank was allowed to use the main corps or division routes. Instead, they had to find their own way cross-country or use secondary roads. If absolutely necessary, they were permitted to cross rivers on bridges, but then return to cross-country movement. The *Sherbrookes* still had eight or nine Stuart tanks and Lt-Col Gordon devised a strategy for dealing with these restrictions. He would send them forward to find a route parallel to the corps or division axis; after advancing 8 to 10 miles, one tank would be sent back to the unit to lead it forward. After another 8 to 10 miles, a second tank would be dispatched to the rear to meet up with the advancing tanks for the next leg of the advance. The same procedure was maintained until the unit got to that night's designated harbour area. This kept the unit moving and prevented traffic jams on the route, and especially at the bridge crossings where the column joined the main corps or division routes.

On 23 August, 2nd Cdn Armd Bde returned to under the command of Second Cdn Corps. The *Sherbrookes* were assigned to support 2nd Cdn Inf Div and were given three FOO tanks and crews for the upcoming operation. The regiment was then ordered to marry-up with the division in the area of Thiberville. At 15.05, the tanks started their move forward in a heavy rainstorm but, as ordered, kept off the main roads. Progress was very slow. The *Sherbrookes* were only one unit moving in a larger movement of formations. The Germans, for their part, were fighting a rearguard action. Two or three tanks, a couple of anti-tank guns and maybe a company of infantry with some mortars were encountered in built-up areas. The enemy resistance was not well organised and occurred mostly in places from which the Germans could easily escape when pressure was applied. The Canadians would brush them out of the way and move on towards the next little hill or village where they ran into another pocket of resistance. The regiment passed through Fervaques at 15.39, Saint Maur at a little past 16.00, and reached Saint-Paul-de-Courtonne at 16.45; the tanks finally reached the area of Thiberville at 19.27. When darkness fell, the troops returned to Point 140 and set up a harbour for the night. A Sqn, less a troop, and the RHQ took up a position just south-west of Thiberville. C Sqn had left its harbour area and moved off for Thiberville. The Camerons were mounted in soft-skinned vehicles and needed the protection of the squadron's tanks. At around 04.00 the next morning, the squadron arrived in its new harbour area in La Buissonnière, near Thiberville, and it would remain there until 19.00.

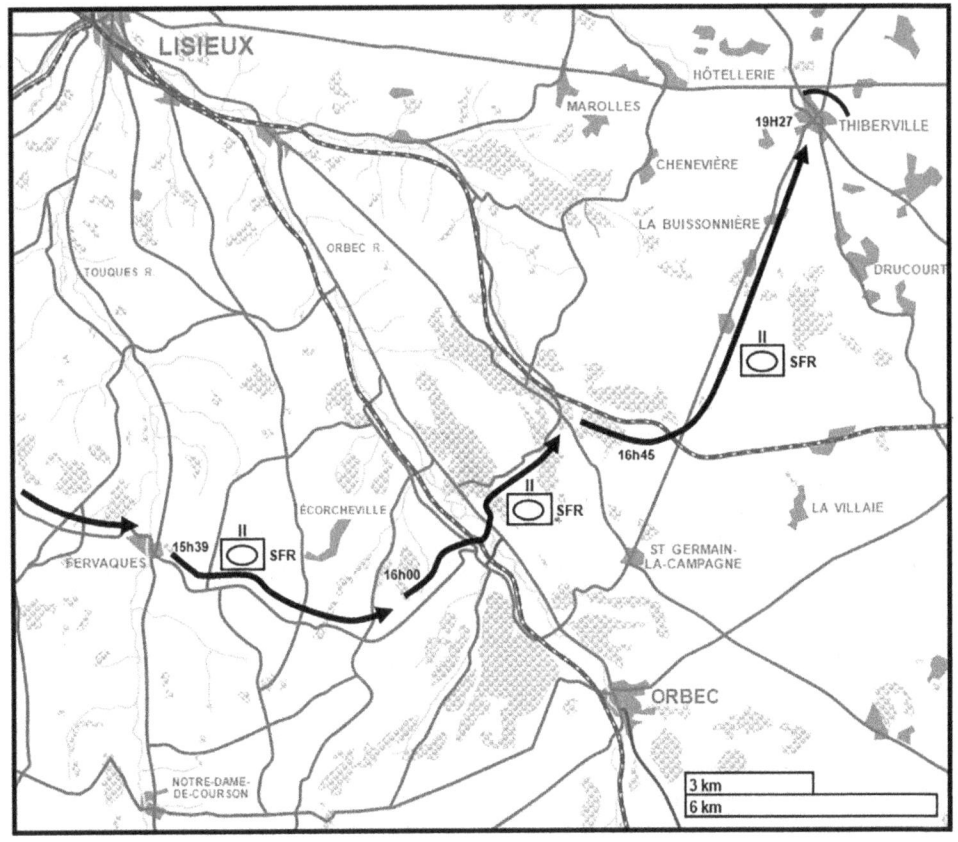

24 August 1944: The advance to Thiberville.

On 25 August, Lt-Gen Crerar issued new instructions. Second Cdn Corps was to plan and make initial preparations for an opposed crossing of the Seine River between Pont-de-l'Arche and Elbeuf. Its task was to clear the enemy from the west bank of the Seine and to establish a bridgehead across the river. However, special attention was to be given to the actions of Second Brit Army and 12th Army Group on their right. Lt-Gen Simonds issued his own orders later that same day. On the right flank, 4th Cdn Armd Div was instructed to seize a bridgehead beyond the Seine River in the area of Pont-de-l'Arche and Criquebeuf-sur-Seine, and to then advance on Forges-les-Eaux. In the centre, 3rd Cdn Inf Div was to seize by 'coup-de-main' a bridgehead including Elbeuf and the railway bridge at Port du Gravier to the north. It would then drive towards Neufchâtel-en-Bray. On the left, 2nd Cdn Inf Div was to clear the meander south of Rouen between Oissel and

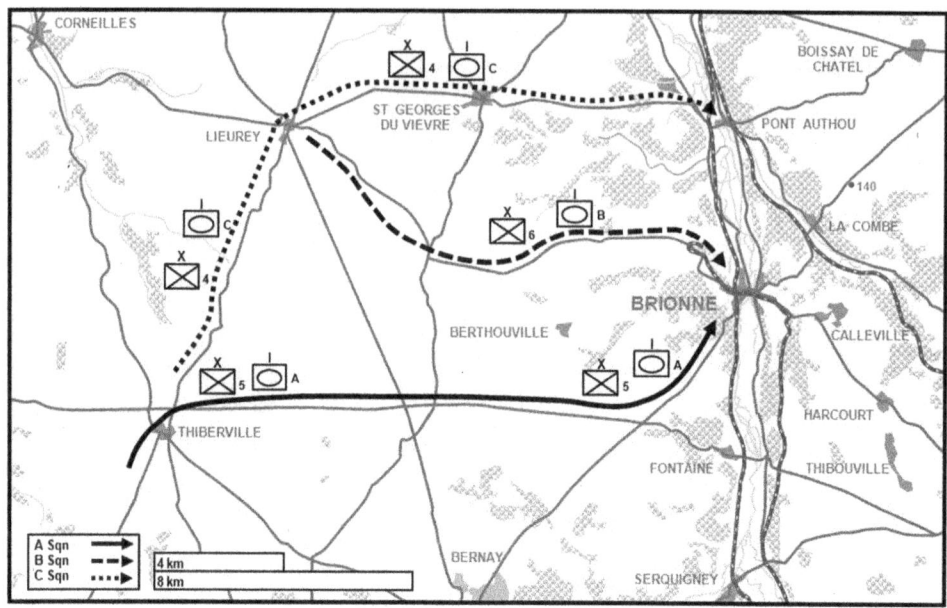

25 August 1944: The advance to Brionne.

Moulineaux and also seize by 'coup-de-main' a bridgehead at the railway bridge at Oissel on the east side of this loop and at bridges south of Rouen.

The Canadian advance continued all day on 25 August; 2nd Cdn Inf Div sent 6th Brigade forward, led by the South Sask, to take Brionne, while 4th Brigade and 5th Brigade remained in the area of Thiberville. The division's engineers were to then construct two bridges across Risle River, one for each of the infantry divisions. One would be established in Brionne for the use of 3rd Cdn Inf Div, while 2nd Cdn Inf Div would have use of a bridge built just north of the town. At 06.00, the *Sherbrookes* resumed their move east. After a move of 8 miles the previous day, the tanks now drove another 13 miles to the village of Boisney, arriving in the late afternoon. This brought them to within 3 miles of the enemy, who were just being cleared out of Brionne by 6th Brigade. While the tanks advanced, Lt-Col Gordon moved off to attend Brig Bingham's O Group at the 2nd Cdn Armd Bde HQ. He returned to the regiment and issued his own orders at 16.30. The *Sherbrookes* were to remain in support of 2nd Cdn Inf Div. The tanks were to dash along to the Seine River in the vicinity of Bourgtheroulde followed by the infantry of 5th Brigade in trucks. The infantry would then make an assault crossing of the river and hold the bridgehead while a bridge was thrown across. The tanks would then cross and turn northward and lead the way to Dieppe where the infantry would seize the town. The whole operation was planned to take three days.

The plan called for the tanks to proceed to the Forêt de la Londe that same night in advance of the infantry. B Sqn was placed in support of 6th Brigade and would lead the advance, crossing the Risle River at Brionne before proceeding up the main road to Bourgtheroulde; C Sqn was sent in support of 4th Brigade with the intention of crossing the Risle River at Pont-Authou and following 6th Brigade to Bourgtheroulde; A Sqn was placed in reserve awaiting further orders and would, in the short term, be located with 5th Brigade. At the close of the O Group, an extensive issue of maps from 2nd Cdn Armd Bde was distributed. They covered a vast area and were another indication of the fabulous advance anticipated. This was a far cry from Saint-André-sur-Orne where the tanks fought hard and long for several yards of terrain. Now, the tanks were advancing miles each day. However, certain questions remained unanswered. It was uncertain if assault boats were available and if the bridging company would follow behind the lead troops. Also, information on the location of the enemy was sparse. Furthermore, little information was available as to the intentions of the other Allied armies or what they were doing.

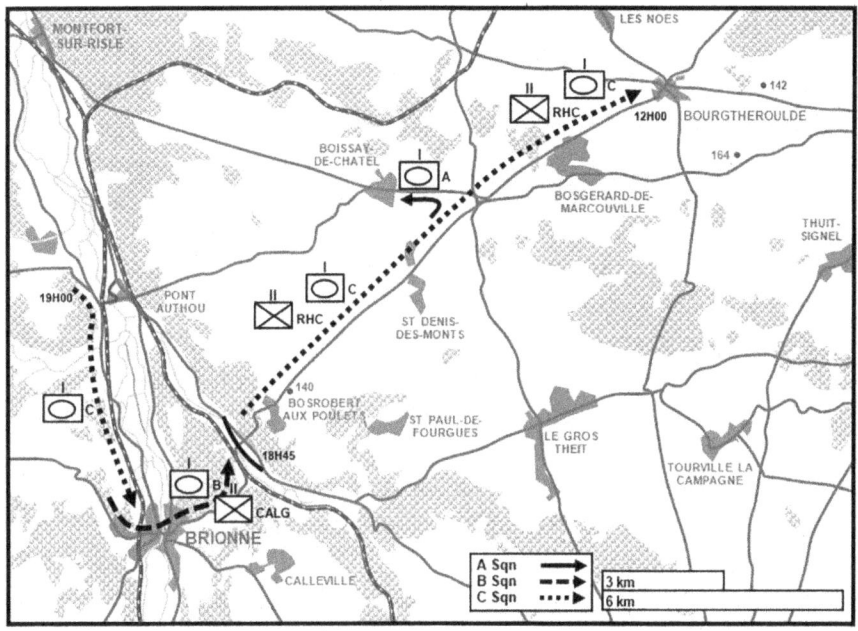

25-26 August 1944: The night advance to Bourgtheroulde.

At 17.10, Lt-Col Gordon and Capt Spielman, the Int O, left in a scout car to join up with 5th Brigade HQ. The Int O advised the brigade's intelligence section that he had received information regarding a suspected 400 German troops from 9.SS-Pzdiv, the equivalent of 6 enemy companies at normal field battle strength, who were acting as rearguard along the main road to Bourgtheroulde on the other side of the tributary of the Risle River. Their suspected mission was to cover the withdrawal across the Seine of the remnants of 21.Pzdiv and any other odds and sods that had joined them during their swift retreat. Lt-Col Gordon also put the same question to Brig Megill, the commander of 5th Brigade, concerning the intelligence report. Brig Megill denied the report in its entirety and so the tanks started moving forward towards Brionne at 17.35.

With the decision to push on towards Bourgtheroulde that night, B Sqn was instructed to lead the way in support of the Calgary Highlanders. C Sqn would move down to Brionne and follow behind B Sqn. B Sqn joined up with the Calgary Highlanders and now marched off towards Brionne. The tanks passed through the town but at 18.45 bumped into trouble 2 miles beyond the town when medium machine-gun fire streamed at them from the village and the woods at La Cambe. The intelligence report that had worried Lt-Col Gordon and which had been so easily tossed aside by 5th Brigade, came back to haunt the *Sherbrookes*. A civilian on the route confirmed that there were approximately 400 German troops in the village. La Cambe was engaged by artillery fire and the tanks corrected the fire themselves. The machine-gun fire was finally silenced. Unfortunately, Lieut Wood was wounded and had to be evacuated. At 19.30, in the growing darkness, the decision was taken to keep the BdeHQ, the *Sherbrooke* tanks and the artillery HQ at Point 140.

Although 2nd Cdn Inf Div had just finished a month of extremely hard fighting, including a week of continuous and strenuous pursuit of the enemy, Maj-Gen Foulkes believed that it still had enough strength to push through what he called 'the weak German defences'. The division, however, was considered by some to be too exhausted for further fighting. As well as the brigades being under strength,[2] the division was now made up of relatively new reinforcements whose standard of training was extremely doubtful. Nonetheless, at 04.15 on 26 August, Maj-Gen Foulkes issued his orders for the next few days. His intentions were for 6th Brigade to clear the Forêt de la Londe of any enemy present there, while 4th Brigade and 5th Brigade were to cross the Seine at Elbeuf by alternating with the brigades of 3rd Cdn Inf Div. 4th Brigade was to first seize Oissel and the territory north and west of the village using the Essex Scottish. The R Regt C would follow behind and occupy the Grand Essart. The RHLI would then occupy the high ground south of the Grand Essart overlooking the Seine River; 5th Brigade would set the stage by first seizing Bourgtheroulde.

Since no further enemy opposition was anticipated, the infantry began to load into trucks and transports for a quick move forward from Brionne. Suddenly, German searchlights lit up Brionne. Fifteen medium bombers from the *Luftwaffe* bombed the Canadians as they prepared to move forward. The *Luftwaffe*'s objective was to destroy the bridge over the Risle River in Brionne in an effort to further delay the Canadian advance. They missed the bridge but hit close to the Canadian positions. The Calgary Highlanders were hit hard and suffered fifteen dead and seventy-two wounded. Several R de Mais were also hit. The A Ech of the *Sherbrookes* was located nearby and craters measuring 20 by 35ft were made not more than 150 yards from its harbour area.

The Black Watch was unharmed and was therefore ordered to assume the lead and push off with C Sqn in support. C Sqn had left its position at 19.00 and arrived in Brionne at about midnight. There, it married up with the Black Watch and pushed through the B Sqn positions at 04.00 and moved up the road at the head of the column towards Bourgtheroulde. About 2 miles northeast of Bosrobert aux Poulets, the Germans made another stand and one of the tanks was brewed up by a *Panzerschreck*. No other enemy was encountered but much enemy materiel was passed along the way; the force arrived in front of Bourgtheroulde and C Sqn formed a laager. When first light arrived, the squadron formed a firm base northeast of the road running north of the town. During the morning, a troop was ordered to recce the town; it saw some enemy, which unfortunately drove off before they could be engaged. Bourgtheroulde was strongly held by the enemy, including a 75mm anti-tank gun in the town square. Lt-Col C.C. Mitchell, the CO of the Black Watch, had orders to bypass the town and head straight for the Seine River. He decided, therefore, that the battalion vehicles would rush through the town as quickly as possible and then resume the advance to the Seine. Unfortunately, every seventh or eighth vehicle was taken out by the anti-tank gun, resulting in heavy casualties to the infantry; C Sqn had bypassed to the north of the town. Just as the Black Watch reached the eastern outskirts, it received orders to clear the town and consolidate there. The A Sqn advance behind C Sqn had been delayed due to enemy action and the Black Watch and C Sqn were therefore threatened with possible encirclement; a troop was sent on patrol towards the northeast to recce the area. Little enemy activity was seen so Lt-Col Mitchell decided to organise an attack from the northeast to take the town since all the German weapons in the town were pointing to the southwest. The enemy was caught by surprise. The battle was a prolonged one hampered by German snipers and the anti-tank gun in the centre of the town. German mortar and artillery fire continued to rain down throughout the day and two German counter-attacks of tanks and infantry, one from the east and then one from the west, were repulsed by C Sqn in the afternoon. Two enemy tanks were destroyed as well as several machine-guns. A number of prisoners were taken, but C Sqn lost one tank in the battle.

During the early morning hours of 26 August, A Sqn had started off with the Calgary Highlanders on its back decks using the same route to Bourgtheroulde as the previous evening. The next objective was to clear the high ground at Point 142 in order to create a firm base of operations for the move into the Forêt de la Londe. At about noon, the squadron was held up at Saint-Denis-des-Monts, but the enemy was quickly pushed aside and the advance continued. About 1,000 yards beyond the village, machine-gun

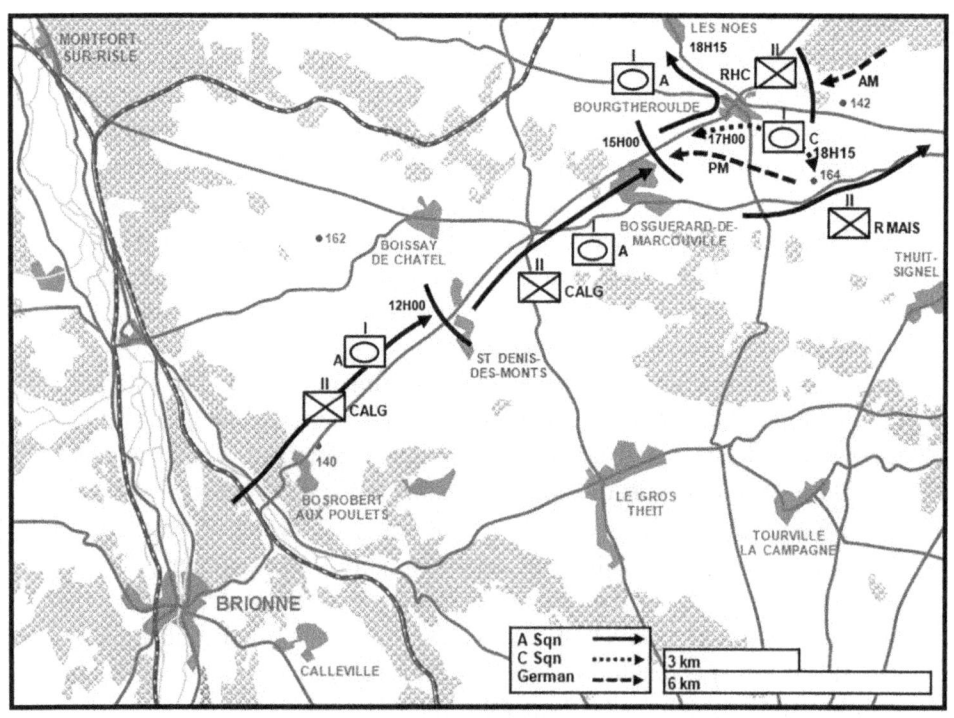

26 August 1944: The battle for Bourgtheroulde.

THE PURSUIT TO THE SEINE

and artillery fire were reported from a wooded area north of the main road. A Sqn had to stop en route when enemy infantry was reported about 1 mile north of the road they were travelling. As a consequence, a troop was sent to make a recce to the right of the main road near Saint-Philbert-sur-Boissey. The area was filled with orchards and sunken roads. Enemy tanks were believed to be dug-in along the main road itself. Once again, the enemy was engaged and forced to retreat. The recce troop on its flank reported a flying bomb launching site in the area of Bas-normand, a few miles south of Bourgtheroulde. It had already been used and then demolished prior to the recce troop moving into the area. The advance once again resumed and the squadron passed through Bosguérard-de-Marcouville. It rolled up a hill and onto a 1.5 mile stretch of flat terrain in front of Bourgtheroulde at about 15.00. Lieut Williams's tank was on the right side of Maj Radley-Walters's tank and he yelled over that something was coming up on the left flank. It turned out to be two *PzKpfw IV* tanks. A German *Kampfgruppe*, formed from the remnants of a reconnaissance battalion and composed of several light tanks, two *PzKpfw IV* and about one company of infantry, had positioned itself to the southwest of Bourgtheroulde. C Sqn was ordered to move back west of Bourgtheroulde to give A Sqn a hand, and friendly artillery fire was brought down. The German *Kampfgruppe* was caught between both squadrons and eliminated. The light tanks and one *PzKpfw IV* were engaged and destroyed. The other *PzKpfw IV* succeeded in knocking out two of A Sqn's tanks before it too was destroyed. Sgt Beardsley's tank was knocked out by anti-tank fire from Point 150. The crew bailed out but Tpr Paul J.H. Elliott was killed and another crewman wounded. Sgt Milne was also wounded in the hand by machine-gun fire and so his crew evacuated him to the rear. Sgt Beardsley moved over to discuss his situation with Maj Radley-Walters and was told to go back to the echelon to get another tank. There, he took over Sgt Milne's tank and returned to the front. About 500 yards behind the *PzKpfw IV* was an eight-wheeled armoured car with a short-barrelled 75mm gun. It fired at Maj Radley-Walters's tank, but missed. He fired back and put a round through its front end; it brewed up and the crew tried to escape. He ordered his tank to advance and when he came alongside one of the crew, he tackled him. He turned out to be the German OC the reconnaissance unit. A Sqn then proceeded into the town at about 17.00.

It was found that the enemy had already evacuated the town. The order was then given to overcome enemy resistance north of the village. Capt G.I. Fripp's tank was knocked out by anti-tank fire from Les Noës. Two crew members were wounded and had to be evacuated. Thirty minutes after first being hit, a Sherman tank went whizzing by Maj Radley-Walters's tank, it was Sgt Beardsley. He waved as he went by and moved forward on the left for another 300 yards before his tank was again hit by anti-tank fire from Les Noës – his driver was badly hurt. Sgt Beardsley got him safely out and administered first aid, but the driver ultimately lost both his legs. After he was evacuated, Capt Fripp and Sgt Beardsley headed back once again to get another tank.[3] The attack continued and the squadron entered and occupied the town with the Calgary Highlanders. By the time the infantry got into defensive positions, daylight was fading, so the squadron moved back and SSM E.A. Howland moved in with the echelon to replenish the tanks. Maj Radley-Walters told him to look after Sgt Beardsley as he had already been knocked out of two tanks that day and had gone back for another. SSM Howland replied that Sgt Beardsley had already come back up with the echelon and was there with a new tank, ready to go. A Sqn harboured for the night in the area of Les Noës. At 18.15, C Sqn was ordered to support the R de Mais onto Point 164. The position was taken and the battalion pushed on to reach the outskirts of the Forêt de la Londe, where they took up a defensive position.

4th Brigade embussed in the afternoon and moved forward to Bourgtheroulde. From there, the brigade was to march along the northeast route through the Forêt de la Londe and take up positions in the general area of Moulineaux. The Essex Scottish was in the lead followed by the RHLI and the R Regt C. As the Essex Scottish approached the town of Bourgtheroulde, it was met with the sounds of the fierce firefight in the town between the enemy and the Black Watch. The battalion passed through the town amid very heavy mortar fire on the main intersection. Once through the town, they met up with the Black Watch which was repulsing another German counter-attack. The Essex Scottish managed to move a short distance forward but had to stop and take up defensive positions.

The mission of 2nd Cdn Inf Div was to capture Rouen and the crossings located there. To do so, it would have to advance up the isthmus which was about 3 miles wide. During the evening, Maj-Gen Foulkes came up with a revised plan for a deliberate attack on the forest with 4th Brigade on the right and 6th Brigade on the left. The final plan which he settled upon was for 5th Brigade to clear and hold Bourgtheroulde while 4th Brigade advanced through Elbeuf. The RHLI would take the lead while the Essex Scottish disengaged itself from the enemy and followed behind it. The R Regt C was to remain as the brigade reserve. The two lead battalions were to seize the high ground overlooking the Seine, north of the hamlet of Port du Gravier. The R Regt C would then pass through and take up a position just south of Grand Essart; 6th Brigade was ordered to clear the Forêt de la Londe. The South Sask would lead off on the left flank along a route through La Bouille to Le Buisson. The Camerons would follow through to La Chênaie and Moulineaux. The FMR would then drive through the isthmus east of the railway triangle, and 5th Brigade would become the 2nd Cdn Inf Div reserve. At 19.20, orders were received from 2nd Cdn Armd Bde instructing Lt-Col Gordon to report for duty as the acting brigade commander during the absence of Brig Bingham, who was admitted to hospital suffering from 'an internal chill'. Lt-Col Gordon was the senior CO of the brigade since both the Hussars and the Garrys had changed COs since D-Day. Maj Walsh, the DCO of the regiment, was detailed as the acting CO during his absence.

The Forêt de la Londe blocks the meander of the Seine that leads directly to Rouen. Its bottleneck is wooded and hilly, with only narrow tracks through the forest. At its widest, the bottleneck of the meander is about 4,000 yards wide. The terrain rises gradually to attain 120 metres above the river. In the northwest corner, there is a north-south depression, possibly an old river bed. Two railway lines, about 100 yards apart, run across the bottleneck and include four tunnels. One branches north through a tunnel built under a steep chalk hill, codenamed 'CHALK PITS HILL'. Close to the river, there is a second hill just east of the railway lines, codenamed 'MAISIE', which controls access to two of the three roads to Rouen. The region was largely uninhabited. A 2nd Cdn Inf Div intelligence summary issued on the night of 26–27 August put the enemy presence as 'nothing more than a local rearguard'. However, the Germans had set up a strong defensive position in the area of MAISIE and it had been ordered to hold the isthmus to gain time for the retreating forces which were trying to escape across the river. The lines of approach through the forest offered excellent positions of fire and defence for the defenders. An estimated two battalions of paratroopers and SS men were believed to be located there. The division intelligence section, however, believed that the enemy had evacuated the area and would offer only limited opposition. In reality, the bottleneck of the meander was held by elements of *559.Infanterie-Regiment*, reinforced by elements of the *6.Fallschirm-Gruppe*. Some of these reinforcements had been flown into the area from Paris on the night of 25–26 August.

On 26 August, 3rd Cdn Inf Div seized Elbeuf, but its advance was held up while it waited for the engineers to complete a bridge over the Seine. It was only at 09.00 the next morning that the division started crossing the river to the cheers of the villagers. By 10.30, two battalions were across and by 17.00 the Regina Rifles were on their objective in the area northwest of Tourville. Farther to the south, 4th Cdn Armd Div had reached the Seine in the area of Criquebeuf and Pont-de-l'Arche. The Algonquins of 10th Brigade crossed in assault boats at Criquebeuf at 07.15 on 27 August and took Sotteville. The Argyll & Sutherland followed suit at 08.15 and occupied Igoville by 18.00. The Lincoln & Welland crossed the Seine in the evening and took up positions on the railway line.

At 23.50 on 26 August, 4th Brigade commenced its advance to Elbeuf and then towards Port du Gravier. The RHLI took over the lead. Its objective

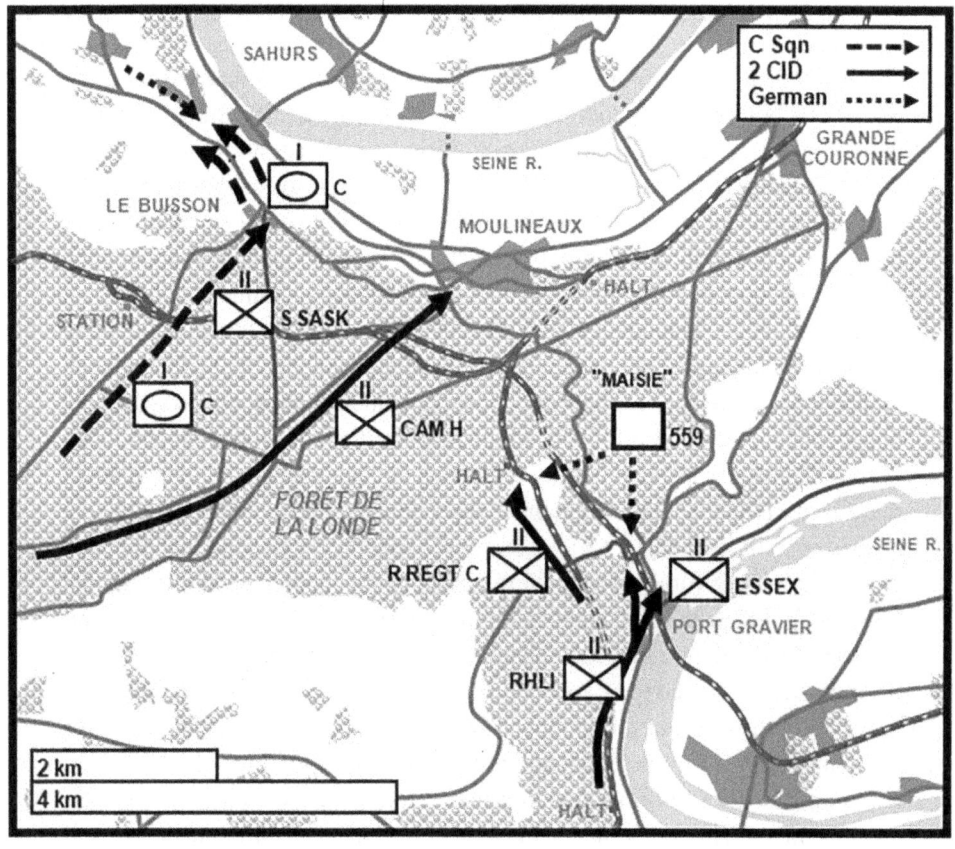

27 August 1944: The Forêt de la Londe.

was to secure the high ground overlooking the Seine in order to give protection to the Elbeuf crossing by 3rd Cdn Inf Div. As they advanced, the roads and villages had to be cleared. As the battalion moved through Bourgtheroulde, it was forced to debus because of heavy shelling. When its advance resumed, it ran into mines. When it finally approached Port du Gravier, the battalion came under attack from small arms and mortar fire, but it was generally inaccurate and the battalion suffered few casualties. When the RHLI finally reached the hamlet at about 02.00, it took the left fork in the road by mistake instead of continuing on up the river; 500 yards up, the road was blocked by machine-gun and mortar fire. The battalion took up a defensive position a little south of there, where the railway tracks and the road to Elbeuf met. The Essex Scottish now became the lead battalion and resumed the brigade's advance towards Oissel. The battalion was also halted at about 03.30 by grenades, machine-guns and mortar fire coming from Port du Gravier. It dug-in on the river banks amid continuous German mortar and artillery fire.

The R Regt C, the brigade reserve, had halted its advance at Orival at first light. At 09.00, Brig Ganong, the commander of 4th Brigade, came to the realisation that neither the RHLI nor the Essex Scottish would be able to take the Germans on MAISIE through a frontal attack. He therefore ordered the R Regt C to make a wide flanking movement; first northwest then east across the Moulineaux-Port du Gravier road, to get behind the enemy positions at CHALK PITS HILL and MAISIE, which were holding up the brigade. The battalion moved out at 11.30 but its progress through the woods was slow. At 15.00, its lead troops encountered a company from the FMR which was acting as the right flank of 6th Brigade. Brig Ganong requested that the FMR be placed under the command of 4th Brigade. The request was granted and the transfer of control was completed by 16.15. The R Regt C was then ordered to make an attack across the Orival-Moulineaux road using the FMR artillery plan. However, this order was remanded shortly after it was issued. Instead, the battalion was ordered to move northward through the forest and rendezvous with C Coy and D Coy of the Essex Scottish which had been ordered to move up from Port du Gravier. At 18.30, it moved off but failed to make contact with the Essex Scottish. Led by a guide from the Maquis,[4] the battalion reached the railway halt-station without incident two hours later and dug in.

Just after midnight, Brig Ganong issued his orders for the next day. The R Regt C was to continue its wide flanking movement and outflank the machine-gun and mortar positions and seize MAISIE. For their part,

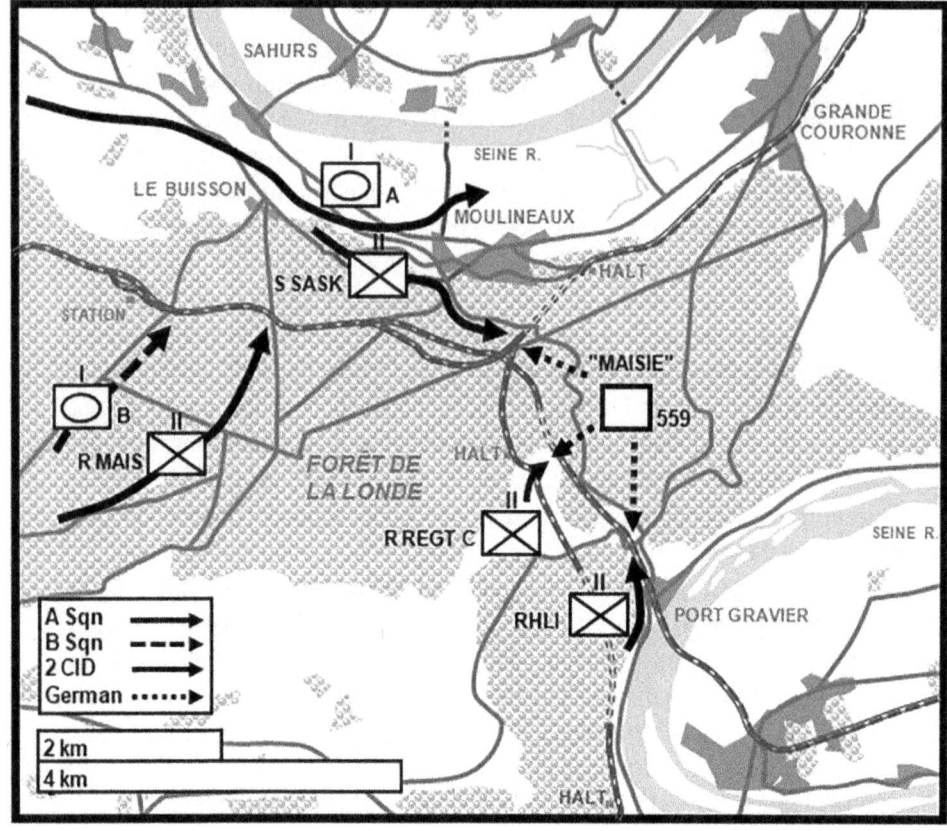

28 August 1944: The Forêt de la Londe.

the Essex Scottish was to punch through on the right, just north of Port du Gravier and take the high ground dominating the river. Just as the R Regt C was preparing to move out, food and water arrived. The troops had not had a solid meal the previous day and no water for eighteen hours. Therefore, the acting CO, Maj T.F. Whitley, allowed his troops time to eat and fill their canteens before moving off. However, rather than the attack starting in darkness as planned, the attack got under way at first light. Its immediate objective was CHALK PITS HILL. Unfortunately, the companies got separated in the woods and the battalion lost its momentum. An initial attack on CHALK PITS HILL by C Coy was repulsed with heavy casualties. The company was ordered to withdraw. The decision was taken to use artillery fire to soften up the position in preparation for a battalion attack. This took some time to arrange and the advance was again delayed.

However, despite mortar and artillery fire, the enemy position was not neutralised. At 11.30, the battalion attack commenced with B Coy on the left and A Coy on the right; D Coy followed behind on the right to support A Coy. The B Coy attack got bogged down in the afternoon, but C Coy was down to only twenty men and could not be sent up to reinforce it. Therefore, the order was given for B Coy to withdraw. On the right, A Coy reached the second railway but met heavy opposition there. Believing A Coy was having a certain measure of success, D Coy was sent forward to reinforce A Coy and resume the advance. Unfortunately, the attack came to a halt. A smoke screen was laid on but, due to the large area it had to cover, it was ineffectual and the companies were forced to remain in their positions under heavy mortar and artillery fire for the remainder of the day.

The Essex Scottish began its attack from the south at 13.30. C Coy and D Coy led the advance and passed through Port du Gravier after an intense artillery barrage. They took the northern road towards Moulineaux but met with heavy fire from machine-guns, light mortars and cup-discharged grenades. It was soon realised that the battalion could not take the high ground without negotiating a steep slope down the railway embankment and then crossing a narrow valley. The companies got into the valley but came under enemy observation. The battalion was pinned down by intense, accurate and sustained machine-gun fire. It suffered heavy casualties and was forced to dig in. After dark, it was withdrawn to its original position along the river road southwest of Port du Gravier.

At 16.00 on 28 August, Maj-Gen Foulkes held a conference attended by Brig Ganong and his three battalion commanders. A new plan was discussed to take MAISIE by sending a battalion through the R Regt C positions in the darkness. The COs of both the RHLI and the R Regt C emphasised to Maj-Gen Foulkes that this operation was beyond the ability of their battalions, which were mainly composed of reinforcement personnel with little training. They suggested that the enemy was actually stronger than earlier intelligence reports indicated and the ground immensely favoured the defence. Despite these arguments, the RHLI was ordered to prepare to pass through the forward lines of the R Regt C and take MAISIE before first light.

Just prior to the move up, the CO of the RHLI, Lt-Col G.M. MacLachlan suddenly took ill and had to be replaced by Maj H.C. Arrell. The RHLI moved up slowly through the woods during the early morning of 29 August, having experienced difficulties in navigation due to the unreliability of the maps provided. As dawn broke on 29 August, the lead elements crossed the

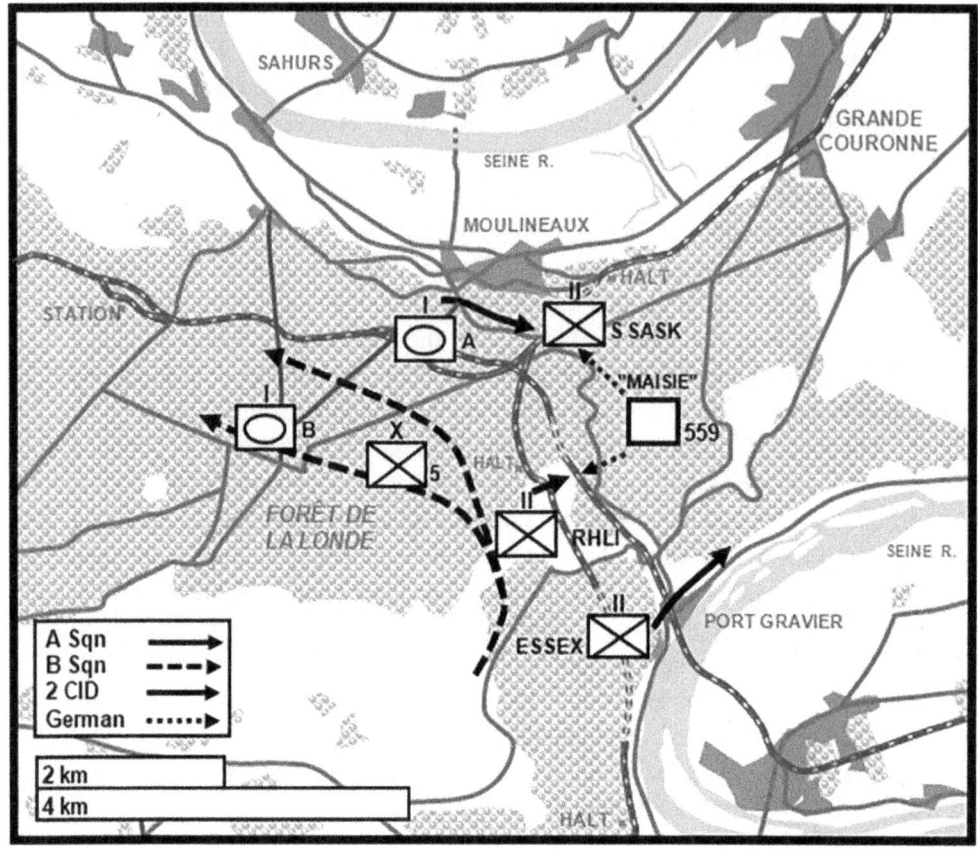

29 August 1944: The Forêt de la Londe.

first railway line and came under heavy machine-gun and mortar fire from MAISIE. Four enemy machine-gun posts were located and an attack from the flank using artillery support was planned. D Coy approached quickly but came under fire from a fifth, previously unseen machine-gun position on the right flank. The company was forced to withdraw after the artillery laid down a smoke screen. A Coy moved forward to the railway bridge when it was also hit by heavy machine-gun fire. At 13.26, the companies moved back and Maj Arrell reported that the position could not be taken. The battalion stayed in its forward positions all afternoon in the rain and without food before it was withdrawn to the R Regt C area. The R Regt C, who had watched the fruitless attack of the RHLI, also stayed in its positions throughout the day. In the afternoon, permission was asked for A Coy and D Coy to withdraw from their advance positions. This was granted and accomplished using artillery smoke. During the evening, the battalion moved into a concentration in the neighbourhood of La Capelle, west of Elbeuf. On the brigade's right flank, the Essex Scottish had discovered that the Germans seemed to have drawn back. Just before noon, the battalion reported it had advanced some 800 yards beyond the railway bridge at Port du Gravier. Both A Coy and B Coy fired on numerous caves with machine-gun fire and a 6-pdr anti-tank gun. That evening, they were informed that they were to be relieved by 8th Cdn Recce Regt and were to be prepared to continue the advance the following morning; 4th Brigade had lost 29 officers and 289 other ranks in the course of the Forêt de la Londe operation.

As part of the 2nd Cdn Inf Div plan, 6th Brigade, now under the command of Brig Clift,[5] was ordered to push through the Forêt de la Londe with the intention of reaching the Seine at La Bouille and La Chênaie. The South Sask was to lead the brigade advance and clear the enemy from Le Buisson and La Bouille. The Camerons were to advance east through the forest to take La Chênaie and Moulineaux. The FMR had been ordered to swing around from the south and move through the forest to join up with the Camerons in the area of the railway triangle south of La Chênaie. At 08.00 on 27 August, the South Sask led off the brigade advance towards Le Buisson. When they reached the entrance to the forest at Saint Martin, they came under fire and were forced to debus. The road was covered by German anti-tank guns set up where the railway crossed the main road and pointing straight down the road. A Coy, B Coy and D Coy started to advance on foot until they reached the vicinity of the railway crossing. There, C Coy made a left flanking via the railway bridge and established that the enemy was absent in the western part of the forest. The position was turned and the battalion prepared for its assault on Le Buisson and then La Bouille.

Capt Belton had taken over command of C Sqn when Maj Walsh had assumed temporary command of the regiment. At 11.00, the squadron moved down the main road from Bourgtheroulde, through the forest and made contact with the South Sask in preparation for its attack on the Seine in the vicinity of La Bouille. The move forward was done without opposition and the South Sask proceeded to clear the high ground south of La Bouille and took up defensive positions on their objective. Once through the forest, C Sqn reached the heights overlooking the banks of the Seine.

There, it caught off guard about 300 German soldiers sunbathing on the far bank. Immediately, the order was given for a squadron shoot and the tanks began to pound HE shells into the area, with devastating results. When word reached them that German tanks were attacking from the west, the squadron wheeled left and advanced westward along two parallel paths to meet the threat; one thrust on the main road and the second on a small track to its right. The German infantry had placed an anti-tank gun screen to look down the track while some tanks were positioned on the main road. The troops tried to outflank the position but were unsuccessful. One tank was lost due to a shot through its bogie wheels. A second tank was lost due to engine trouble. The former was later recovered and the latter was withdrawn from the battle prior to suffering a complete engine failure. Nonetheless, the German counter-attack was halted. In the meantime, the Camerons, following behind the South Sask, now debussed at the forward edge of the forest and pushed forward on foot towards the Seine. Passing through the forest, the battalion pushed on, arriving in the vicinity of La Chênaie at about 20.00. There, it took heavy fire from an enemy position about 1,000 yards forward of its position which halted the battalion's advance just short of its final objective. It established a defensive position in La Vacherie, just south of Moulineaux. Unfortunately, little of much consequence was accomplished by the tanks during the day. Great difficulty was encountered due to the natural cover offered to the German anti-tank gun defences, the inability of the tanks to leave the roads, and the infantry going to ground rather than outflanking the enemy strong points and destroying them to allow the tanks to proceed. Considerable friction developed between commanders at all levels, and this was due to a lack of appreciation on the part of the infantry of the problems that occur in the employment of armour in close country – particularly in woods where it is often so dense that traversing the main guns is greatly limited. When darkness had fallen, the infantry released the tanks for the night and they returned to Bourgtheroulde.

Brig Clift held another O Group just after midnight. The main objective of 6th Brigade for 28 August would be to move towards Oissel with the hope of outflanking the enemy positions which were holding up 4th Brigade. The Camerons were to stay put in their present position and continue to dominate the German escape route at La Vacherie. The South Sask, in the lead, was to take the first brigade objective, La Roquette. The FMR, which had been released by 4th Brigade during the evening and was to rejoin the brigade during the night, would then pass through the South Sask and take the second brigade objective – the high ground just north of and overlooking Oissel. The South Sask made an early start southeast from Le Buisson towards the railway bridges south of La Chênaie. C Coy was in the lead and reached the railway triangle south of La Chênaie without encountering the enemy. When the troops were half-way across the first bridge, they came under sniper and machine-gun fire from the left flank. Two separate flanking attacks on either side of the enemy failed to make any progress. C Coy was ordered to withdraw and it was again hit by heavy fire as it moved. It lost all its officers and was down to thirteen men. The battalion withdrew to the road junction at Le Buisson and reorganised in a defensive position. The FMR should have followed the South Sask, but machine-gun and mortar fire kept them virtually immobilised throughout the day in the area west of Port du Gravier. Therefore, new instructions were issued during the afternoon ordering the South Sask to make a second attempt. However, with the FMR unable to move, the Camerons were ordered to be the follow-on battalion and take over the FMR objectives. The Calgary Highlanders from 5th Brigade would relieve the Camerons and watch La Vacherie.

The division reserve was 5th Brigade. It was tasked with mopping up the remnants of Germans in Bourgtheroulde and securing the left flank of the division. On 27 August, A Sqn was put in support of the Calgary Highlanders and pushed forward from Bourgtheroulde northward through Les Noës towards Bosc-Bénard-Commin. When the squadron reached Les Noës, it found that the enemy had cleared away during the previous night. It stayed in the area most of the day before it withdrew at 19.00 to refuel and rest. First thing the next morning, A Sqn was ordered to move in support of the Camerons, which was well-entrenched in a position west of Moulineaux overlooking the Seine River and cutting off the German escape route by way of the La Vacherie ferry. A Sqn worked its way from Les Noës, around the west end of the Forêt de la Londe and then eastward until it reached a point on the riverbank about 2 miles east of where C Sqn had been the day before. There, it patrolled the river and engaged the enemy along the northern bank. It destroyed barges on the river and caused a lot of damage to German equipment on the opposite bank. The Germans still on the south side of the Seine were under continuous harassment from Allied artillery and Typhoons. They tried to move closer to the Camerons' positions under the cover of the woods in an attempt to find sanctuary from the attacks. Both sides fought a battle of mortar fire with heavy casualties inflicted on both sides. That evening, A Sqn was ordered to give support to the South Sask of 6th Brigade in its renewed attack towards Oissel.

At 21.30, the South Sask began a new attempt to take Oissel. The planned route was an advance from Le Buisson to the crossroads just west of Moulineaux, and then to turn south along the main Moulineaux-Port du Gravier road. Once at Port du Gravier, the advance would take a left turn and move along the river road to La Roquette. A Coy led off, followed by D Coy; just before the crossroads, the advance came upon a castle that had belonged to Robert 'Diablo', the brother of William the Conqueror. A Coy set up a position by the castle, while D Coy assumed the lead. When the battalion reached the crossroads, D Coy was hit by considerable small arms and mortar fire. A Coy moved off from its position by the castle and began to clear up the machine-gun and sniper positions beyond. At 22.30, the advance resumed and the South Sask turned south down the main road to Port du Gravier. Shortly after midnight, D Coy was once again halted 300 yards beyond the railway triangle. B Coy did a right flanking and succeeded in getting to the railway triangle at 02.30, but the battalion could get no further. The battalion commander was killed when his vehicle hit a mine, so the battalion took up firing positions and dug in along the road. Owing to the darkness and heavy opposition from *Panzerschreck* and machine-guns, A Sqn was released and went back to Le Buisson to spend the night. At first light, a German counter-attack drove the companies back to the area of the crossroads southeast of Moulineaux. There they set up a defensive position with the help of the A Sqn tanks. At first light on 29 August, SSM Howland and the squadron A Ech moved up to refuel and rearm A Sqn.

The forest roads were filled with enemy so they wasted no time moving up to Le Buisson. An attack by 6th Brigade was launched that morning on the crossroads east of La Chênaie. The CO of the Camerons, Lt-Col A.S. Gregory, was wounded and had to be evacuated. At 10.00, Sgt James A. Woodward's tank hit a mine. The crew remained in the tank until 18.45 and succeeded nonetheless in firing on the enemy with some effect. For the rest of the day, the squadron remained in the vicinity of Moulineaux and patrolled the river; A Sqn set up a defensive position based around the castle. Brig Clift came forward and was talking to Maj Radley-Walters when suddenly a machine-gun opened up and hit him in the left leg and the right ankle. He rolled off the high ground and Maj Radley-Walters had to carry him to the side of his tank for protection. Once he was loaded onto the tank, they moved back to an infantry aid station where a stretcher was waiting. From there, Brig Clift was evacuated to the rear.[6] Unfortunately, when Maj Radley-Walters moved his tank, 'Caribou II', forward towards his previous position, the tank hit an improvised mine made from two Teller mines on top of a large artillery or naval gun shell. It blew the bottom out of the tank and it started to brew up. Tpr James A. MacDougall and Tpr Paquette panicked when Maj Radley-Walters was slow to exit the tank – they pushed his backside from below and he went right out the top. The crew followed. Each member of the crew suffered varying degrees of burn, but Maj Radley-Walters was badly burned on his hands, his face and his ears, and he had a nasty gash where his head had hit the hatch cover. He was evacuated back to Bourgtheroulde along with his driver, Tpr McDougall.

5th Brigade had spent a day resting, but on 28 August it was ordered to lend a hand in the Forêt de la Londe. The plan was for the infantry to sweep through the forest from the east and flush the enemy troops westward towards the tanks of B Sqn. The road through the forest was supposed to be secure since C Sqn and 6th Brigade had passed through the day before. Therefore, the Black Watch moved forward and established itself in the area of Le Buisson where it came under heavy mortar- and shell-fire. The R de Mais carried out patrols on the brigade's far right flank from Bas de la Vigne. However, in order to support the infantry, the B Sqn tanks had to push in among the trees. The forest was so dense that the trees prevented the turrets from traversing. To make matters worse, the Germans tank-hunting teams had infiltrated the forest during the night with their deadly *Panzerfaust* and stealth snipers. B Sqn was unable to get through, however, and the original 5th Brigade plan had to be abandoned. B Sqn spent the day of 29 August on the right flank and joined the main body of 5th Brigade in a steady pushing advance through the woods. The Calgary Highlanders had relieved the Camerons in their watch of the ferry crossing at La Vacherie on 28 August, but all the next day they were subject to small arms and artillery fire.

During the morning of 29 August, the 2nd Cdn Inf Div HQ paid a visit to Maj Walsh to discuss the proper use of tanks in an effort to avoid the recurrence of instances of misemployment. After the meeting, the Int O was sent to 2nd Cdn Armd Bde HQ to brief Lt-Col Gordon on the course adopted. Lt-Col Gordon, as acting brigade commander, followed suit and went to the 2nd Cdn Inf Div HQ, where he discussed the situation with Maj-Gen Foulkes. He criticised the division's planned method of using tanks in close country such as the Forêt de la Londe. He urged Maj-Gen Foulkes to call off the 2nd Cdn Inf Div attempt to clear the Germans out of the forest before throwing a bridge across the Seine. Instead, he suggested that the division cross the river at Elbeuf which was already in the hands of 3rd Cdn Inf Div. The division had already lost one brigade commander and two COs to date in the fruitless struggle. At the O Group held later that afternoon at

6th Brigade HQ, Maj-Gen Foulkes called off the remaining attacks planned for 6th Brigade. Instead, 6th Brigade was told to hold a line from La Chênaie to Elbeuf to prevent the enemy from infiltrating back into the forest. In the meantime, 4th Brigade and 5th Brigade were to move into the area of Elbeuf in anticipation of crossing the Seine River using 3rd Cdn Inf Div's bridges. All day, the Camerons had received harassing long-range shellfire, interspersed with 88mm fire from La Chênaie. Late that evening, they were relieved and moved to a quieter area near Elbeuf; 6th Brigade had also suffered heavy casualties. At 14.00, the fighting strength of the South Sask was down to four officers and sixty other ranks. Twenty reinforcements, the dismounted carrier platoon, were brought up and distributed between the decimated rifle companies. During the night, a German patrol slipped through in the region of Moulineaux and planted demolition charges on two A Sqn tanks and destroyed them before being discovered. Maj Radley-Walters complained to the division commander of the unnecessary risks that the tanks were taking in the woods. He was taken back to the Second Cdn Corps HQ with Lt-Col Gordon and he spoke to Lt-Gen Simonds. The decision was taken to stop the fighting and to pull out 2nd Cdn Inf Div. Instead, the Free French were to cordon off the area and the Germans left to starve. In the course of events, they surrendered four days later.

In the course of the night of 29–30 August, the majority of the German defenders withdrew from the isthmus. Suddenly, 6th Brigade was no longer faced with the heavy mortar- and shell-fire that had assailed them for the last three days. The brigade spent a quiet day reorganising and received much needed reinforcements; 6th Brigade had suffered 17 officer casualties and 287 other ranks, and 4th Brigade had suffered 273 casualties. While 6th Brigade reorganised, the balance of 2nd Cdn Inf Div crossed the Seine River and proceeded north towards Rouen; 5th Brigade crossed the bridges at Elbeuf on 30 August and occupied positions northeast of Tourville vacated by 7th Brigade. The next day, the brigade, with B Sqn in support, pushed along the meander and entered Rouen without encountering much resistance. Each tank had eight to ten infantrymen riding on top. The citizens of the city turned out by the thousand to welcome the Canadians and passed up endless bottles of wine to the troops. The going got so congested that it took several hours to go through the city. By 18.00, the tanks finally reached the neighbourhood of Tôtes, some 10 miles north of Rouen; 4th Brigade had established itself near Elbeuf in anticipation of a two to three day period of rest. However, orders were received during the day to resume the advance on

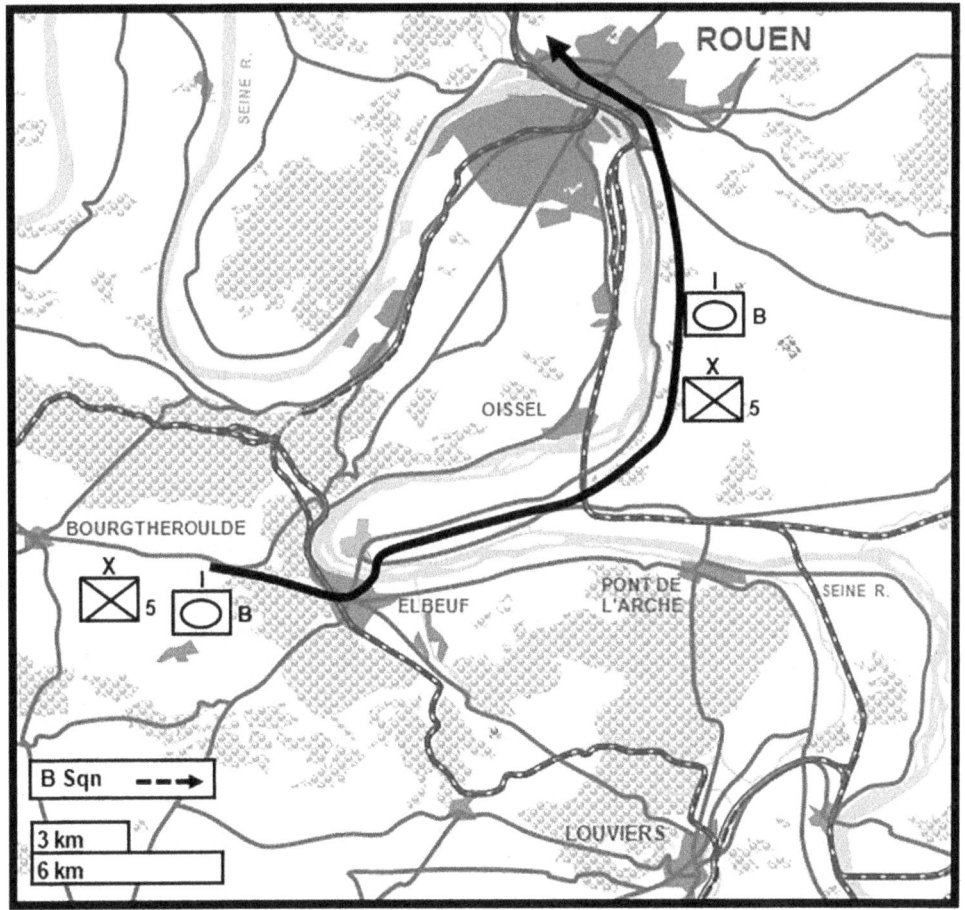

31 August 1944: The move through Rouen.

Dieppe the next day; 4th Brigade followed 5th Brigade across the Seine and took over 9th Brigade's area south of the city. C Sqn also crossed the Seine on 31 August and moved up to Rouen using secondary roads; 3 Troop was given the task of clearing a short but difficult stretch of road. On the right side of the road, there was an almost sheer drop, and it was just as sharp a drop on the left side. As Lieut Reginald Bickford Hoar's tank approached a sharp curve, it was fired upon by a German tank. A bogey wheel was badly damaged to the extent that the tank could neither move forward nor backwards. Tpr D.T. Smith, his gunner, sat there and fired round after round until the drivers were able to free the track and get the tank mobile once again. The tanks pushed ahead and established a harbour area in Criquetot-sur-Longueville, about 16 miles west of Neufchâtel-en-Bray.

During the four-day battle, the Canadians had suffered 791 killed, wounded or missing. These were soldiers that would prove difficult to replace in the coming months, and those replacements received would be sent up regardless of their lack of adequate training. The Forêt de la Londe had another long-lasting effect: the infantry lost faith in the tanks. The tanks couldn't get around the trees that lined each side of the narrow logging roads that crisscrossed the forest. The woods were so dense that the guns couldn't traverse. When a target was visible, the main gun couldn't be used with effect since HE rounds would detonate after hitting a tree or branch. If the tanks went into the open fields, they got clobbered. The Germans had 88mm anti-tank guns positioned on the top of the hills with the open ground well-sited, or positioned to aim directly down the roads and tracks. When the guns opened up, the infantry usually went to ground rather than advance to take out the threat. The situation proved that the tank should not be used as a direct support weapon for the infantry in that type of terrain. To make matters worse, the commanding generals continued to send the troops in day after day against the same positions, with the same devastating results day after day. Confidence in its leadership also became a subject of discussion.

On 26 August, Gen Montgomery issued a new directive for the next phase of the pursuit: 21st Army Group was to destroy all the enemy forces in northeast France and Belgium. In doing so, it would secure the Pas-de-Calais area and the airfields in Belgium. It would then secure Antwerp as a supply base. Eventually, 21st Army Group was to advance eastward towards the Ruhr River and its industrial centres. During the advance, the main weight would be on its right flank. Enemy resistance would be dealt with by out-flanking movements and 'right hooks'. Second Brit Army was to be the spearhead of the general advance towards Belgium. It was ordered to cross the Seine and advance rapidly northwards and to establish itself as soon as possible in the Arras-Amiens-Saint-Pol-sur-Ternoise area. It was to advance with its armoured strength deployed well ahead. First Cdn Army received the task of pushing north and securing the port of Dieppe. It would then proceed quickly with the destruction of all the enemy forces in the coastal belt up to Bruges. First Brit Corps was to turn westward into the Le Harve Peninsula and secure Le Havre.

THE PURSUIT TO THE SEINE

On the Canadian front, 3rd Cdn Inf Div had crossed the Seine at Elbeuf on 30 August. With 9th Brigade leading, the division cleared the main routes through Rouen and sent patrols 4 miles beyond the city; 7th Brigade moved up to the Boos area while 8th Brigade moved up and took up positions 5 miles north of Boos in the Fontaine-sous-Preaux-Rocherolle area. That evening, orders were received for the division to resume its advance the next morning from Le Mesnil-Esnard along the Rocherolle-Fontaine-le-Bourg-Saint-Saëns axis. Before 3rd Cdn Inf Div reached Saint-Saëns, it was ordered to push through to Pommeréval. In fact, it got as far as Neufchâtel-en-Bray where the division bivouacked for the night. On 27 August, the decision had been taken for 4th Cdn Armd Div to cross the Seine River using the Bailey pontoon bridge built by 3rd Cdn Inf Div engineers in Elbeuf. The armoured division crossed the next day and 4th Cdn Armd Bde concentrated in the Sotteville area, while 10th Brigade consolidated at Igoville. In the meantime, an additional pontoon bridge was started at Criquebeuf but had to be stopped when the site came under enemy fire. On 29 August, Polish engineers arrived and the work started once again. It was completed the next day and baptised 'WARSAW' by the Polish.

Lt-Gen Crerar issued new orders on 30 August. First Brit Corps was to clear Le Havre Peninsula while Second Cdn Corps was to capture Dieppe by 2 September. Any troops not being used in the attack on Dieppe were to continue in a thrust along the main Neufchâtel-en-Bray-Abbeville axis as a preliminary move for an early crossing of the Somme River. Lt-Gen Simonds gave the lead role to 4th Cdn Armd Div. It was to advance along the Pont-Saint-Pierre-Boos-Mesnil-Esnard axis; 10th Brigade was to seize the high ground at Ymare, while 4th Cdn Armd Bde seized the general area Les Grandes Masures-Pont-Saint-Pierre. From there, 10th Brigade would take Le Mesnil-Esnard and Notre Dame de Franqueville and 4th Cdn Armd Bde would capture the Neuville-Champs-d'Oisel-Boos area. The armoured brigade would then exploit to the area of Buchy. On 31 August, 4th Cdn Armd Div seized its objectives in the Buchy area, having passed some V-1 launch sites en route.

With Maj Radley-Walters incapacitated, Capt Welsh of B Sqn was loaned to A Sqn on 30 August to act as its squadron commander. The squadron was down to eight tanks and so the decision was taken to split the squadron in two. Four tanks, under Lieut Harold James Butler and Lieut George Lloyd Marshall, went with the RHQ while the other four were sent to C Sqn under the command of Lieut Martin. That same day, the regiment, less B Sqn, crossed the Seine River at Elbeuf and concentrated in the area of Les Authieuxsur-le-Port-Saint-Ouen. The tanks under Lieut Marshall and Lieut Butler continued on to Tôtes and came under the command of B Sqn. Lieut Butler went into Torcy-le-Grand with the Black Watch but found it clear of enemy. The balance of B Sqn went to the crossroads just north of Belmesnil and watched 2nd Cdn Inf Div pass by on its way to Dieppe. The squadron later moved to join the RHQ and C Sqn which had arrived in the area of Criquetot-sur-Longueville. With the enemy gone or isolated, 6th Brigade proceeded by road from Moulineaux up the Rouvray peninsula to Rouen, reaching the town at 15.00. The brigade used a repaired railway bridge to cross the river and moved through the city to a concentration area on its northern outskirts.

On 31 August, Brig Bingham resumed his command of 2nd Cdn Armd Bde at 15.50. Lt-Col Gordon briefed him before moving off the next day to rejoin the regiment in Criquetot-sur-Longueville. The *Sherbrookes* were tasked to act as the brigade's reserve and settled down to two days of rest and maintenance. 2nd Cdn Inf Div was advancing on Dieppe and the British armoured divisions were streaking through Arras and were already entering Belgium as the regiment set up its harbour amid the green pasturelands south of Dieppe. For the first time since the beginning of the Canadian drive south from Caen, the unit had time to catch up on long overdue maintenance. At his afternoon O Group, the CO emphasised that all the unit's vehicles were to be cleaned and painted where necessary; 85th LAD was also tasked to complete an entire vehicle engine check by the end of the week.

Brig Bingham issued new orders at 08.00 on 2 September. He advised Lt-Col Gordon that the next move for the *Sherbrookes* was expected to be about 100 to 200 miles at a rate of 50 miles per day. Each move would commence at first light at a maximum speed of 15 mph, the maximum limit for tanks. Military Provost would monitor the move and anyone caught speeding would face disciplinary action. The column would take the normal maintenance halt parades but drive as long as possible each day. The *Sherbrookes* were also promised eight new tanks. The regiment needed more, but eight corresponded to the maximum number for which competent crew commanders could be found. Efforts would have to be made internally to fill crew vacancies with tradesmen. The *Sherbrookes* had been operating for several days now as two squadrons since Maj Radley-Walters' injuries. Orders were now given for the unit to reorganise back into three squadrons by the next day.

When Lt-Col Gordon got back to the regimental lines, he held his own information conference at 10.00. He declared that the tank had come into its own. Up to Falaise, it was a close support weapon for the infantry. It was now leading the pursuit, which should be considered as normal. Leading tanks should not move up the road, but on either side whenever possible, and use the power of manoeuvre to avoid casualties. In rolling ground, they should outflank the guns that covered the roads and, if seen, call down artillery fire. Once the upcoming move started, the unit would have to get a certificate of satisfactory occupation from the owners of the ground on which they would harbour. This would be the responsibility of the Capt-Adjt; Maj Baldwin, the OC of HQ Sqn, stated that he considered that the B Ech vehicles were substandard. He would inspect all the vehicles and issue directives on maintenance. Furthermore, any German vehicle being used by the echelons must be immediately dispatched to the Enemy Equipment Park. In closing, Lt-Col Gordon instructed the squadron officers to prepare a 'lessons learnt' report in preparation for a meeting with him later that evening and then one with Lt-Gen Simonds at a later date.

That evening, all the officers attended the conference to discuss the lessons learnt over the past month. All agreed that a night thrust was an excellent method of bypassing enemy positions, provided no enemy counter-attacks were met. In such an event, the tanks were practically helpless. The reason was that the gunner had very poor vision through both the periscope and the telescope. The driver, if closed down, also had poor vision and was likely to go off the road. Consequently, the crew commander's job was greatly increased. In addition, travelling by night greatly fatigued a crew because of the loss of sleep and the added strain of the move. Confusion at the head of a column could occur quickly in the darkness, thereby increasing the chances of accidents. If the head of the column was stopped, then the enemy could easily block the rear as well. The vehicles in the centre would then be helpless, the attack halted and the tanks vulnerable to enemy attack.

At 08.00 the next day, a proposed possible move to Foucarmont was cancelled. At 15.50, however, the regiment was advised to be prepared to move to the area of Saucourt on 5 September. Three hours later, the route to be used was confirmed. The tanks were to move independently off the main roads while the wheeled vehicles were to take the route from Tôtes to Dieppe and then follow the coast via Eu to Saucourt. At 21.00, Lt-Col Gordon issued his orders for the move. Lieut Normand Arnold John Dann, the recce troop leader, was to act as the regimental path finder. The order of march would be the recce troop, followed by the ack-ack troop and then C Sqn. The RHQ would then follow with B Sqn and A Sqn closing up the rear. H-Hour for the move would be 06.30 for the tanks and 07.30 for the wheeled vehicles; 85th LAD had already moved off in convoy at 07.30 that morning and arrived in Abbeville at 16.00, having covered some 80 miles.

At 06.30 on 5 September, the tanks rolled off towards Saucourt, a move of 35 miles. The route took the regiment through Arques, a suburb of Dieppe, and Eu to Saucourt, a village 9 miles west of Abbeville. The wheeled vehicles arrived at 13.00, while the tanks arrived later in the afternoon. The trip had been slow, circuitous and tiresome for the tanks, the last part under torrential rains. Several tanks failed to arrive in harbour before 06.30 the next morning having run out of fuel. The rest of 6 September was spent in conducting maintenance in anticipation of the unit's next move. Spirits were raised at around noon when word reached the regiment that Capt Côté, who had been reported missing on the evening of D-Day and believed to be a prisoner of war, had returned to England after escaping German captivity. The unit immediately asked to get him back again.

At 02.00, orders were received from 2nd Cdn Armd Bde to prepare for a brigade move to Sercus near Hazebrouck. That evening, Lt-Col Gordon issued his orders for the move. Once again, Lieut Dann would be the regimental path finder. Maj Walsh would command the tank column and its start time was set for 07.00 on 8 September. The wheeled vehicles would leave at the same time but once again follow a separate route from the tanks. An intelligence report received at 21.30 reported 500 SS troops in the area of Hazebrouck and so, at 22.45, the time for the move was postponed to 'Not before noon'. At 08.30 the next morning, word was received that the move would finally begin at 14.15. The *Sherbrookes* would lead the brigade move, followed by the Hussars, the 2nd Cdn Armd Bde HQ and 17th Light Field Ambulance in the rear. At 14.30, the tanks moved off on their 80-mile trek in a heavy downpour of rain. They travelled all night and reached their new harbour area at 08.00 the next day. On the outskirts of the town, a young woman, in her joy of liberation, threw great bunches of flowers at the tanks. 85th LAD had received orders to move out at 10.00 but only left the harbour at 13.00. It arrived at Hazebrouck ahead of the tanks at 23.45 on 8 September and had to set up a bivouac in the darkness and in a heavy downpour.

At 23.45, orders came down that, due to a petrol shortage and effective immediately, only essential vehicle movement was allowed until further notice. The distances from the beaches in Normandy to the forward lines were growing on a daily basis. Until new port facilities were acquired, only essential movements were allowed. For the *Sherbrookes*, this would mean no further moves for twelve days.[7] During the twelve-day period, the first priority was to get the regiment back up to full fighting strength. The regiment was down to only thirty-three Sherman, nine Firefly and four

THE PURSUIT TO THE SEINE

Stuart tanks; 85th LAD had started doing a mechanical inspection of the tanks in Criquetot-sur-Longueville, and by 12 September they reported that all the tanks were declared up to mechanical standards. The 85th LAD boys now turned their attention to doing the same with the armaments. All the tanks were ordered repainted and squadron signs, numbers and tank names put back on. On 14 September, eight tanks were received that put the regiment strength up to two command tanks, thirty-seven Shermans, eleven Fireflies and four Stuarts.

The regiment also went through a transformation in its personnel structure. Capt Bradley, who had replaced Capt Côté as the Capt-Adjt when the later went missing on D-Day, left the position to become the squadron 2i/c for A Sqn. In his place, Capt Dann took over the position. Capt Fripp took over Capt Dann's position as the recce troop leader, and Lieut Gould also returned to the unit from medical leave after having been injured during Operation TOTALIZE. The unit also received a new dentist, Capt R. Silverstone, who immediately got down to inspecting the dental health of the men. A Canadian Army Rest Camp was established in Deauville on the coast and it provided seventy-two-hour short leaves for the men. On 17 September, a visit was organised under the command of Maj Houston, the OC of B Sqn, for the unit's personnel and some men from 85th LAD to the Vimy Ridge Memorial. The men found the memorial and the surrounding military cemeteries undamaged, carefully tended, and the graves still bright with flowers. First World War craters and trenches were still clearly visible.

At 15.30 on 17 September, 2nd Cdn Armd Bde, less the *Sherbrookes*, was placed under the command of 3rd Cdn Inf Div for Operation UNDERGO, the planned capture of Calais. The *Sherbrookes* were to be the Second Cdn Corps reserve during the operation. At 10.10 the next day, the regiment was placed on one-hour notice to move by 2nd Cdn Armd Bde. That afternoon, Lt-Col Gordon issued orders for a regimental move by tank transporters to Antwerp on 19 September. Guides were to meet the transporters at 06.00 and the regiment was to be ready on a two-hour notice to move. Just before midnight, 2nd Cdn Armd Bde advised the regiment that the transporters would not arrive until the evening of 19 September, and that there would be no move before 20 September.

The next day, a message arrived at 13.15 that the A Ech was to have a harbour recce representative stand by for a 2nd Cdn Armd Bde liaison officer (LO), who would be in the regiment's area at 14.30. The brigade LO finally arrived at 16.20 and informed the regiment that the *Sherbrookes* would move to the area of Contich, Belgium, on the outskirts of Antwerp.

The regiment was to send recce parties separately and as early as possible that day. At 17.00, Lt-Col Gordon held an O Group and began by painting the situation as it existed. Boulogne was expected to be cleared that night; one of the great German guns at Cap Gris-Nez was reported knocked out by a direct hit from a British gun at Dover. Fire bombs, which burn for up to five days, were authorised to precipitate its capitulation. The Calais area was flooded and could be reached using only three approaches: a footpath, by assault boats, and by sea. The only hindrance to the Allies was the question of supplies, ammo and fuel. Lt-Col Gordon's intentions for the next day were for the *Sherbrookes* to move to Contich in three groups. The first and second groups were to travel on sixty tank transporters, while the third group would be the wheeled column. The first tank group would be under the command of Maj Walsh, while the second group would move under the command of Maj Radley-Walters. The first group of tank transporters would leave at 08.00 and the second group one hour later. The wheeled column would move along a separate route, leaving at 08.00. The harbour parties were to leave immediately under the command of Lieut Joseph Sterling Goodfellow and RSM J.G.L.L. Dufault. The regiment's tank strength now stood at two command tanks, thirty-nine Shermans, eleven Fireflies and four Stuarts.

The wheeled column set off as planned at 08.00; at 23.50, the column arrived in its new harbour area. The trip was tiresome but a great morale booster after twelve days of inactivity, and the reception by the Belgian population was overwhelming. The *Sherbrookes* found the Belgians to be a clean and industrious people. The country showed little of the appearance of superficial material suffering or damage at the hands of the Germans; the houses were modern and neat. The welcome was utterly spontaneous and delightful, with the population giving out fruit and drinks en route – and this despite the privations they had suffered under the Germans. Posters in the store windows carried the greeting: 'Thanks to our Liberators for the quick liberation of our dearest Belgium.'

At 07.00, the tanks were ready to roll down to meet the tank transporters at the planned rendezvous point 2 miles away. Unfortunately, the transporters had difficulty getting through the crowded road, and it would be 16.00 before the tanks finally met up with them. Half the tanks went off along a route that led through Roulers, Ghent and Termonde, while the other half went via Roulers and Brussels. Unfortunately, because of the tremendous weight of the loaded transporters, the columns were forced to take a diversion in order to find bridges strong enough to carry them. At many bridges, it was necessary to dismount the tanks and drive them over separately and then reload them. When the column got to Grembergen on 21 September, it found that the bridge over the Escaut Canal had been so weakened by traffic that the column could not travel over it. The column had to stop for the night while a new route was decided on by higher authority and another bridge built. The tanks travelled for three days before reaching their harbour areas. Most of the tanks arrived at about 19.30 after frequent re-routings and two re-loadings over bridges. The recovery section of 85th LAD was busy all day bringing up several vehicle casualties. Once repaired, these tanks would slowly rejoin their squadrons over the course of the next few days.

The order of the day for 23 September was the complete maintenance of all the regiment's vehicles and the cleaning of the vehicles and equipment. That night a dance was organised at the Contich church hall for 200 men, 50 from each squadron, and with young women from the village acting as partners. Beer and soft drinks were available. Sign language was used for conversation as most of the women spoke only Flemish and very few were conversant in French or English. The remaining troops were restricted to the harbour area. The men would remain in Contich for three more days before they re-entered the battle on the Antwerp-Turnhout Canal.

The Aftermath

On 1 September 1944, Gen Eisenhower took over the direct operational command of the Allied Expeditionary Force. That same day, Gen Montgomery was promoted to the rank of Field-Marshal (Fd-Mar) in recognition of his many successes both in Africa and Europe. In his first directive, Gen Eisenhower instructed 21st Army Group to secure Antwerp, to breach the sector of the Siegfried Line covering the Ruhr River, and to seize the Ruhr industrial pocket; 12th Army Group was given the task of occupying the sector of the Siegfried Line covering the Saar and to seize Frankfurt. On 10 September, Fd-Mar Montgomery proposed a plan to seize crossings over the Rhine River by using airborne troops to seize a number of strategic river crossings with, as the ultimate objective, the capture of Arnhem. The armoured divisions of XXX Brit Corps would link up with each captured crossing as it advanced along the corridor created and, in a 'rapid and violent' advance, secure the crossings seized by the airborne troops. The offensive was codenamed Operation MARKET GARDEN. To achieve success, Gen Eisenhower agreed to give the operation his top priority for logistics.

As a consequence, after crossing the Seine River at Rouen, the *Sherbrookes* were ordered to stop their advance in an effort to preserve fuel for the tanks of XXX Brit Corps. The Canadian infantry divisions were ordered to clear the Channel ports, the Scheldt Estuary and to open the harbour in Antwerp as quickly as possible. When Operation MARKET GARDEN ground to a halt in Nijmegen on 25 September, a wide gap was formed between First Cdn Army fighting in the Scheldt region and Second Brit Army holding the corridor created by Operation MARKET GARDEN. The *Sherbrookes* were ordered to move forward and were placed under the command of 49th (West Riding) Division (49th Brit Inf Div) with the role of giving support to the Polar Bears, as the division was known, as it cleared the area from the Antwerp-Turnhout Canal to the Tilburg-Breda line. A Sqn crossed the canal on the morning of 26 September near Ryckevorsel and

THE AFTERMATH

the other two squadrons did the same later that afternoon. Throughout the month of October, the regiment gave support to the British infantry and, after Breda was secured on 30 October, the tanks returned to under the command of 2nd Cdn Armd Bde.

After a few days of rest and maintenance, the *Sherbrookes* were sent to the region of Nijmegen. Fd-Mar Montgomery had ordered First Cdn Army to protect the forward Allied line along the Lower Maas and Maas rivers; 3rd Cdn Inf Div was to establish itself in the region east of Nijmegen, while 2nd Cdn Inf Div established positions opposite the Reichswald forest. The *Sherbrookes* were initially placed in support of 82nd US Airborne Div in the area south of Nijmegen, but were later transferred to support 2nd Cdn Inf Div. With the battle to clear the Scheldt over, 2nd Cdn Armd Bde set up a Brigade Study School to train all the officers of the brigade down to and including the rank of captain. The regiment also set up a junior officers' course, a non-commissioned officers' course and a crew commanders' course. Over the course of the winter months, the regiment slowly regained its war establishment.

While Fd-Mar Montgomery planned a new offensive, Operation VALEDICTION, with as its objective to clear the west banks of the Rhine River, the Germans were also planning a new offensive, Operation *Herbstnebel*, that aimed at driving a wedge between the British and American armies. In the early hours of 16 December, the Germans launched their attack using forty divisions. Initially, the offensive was successful. As a result, Operation VALEDICTION was put on hold while the Allies dealt with the advancing German troops. However, once the skies cleared and the Allies regained air superiority, and the German drive petered out due to a shortage in petrol, the German advance halted. Gen Eisenhower then ordered a counter-attack by Third US Army and the Germans were pushed back beyond the Moder River. On 25 January, the German forces withdrew back over the Rhine River and the front returned to pre-16 December lines.

With the front re-established, Fd-Mar Montgomery ordered the resumption of the planning for the offensive to cross the Rhine River, renamed Operation VERITABLE. First Cdn Army was to push southward through the Rhineland while Ninth US Army pushed northward. Both armies were to converge at Wesel, and then Second Brit Army was to cross the Rhine River. Originally planned to begin in the beginning of January, the start date was now set for 8 February for the Canadians and 10 February for the Americans. Phase 1 of the operation would see XXX Brit Corps advance to the forward edge of the Reichswald. Second Cdn Corps would then enter the battle in Phase 2. The British would move south with their right flank along the Maas River and take Goch. The Canadians would enter the line on the left flank and take Cleve and the Calcar Ridge. During the final phase, Second Cdn Corps would continue its advance and clear the Hochwald and capture Xanten, while XXX Brit Corps would meet the Americans moving northward and advance to Wesel.

The *Sherbrookes* were not implicated in Phase 1 of the operation. However, after clearing the Moyland woods on 20–21 February, the regiment was assigned to give support to 6th Brigade in a night attack onto the Calcar Ridge. The H-Hour was set for 04.30 on 26 February, the beginning of Operation BLOCKBUSTER I. The initial advance went relatively well for the *Sherbrookes*; the tanks led the infantry onto their objectives, and this despite the water-soaked fields. However, at first light 4th Cdn Armd Div rolled down the ridge and, mistaking 6th Brigade for Germans, shot up everything they saw. A ceasefire was finally called and the division pushed through to the high ground overlooking the Hochwald and Balberger Wald. For Phase 3 in Lt-Gen Simonds plan, the Canadians had to clear the enemy from the two forests before taking Xanten. The task had been given to 4th Cdn Armd Div. However, Lt-Gen Simonds soon realised that a corps attack was required to dislodge the enemy. He tasked 2nd Cdn Inf Div with clearing the Hochwald while 3rd Cdn Inf Div was tasked with clearing the Balberger Wald.

The *Sherbrookes* were assigned to give support to 2nd Cdn Inf Div. Each squadron was assigned to a brigade and the advance began at first light on 27 February. C Sqn gave support to 4th Brigade on the left flank, but the dense woods prevented the tanks from being used in direct support. Instead, the tanks gave indirect fire support to the infantry as they moved through the woods. A Sqn, in support of 6th Brigade, moved down and secured the entrance to the Hochwald Gap on 1 March. The next day, the brigade moved through the forest towards Marienbaum with the tanks in direct support. The lessons learned from the battle for the Forêt de la Londe were forgotten as the infantry grew exasperated at the limited support the tanks could give them. However, the forest was cleared and the tanks established blocking positions on the eastern edge of the forest facing Xanten. Meanwhile, 5th Brigade with B Sqn had followed 6th Brigade into the gap. With 6th Brigade fighting in the Hochwald, 5th Brigade pushed through the gap to a small wood a couple of miles beyond it.

On 5 March, the Hochwald was declared secure and Lt-Gen Simonds ordered 6th Brigade to launch a hasty attack on Xanten the next day. However, the attack was successfully repulsed by the German defenders.

THE AFTERMATH

Therefore, Lt-Gen Simonds ordered Operation BLOCKBUSTER II for the capture of the town; 4th Brigade led the 2nd Cdn Inf Div attack on 7 March with B Sqn in support. The next day, 5th Brigade with C Sqn passed through the town and captured the high ground south of the town; 6th Brigade leap-frogged through on 9 March with the aim of taking Wesel, but were stopped while waiting for the engineers to build a bridge over the canal south of Birten. In the meantime, 3rd Cdn Inf Div cleared the Balberger Wald and took Veer. 4th Cdn Armd Div had passed south around the forest and now faced Xanten while XXX Brit Corps was fast approaching Wesel. However, Ninth US Army had faced lighter resistance and captured Wesel on 10 March. All German resistance on the west side of the Rhine ceased the next day.

By 10 March, the Allied armies controlled the entire west banks of the Rhine River, the last great river barrier left to the Germans on the Western Front. The Americans had seized a bridgehead over the river at Remagen three days earlier and were pushing troops onto the east banks. Gen Eisenhower realised that the Ruhr industrial area, the final objective of Operation MARKET GARDEN in September 1944, had to be isolated to prevent it from continuing to supply the German war machine with armaments, and then eliminated. He decided this could be accomplished using a pincer movement with 21st Army Group on the left and 12th Army Group on the right. Fd-Mar Montgomery elaborated a plan nicknamed Operation PLUNDER which aimed at initially putting Second Brit Army and Ninth US Army across the Rhine River between Rheinberg and Rees. Once the bridgehead was established, First Cdn Army would be inserted into the battle over a bridge across the river at Emmerich. It was to turn northward to liberate Holland and then exploit along the northern coast of Germany. Ninth US Army would veer east and meet up with 12th Army Group, thus encircling the Ruhr; Second Brit Army would exploit north towards Berlin.

For the initial crossing, Second Cdn Corps was placed under the command of Second Brit Army. The date for the attack was set for 31 March, but on 9 March the date was advanced to 24 March. The plan developed by Second Cdn Corps was for 3rd Cdn Inf Div to cross the river and, after clearing Rees, move to secure Emmerich and the high ground of the Hochelten feature. Once Emmerich was captured, 2nd Cdn Inf Div was to exploit northward to Terborg. 4th Cdn Armd Div would take the advantage offered by the German plain to push towards the Elbe River. Lt-Gen Simonds then planned for 3rd Cdn Inf Div to clear Zutphen, Deventer, Zwolle and Leeuwarden, while

2nd Cdn Inf Div advanced parallel to it towards Groningen. The tanks of C Sqn were assigned to 3rd Cdn Inf Div for the crossing; 7th Brigade was to clear Rees while the tanks formed a semi-circle around the town, thereby cutting off all the roads in and out of it. However, the town was quickly secured by the infantry so the squadron was ordered to push forward towards Emmerich during the early hours of 28 March.

On 29 March, C Sqn teamed up with 7th Brigade for the assault on Emmerich and, despite heavy resistance, took the city the next day. While 7th Brigade continued to mop up the city, 8th Brigade began its advance towards the Hochelten feature, and 9th Brigade with A Sqn cleared the northern suburbs of the city and then cleared the Stokkammer Bosch the next day. After a day of rest, 7th Brigade veered west to liberate Zevenaar and the town was taken on 3 April. With 7th Brigade fighting in Zevenaar, 8th Brigade with B Sqn took Doetinchem before pushing further towards Doesburg, which was captured on 5 April; 9th Brigade leap-frogged through and cleared the area south of Zutphen, and 7th Brigade then pushed through to the north of the town while 8th Brigade was tasked with capturing it. A Sqn led the battalions of 9th Brigade and cleared the approaches to and beyond Deventer; 8th Brigade attacked the town, which fell on 10 April. This paved the way for 3rd Cdn Inf Div to complete the liberation of Friesland and the capture of Leeuwarden; 2nd Cdn Inf Div, on the other hand, had captured Groningen.

Fd-Mar Montgomery issued his last directive on 22 April. His intention was for 21st Army Group to capture Emden, Bremen, Hamburg and Lübeck. First Cdn Army was to clear the north German coast and advance on Oldenburg, while Second Brit Army seized Bremen. The Canadians would then turn north and capture Emden and Wilhelmshaven. The *Sherbrookes* were again married up with 3rd Cdn Inf Div for the operation. A Sqn and 8th Brigade were ordered to clear the west banks of the Ems River opposite Leer. The division then pushed forward, crossed the Ems and Leda rivers, and seized Leer. The town was captured on 30 April and the division pushed on towards Aurich. However, the day before the town was to be attacked, a news flash from the Supreme Headquarters Allied Expeditionary Force (SHAEF) was heard on the BBC:

> German forces in northwest Germany, Holland and Friesland have surrendered unconditionally (effective 0800 hours on May 5th) to Field-Marshal Montgomery's 21 Army Group.[1]

The war was over for the *Sherbrookes*.

Conclusion

The Sherbrooke Fusilier Regiment was created in July 1940 as an infantry battalion. However, when 4th Cdn Armd Div was created in January 1942, the battalion was converted into a tank regiment. After seven months of conversion training, the new regiment was shipped overseas to the United Kingdom where it continued to perfect its armoured training. In 1943, the regiment, now a part of 2nd Cdn Armd Bde, was selected to participate in the planned invasion of Nazi Europe. There followed a period of intense training with 9th Brigade on the assault phase of Operation OVERLORD. At 11.40 on 6 June 1944, the tanks of the *Sherbrookes* landed on NAN WHITE Beach and moved inland to their assembly area in Bény-sur-Mer. The next day, the *Sherbrookes* fought the first tank battle on the Western Front against the *Panzer* tanks of 12.SS-Pzdiv. While the battle can be considered to be a draw with no outright winner, the battle did halt the German attempt to push the Canadians back into the English Channel.

The *Sherbrookes* were to fight in every major Canadian operation in the war. The tanks of the regiment went on to support 3rd Cdn Inf Div, and then the units of Second Cdn Corps. The tanks led the battle into Caen before leading the charge southward towards Falaise in Operations SPRING, TOTALIZE and TRACTABLE. During the pursuit phase of the battle, the squadrons raced towards Rouen to assist 2nd Cdn Inf Div with the clearing of the Forêt de la Londe and the crossing of the Seine River. After a temporary halt to operations to conserve fuel for the tanks of Second Brit Army during Operation MARKET GARDEN, the regiment was placed under the command of 49th Brit Inf Div with the task of clearing the left flank of Second Brit Army holding the corridor to Nijmegen created by Operation MARKET GARDEN. The planned 21st Army Group attack across the Rhine River, however, had to be postponed after the Germans counter-attacked on 16 December in an attempt to divide the British and American armies in what became known as the Battle of the Bulge.

After the German offensive was repulsed, Fd-Mar Montgomery once again ordered 21st Army Group to execute Operation VERITABLE, the crossing of the Rhine River and the encirclement of the Ruhr industrial region. First, the west banks of the Rhine had to be cleared. The *Sherbrookes* were again front and centre as Second Cdn Corps pushed south along the Rhineland towards Wesel. The Rhine was crossed at Rees and First Cdn Army then pushed northward and 3rd Cdn Inf Div with the *Sherbrookes* in support cleared Emmerich, Zutphen, Deventer, Zwolle and Leeuwarden, before pushing eastward and taking Leer. When the German forces in northwest Germany and Holland surrendered on 5 May, the *Sherbrookes* put on a show of force in Aurich and Emden before retiring, first to Germany and then to Holland before returning to Canada in January 1946. The regiment suffered 102 officers and other ranks killed in action; 26 died of the wounds they received and 1 member was missing, presumed dead; 262 other ranks had been wounded and 17 had been taken as prisoners of war.

Annex A

Honour Roll

	Killed in Action or Died of Wounds Received	
6 Jun 44	Lieut J.H. Casey	Lieut T.C. Stevens
7 Jun 44	H/Capt W.L. Brown	Lieut W.H. Trenholme
	Lieut T.A.L. Windsor	Sgt F.J. Allsop
	Sgt E.B. McMillan	L/Sgt L.G. Ride
	Cpl E.J. Klose	A/Cpl J.P. Fountain
	L/Cpl J.H. Greenwood	L/Cpl J. Kachor
	Tpr H.W. Balkwill	Tpr J.E. Bolt
	Tpr J.H. Davidson	Tpr G. Fontaine
	Tpr W.M. Forbes	Tpr G.V. Gill
	Tpr W.G. Hardy	Tpr T.H. Henry
	Tpr R. Lockhead	Tpr M. MacKenzie
	Tpr H.G. Philp	Tpr H.J. Provencher
	Tpr J.M. Severeid	Tpr J. Sosnowski
	Tpr D.H. Stewart	Tpr A. White
	Tpr N.E. Wilkinson	
9 Jun 44	Lieut P.H. Morgan	Tpr K.B. Keith
15 Jun 44	Tpr S. Hancharyk	
8 Jul 44	A/Capt M.J. Fitzpatrick	Lieut N.S. Boyd
	Tpr J.A. Clark	Tpr J.E.V. Leblanc
	Tpr G.G. Legge	Tpr K.M. MacKay
	Tpr C.F. Nadon	Tpr B.E. Nicks
	Tpr G.V. Reno	Tpr D.A. Sarr
	Tpr E.H.J. Schneider	Tpr S.F. Stinson
10 Jul 44	Tpr J. Pettitt	
18 Jul 44	A/Cpl J.M. Mutter	Tpr E.M. Loveday
	Tpr L.C. Nelson	Tpr J.L. Rodgers
20 Jul 44	Lieut H.W. Bancroft	Lieut W.J. Charters
	Lieut C.F. Thompson	A/Sgt M. Lefebvre
	Tpr A. Jelly	

\	Killed in Action or Died of Wounds Received	
21 Jul 44	Sgt T.B. Murray Cpl K. Hill Tpr D.W. MacKenzie	A/Sgt C.H. McMurdo Tpr W.R. Jones
22 Jul 44	Sgt T.C. Reid	L/Cpl G.S. Rice
24 Jul 44	Tpr F.A. Seastrand	
26 Jul 44	L/Cpl A.L. Evans	
27 Jul 44	Tpr E.C. Nordin	
4 Aug 44	Tpr F. Goodall	
8 Aug 44	L/Sgt L.M. Jenne Tpr L.E. Harvey Tpr F.W. Quann	Tpr D. Gelman Tpr F.J. Munro
12 Aug 44	Lieut J.E.M. Logan Trp E. Fidler Tpr H.V. Kenny Tpr W.J. Smith	Tpr C. Elsby Tpr M.J. Gaffney Tpr A. McLean Tpr C.E. Wood
13 Aug 44	Lieut I.J. McCrimmon Sgt R.N. Joudrey Tpr H. McChesney Tpr M.C. Uhlman	Lieut M.V. Mondor Tpr D. Andres Tpr L.J. Shepherd
14 Aug 44	Cpl H.A. McCormick	Tpr G.C. Gareau
16 Aug 44	Tpr J.W. Davis	
17 Aug 44	Tpr R.B. Gilroy	
25 Aug 44	Tpr P.J.H. Elliott	Tpr R.G. Purdy
26 Aug 44	Tpr J. Brown	Tpr E.W. Reid
28 Aug 44	Tpr L.W.M. Jennings	

Annex B

Decorations and Awards

Member of the Order of the British Empire (MBE)
Lt-Col F.T. Jenner   Maj K.A. Bryce
Maj C.C. MacLachlan   SSM G.W. Hull

Distinguished Service Order (DSO)
Lt-Col M.B.K. Gordon   Lt-Col S.V. Radley-Walters
Maj R.M. Houston   Maj V.O. Walsh

Military Cross (MC)
Maj S.V. Radley-Walters   Maj J.P. Brennan
Maj E.A. Spafford   Capt (A/Maj) E.A. Clout
Capt T.G. Gould   Lieut G.D. Goodwin
Lieut J.W. Neill   Lieut R.A. Warriner

Distinguished Conduct Medal (DCM)
Sgt L.W. Cuddie

Military Medal (MM)
RSM C.L. Nicholson   SSM E.A. Howland
Sgt R.R. Beardsley   Sgt V.R. Bowers
Sgt A. Rigby   L/Sgt A.T.P. Connell
L/Cpl M.D. Davis   Tpr D.D. Bartlett
Tpr V.P. Schuler

King's Commendation
Capt R.F. Garrow

Mentioned in Despatches
Maj F.H. Baldwin   Maj E.A. Spafford
Maj N.H. Welsh   Capt M.J. Fitzpatrick

Capt R.F. Garrow
Capt B.M. Veilleux
A/Capt S.W. Wood
QM Sgt J. Désy
Sgt J.G. Jones
Sgt R.V. Oliver
Sgt G.H. Stewart
L/Sgt J.F. Larkin
Cpl R.E. Hutcheson
L/Cpl R. Olimb
Tpr E. Fidler

Capt C.C. MacLachlan
A/Capt L.N. Davies
Lieut S.L. Dunn
Sgt R.A. Cathcart
Sgt P.G. Myrtle
Sgt J.S. Savard
L/Sgt L.M. Jenne
Tpr (A/Sgt) A.F. Hall
L/Cpl A. Cornish
Tpr (A/Cpl) R.M. Temple
Tpr J.L. Leclerc

Chevalier, Ordre de Léopold II avec Palme (Belgium)
Capt S. Breen
Capt G.L. Marshall

Croix de Guerre, 1940, avec Palme (Belgium)
Capt S. Breen
Sgt L.S. Anton
Tpr L.P. Clutterbuck

Capt G.L. Marshall
Sgt J.S. Savard
Tpr A.E. Lick

Croix de Guerre, 1939–1945 (France)
Avec Palme de bronze
Avec Étoile de vermeil
Avec Étoile d'argent
Avec Étoile de bronze

Sgt C.R. Barr
Tpr W.R. Thomas
Lieut J.D. Corless
Tpr P.A. Paquette

Bronze Lion (Netherlands)
A/Sgt P.J. Hart
Pte (A/Cpl) E.G. Harvey

Silver Star (United States)
Tpr O.N. Nesdoly

Annex C

Command Appointments

Commanding Officers
Lt-Col Mathias William McA'Nulty
(23 July 1940 – 31 January 1943)
Lt-Col Melville Burgoyne Kennedy Gordon
(31 January 1943 – 5 February 1945)
Lt-Col Frederick Thomas Jenner
(5 February 1945 – 29 July 1945)
A/Lt-Col Sydney Valpy Radley-Walters
(30 July 1945 – 15 February 1946)

Deputy Commanding Officers
Maj Aimé Biron
(23 July 1940 – 26 January 1942)
Maj John Clifford Cave
(26 January 1942 – 12 June 1944)
Maj Vincent Owen Walsh
(12 June 1944 – 21 July 1945)
Maj Sydney Valpy Radley-Walters
(21 July 1945 – 29 July 1945)
Maj Merritt Hayes Bateman
(30 July 1945 – 15 February 1946)

Regimental Sergeant-Majors
RSM G.C.H. Barlow
(16 October 1940 – 7 January 1942)
A/RSM E. Burke
(7 January 1942 – 1 March 1942)
RSM E.J. Wolfe
(1 March 1942 – 9 July 1943)
A/RSM D.E. MacLeod

ARMOURED THUNDER

(10 July 1943 – 10 October 1943)
RSM J.G.L.L. Dufault
(10 October 1943 – 1 June 1944)
RSM D.E. MacLeod
(1 June 1944 – 2 July 1945)
RSM E.A. Howland
(2 July 1945 – 10 August 1945)
A/RSM C.L. Nicholson
(10 August 1945 – 15 February 1946)

Annex D

Order of Battle

First Canadian Army

First Canadian Corps
    First Canadian Armoured Brigade
        The Ontario Regiment
        Three-Rivers Regiment
        The Calgary Regiment
    5th Canadian Armoured Division
        3rd Reconnaissance Regiment (The Governor General's Horse Guard)
        5th Canadian Armoured Brigade
            Lord Strathcona's Horse (Royal Canadian)
            8th Princess Louise's (New Brunswick) Hussars
            The British Columbia Dragoons
        11th Canadian Infantry Brigade
            Princess Louise Fusiliers
            The Perth Regiment
            The Cape Breton Highlanders
            The Irish Regiment of Canada
    1st Canadian Infantry Division
        4th Canadian Reconnaissance Regiment (4th Princess Louise Dragoon Guards)
        Saskatoon Light Infantry (MG)
        1st Canadian Infantry Brigade
            The Royal Canadian Regiment
            The Hastings and Prince Edward Regiment
            48th Highlanders of Canada
        2nd Canadian Infantry Brigade
            Princess Patricia's Canadian Light Infantry
            The Seaforth Highlanders of Canada
            The Loyal Edmonton Regiment

3rd Canadian Infantry Brigade
    Royal 22e Régiment
    The Carleton and York Regiment
    The West Nova Scotia Regiment

Second Canadian Corps
Second Canadian Armoured Brigade
    First Hussars
    The Fort Garry Horse
    The Sherbrooke Fusilier Regiment
    The Elgin Regiment (25th Cdn Armd Del Regt)

4th Canadian Armoured Division
    29th Canadian Reconnaissance Regiment (South Alberta Regiment)
    The Lake Superior Regiment (Motor)
    4th Canadian Armoured Brigade
        The Governor General's Foot Guards
        The Canadian Grenadier Guards
        The British Columbia Regiment
    10th Canadian Infantry Brigade
        The Lincoln and Welland Regiment
        The Algonquin Regiment
        The Argyll and Sutherland Highlanders of Canada (Princess Louise's)

2nd Canadian Infantry Division
    8th Canadian Reconnaissance Regiment (14th Canadian Hussars)
    The Toronto Scottish Regiment (MG)
    4th Canadian Infantry Brigade
        The Royal Regiment of Canada
        The Royal Hamilton Light Infantry
        The Essex Scottish Regiment
    5th Canadian Infantry Brigade
        The Black Watch (Royal Highland Regiment) of Canada
        Le Régiment de Maisonneuve
        The Calgary Highlanders
    6th Canadian Infantry Brigade
        Les Fusiliers Mont-Royal

ORDER OF BATTLE

    The Queen's Own Cameron Highlanders of Canada
    The South Saskatchewan Regiment

3rd Canadian Infantry Division
    7th Canadian Reconnaissance Regiment (17th Duke of York's Royal Canadian Hussars)
    Cameron Highlanders of Ottawa (MG)
    7th Canadian Infantry Brigade
        The Royal Winnipeg Rifles
        The Regina Rifle Regiment
        1st Battalion, The Canadian Scottish Regiment
    8th Canadian Infantry Brigade
        The Queen's Own Rifles of Canada
        Le Régiment de la Chaudière
        The North Shore (New Brunswick) Regiment
    9th Canadian Infantry Brigade
        The Highland Light Infantry of Canada
        The Stormont, Dundas and Glengarry Highlanders
        The North Nova Scotia Highlanders

Attached troops
1st Polish Armoured Division
    10th Mounted Rifle Regiment
    10th Polish Armoured Cavalry Brigade
        1st Polish Armoured Regiment
        2nd Polish Armoured Regiment
        24th Polish Uhlan Regiment
        10th Polish Dragoons Regiment
    3rd Polish Infantry Brigade
        10th Podhane Rifles Battalion
        8th Polish Rifles Battalion
        9th Polish Rifle Battalion

49th (West Riding) Infantry Division
    49th British Reconnaissance Regiment
    2nd Battalion, Princess Louise's Kensington Regiment
    56th British Infantry Brigade
        2nd Battalion, Essex Regiment
        2nd Battalion, Gloucestershire Regiment
        2nd Battalion, South Wales Borderers

146th British Infantry Brigade
    4th Battalion, Lincolnshire Regiment
    1/4th Battalion, King's Own Yorkshire Light Infantry
    Hallamshire Battalion, York and Lancaster Regiment

147th British Infantry Brigade
    1/7th Battalion, Duke of Wellington Regiment
    11th Battalion, Royal Scot Regiment
    1st Battalion, Leicestershire Regiment

Annex E

German Forces opposing the Canadians in Normandy

7.Armee
  21.Panzerdivision
    Panzer-Regiment 22
    Panzergrenadier-Regiment 125
    Panzergrenadier-Regiment 192
  Schwere.Panzerabteilung 503
  716.Infanterie-Division
    Grenadier-Regiment 726
    Grenadier-Regiment 736
  16.Luftwaffe-Feld-Division

Other Formations in Support of 7.Armee
  Panzergruppe West
    I.SS-Panzerkorps
      12.SS-Panzerdivision (Hitlerjugend)
        SS-Panzer-Regiment 12
        SS-Panzergrenadier-Regiment 25
        SS-Panzergrenadier-Regiment 26
      Panzer-Lehr-Division
        Panzer-Lehr-Regiment 130
        Panzergrenadier-Lehr-Regiment 901
        Panzergrenadier-Lehr-Regiment 902
      17.SS-Panzergrenadier-Division (Götz von Berlichingen)
        SS-Panzergrenadier-Regiment 37
        SS-Panzergrenadier-Regiment 38
        SS-Panzerabteilung 17
      Schwere.SS-Panzerabteilung 101

II.SS-Panzerkorps
  1.SS-Panzerdivision (Leibstandarte SS Adolf Hitler)
    SS-Panzer-Regiment 1
    SS-Panzergrenadier-Regiment 1
    SS-Panzergrenadier-Regiment 2
  9.SS-Panzerdivision (Hohenstaufen)
    SS-Panzer-Regiment 9
    SS-Panzergrenadier-Regiment 19
    SS-Panzergrenadier-Regiment 20
  10.SS-Panzerdivision (Frundsberg)
    SS-Panzer-Regiment 10
    SS-Panzergrenadier-Regiment 21
    SS-Panzergrenadier-Regiment 22
  Schwere.SS-Panzerabteilung 102
116.Panzerdivision
  Panzer-Regiment 16
  Panzergrenadier-Regiment 60
  Panzergrenadier-Regiment 156
85.Infanterie-Division
  Grenadier-Regiment 1053
  Grenadier-Regiment 1054
89.Infanterie-Division
  Grenadier-Regiment 1055
  Grenadier-Regiment 1056
271.Infanterie-Division
  Grenadier-Regiment 977
  Grenadier-Regiment 978
  Grenadier-Regiment 979
272.Infanterie-Division
  Grenadier-Regiment 980
  Grenadier-Regiment 981
  Grenadier-Regiment 982

III.Flakkorps

Annex F

Abbreviations

Ranks

Fd-Mar	Field-Marshal
Gen	General
Lt-Gen	Lieutenant-General
Maj-Gen	Major-General
Brig	Brigadier-General
Col	Colonel
Lt-Col	Lieutenant-Colonel
Maj	Major
Capt	Captain
H/Capt	Honorary Captain
Lieut	Lieutenant
RSM	Regimental Sergeant-Major
WO1	Warrant Officer, 1st Class
SSM	Squadron Sergeant-Major
CSM	Company Sergeant-Major
WO2	Warrant Officer, 2nd Class
Sgt	Sergeant
L/Sgt	Lance-Sergeant
Cpl	Corporal
L/Cpl	Lance-Corporal
Tpr	Trooper
Pte	Private

Other Abbreviations Used

2i/c	Second-in-command
AFV	Armoured Fighting Vehicle
AP	Armour piercing

ARV	Armoured Recovery Vehicle
Bde	Brigade
BdeHQ	Brigade Headquarters
Bdr	Bombardier
Bn	Battalion
BnAS	Battalion Aid Station
BnHQ	Battalion Headquarters
CAC	Canadian Armoured Corps
CACRU	Canadian Armoured Corps, Reinforcement Unit
Cal	Calibre
CASF	Canadian Active Service Force
CO	Commanding officer
DCO	Deputy commanding officer
Div	Division
DivHQ	Division Headquarters
FOO	Forward Observation Officer
FUP	Forming-up point
HE	High-explosive
HQ	Headquarters
Int O	Intelligence officer
Int Sgt	Intelligence sergeant
LCA	Landing craft, assault
LCI	Landing craft, infantry
LCT	Landing craft, tank
LO	Liaison officer
LST	Landing ship, tank
Med O	Medical officer
mm	Millimetre
MQMS	Mechanical Quarter-Master Sergeant
MTC	Militia Training Centre
NAAFI	Navy, Army and Air Force Institute
NPAM	Non-Permanent Active Militia
O Group	Orders Group
OC	Officer commanding
OP	Observation post
PAM	Permanent Active Militia
PoW	Prisoner of War
RAF	Royal Air Force
RAS	Regimental Aid Station

ABBREVIATIONS

RCAC	Royal Canadian Armoured Corps
RCAF	Royal Canadian Air Force
RCN	Royal Canadian Navy
Recce	Reconnaissance
Regt	Regiment
RHQ	Regimental Headquarters
RLO	Reconnaissance/liaison officer
SHQ	Squadron Headquarters
SP	Self-propelled
SQMS	Squadron Quarter-Master Sergeant
Sqn	Squadron
TULO	Tank Unit Landing Officer

Bibliography

Unpublished Sources

I. Library and Archives Canada/Department of National Defence, Ottawa

Historical Section, Canadian Military Headquarters, Series of Reports on the Canadian Participation in the Operations in North-West Europe:
  Report No. 94: 'G.H.Q. Exercise "SPARTAN", March, 1943', (1943)
  Report No. 147: 'Part I: The Assault and Subsequent Operations of 3 Cdn Inf Div and 2 Cdn Armd Bde, 6–30 Jun 44', (1945)
  Report No. 150: 'The Black Watch (Royal Highland Regiment) of Canada in Operation "Spring", 25 Jul 44', (1946)
  Report No. 162: 'Part II: Canadian Operations in July', (1946)
  Report No. 169: 'Part III: Canadian Operations, 1–23 August', (1948)
  Report No. 183: 'Part IV: Canadian Army in the Pursuit, 23 Aug–30 Sep 44', (1947)

Historical Section, First Canadian Army Headquarters, Series of Reports on the Canadian Participation in the Operations in North-West Europe:
  Report No. 50: 'The Campaign in North-West Europe: Information from German Sources. Part II: Invasion and Battle of Normandy (6 Jun–22 Aug 44)', (1952)
  Report No. 61: 'Policy and Organization for Scientific Research and Technical Development in the Canadian Army 1939–1945', (1953)

Records Group 24, Series C-3, Records of the Department of National Defence:
  War Diaries:
    The Sherbrooke Fusilier Regiment (27th Canadian Armoured Regiment)
    No. 85 Light Aid Detachment, RCEME
    Headquarters, Second Canadian Armoured Brigade

BIBLIOGRAPHY

1st Battalion, Black Watch R.H.R. of Canada
The Calgary Highlanders
The Fusiliers Mont-Royal
North Nova Scotia Highlanders
The Queen's Own Cameron Highlanders of Canada
1st Battalion, The Regina Rifles Regiment
Stormont, Dundas & Glengarry Highlanders
Royal Hamilton Light Infantry
1st Battalion, Royal Regiment of Canada

Miscellaneous documents:
Report of shooting of Allies by 12th SS 7–21 June 44, Vol 10427, 205S1.023(D9)
Interrogation report of Kurt Meyer, Vol 10474, 212C1.3009(D60)
History of 'BOMB', Vol 10622, 215C1.009(D185)
2 Cdn Corps op instructions No 1 / 1 May 44 for Op Overlord, Vol 10835, 229C2 (D3)
Weekly and monthly summaries of ops 2CID July 44–May 45, Vol 10898, 235C2.013(D21)
Report ops 3CID to 31 July 44, Vol 10908, 235C3.013(D10)
Report for D-Day ops by 3CID, Vol 10908, 235C3.013(D11)
Op reports 2CAB, Vol 10992
Op 'Totalize': An account of ops by 2 Cdn Amrd Bde in France 5 to 8 Aug 1944
Op 'Tractable': An account of ops by 2 Cdn Armd Bde in France 14 to 16 Aug 44, Vol 10992, 275C2.013(D1)

II. Other Allied Military Reports or Documents
Great Britain:
21 Army Group. 'Notes on the Operations of 21 Army Group 6 June 1944–5 May 1945', (September 1945)

III. Axis Military Reports or Documents
Germany
Kraemer, *Generalmajor* Fritz (translated by Rosenwald, A.). 'I SS Pz Corps in the West in 1944'. (Landsberg Prison, 1948)
'Fuehrer Directives and other Top-level Directives of the German Armed Forces 1942–1945'. Translated by US Department of the Army (Washington, 1948)

IV. Memoirs and Diaries

Gould, T. Garry. 'The Memory Project: Digital Archive.' https://www.thememoryproject.com

Love, James V. 'The Memory Project: Digital Archive.' https://www.thememoryproject.com

MacLean, Ian. 'Prisoner of War Diary, 1944–1945.' http://www.thousandislandslife.com

Neill, John W. 'One Soldier's War: The War and Post War Memories of Major (Rtd) John W. Neill, MC, CD, BSA, PhD, FCSLA'

Taylor, J.L. 'B4443 Sgt. J.L. Taylor – War Diary: June 1 to Sept 17, 1944'

White, Walter M. 'Lieutenant Walter M. White'

Published Sources

V. Memoirs and Diaries

Gardam, John. *Fifty Years After*. (Burnstown: General Store Publishing House Inc, 1990)

Isby, David C., ed. *Fighting in Normandy: The German Army from D-Day to Villers-Bocage*. (Mechanicsburg: Greenhill Books, 2001)

Meyer, Kurt. *Grenadiers*. (Winnipeg: Stackpole Books, 1994)

Portugal, Jean E. *We Were There: A Record for Canada, Vols 3, 4 and 5: The Army*. (Shelburne: Self-published, 1998)

VI. Regimental and Corps Histories

----------------. *A History of the First Hussars Regiment*. (London: Hunter Printing London Limited, 1951)

Bird, Will R. *No Retreating Footsteps: the story of the North Novas*. (Amherst: Furlong's Rapid Print & Digital Design, 2007)

Braün, Daniel. *Green Fields Beyond: The Story of the Sherbrooke Fusilier Regiment*. (Durham, NC: Lulu Publishing Services, 2021)

Castonguay, Jacques et Ross, Armand. *Le Régiment de la Chaudière*. (Lévis: Le Régiment de la Chaudière, 1983)

Jackson, H.M. *The Sherbrooke Regiment (12th Armoured Regiment)*. (Sherbrooke: The Sherbrooke Regiment, 1958)

Marteinson, John & McNorgan, Michael R. *The Royal Canadian Armoured Corps: An Illustrated History*. (Toronto: The Royal Canadian Armoured Corps Association, 2000)

Stacey, Colonel C.P. *History of the Canadian Army in the Second World War. Volume I: The Army in Canada, Britain and the Pacific.* (Ottawa: The Queen's Printer and Comptroller of Stationary, 1957)

------------------. *Official History of the Canadian Army in the Second World War. Volume III: The Victory Campaign: The Operations in North-West Europe, 1944–1945.* (Ottawa: The Queen's Printer and Comptroller of Stationary, 1960)

VII. Books

Agte, P. *Michael Wittmann and the Waffen SS Tiger Commanders of the Leibstandarte in WWII.* (Mechanicsburg, PA: Stackpole Military History, 1996)

Bernage, George. *The Panzers and the Battle of Normandy, 5 June to 20 July 1944.* (Bayeux: Editions Heimdal, 2000)

Blackburn, George G. *The Guns of Normandy: A Soldier's Eye View, France 1944.* (Tornoto: McClelland & Stewart Ltd, 1995)

Bowden, Mark. *D-Day: June 6, 1944.* (San Francisco: Chronicle Books, 2002)

Broadfoot, Barry. *Six War Years, 1939–1945: Memories of Canadians at Home and Abroad.* (Don Mills: Double Day, 1974)

Carafano, James Jay. *After D-Day: Operation Cobra and the Normandy Breakout.* (Boulder, CO: Lynne Rienner Publishers, Inc, 2000)

Chambers, Captain Ernest J. *The Canadian Militia: A History of the Origin and Development of the Force.* (Montreal: L.M. Fresco, 1907)

Copp, Terry. *Fields of Fire: The Canadians in Normandy.* (Toronto: University of Toronto Press, 2003)

Copp, Terry ed. *Montgomery's Scientists: Operational Research in Northwest Europe – The Work of No.2 Operational Research Section with 21 Army Group Jun 1944 to July 1945.* (Waterloo: Wilfrid Laurier University, 2000)

Edwards, Roger. *Panzer: A Revolution in Warfare, 1939–1945.* (London: Arms and Armour Press, 1989)

Fowler, Will. *D-Day: The First 24 Hours.* (Miami: Amber Books Ltd, 2003)

Goddard, Lance. *D-Day: Juno Beach, Canada's 24 Hours of Destiny.* (Toronto: The Dundurn Group, 2004)

Hart, Dr Stephan A. *No. 5 Second World War 60th Anniversary: The Final Battle for Normandy: Northern Francem 9 July–30 August 1944.* (London, 2005)

Isby, David C. ed. *Fighting in Normandy: The German Army from D-Day to Villers Bocage.* (Mechanicsburg: Stackpole Books, 2001)

Keggan, John. *The Second World War*. (New York: Viking Penguin, 1989)

Kesteman, Jean-Pierre. *Histoire de Sherbrooke*. (Sherbrooke, 2001–2002)
  Tôme 1 : De l'âge de l'eau à l'ère de la vapeur (1802–1866)
  Tôme 2 : De l'âge de la vapeur à l'ère de l'électricité (1867–1896)
  Tôme 3 : La ville de l'électricité et du tramway (1897–1929)
  Tôme 4 : De la ville ouvrière à la métropole universitaire (1930–2002)

Morton, Desmond. *A Military History of Canada*. (Edmonton: Hurtig Publishers, 1985)

Gardam, John. *Fifty years After*, (Burnstown: The General Store Publishing House Inc, 1990)

Granatstein, J.L. & Morton, Desmond. *Bloody Victory: Canadians and the D-Day Campaign, 1944*. (Toronto: Lester Publishing Ltd, 1984)

------------------. *A Nation Forged in Fire: Canadians and the Second World War, 1939–1945*. (Toronto: Lester & Orpen Dennys, 1989)

Lewis, Brenda Ralph. *Hitler Youth: The Hitlerjugend in War and Peace 1933–1945*. (Osceola: MBI Publishing Company, 2000)

McAndrew, B., Rawling, B. & Whitby, M. *La Libération: Les Canadiens en Europe*. (Montreal: Art Global, 2005)

Patrick, Stephen A. *The Normandy Campaign: June and July, 1944*. (South Melbourne: Wieser & Wieser Inc, 1986)

Reid, Brian A. *No Holding Back: Operation Totalize, Normandy, August 1944*. (Toronto: Stackpole Books, 2005)

Zuehlke, Mark & Daniel, C. Stuart. *The Canadian Military Atlas: The Nation's Battlefields from the French and Indian Wars to Kosovo*. (Toronto: Stoddart Publishing Co Limited, 2001)

VIII. Dissertations

Kavanagh, Robert L. *W Force: The Canadian Army and the Defence of Newfoundland in the Second World War*. MA Thesis (Memorial University of Newfoundland, 1995)

Zaporzan, James Lawrence. *Rad's War: A Biographical Study of Sydney Valpy Radley-Walters from Mobilization to the end of the Normandy Campaign 1944*. MA Thesis (Queen's University, 2001)

IX. Periodicals

Barbé, Dominique. 'The Sherbrooke Fusiliers Regiment – 27th Canadian Armoured Regiment: Buron – St-Contest 6–7 June 8–9 July 1944'. (St Contest, 1977)

------------------. 'The Canadians Facing Buron: June 7–July 8 1944'

BIBLIOGRAPHY

Brown, Gordon. 'The Capture of the Abbaye D'Ardenne by the Regina Rifles, 8 July 1944'. *Canadian Military History*, (Spring 1995, Vol 4, No 1), pp.91–99

Burns, Ray 'Remembering D-Day'. *The News*, (New Glasgow, Nova Scotia, 5 June 2009)

Campbell, Ian J. 'Abbaye d'Ardenne June 1944: Twenty Canadian Prisoners of War' (Buron, 1984)

------------------. 'Nineteen or Twenty Canadians at the Abbaye d'Ardenne'

Canadian Army Commanders. 'The Techniques of the Assault: The Canadian Army on D-Day: After-Action Reports by Commanders'. *Canadian Military History*, (2005, Vol 14, Issue 3), pp.57–70

Copp, Terry. 'Clearing Buron'. *Legion Magazine*, (2011)

------------------. 'Lessons of Carpiquet'. *Legion Magazine*, (2011)

------------------. 'The March to the Seine'. *Legion Magazine*, (2000)

------------------. 'Murder in Normandy'. *Legion Magazine*, (2010)

------------------. 'A Well-entrenched Enemy'. *Legion Magazine*, (2011)

Demaney, Major Douglas E., CD, PhD. 'Looking Back on Canadian Generalship in the Second World War'. *Canadian Army Journal*, (Spring 2004, Vol 7, No 1), pp.13–22

Dykman, Henk. 'The Liberation of Leesten'. *Canadian Military History*, (1995, Vol 4, No 1), pp.21–35

Fitzgerald-Black, Alexander. 'Investigating the Memory of Operation Spring: The Inquiry into the Black Watch and the Battle of St. André-sur-Orne, 1944–46'. *Canadian Military History*, (Spring 2012, Vol 21, No 2), pp.21–32

Gillis, Roger. 'Into Harm's Way: Canadian Forces in Operation "Totalize"'. *Timepieces: A Journal of Undergraduate History at UNB*, pp.26–37

Jarymovycz, Roman Johann. 'Der Gegenangriff vor Verrières: German Counterattacks during Operation "Spring": 25–26 July 1944'. *Canadian Military History*, (1993, Vol 2, Issue 1, Article 6), pp.74–89

------------------. 'Canadian Armour in Normandy: Operation "Totalize" and the Quest for Operational Manoeuvre'. *Canadian Military History*, (1998, Vol 7, Issue 2, Article 3), pp.19–40

Laurent, Boris. 'Opération Totalize et Tractable (Normandie, 1944): Victoire retentissante ou défaillance des armées Alliées?'. *Axe & Alliés*, (2011, No 24), pp.32–33

Learment, Don. 'Soldier, POW, Partisan: My Experiences during the Battle of France, June-September 1944'. *Canadian Military History*, (Spring 2000, Vol 9, No 2), pp.91–104

Liedtke, Gregory. 'Canadian Offensive Operations in Normandy Revisited'. *Canadian Military Journal*, (Summer 2007), pp.60–68

Magdelaine, Yvan. 'Les Alliés dans l'impasse: Genèse de Totalize'. *Axe & Aliés*, (2011, No 24), pp.34–41

------------------. 'Opération Totalize : Les Canadiens s'enlisent'. *Axe & Aliés*, (2011, No 24), pp.42,51

------------------. 'Opération Tractable: La Wehrmacht échappe à la destruction totale'. *Axe & Aliés*, (2011, No 24), pp.52–59

Mantle, C.L. & Zaporzan, Lt-Col L. 'The Leadership of S.V. Radley-Walters: Enlistment to D-Day'. *Canadian Military Journal*, (2009, Vol 9, No 4), pp.61–71

------------------. 'The Leadership of S.V. Radley-Walters: The Normandy Campaign'. *Canadian Military Journal*, (2010, Vol 10, No 1), pp.56–67

McIntyre, D.W. 'Pursuit to the Seine: The Essex Scottish Regiment and the Forêt de la Londe, August 1944'. *Canadian Military History*, (1998, Vol 7, No 1), pp.50–72

Milner, Marc. 'No Ambush, No Defeat: The Advance of the Vanguard of the 9th Canadian Infantry Brigade, 7 June 1944'. Chapter 15 of *Canada and the Second World War: Essays in Honour of Terry Copp*

O'Keefe, David R. 'Double-edged Sword: Part 1: Ultra and Operation Totalize, Normandy, August 8, 1944'. *Canadian Army Journal*, (2010, Vol 12, No 3), pp.85–93

Perrun, Jody. 'Best Laid Plans: Guy Simonds and Operation Totalize, 7–10 August 1944'. *The Journal of Military History*, (2003, Vol 67, No 1), pp.137–173

Rickard, John Nelson. 'The Test of Command: McNaughton and Exercise "Spartan," 4–12 March 1943'. *Canadian Military History*, (Summer 1999, Vol 8, No 3), pp.22–38

Windsor, Lee A. '"Too Close for the Guns!" 9 Canadian Infantry Brigade in the Battle for the Rhine Bridgehead'. *Canadian Military History*, (2003, Vol 12, No 1 & 2), pp.5–28

Endnotes

Chapter 1

1. Halifax to Henderson (Berlin) 3 September 1939. Great Britain, Foreign Office. *Documents on British Foreign Policy, 1919–1939.* (London: 1949–1977), Series 3, Volume VII, Document #757, p.535.
2. $98.9 million to the PAM and NPAM, $25.8 million to the RCN and $74.7 million to the RCAF. Stacey, Colonel C.P. *History of the Canadian Army in the Second World War. Volume 1: The Army in Canada, Britain and the Pacific.* (Ottawa, The Queen's Printer and Controller of Stationary, 1957), p.19.
3. *Sherbrooke Daily Record*, 16 August 1939.
4. Granastein, J.L. & Morton, Desmond. *A Nation Forged in Fire: Canadians and the Second World War, 1939–1945.* (Toronto: Lester Publishing Limited, 1989), p.7.
5. All future references to Canadian brigades are by their brigade number and the word Brigade.
6. *Sherbrooke Daily Record*, 4, 6 and 10 June 1940.
7. After the war, Newfoundland joined Canada as its tenth province in 1949.
8. In order to maintain the sequential numbering of the divisions, it would later be renamed as 5th Canadian Armoured Division.
9. Three types of targets were generally used on tank ranges. Stationary targets were permanently positioned to represent concrete pillboxes or bunkers or vehicles. Moving targets represented vehicles driving on a road or path, and aimed at perfecting the gunner's ability to engage a moving vehicle. Snapped targets became visual for a period of about 5 to 10 seconds, and measured the crew's ability to observe, identify and engage a target in a very short period of time.
10. Armoured Fighting Vehicle.
11. Projector Infantry, Anti-tank, Mark I – a British man-portable anti-tank weapon (effective range: 100 meters; maximum armour penetration: 55mm).

12. Reconnaissance-liaison officer.
13. The surface of all the highways near the coast had been divided into rectangles, painted yellow and numbered. These 'standings' were assigned to vehicles and the crew, less the driver, placed in a transition camp.
14. Naval assault force 'U' for American forces landing on Utah Beach had already conducted its final rehearsal separately at the end of April as Exercise TIGER.
15. Included with the forty-three Sherman and fifteen Firefly tanks to be used on D-Day, the regiment received eight Sherman and six Firefly tanks to replace vehicle casualties in the fighting.
16. The No. 77 grenade is a small white phosphorous grenade intended for signalling and screening purposes.
17. Porpoises were large, metal sleds 4–5ft wide, 1ft high and 8ft long. They were used to transport extra ammunition and equipment. Once loaded, they were waterproofed. They would be removed in the assembly area and their contents pooled for future regimental disbursement.

Chapter 2

1. A whole series of specialised landing craft would be required. The landing ship, tank (LST) was a ship capable of putting as many as twenty tanks, and their wheeled support vehicles, directly on the beach if the gradient was modest. The landing craft, tank (LCT) could carry up to eight tanks. The landing craft, infantry (LCI) could carry a 200 man company of infantry ashore. The landing craft, assault (LCA) could put the equivalent of a platoon of infantry ashore, while an amphibious vehicle nicknamed the DUKW could carry men and supplies from ship to shore and inland.
2. On 19 August 1942, 2nd Cdn Inf Div conducted a raid on the port town of Dieppe. The aim of the raid was three-fold: first, to test Hitler's Atlantic Wall; second, as a limited dress rehearsal for Operation ROUNDUP; and third, to gather intelligence information on the radar stations that were located there. The raid was a disaster for 2nd Cdn Inf Div with a casualty rate over 68 per cent. It resulted in the loss of 3,367 men out of the attacking force of 4,963; 907 were killed on the beaches or would die in captivity, 586 were wounded, and the Germans took a further 1,946 as prisoners.
3. Brig Eisenhower had rapidly risen in rank to attain the rank of a four-star general and the position of Supreme Allied Commander in northwest Europe.

4. One of the biggest 'beefs' from the men was that they drove off into only 3 to 4ft of water while they had spent weeks waterproofing their tanks in anticipation of wading ashore in 6ft of water.
5. It didn't upset him too much, though. He could easily have obtained another but he didn't like having to wear it in the first place.
6. The next day, he got another truck and spent the week with Honorary Captain (H/Capt) E.J. Gleason, the Protestant padre of the *Sherbrookes*, picking up the bodies of dead Canadian soldiers.
7. The timetable for Operation OVERLORD called for the reserve brigade to land at 10.30 and to commence its advance on Carpiquet from ELDER at about 12.00.
8. *Heeresgruppe B* was under the command of *Generalfeldmarschall* Erwin Rommel who had the responsibility for the defence of the Atlantic Wall from Holland, through Belgium and France to Spain. Under his command were *15.Armee* and *7.Armee*.
9. Interview with Maj Walsh as quoted in *We Were There: A Record for Canada. Volume 5: The Army* by Jean E. Portugal. (Shelburne: Self-published, 1998), p.2418 (hereafter referred to as *We Were There* and the page).
10. Lieut Douglas Hamilton Bradley was appointed acting Capt-Adjt to cover off the vacancy left by Capt Côté and was promoted to acting Captain. Capt Côté would later escape from German custody when the Allies entered Paris while Sgt Barter would only find his freedom at the end of the war. In October 1944, Capt Côté would return to the *Sherbrookes* and describe his adventures to a war correspondent.

   When on their way to the headquarters, the two scout cars found themselves in the midst of a strong German motorised patrol. In an effort to escape, he and Sgt Barter abandoned their vehicle and succeeded in eluding the enemy force. They crawled through no-man's-land in an attempt to return to friendly lines. But, the infantry of 3rd Cdn Inf Div didn't recognise them and so opened fire with rifles and machine-gun fire as they approached their positions. When Capt Côté realised they couldn't get back, they wandered aimlessly through the fields seeking some avenue of escape. They finally spotted an outpost they believed to be occupied by friendly troops. They headed for it only to find it occupied by the enemy. They were forced to surrender at bayonet point. Capt Côté finally ended up in a German hospital in Paris. With the help of a French nurse who got him fake papers, he escaped from the institution. He made his way through Paris and found refuge in an apartment house and hid there for two weeks while the Allies assaulted the city. When he realised that the Germans had left Paris, he came out of hiding and reported to an American Army headquarters. He was welcomed, put on a plane and sent back to London.

Sherbrooke Fusilier Regiment War Diary, 19 October 1944. (Library and Archives Canada – Department of National Defence – Records Group 24, Series C-3, Volume s T-12754 to T-12762) (hereafter referred to as *SFR WD* and the relevant date).
11. Operation OVERLORD had foreseen the possibility that 3rd Brit Inf Div might not be able to capture Caen on D-Day. If so, a renewed frontal assault would be avoided. Instead, the city would be 'subjected to heavy air bombardment to limit its usefulness to the enemy and to make its retention a costly business.'
12. http://www.tanks-encyclopedia.com.

Chapter 3

1. It turned out to be a *Reihenwerfer*, a sixteen-barrelled rocket projector mounted on a half-track.
2. The Forward Observer Bombardment (FOB), a young naval officer from the cruiser *HMS Belfast*, lost contact with the cruiser when his wireless set failed and he had no backup unit.
3. Speculative fire (spec fire) was fire laid down on a suspected enemy position in the hope that the enemy would return fire thereby giving away its locations.
4. Three miles of no-man's-land separated the two brigades.
5. In order to gain the advantage of light, the Allies were on British double summer time. The Germans, on the other hand, operated one hour behind the Allies (9.30 German time was 10.30 Allied time). All the references to the German time movements have been converted into British double summer time.
6. Kurt Meyer had also earned another nickname 'SchnellMeyer' in reference to the speed with which he reacted to new situations on the battlefield. Meyer would later be able to claim fame for being the youngest German Division Commander of the war.
7. Meyer, Kurt. *Grenadiers*. (Winnipeg: Stackpole Books, 1994), p.222, (hereafter referred to as *Grenadiers*).
8. *Grenadiers*, p.223.
9. When a tank was hit, the shell drilled a hole through the tank and released a whole shower of shrapnel that would ricochet around inside the tank and result in some dreadful injuries. If the shell hit either the fuel tanks

ENDNOTES

or the ammunition bins, then an explosion would most likely occur and the tank would brew up. If the tank was fuelled by gasoline, then the delay to get out of the tank alive was about six seconds. If it was fueled by derve (diesel) the delay was nine seconds.
10. The .50-cal Browning anti-aircraft gun.
11. The remnants of the squadron went back via Gruchy. Lieut Davies's tank ran out of fuel and had to be towed to les Buissons by Sgt R. Allison's tank. After consolidation and refuelling, it was confirmed that only five tanks remained of the twenty tanks from B Sqn which had gone into battle.
12. In hind sight, Maj Walsh believed that Lt-Col Gordon had ordered C Sqn to attack because he knew the enemy was listening to his orders and he wanted them to think that C Sqn still had nineteen tanks.
13. Only thirty-five men got back from both A Coy and C Coy combined; while sixty returned for B Coy.
14. Among the casualties were 175 missing, including 17 officers. Lost were three company commanders and all four company 2i/c.
15. The *Sherbrookes* war diary noted that Lieut Stevens and Lieut Trenholme had been killed; Maj Mahon, Lieut Steeves, Lieut Kraus and Lieut Thompson had been wounded; while Capt Côté, Lieut Windsor and Lieut MacLean were missing.
16. On 16 June 1944, H/Capt K.M. Cutler was taken on strength to replace padre Brown.
17. Tpr Dagenais would be liberated from a PoW Camp in April 1945.
18. Meyer visited the Abbaye d'Ardenne in the late 1950s. When questioned by Jean-Marie Vico as to why he had lied at his trial, Meyer is reported to have stated that it was difficult for an officer to admit to an enemy court that such things had been done. Campbell, Ian J. 'Abbaye d'Ardenne June 1944: Twenty Canadian Prisoners of War.' (Buron, 1984), pp.8–16.

Chapter 4

1. 3.Pzkom was commanded by *SS-Obersturmführer* Rudolf von Ribbentrop, the son of the Nazi Foreign Minister.
2. Armoured Vehicle, Royal Engineers.
3. The Allies had captured the German encryption machine, codenamed ENIGMA, and a secret operation nicknamed ULTRA was set up at Bletchley Park to intercept and interpret German signals. Therefore, the Allies were privy to secret German intelligence during most of the European campaign.

4. *SS-Brigadeführer* Witt had been killed on 14 June during a naval gun barrage on his HQ. Two days later, as the senior officer of 12.SS-Pzdiv, Meyer was promoted to the rank of *SS-Brigadeführer* and given its command.
5. The *Panzerschreck*, officially known as the *Raketenpanzerbüchse 54*, was a German 88mm reusable anti-tank rocket launcher (maximum effective range: 180 meters; maximum armour penetration: 160mm).
6. The *Panzerfaust* was a German inexpensive, hand held, single shot, recoilless anti-tank weapon, similar to the British PIAT (maximum effective range: 60 meters; maximum armour penetration: 200mm).
7. The fighting in Buron was still intense and the town remained in German hands. It would not be until 14.30 before the North Novas could start their move forward to their line of departure south of the town.
8. It was lucky for the population, as it was later learned that as many as 2,000 civilians were taking refuge in the church at the time.
9. 'Sunray' was the nickname used to designate a commander, whether it was for a tank, a troop, a squadron or, as in this case, the CO of the *Sherbrookes*.
10. The *Nebelwerfers* were nicknamed the 'Moaning Minnies' by the Allied troops because of the sound they generated when fired.
11. That same day, the body of H/Capt Brown, the regimental Catholic padre, who had gone missing on D-Day evening, was found on the edge of some woods near Caen, his hands tied behind his back.

Chapter 5

1. Although 85th LAD painted the interior of the tank, they couldn't get rid of the smell of death. A tank delivery crew arrived but refused to get in it no matter what. The crew thought it would bring them bad luck. James Lawrence Zaporzan. *Rad's War: A Biographical Study of Sydney Valpy Radley-Walters from Mobilization to the end of the Normandy Campaign 1944*. MA Thesis. (Queen's University, 2001), pp.208–209.

Chapter 6

1. Also known as the King Tiger.
2. The gun, gun mantle, seats and communication bins were removed from the Priests. A piece of armoured plate was welded over the opening in

the front where the gun had been. When all available armour plating had been used up, the fitters welded two mild steel plates about two inches apart and filled the gap in between them with sand. The engine was also overhauled. The new armoured personnel carriers were nicknamed by the troops as either *'Unfrocked Priests'* or *'Holy Rollers'*. By 6 August, seventy-six Priests would be converted. This same idea would be later applied to left over Ram tanks.
3. Self-propelled anti-tank guns.
4. In reality, it would take four hours before the lead elements of 4th Cdn Armd Div passed through the position.
5. 5.Pzarmee was created on 2 July from the units of *Panzergruppe West*.
6. *SS-Hauptsturmführer* Michael Wittmann was one of Germany's top scoring *Panzer* aces and a national hero for the German people. On 25 July 1944, he had received, directly from the hands of Adolf Hitler, the Swords to his Knight's Cross with Oak Leaves for his actions in Normandy, making him the most decorated tank ace of the war. During the war, he was accredited with having destroyed 138 tanks, 141 artillery pieces and an unknown number of other armoured vehicles. He had fought in Poland (1939), the Balkans (1940–1941) and on the Eastern Front (1941–1944) before being sent to Normandy.
7. An AP shell had entered the upper hull of Wittmann's tank and it caught fire. The fire ignited the Tiger's ammunition and the resulting explosion blew the turret off. The remains of Wittmann and his crew were later recovered and buried near the spot. The 1st Yeomanry would later claim to have killed the German tank ace but it wasn't until the mid-1980's that a review of the evidence raised the possibility that the *Sherbrookes* might have got him. See Appendix 1.
8. It was named after Lt-Col Donald Grant Worthington, the CO of the BCR.
9. It was named after Lt-Col W.W. Halfpenny, the CO of the CGG.
10. Reid, Brian A. *No Holding Back: Operation Totalize, Normandy, August 1944*. (Toronto: University of Toronto Press, 2005), p.242.
11. P. Agte, *Michael Wittmann and the Waffen SS Tiger Commanders of the Leibstandarte in WWII*. (Stackpole Military History, 1996).
12. The German version of a jeep.
13. Global Positioning System.
14. Michelburgh, Rod and Griffiths, Rudyard. *Rare Courage: Veterans of the Second World War Remember*. (Toronto: McClelland & Stewart, 2005).

Chapter 7

1. A tactical grouping of 12.SS-Pzdiv and 21.Pzdiv.
2. The M1 Bazooka was an American hand held, anti-tank weapon (maximum effective range: 200 meters; maximum armour penetration: 76mm).
3. Quoted in Stacey, Colonel C.P. *Official History of the Canadian Army in the Second World War. Volume III: The Victory Camapign: The Operations in North-West Europe, 1944–1945*. (Ottawa: The Queen's Printer and Controller of Stationary, 1960), p.285 (Hereafter referred to as *The Victory Campaign*).

Chapter 8

1. In order to prevent confusion, the initial designation of 21st Army Group composed of First US Army and Third US Army was changed to 12th Army Group on 1 September 1944.
2. 4th Brigade had 639 troops; 5th Brigade had 627 and 6th Brigade had 746 persons. The strongest battalion was the FMR with 331 soldiers and the lowest was the Black Watch with 176 infantrymen.
3. In the space of less than two hours, Sgt Beardsley had had two tanks knocked out under him.
4. The French Underground.
5. Lt-Col Clift had been promoted to the rank of brigadier and had taken command of the brigade from Brig Young on 26 August. He had been the CO of the South Sask and Maj F.B. Courtney was appointed as the acting CO for the operation.
6. He was replaced by Lt-Col J. Guy Gauvreau, the CO of the FMR.
7. It would be later learned that what petrol was available was being reserved for Operation MARKET GARDEN.

The Aftermath

1. *Victory Campaign*, p.609.

Index

I. PERSONNEL

a. Sherbrooke Fusilier Regiment

Allen, W., Tpr, 115
Allsop, F.J., Sgt, 43, 219
Andrees, D., Tpr, 220
Anton, L.S., Sgt, 222
Archibald, A.J., Lieut, 162
Arnold, E.W.L., Maj, 8, 13, 47, 71–2, 74, 76
Arsenault, C.R., Sgt, 56–8, 73–4
Aulis, G.E., Sgt, 72
Ayriss, P.W., Capt, 170

Bailey, D.C., Cpl, 36, 43–4
Baldwin, F.H., Maj, 13, 31, 33, 62, 207, 221
Balkwill, H.W., Tpr, 219
Bancroft, H.W., Lieut, 219
Barlow, G.C.H., RSM, 8, 223
Barr, C.R., Sgt, 222
Barter, N.H., Sgt, 37
Bartlett, D.D., Tpr, 85, 115, 221
Bateman, M.H., Capt, 32, 46, 55, 76, 136; Maj, 223
Beardsley, R.R., Sgt, 36, 85, 102, 117, 125, 189–90, 221
Beaudry, D.W., Maj, 8, 12
Bégin, D.E., Sgt, 84
Belton, H.M., Capt, 34, 60, 161, 197

Bennett, C.W., Lieut, 78
Bingham, F.W.K., Maj, 77, 87, 95–7
Birch, H., Cpl, 170
Biron, A., Maj, 7, 10, 223
Bolt, J.L., Tpr, 67–8, 219
Bowers, V.R., Sgt, 221
Boyd, A.B., Tpr, 31
Boyd, N.S., Lieut, 56, 60, 90, 219
Bradley, D.H., Lieut, 62, 71, 73; Capt, 209
Breen, S., Capt, 222
Brennan, J.P., Maj, 221
Brokovski, T.W., Capt, 33, 37
Brown, J., Tpr, 220
Brown, W.L., H/Capt, 66, 76, 219
Bryant, R.A., Cpl, 66, 159–60
Bryce, K.A., Maj, 221
Buckley, H.W.M., Tpr, 52
Burke, E., A/RSM, 223
Butler, H.J., Lieut, 205–206

Camirand, A.J., Maj, 8, 10
Casey, J.H., Lieut, 36, 219
Cathcart, R.A., Sgt, 45, 47, 54, 57, 61–2, 90, 116, 222
Cave, J.C., Maj, 12, 72, 75–7, 223
Charters, W.J., Lieut, 89–91, 98, 112, 219
Clare, J., Tpr, 98, 219

Clout, E.A., Capt, 221
Cloutier, A.N., Lieut, 129–30
Clutterbuck, L.P., Tpr, 222
Colbeck, H.G.M., Lieut, 162
Connell, A.T.P., L/Sgt, 221
Corless, J.D., Lieut, 80, 91, 115, 222
Cormier, A.J., Sgt, 54
Cornish, A., L/Cpl, 222
Côté, G.W., Capt, 37, 208–209
Coveny, P.W., L/Cpl, 41, 43–4, 52
Craig, J.D., Lieut, 138
Cuddie, L.W., Sgt, 117, 221
Cutler, H/Capt, 76

Dagenais, M.J.A., Tpr, 68
Dann, N.A.J., Lieut, 207–208; Capt, 209
Davidson, J.H., Tpr, 52, 219
Davies, L.N., Lieut, 33, 43, 46, 55, 58, 96, 100, 222
Davis, J.W., Tpr, 220
Davis, M.D., L/Cpl, 221
Désilet, E.L., Cpl, 91–2
Désy, J., QM Sgt, 222
Dick, K.Y., Capt, 159–60
Drodge, G.M., Cpl, 46
Dufault, J.G.L.L., RSM, 12, 23–4, 210, 224
Dundas, D.M., Cpl, 88
Dunn, S.L., Lieut, 222

Elliott, P.J.H., Tpr, 189, 220
Elsby, C., Tpr, 220
Evans, A.L., L/Cpl, 220

Fidler, E., Tpr, 117–18, 160, 220, 222
Fisher, H.G., L/Sgt, 57
Fitzpatrick, M.J., Lieut, 47–8, 52, 73, 80, 219; Capt, 221
Flavelle, L.D., Tpr, 43

Fletcher, J.R., Tpr, 98
Fontaine, G., Tpr, 219
Forbes, W.M., Tpr, 219
Foster, H.D., Lieut, 87–8, 94, 97
Fountain, J.P., Cpl, 43, 52, 219
Fowlis, H., Sgt, 91, 98, 114
Fripp, G.I., Capt, 189–90, 209
Fuger, J.E., Capt, 117
Futter, H.A., Sgt, 97–8

Gaffney, M.J., Tpr, 220
Galley, W.A., Tpr, 54
Gannaw, P.E., Lieut, 129, 138
Gareau, G.C., Tpr, 220
Garrow, R.F., Capt, 221–2
Gelman, D., Tpr, 220
Gilbert, H.J., Tpr, 54
Gilbert, J.H., Capt, 62, 76, 96
Gill, G.V., Tpr, 67–8, 219
Gilroy, R.B., Tpr, 220
Goodall, F., Tpr, 220
Goodfellow, J.S., Lieut, 210
Goodwin, G.D., Lieut, 221
Gordon, M.B.K., Lt-Col, 12, 16, 18–19, 34, 45, 54–6, 58, 60–1, 72, 76–7, 90, 92, 96, 98, 107, 112, 117–19, 130, 132, 137, 139, 158, 161, 182, 184, 186, 191, 201–202, 206–210, 221, 223
Gould, T.G., Lieut, 138, 153, 209, 221
Grainger, W.F., Lieut, 66
Greenwood, J.H., L/Cpl, 66, 219

Hall, A.F., Tpr, 222
Hammond, E.M., Cpl, 163
Hancharyk, S., Tpr, 219
Hardy, W.G., Tpr, 52, 219
Harris, R.V., Tpr, 161

INDEX

Hart, P.J., Cpl, 138; A/Sgt, 222
Harvey, E.G., Pte, 222
Harvey, L.E., Tpr, 220
Henry, T.H., Tpr, 67–8, 219
Herman, E.J., Tpr, 34
Hill, K., Cpl, 118, 220
Hoar, R.B., Lieut, 203
Houston, R.M., Maj, 117, 119, 125, 209, 221
Howland, E.A., SSM, 190, 200, 221; RSM, 224
Hull, G.W., SSM, 221
Hunter, T.H., Lieut, 76
Hutcheson, R.E., Tpr, 61, 88; Cpl, 222

Jelly, A., Tpr, 113, 219
Jenkins, H.M., Tpr, 52
Jenne, L.M., Sgt, 140, 220, 222
Jenner, F.T., Lt-Col, 221, 223
Jennings, L.W.M., Tpr, 220
Johnston, W.M., Tpr, 62
Jones, J.G., Cpl; 74; Sgt, 222
Jones, W.R., Tpr, 220
Joudrey, R.N., Sgt, 220

Kachor, J., L/Cpl, 46, 219
Keith, K.B., Tpr, 219
Kenny, H.V., Tpr, 220
Klose, E.J., Tpr, 55, 219
Kraus, G.A., Lieut, 34, 41–4, 52

Larkin, J.F., L/Sgt, 222
Lavallière, D.R., L/Sgt, 56
Leblanc, J.E.V., Tpr, 219
Leclerc, J.L., Tpr, 222
Lefebvre, M., Sgt, 90, 113, 219
Legge, G.G., Tpr, 219
Leonard, G.A., Cpl, 36, 160
Lick, A.E., Tpr, 222

Litchfield, O.C.J., Tpr, 129
Lockhead, R., Tpr, 68, 219
Logan, J.E.M., Lieut, 138, 153, 160, 220
Loveday, E.M., Tpr, 219
Lyon, B.D., Maj, 8, 12

MacDougall, J.A., Tpr, 201
MacKay, K.M., Tpr, 219
MacKenzie, D.W., Tpr, 220
MacKenzie, M., Tpr, 52, 219
MacLachlan, C.C., Capt, 222; Maj, 221
MacLean, I.A., Lieut, 43, 45, 47, 54, 56–7, 60
MacLeod, D.E., SSM, 24; RSM, 24, 223–4
McA'Nulty, M.W., Col, 7; Lt-Col, 10, 12, 223
McChesney, H., Tpr, 220
McClure, L.G., Tpr, 161
McCormick, H.A., Cpl, 220
McCrimmon, I.J., Lieut, 112–13, 220
McLean, A., Tpr, 160, 220
McMillan, E.B., Sgt, 46, 55, 219
McMurdo, C.H., A/Sgt, 220
Mahon, G.S., Maj, 13, 46, 76
Mann, G.K., Tpr, 33
Marshall, G.L., Lieut, 205–206; Capt, 222
Martin, W.R., Lieut, 169–70, 205
Miller, D.J., Sgt, 112
Milne, H.A., Sgt, 135, 189
Mondor, M.V., Lieut, 220
Morgan, P.H., Lieut, 219
Munro, F.J., Tpr, 220
Munroe, R.W., Tpr, 55
Murray, T.B., Sgt, 220
Mutter, J.M., A/Cpl, 219
Myrtle, P.G., Sgt, 222

Nadon, C.F., Tpr, 219
Neill, J.W., Lieut, 170, 221
Nelson, L.C., Tpr, 219
Nesdoly, O.N., Tpr, 222
Neuman, J., Tpr, 84
Nicholson, C.L., SSM, 62, 221; A/RSM, 224
Nicks, B.E., Tpr, 219
Nordin, E.C., Tpr, 220
Norris, R.P., Tpr, 115

Olimb, R., L/Cpl, 222
Olivier, R.V., Sgt, 90–1, 114, 222

Parsons, A.J., Sgt, 33, 46, 58, 136
Paquette, P.A., Tpr, 86, 201, 222
Pépin, H.W., L/Cpl, 52
Pettitt, J., Tpr, 219
Philp, H., Tpr, 68, 219
Pinning, R.E., Lieut, 109, 112
Provencher, H.J., Tpr, 219
Purdy, R.G., Tpr, 220

Quann, F.W., Tpr, 220
Quinn, T., Cpl, 45, 47, 57, 89, 96

Radley-Walters, S.V., Capt, 34, 60–2, 71; Maj, 76, 79–80, 85–6, 92, 95, 99, 110–12, 115, 118, 120, 125, 135, 138, 141–2, 151, 159, 164–5, 169–70, 176, 189–90, 201–202, 205–206, 210, 221, 223
Raites, R., Capt, 136
Reid, E.W., Tpr, 220
Reid, T.C., Sgt, 43, 45, 54, 58, 99, 116, 136, 220
Reno, G.V., Tpr, 219
Rice, G.S., Cpl, 95, 115, 220
Ride, L.G., L/Sgt, 61, 219

Rigby, A., Sgt, 221
Rodgers, J.L., Tpr, 219

Sambrook, A.E., Cpl, 46
Sarr, D.A., Tpr, 219
Sauvé, H.R., Sgt, 41, 44, 52
Savard, J.S., Sgt, 55, 71, 222
Schneider, E.H.J., Tpr, 219
Schuler, V.P., Tpr, 221
Seastrand, F.A., Tpr, 220
Seigrist, H.O., Cpl, 88
Severeid, J.M., Tpr, 55, 71, 219
Shannon, C.M., Tpr, 62
Shepherd, L.J., Tpr, 220
Silverstone, R., Capt, 209
Slater, J.G., L/Cpl, 33
Smith, D.T., Tpr, 203
Smith, W.J., Tpr, 220
Sosnowski, J., Tpr, 219
Spafford, E.A., Lieut, 45, 47, 56–7, 62, 73–4, 90–1, 98, 116, 221
Spielman, H.D., Lieut, 70, 186
Steer, A.J., Tpr, 57
Steeves, K.L., Lieut, 46, 57, 71
Stevens, T.C., Lieut, 37, 219
Stewart, D.H., Tpr, 219
Stewart, G.H., Sgt, 222
Stinson, S.F., Tpr, 219
Stone, W.S., Tpr, 92

Tanner, R.W.W., L/Cpl, 161
Taylor, J.W., Sgt, 87–8, 115, 160
Temple, R.M., Tpr, 222
Thistle, H., Tpr, 57
Thomas, W.R., Tpr, 222
Thompson, C.F., Lieut, 34, 37, 56, 73, 91–2, 109, 112–14, 219
Thwaites, M.E., Sgt, 160
Tomkins, W.L., Maj, 8

INDEX

Trenholme, W.H., Lieut, 46, 55, 219
Truax, A.R., Lieut, 44, 80, 85

Uhlman, M.C., Tpr, 220

Veilleux, B.M., Capt, 222

Walsh, V.O., Maj, 13, 37, 56, 60–2, 71–3, 86, 92, 129–30, 191, 197, 201, 208, 210, 221, 223
Warnes, E., Cpl, 52
Warriner, R.A., Lieut, 221
Weber, W.C., Maj, 77, 102
Welsh, N.H., Capt, 170, 205, 221
White, A., Tpr, 219
Wilkinson, N.E., Tpr, 55, 219
Williams, C.M., Lieut, 135, 169–70, 176
Williams, L.D., Cpl, 90–1, 109
Windsor, T.A.L., Lieut, 47–8, 52, 68, 219
Wolfe, E.J., RSM, 9, 12, 223
Wood, C.E., Tpr, 220
Wood, F.J., Tpr, 115
Wood, S.W., Lieut, 37, 46, 186; A/Capt, 222
Woodward, J.A., Sgt, 200

Young, J.A., Tpr, 55

b. Other persons

Alexander, Sir H., Gen, 26
Arrell, H.C., Maj, 195–6

Bingham, J.F., Col, 139; Brig, 184, 191, 206
Blackader, K.G., Brig, 27, 88–9, 140

Boardman, T., Capt, 149
Booth, E.L., Brig, 145
Bradley, O.N., Lt-Gen, 26, 79, 104, 126; Gen, 155, 178
Burgess, J., Maj, 138

Campbell, C., Lieut, 86
Cantlie, S.S.T., Lt-Col, 124
Churchill, W.S., 25–6
Clift, F.A., Lt-Col, 169; Brig, 197–8, 200
Crerar, H.D.G., Lt-Gen, 14, 22, 27, 121, 126, 155, 166–7, 172, 179, 183, 205
Crocker, J.T., Lt-Gen, 81, 83
Cunningham, D.G., Brig, 27, 34, 37, 63

Dempsey, M.C., Lt-Gen, 26, 37, 76, 79, 104, 121
Durward, D., Maj, 87

Eberbach, H. *General der Panzertruppe*, 140, 144
Eisenhower, D.D., Brig, 25; Gen, 23, 26, 155, 212–13, 215
Ekins, J., Tpr, 148–9

Feuchtinger, E., *Generalleutnant*, 36, 50
Foster, H.W., Brig, 27
Foulkes, C.H., Maj-Gen, 109, 111, 117–18, 130, 158, 161, 186, 190, 195, 201–202

Ganong, J.E., Brig, 133, 193, 195
Gordon, Sgt, 149
Gregory, A.S., Lt-Col, 200
Griffin, F.P., Maj, 124
Griffiths, F.M., Lt-Col, 86–7

Hitler, A., 1, 48, 78, 103, 167, 171, 176, 180
Hodges, C.H., Lt-Gen, 126
Hodgins, R.G., Maj, 87
Höfflinger, H., *SS-Hauptsturmführer*, 149–51

Ihrion, *SS-Untersturmführer*, 149–50

James, Lieut, 149
Jodl, A., *Generaloberst*, 171
Jones, C.E.F., Lt-Col, 138

Keller, R.F.L., Maj-Gen, 16–17, 27, 34, 79, 82, 88, 93, 95, 140
King George VI, 22
Kitching, G., Maj-Gen, 145
Kluge, G. von, *Generalfeldmarschall*, 125–6, 171, 180

Macdonald, Lt-Col, 114, 117
MacLachlan, G.M., Lt-Col, 195
Marshall, G.C. Jr, Gen, 25
Matthews, G.R., Maj, 114
Megill, W.J., Brig, 124, 186
Meyer, K., *SS-Standartenführer*, 49–51, 61, 68–70, 73, 79, 93; *SS-Brigadeführer*, 140–1, 144, 148, 154, 156
Mitchell, C.C., Lt-Col, 187–8
Model, W., *Generalfeldmarschall*, 171, 180
Montgomery, Sir B.L., Gen, 20, 26, 76–9, 104, 121, 125–6, 128, 147, 154–5, 166, 172, 174, 177–9, 204; Fd-Mar, 212–13, 215–17
Morgan, F.E., Lt-Gen, 25–6
Morton, R.E.A., Lt-Col, 72

O'Connor, Sir R.N., Lt-Gen, 77

Patton, G.S., Lt-Gen, 121, 126, 155, 166
Paulus, F. von, *Generalfeldmarschall*, 48
Petch, C., Lt-Col, 34, 47–8, 54, 58, 62–3

Rabe, *SS-Hauptsturmführer Doktor*, 150
Richter, W., *Generalleutnant*, 50
Rommel, E., *Generalfeldmarschall*, 78
Roosevelt, F.D., 25–6
Rundstedt, G. von, *Generalfeldmarschall*, 78

Saucken, D. von, *General der Panzertruppe*, 174
Scheweppingburg, G. von, *General der Panzertruppe*, 70
Simonds, G.G., Lt-Gen, 27, 105–106, 110, 121, 126–8, 130, 139, 145–7, 154, 156, 167, 172, 179–0, 205, 207, 214–15

Vokes, C., Maj-Gen, 69

Whitley, T.F., Maj, 194
Witt, F., *Brigadeführer*, 50
Wittmann, M., *SS-Hauptsturmführer*, 141–2, 148–53
Wyman, R.A., Brig, 27, 58, 71, 75, 130, 139

Young, H.A., Brig, 110, 164

INDEX

II-GENERAL

a. Military Operations (by calendar events)

Operation OVERLORD, 14, 217
  amphibious training, 14–16
    Exercise HAMMER, 14–15
    Exrecise ADAM, 15
    Exercise PICKAXE, 15
    Exercise EVE I, 15
    Exercise EVE II, 15
  basic training, 14, 16–20
    Exercise CHASER, 16
    Exercise ROUNDABOUT, 16
    Exercise PUSH, 16–18, 33
    Exercise FROST, 18–19
    Exercise NUDGER II, 18
    Exercise POPLIN, 19–20
  assault training, 14, 20–22
    Exercise PEDAL, 20, 33
    Exercise PRANK, 20–1
    Exercise PEDAL II, 22
  collective assault training, 14, 22
    Exercise FABIUS III, 22, 33
  Planning;
    Operation ROUNDABOUT, 16
    Atlantic Wall, 26
    21st Army Group plan, 26–7, 71
    3rd Canadian Infantry Division plan, 27–9
    D-Day objectives, 29
    MIKE Beach, 29
    NAN Beach, 29
    execution, 29–38
Battle for Carpiquet, 40–64
  Normandy;
    topography, 40
  3rd Canadian Infantry Division plan, 41
  9th Canadian Infantry Brigade plan, 41
  tactics used, 40–1
  execution, 40–65
  Abbaye d'Ardenne, 40, 50, 60
    German onservation post, 51
    executions at, 67–9
    trial of Meyer, 68–9
Operation ABERLOUR, 77–82
  plan, 77–8, 81–2
  preparations, 78
  postponement, 77
  cancellation, 79
Operation EPSOM, 77
Operation CHARNWOOD;
  21st Army Group plan, 76–9
  First British Corps
    plan, 81–2
    execution, 83, 90
  3rd Canadian Infantry Division
    plan, 79, 82
    9th Brigade plan, 82–3
    execution, 83–101
Operation WINDSOR;
  objective, 79–80
  plan, 80
  execution, 80–81
Operation GOODWOOD, 104–21, 154
  German dispositions, 103–104
  21st Army Group plan, 104–106
  execution, 107–120
  see also Operation ATLANTIC
Operation ATLANTIC, 106–20, 125
  German dispositions, 104
  Second Canadian Corps plan, 105–106, 121

execution, 121–5
2nd Canadian Infantry Division
   plan, 106–107
   execution, 107–20
   failure, 114, 120
Operation SPRING, 121–5, 154, 217
   Second Canadian Corps plan, 121–2
   2nd Canadian Infantry Division plan, 122–3
   3rd Canadian Infantry Division plan, 122–5
   execution, 122–5
Operation COBRA, 121
Operation TOTALIZE, 128–47, 154–5, 217
   situation, 127–8
   Second Canadian Corps plan, 126, 128–33
   tactical innovations, 128–9
   training, 133
   preparations, 133
   execution, 134–46
   German reaction, 140–1
   death of Michael Wittmann, 148–53
Operation LÜTTICH, 126, 155
Operation TULLULAH, 156
   Second Canadian Corps plan, 156
   modifications to, 156
   renamed Operation TRACTABLE, 156
Operation TRACTABLE, 156–77, 217
   Second Canadian Corps plan, 156–7
   2nd Canadian Infantry Division plan, 158
   topography, 158
   situation, 157–8
   execution, 158–72
   closing the Falaise Gap, 170–7
Pursuit to the Seine, 178–211
   21st Army Group plan, 178–9
   topography, 178–9
   objectives, 178–9
   execution, 180–6
   Second Canadian Corps plan, 179, 186–90
   topography, 180–1
   execution, 180–90
   Forêt de la Londe, 191–202
   Operation UNDERGO, 209–10
Operation MARKET GARDEN, 212, 215, 217
   21st Army Group plan, 212
Operation VALEDICTION, 213
Operation VERITABLE, 213–14, 217
   Operation BLOCKBUSTER I, 214
   Operation BLOCKBUSTER II, 215
Operation PLUNDER, 215

b. General

Canada;
   declaration of war, 2–4
   military preparedness, 2–4
   organization, 2
   defence spending, 2–3
   Defence Scheme No. 3, 3
   mobilization, 4–5
Eastern Townships, 5
   topography, 5

INDEX

military heritage, 5
actions on declaration of war, 5–6
   1st General Base Depot, 5–6
   35th (Howitzer) Battery, 6
France;
   declaration of war, 2
Germany;
   invasion of Poland, 1
   invasion of Norway and Denmark, 6
   invasion of Holland, Belgium and France, 6
Great Britain;
   declaration of war, 2
   evacuation from Dunkirk, 6

III. ORDER OF BATTLE

a. Canada

First Canadian Army, 121, 126, 155–6, 166, 172, 174–5, 178–80, 204, 215–16
   creation, 13
Canadian Armoured Corps;
   creation, 10
First Canadian Corps;
   creation, 5
   1st Canadian Armoured Division, 10
   1st Canadian Infantry Division, 5
      1st Canadian Infantry Brigade, 5
      2nd Canadian Infantry Brigade, 5
      3rd Canadian Infantry Brigade, 5
Second Canadian Corps, 27, 104–106, 121, 125–6, 147, 154–6, 165–7, 172, 176, 178–80, 182–3, 202, 205, 209, 213, 215, 217
4th Canadian Armoured Division, 27, 69, 105, 128, 130, 139, 143–8, 157, 171–2, 174, 179–80, 183, 192, 205, 214–15
   creation, 10
   training in Debert, Nova Scotia, 10–12
   29th Canadian Recce Regiment (The South Alberta Regiment), 146
   Lake Superior Regiment (Motor), The, 146
   see 4th Canadian Armoured Brigade; 10th Canadian Infantry Brigade
   deployment to the United Kingdom, 12
2nd Canadian Infantry Division, 6, 27, 105–107, 109–10, 114, 121–2, 126, 128, 130, 143, 146–7, 156–8, 172, 176, 178–80, 182–4, 186, 190–1, 197, 201–202, 206, 213–17
   creation, 5
   8th Canadian Recce Regiment (14th Canadian Hussars), 132, 135, 138, 197
   Toronto Scottish Regiment (MG), 137
   See 4th Canadian Infantry Brigade; 5th Canadian Infantry Brigade;

6th Canadian Infantry Brigade;
deployment to the United Kingdom, 6
Dieppe, 26, 105
3rd Canadian Infantry Division, 14, 16, 22, 24, 27, 37–8, 64, 70, 76–9, 82, 94, 105–108, 110, 114, 122, 128, 140, 146–7, 156, 172, 179, 183–4, 186, 192–3, 201–202, 205, 209, 213–17
creation, 6
7th Canadian Recce Regiment (17th Duke of York's Royal Canadian Hussars), 101
Cameron Highlanders of Ottawa, 41
See 7th Canadian Infantry Brigade; 8th Canadian Infantry Brigade; 9th Canadian Infantry Brigade
training in England, 16–24
4th Canadian Infantry Division, 7
creation, 6, 217
conversion to armoured, 10
2nd Canadian Armoured Brigade, 13, 16–18, 20–1, 27, 29, 32, 37, 58, 70–1, 76–7, 81–2, 95, 98, 105–106, 118, 126, 128, 139–40, 147–8, 156–7, 161, 172, 174–6, 182, 184–5, 191, 201, 206, 208–209, 213, 217
creation, 13
organization, 13

See First Hussars, The; Fort Garry Horse, The; Sherbrooke Fusilier Regiment, The;
4th Canadian Armoured Brigade, 130, 143, 172, 174–5, 205
British Columbia Regiment, 145
Canadian Grenadier Guards, 144–6, 148
Governor General's Foot Guard, 145
4th Canadian Infantry Brigade, 5, 106–107, 113, 122, 133, 147, 158, 161–2, 166–8, 184–6, 190, 192–5, 197–8, 202–203, 214–15
Essex Scottish Regiment, The, 113–14, 117, 133, 136, 138–9, 143, 158, 161, 163, 187, 190, 193, 197
Royal Hamilton Light Infantry, 92, 124–5, 133, 135–7, 158–60, 163, 187, 190, 192–3, 195–6
Royal Regiment of Canada, 124–5, 133, 135–6, 138, 141, 143, 158, 160–3, 167, 187, 190–1, 193–5
5th Canadian Infantry Brigade, 5, 106–109, 122, 124, 133, 147, 161, 166, 176, 180, 184–7, 191, 199, 201–203, 214–15
Black Watch (Royal Highland Regiment) of Canada, 109, 112, 115, 117–18, 120, 124, 187, 190, 201, 206
Calgary Highlanders, The, 108–109, 124–5, 128, 143, 161, 163, 186–90, 199, 201

INDEX

Régiment de Maisonneuve, Le, 108–109, 118–19, 143, 161, 163, 187, 201
6th Canadian Infantry Brigade, 5, 14, 106–10, 113, 115, 120, 122, 128, 133, 166, 184–6, 190–1, 193, 197–200, 202, 206, 214–15
    Fusiliers Mont-Royal, Les, 110, 112–14, 117, 120, 122, 133, 143, 164–5, 170, 172, 191, 193, 197–9
    Queen's Own Cameron Highlanders of Canada, The, 110–11, 114–15, 117, 122, 128–9, 133, 164–5, 168–72, 191, 197–9, 201–202
    South Saskatchewan Regiment, The, 110–14, 133, 148, 164–5, 167–71, 184, 197–200, 202
7th Canadian Infantry Brigade, 17, 27, 29, 48, 63, 71–5, 82, 93–4, 106, 202, 205, 216
    Canadian Scottish Regiment, 1st Battalion, 81, 94
    Regina Rifles Regiment, 72–3, 94, 107, 192
    Royal Winnipeg Rifles, 69
8th Canandian Infantry Brigade, 17, 27, 29, 82, 106–107, 146, 157, 205, 216
    North Shore (New Brunswick) Regitment, 31, 140
    Queen's Own Rifles of Canada, The, 31
    Régiment de la Chaudière, Le, 37, 58
9th Canadian Infantry Brigade, 15, 22, 27, 32, 37, 41, 64–5, 77, 81–3, 88, 94–5, 122–3, 172, 203, 205, 216
    Highland Light Infantry of Canada, 20, 41, 62, 82–7, 95, 98
    North Nova Scotia Highlanders, 20–1, 23, 37, 82, 88, 92, 94, 98, 122–3, 125
        training with Sherbrooke Fusilier Regiment, 17–20
        advance on D-Day, 34, 37
        advance on D+1, 41–65
    Stormont, Dundas and Glengarry Highlanders, 20, 41, 62–3, 81–2, 84, 87–8, 92, 95–6, 98–9
10th Canadian Infantry Brigade, 143, 145–6, 172, 192, 205
    Algonquin Regiment, The, 146, 192
    Argyll and Sutherland Highlanders of Canada, The, 146, 192
    Lincoln and Welland Regiment, The, 146, 180, 192
1st Canadian Parachute Battalion, 27
    D-Day objectives, 27
3rd Anti-tank Regiment, 115
14th Field Regiment, FCA, 41, 47
17th Light Field Ambulance, 208
First Hussars, The, 13, 17, 29, 32, 58, 94–5, 106–107, 191, 208
Fort Garry Horse, The, 13, 18, 29, 32, 71–2, 79, 95, 106–107, 191
Sherbrooke Fusilier Regiment, The;
    creation, 7
    organization, 8
    command personnel, 8
    recruitment, 8
    training in Sherbrooke, 8

march to Ottawa, 9
deployment to Newfoundland, 9
conversion to armoured, 10
training in Debert, 10–12
deployment to the United
    Kingdom, 12
Warburg Barracks, 12
training in the United Kingdom, 12
    see also Operation
        OVERLORD, training,
Normandy landings;
    crossing the English
        Channel, 30–1
    move to Bény-sur-Mer, the
        assembly area, 34
    advance toward Carpiquet;
    D-Day, 34–7
    D+1, 40–65
    German counter-attack,
        48–64
    restructure, 75–6
    See Operation WINDSOR;
        Operation CHARNWOOD;
        Operation ATLANTIC;
        Operation SPRING;
        Operation TOTALIZE;
        Operation TRACTABLE;
        pursuit to the Seine;
11th Field Engineer Company, 128
85th Light Aid Detachment, 62, 96,
    206–209, 211

b. Great Britain
21st Army Group, 19–20, 26, 178,
    204, 212, 215–17
2nd British Tactical Air Force,
    107, 148
First Allied Airborne Army;
    6th British Airborne
        Division, 27

82nd United States Airborne
    Division, 27, 213
101st United States Airborne
    Division, 27
    See Operation OVERLORD
    plan; First Canadian Army;
    First United States Army;
    Second British Army;
Second British Army, 26–7, 76,
    121, 126, 156, 166, 174, 183,
    204, 212–13, 215–17
First British Corps, 27, 81, 83,
    89, 104, 121, 126, 178,
    204–205
Inns of Court Regiment, 90
3rd (United Kingdom) Infantry
    Division, 38, 48, 77, 81
27th British Armoured
    Brigade, 82
51st (Highland) Infantry
    Division, 106, 130, 178
59th (Straffordshire) Infantry
    Division, 81–2
Second British Corps, 156
Third British Corps, 77, 105
Eighth British Corps, 77, 104,
    107, 121
11th British Armoured Division,
    77, 110
XXX British Corps, 27, 212, 215
    7th British Armoured Division,
        122
    43rd (Wessex) Infantry
        Division, 118
    49th (West Riding) Infantry
        Division, 212, 219
    33rd British Armoured
        Brigade, 81
    1st Northamptonshire
        Yeomanry, 148–51, 153

INDEX

50th (Northumbrian) Infantry Division, 38, 70
8th British Infantry Brigade, 78

c. Poland

1st Polish Armoured Division, 128, 130, 140, 143, 147–8, 166–7, 171, 173–4, 176, 205
24th Polish Uhlan Regiment, 144

d. United States

12th Army Group, 126, 178, 183, 212, 215
8th United States Army Air Force, 107, 140, 148
First United States Army, 26–7, 76, 121, 126
5th United States Corps, 173
Third United States Army, 121, 126, 155, 174, 213
Ninth United States Army, 213, 215

e. Germany

Heeresgruppe B, 36, 49
6.Fallschirm-Gruppe, 191
  559.Infanterie-Regiment, 191
5.Panzer-Armee, 140, 155, 167, 171, 176, 178, 180
  LXXXVI.Korps, 180
7. Armee, 36, 140, 155, 171–2, 174, 176, 178, 180
  XLVII.Panzer-Korps, 171
    see *21.Panzerdivision*;
    716.Infanterie-Division, 50, 64
    16.Luftwaffe-Feld-Division, 50, 103

Panzergruppe West, 70, 93
  I.SS-Panzer-Korps, 50, 103–104, 121–2, 155, 167
    see *12.SS-Panzerdivision (Hitlerjugend)*;
    Panzer-Lehr-Division, 50, 70, 103
    schwere.SS-Panzerabteilung 101, 140–1, 148–50
  II.SS-Panzer-Korps, 78, 122, 171, 174
    1.SS-Panzer-Division (Leibstandarte SS Adolf Hitler), 48, 103, 107, 113, 122, 130, 139
    9.SS-Panzerdivision (Hohenstaufen), 103, 122, 125–6, 145, 186
    see *10.SS-Panzerdivision (Frundsberg)*;
    schwere.SS-Panzerabteilung 102, 122, 145
    8.SS-Kavalerie-Division (Florian Geyer), 126
  III.Flak-Korps, 140
2.Panzerdivision, 122, 177
85.Infanterie-Division, 167
89.Infanterie-Division, 139–40, 163
116.Panzerdivision, 103, 122
271.Infanterie-Division, 162, 164
272.Infanterie-Division, 103, 177
10.SS-Panzerdivision (Frundsberg), 122
  SS-Panzergrenadier-Regiment 22, 122
12.SS-Panzerdivision (Hitlerjugend), 64–6, 70, 78–9, 93–4, 103–104, 122, 140, 144, 155–6, 167, 172, 177, 217

creation and organization, 48–9
see *SS-Panzer-Regiment 12*
SS-Panzergrenadier-Regiment 25, 49, 63–5, 68, 73, 79–80, 88
   I Bataillone SS-Panzergrenadier-Regiment 25, 50, 66
   II Bataillone SS-Panzergrenadier-Regiment 25, 50–1, 55, 61, 63
   III Bataillone SS-Panzergrenadier-Regiment 25, 50–2, 55, 60, 63, 79, 93
SS-Panzergrenadier-Regiment 26, 49–50, 63, 69, 73, 165
   III Bataillone SS-Panzergrenadier-Regiment 26, 144
21.Panzerdivision, 36, 50, 63–4, 70, 103, 122, 177, 186
   Panzer-Regiment 22, 36
   Panzergrenadier-Regiment 192, 36–7
schwere.Panzerabteilung 503, 122
SS-Panzer-Regiment 12, 49, 64, 79, 84, 144
   I Bataillone SS-Panzer-Regiment 12, 50
      3.Panzerkompanie, 73, 92
   II Bataillone SS-Panzer-Regiment 12, 49
      5.Panzerkompanie, 51–2
      6.Panzerkompanie, 55
      7.Panzerkompanie, 55, 84